Frazz

Live from Bryson Elementary

Jef Mallett

Foreword by Gene Weingarten

Andrews McMeel
Publishing

Kansas City

Frazz is distributed internationally by United Feature Syndicate.

Frazz copyright © 2005 by Jef Mallett. All rights reserved. Printed in the United States of America. No part of this book may be used or reproduced in any manner whatsoever without written permission except in the case of reprints in the context of reviews. For information, write Andrews McMeel Publishing, an Andrews McMeel Universal company, 4520 Main Street, Kansas City, Missouri 64111.

05 06 07 08 09 BBG 10 9 8 7 6 5 4 3 2

ISBN-13: 978-0-7407-5447-0
ISBN-10: 0-7407-5447-5

Library of Congress Control Number: 2005925661

Frazz can be viewed on the Internet at
www.comics.com/comics/frazz.

ATTENTION: SCHOOLS AND BUSINESSES

Andrews McMeel books are available at quantity discounts with bulk purchase for educational, business, or sales promotional use. For information, please write to: Special Sales Department, Andrews McMeel Publishing, 4520 Main Street, Kansas City, Missouri 64111.

To my parents, for the foundation;
to my wife, for the framework;
and to my teachers and mentors, for all that crap in the attic.

Foreword
by Gene Weingarten

Before getting to the question I know you are all wondering about—Does Jef Mallett, as rumored, shave his legs? And for God's sake, why?—I thought I would tell you a little bit about his comic strip.

I was a fan of *Frazz* long before I met its creator. Because I critique the comics pages for a living, I read lots of comics. But I can count on a cartoon character's hand (four fingers, tops) how many times I have read only a single episode of a new strip and instantly known that it was going to be great. It happened with *Bloom County* and *The Far Side*. The third was a single-panel comic by John Callahan, the blindingly brilliant quadriplegic cartoonist from Seattle. And the fourth time, as you have no doubt guessed, was with *Broom Hilda*.

Kidding, kidding. The fourth was *Frazz*. Specifically, this one:

FRAZZ, HOW WILL I KNOW WHEN I'M A GROWN-UP?
YOU'LL BE ABLE TO MAKE THAT LOUD HONKING SOUND WHEN YOU BLOW YOUR NOSE.
HOW INAUSPICIOUS.
I THOUGHT IT WOULD HAVE SOMETHING TO DO WITH THE DRINKING AGE.
THAT HASN'T PROVEN TO BE AT ALL RELIABLE.
MALLETT

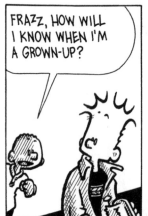

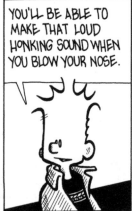

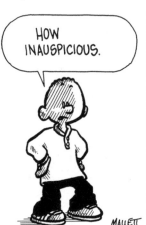

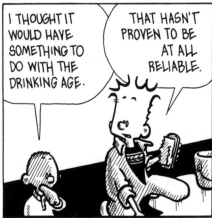

What's so special about it? In four elegantly drawn panels, we have:

1. A booger joke. (And a darned good one!)
2. A vocabulary-list word for kids to bug their parents about.
3. An original, hysterical, illuminating, eccentric observation about human behavior.
4. An existential examination of the nature of aging and the myth of adulthood.
5. A moral, delivered in good humor and without a hint of condescension.

Frazz is an extraordinary comic strip because it has nestled itself comfortably in two worlds at once. It is appealing to children and adults alike, in equal measure and in equal depth, without resorting to in-jokes or double entendre. Try to think of another current strip that accomplishes this. I did. I couldn't.

The ultimate triumph of *Frazz* is that it has found common ground for humor. It recognizes that adults are just bigger kids with more versatile body parts (you know, the ability to honk).

In the interplay between a humongously cool elementary school janitor and the students—most notably Caulfield, of the Salingeresque name and sweetly jaded attitude—Jef Mallett entertains adults by deftly exploring the meaning of childhood. He's Piaget with pen and ink.

As you will see in this first *Frazz* collection, Jef Mallett fearlessly mines truths—sometimes uncomfortable truths—with humor and wit, and occasionally with a poignancy that can summon tears. And through it all, he painlessly sprinkles lessons—spelling lessons, logic lessons, grammar lessons, ethics lessons—that kids absorb. (Some stunningly ignorant adults absorb them, too. One day, Caulfield informed me about an error in word usage that I'd been making all my life.)

The most frequent questions *Washington Post* readers ask me about this strip is whether Frazz himself is a grown-up Calvin of *Calvin and Hobbes*. They're focusing not only on hair (Frazz's frizz) but also on his station in life: a brilliant underachiever. Well, Jef assures me that any similarity is unintentional. Jef also assures me that, yes, he shaves his legs, but only because it helps him compete in bike races and triathlons.

Let's take him at his word. He hasn't lied to us yet.

Introduction

Frazz has been in newspapers about four years now. That may seem like a bit too soon for a retrospective, but that's what this book feels like. And hey, if any nineteen-year-old pop star can write an autobiography, I suppose a forty-three-year-old who still feels like a rookie cartoonist can decide a book of his previous comic strips feels like a retrospective.

I was never one for looking backward, so this has been an education.

Educational item number 1: Now I know why I don't tend to look backward. Who drew those early Frazzes, anyway? Good God.
Educational item number 2: Whoops. I already did the banana gag.
Educational item number 3: I really ought to look backward more often, and not just so I don't repeat the banana gag.

Since *Frazz* is really just my own grossly premature and shamelessly inflated autobiography—come on, you don't really think I'm bright enough to just make stuff up—I'm flipping through more than just old comics.

The path down memory lane (did I actually just use that fetid cliché?) isn't a trail so much as what we in Michigan call a two-track: twin ruts of mud and gravel separated by weeds (that's better). Here. Join me. You take the left rut, the comic-strip rut, and I'll follow on the right and talk your ear off along the way.

While you marvel at how pointy everybody's heads are in the early strips, I'll tell you how hard it was to keep my own head straight during those early, sleep-deprived days before I felt like the strip was secure enough to quit my day job. While you watch the size of the lettering fluctuate until we got it right, I'll tell you about my wife, Patty, who does that lettering (her handwriting's perfect, and since she's a professional editor, it's an automatic chance for her to go over the text and save me from myself). While you notice some of the inside jokes and T-shirt logos, I'll go on about some of the heroes and friends I've met, nudged, and, in at least one case, inadvertently, regrettably, and apparently irrevocably offended through that sort of self-indulgent behavior.

Point out a couple of my more obvious influences, and I'll give you the long list of subtler ones you've missed. Look closer, and I'll tell you how hard it is to take advice sometimes, and how it's even harder—unbelievably hard—to ignore it from your idols when that's what it takes to make your art your own. Comment on Frazz's cycling and triathlon addiction and regret it immediately as I go on about my own love for those sports. Mention the book in general, and I'll tell you how I met my editor talking not about comics but triathlons (she's one of those guys, too).

Suggest how incredibly cool it must be to have a comic strip, and I'll shut right up. I still can't believe it myself.

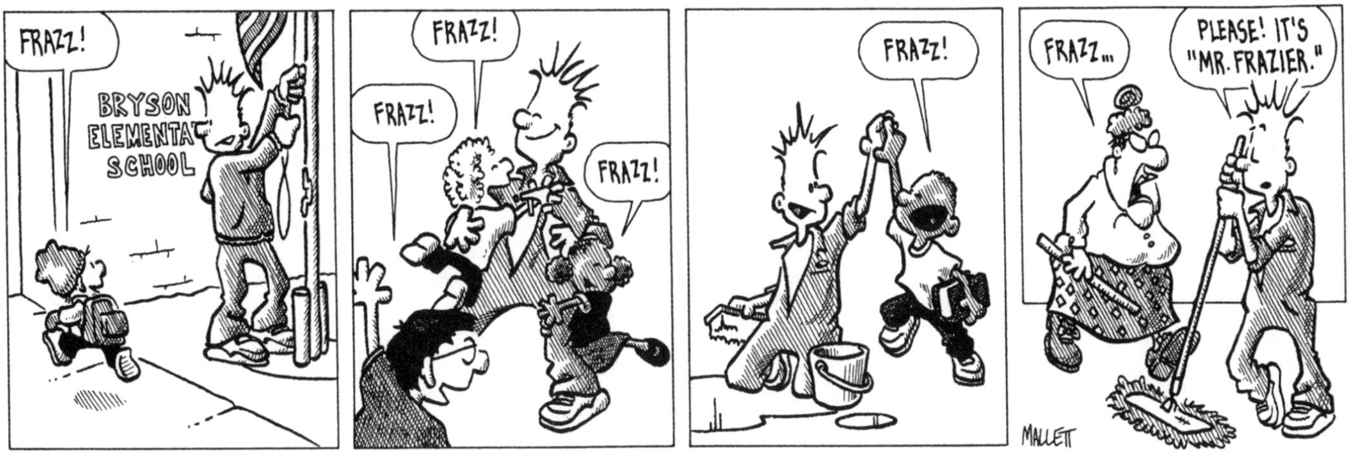
FRAZZ!
BRYSON
ELEMENTA
SCHOOL
FRAZZ!
FRAZZ!
FRAZZ!
FRAZZ!
FRAZZ...
PLEASE! IT'S "MR. FRAZIER."
MALLETT

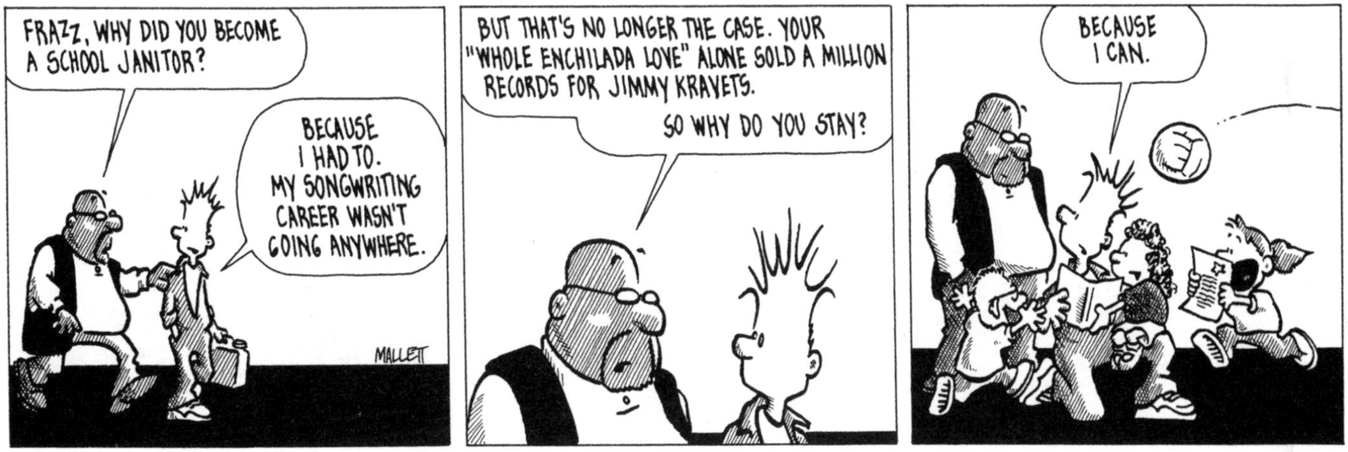
FRAZZ, WHY DID YOU BECOME A SCHOOL JANITOR?
BECAUSE I HAD TO. MY SONGWRITING CAREER WASN'T GOING ANYWHERE.
MALLETT
BUT THAT'S NO LONGER THE CASE. YOUR "WHOLE ENCHILADA LOVE" ALONE SOLD A MILLION RECORDS FOR JIMMY KRAVETS.
SO WHY DO YOU STAY?
BECAUSE I CAN.

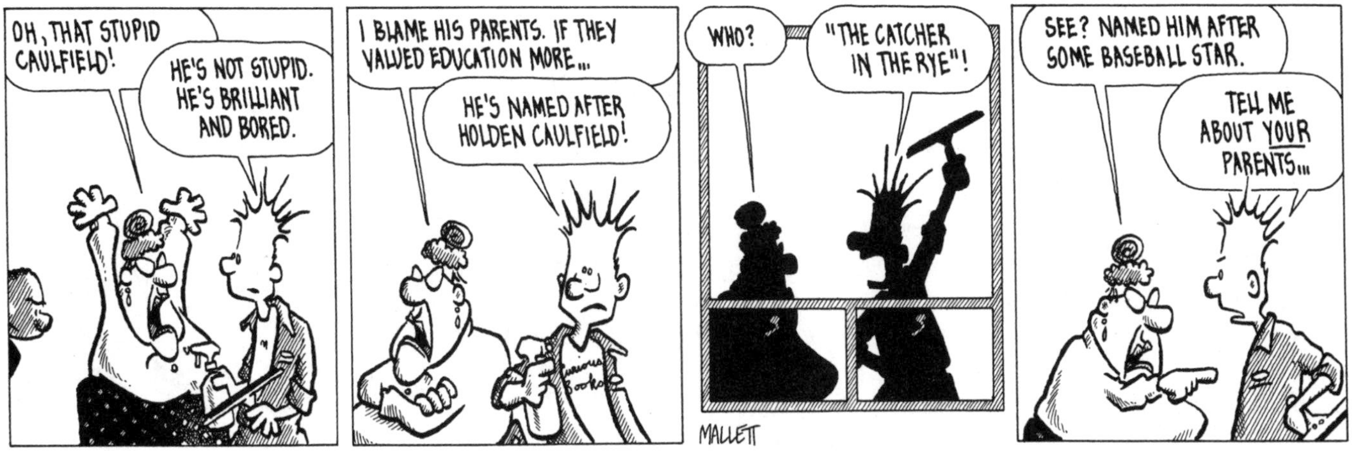
OH, THAT STUPID CAULFIELD!
HE'S NOT STUPID. HE'S BRILLIANT AND BORED.
I BLAME HIS PARENTS. IF THEY VALUED EDUCATION MORE...
HE'S NAMED AFTER HOLDEN CAULFIELD!
WHO?
"THE CATCHER IN THE RYE"!
MALLETT
SEE? NAMED HIM AFTER SOME BASEBALL STAR.
TELL ME ABOUT YOUR PARENTS...

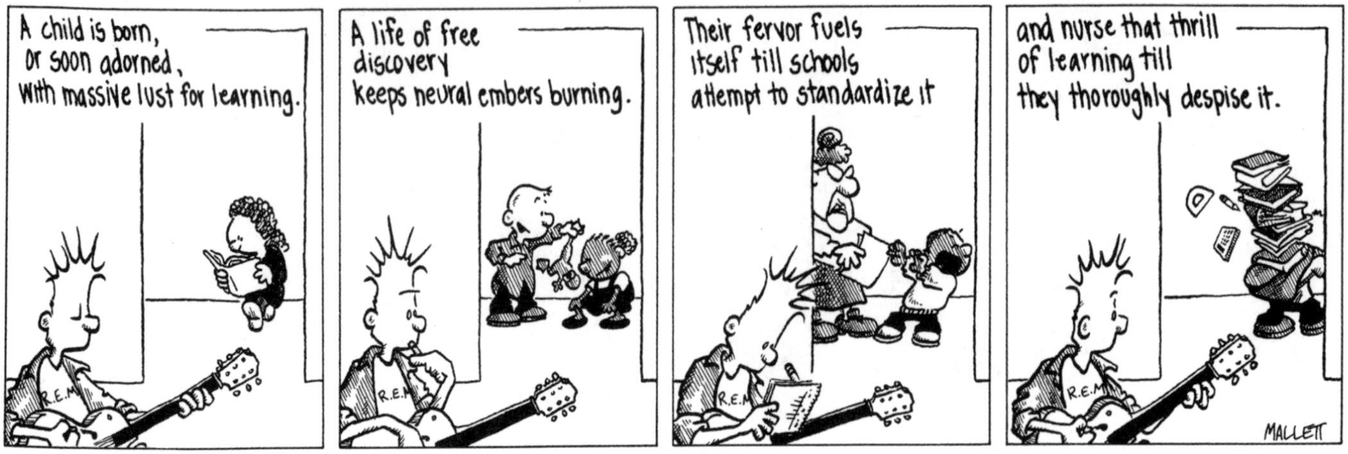
A child is born, or soon adorned, with massive lust for learning.
A life of free discovery keeps neural embers burning.
Their fervor fuels itself till schools attempt to standardize it
and nurse that thrill of learning till they thoroughly despise it.
MALLETT

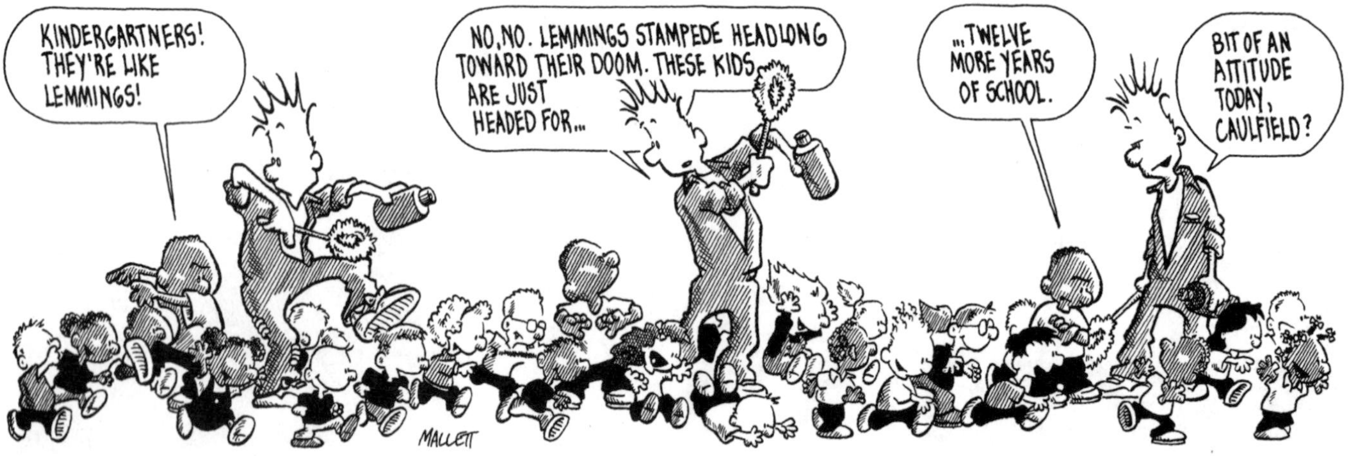
KINDERGARTNERS! THEY'RE LIKE LEMMINGS!
NO, NO. LEMMINGS STAMPEDE HEADLONG TOWARD THEIR DOOM. THESE KIDS ARE JUST HEADED FOR...
...TWELVE MORE YEARS OF SCHOOL.
BIT OF AN ATTITUDE TODAY, CAULFIELD?
MALLETT

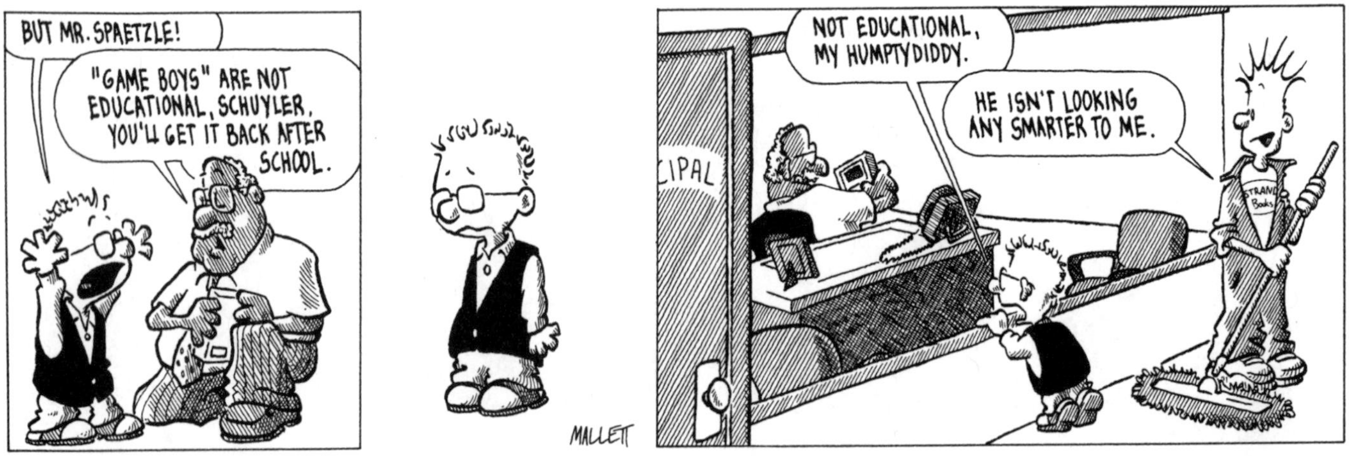
BUT MR. SPAETZLE!
"GAME BOYS" ARE NOT EDUCATIONAL, SCHUYLER. YOU'LL GET IT BACK AFTER SCHOOL.
MALLETT
NOT EDUCATIONAL, MY HUMPTYDIDDY.
HE ISN'T LOOKING ANY SMARTER TO ME.

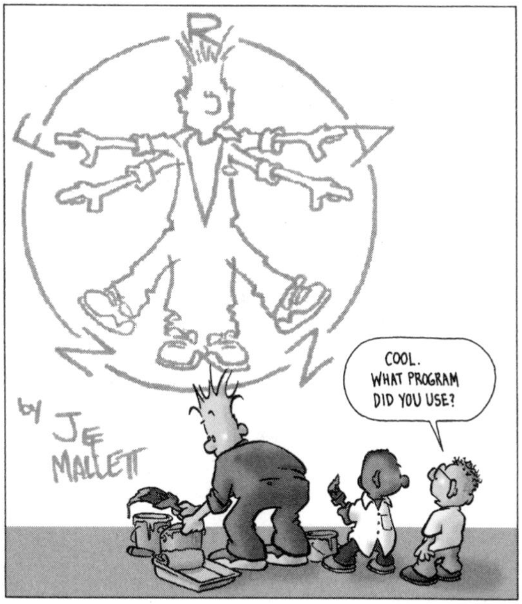
by JEF MALLETT
COOL. WHAT PROGRAM DID YOU USE?

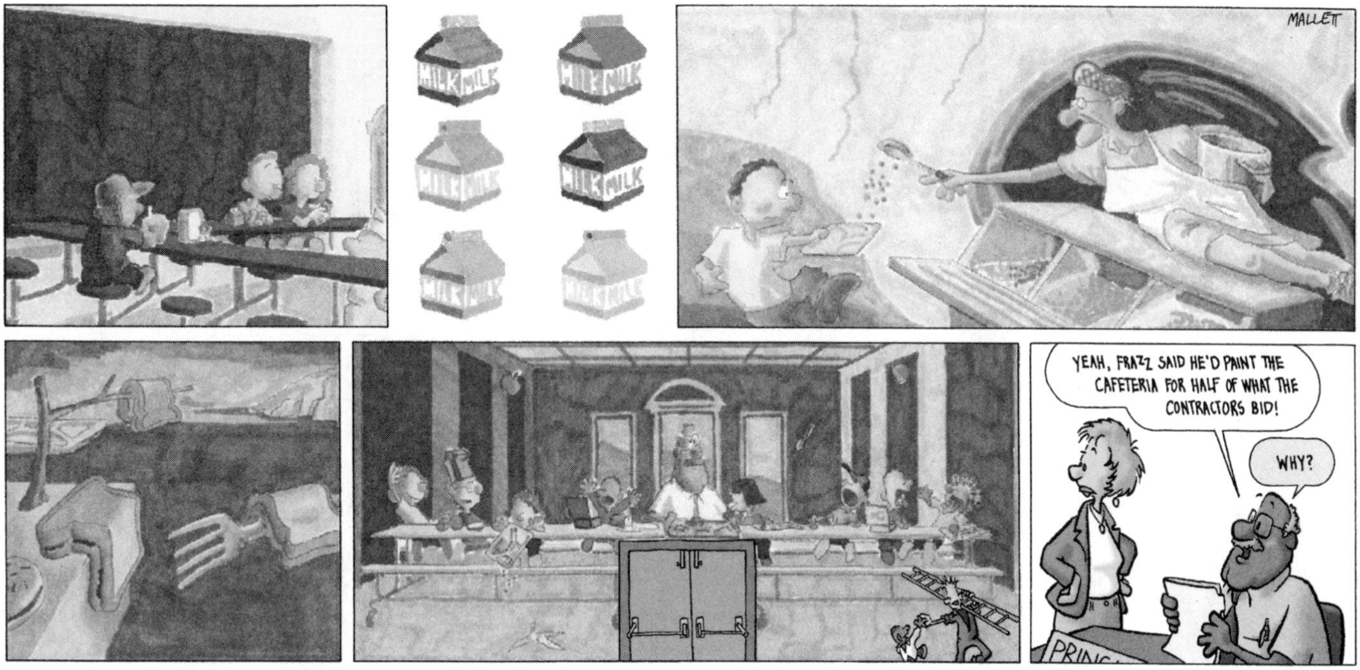
MALLETT
YEAH, FRAZZ SAID HE'D PAINT THE CAFETERIA FOR HALF OF WHAT THE CONTRACTORS BID!
WHY?

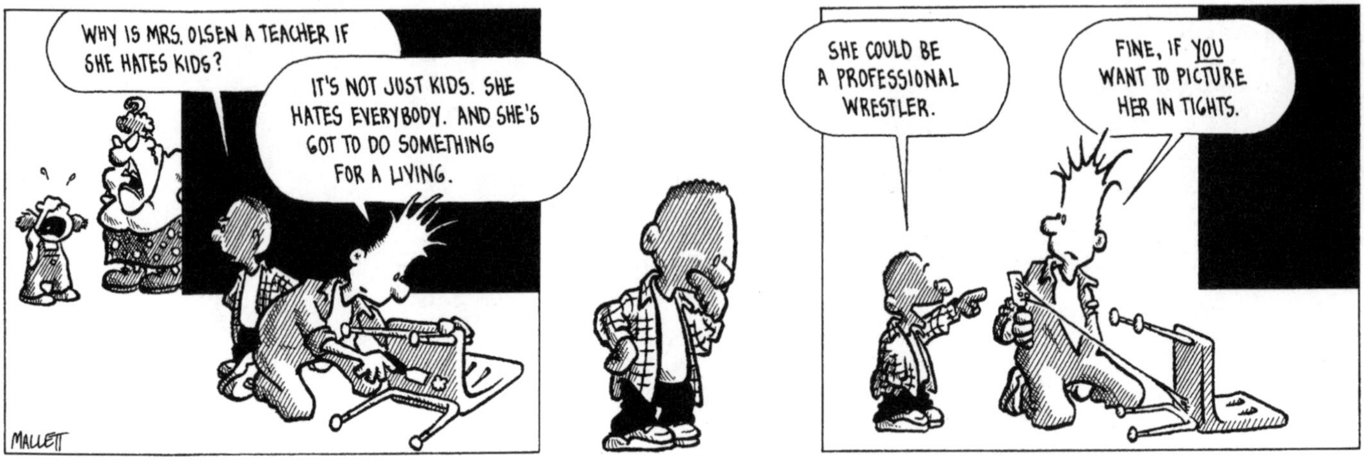
WHY IS MRS. OLSEN A TEACHER IF SHE HATES KIDS?
IT'S NOT JUST KIDS. SHE HATES EVERYBODY. AND SHE'S GOT TO DO SOMETHING FOR A LIVING.
SHE COULD BE A PROFESSIONAL WRESTLER.
FINE, IF YOU WANT TO PICTURE HER IN TIGHTS.
MALLETT

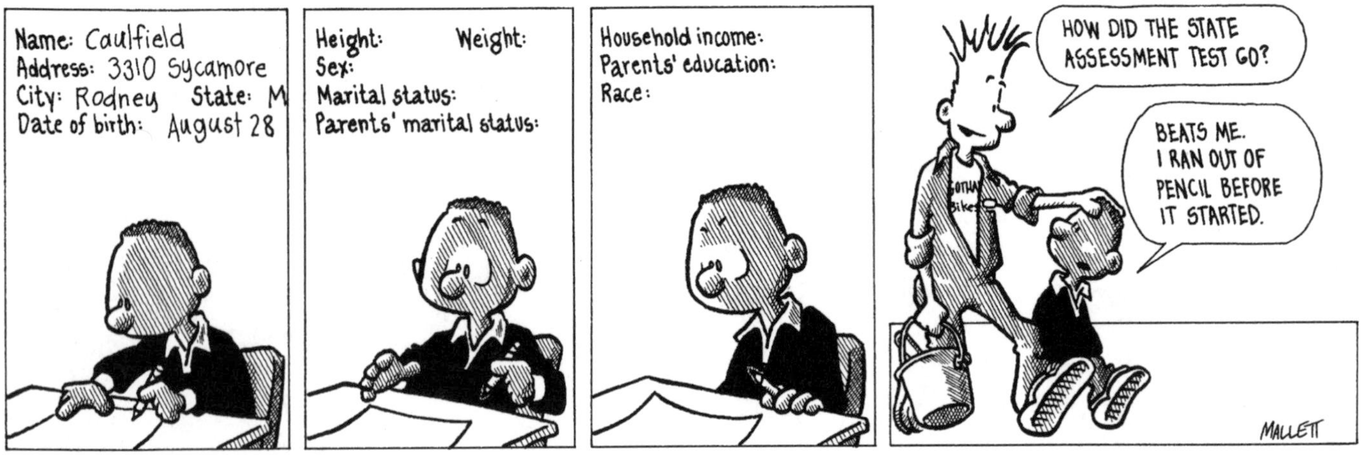
Name: Caulfield
Address: 3310 Sycamore
City: Rodney State: M
Date of birth: August 28
Height: Weight:
Sex:
Marital status:
Parents' marital status:
Household income:
Parents' education:
Race:
HOW DID THE STATE ASSESSMENT TEST GO?
BEATS ME. I RAN OUT OF PENCIL BEFORE IT STARTED.
MALLETT

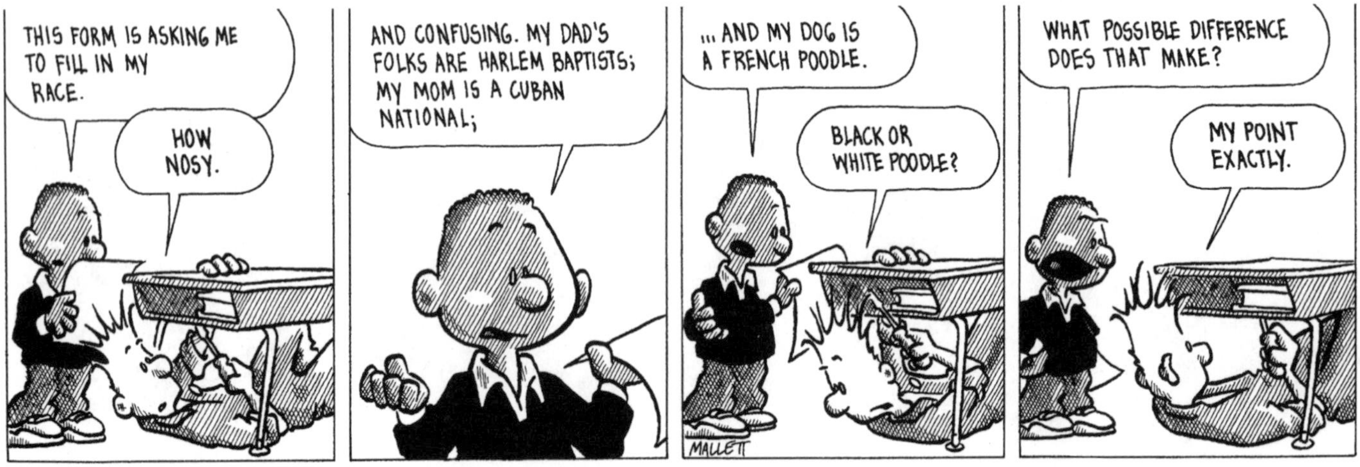
THIS FORM IS ASKING ME TO FILL IN MY RACE.
HOW NOSY.
AND CONFUSING. MY DAD'S FOLKS ARE HARLEM BAPTISTS; MY MOM IS A CUBAN NATIONAL;
... AND MY DOG IS A FRENCH POODLE.
BLACK OR WHITE POODLE?
MALLETT
WHAT POSSIBLE DIFFERENCE DOES THAT MAKE?
MY POINT EXACTLY.

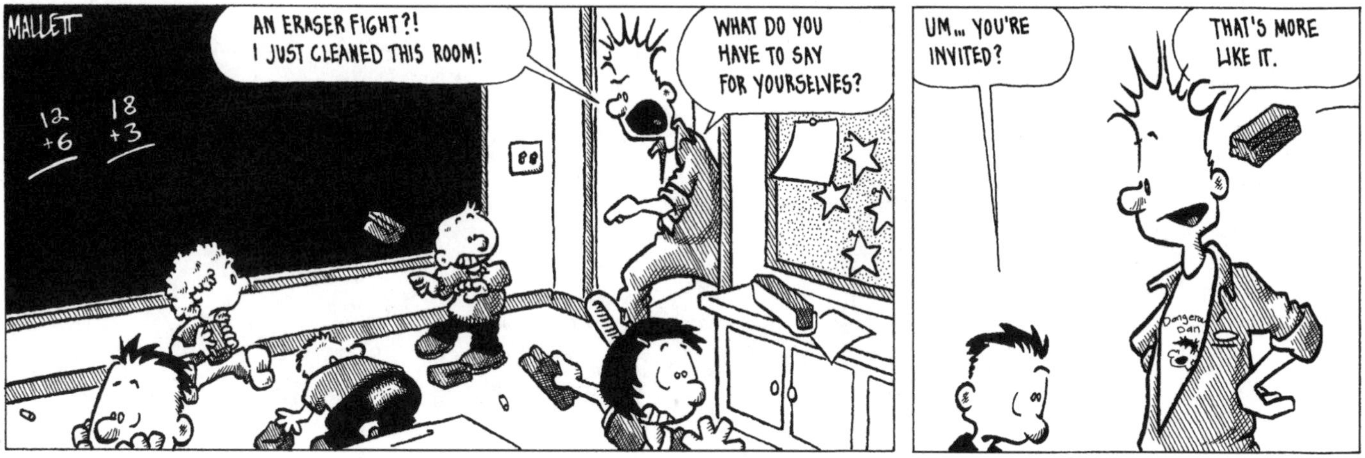
MALLETT
AN ERASER FIGHT?! I JUST CLEANED THIS ROOM!
WHAT DO YOU HAVE TO SAY FOR YOURSELVES?
12 +6
18 +3
UM... YOU'RE INVITED?
THAT'S MORE LIKE IT.

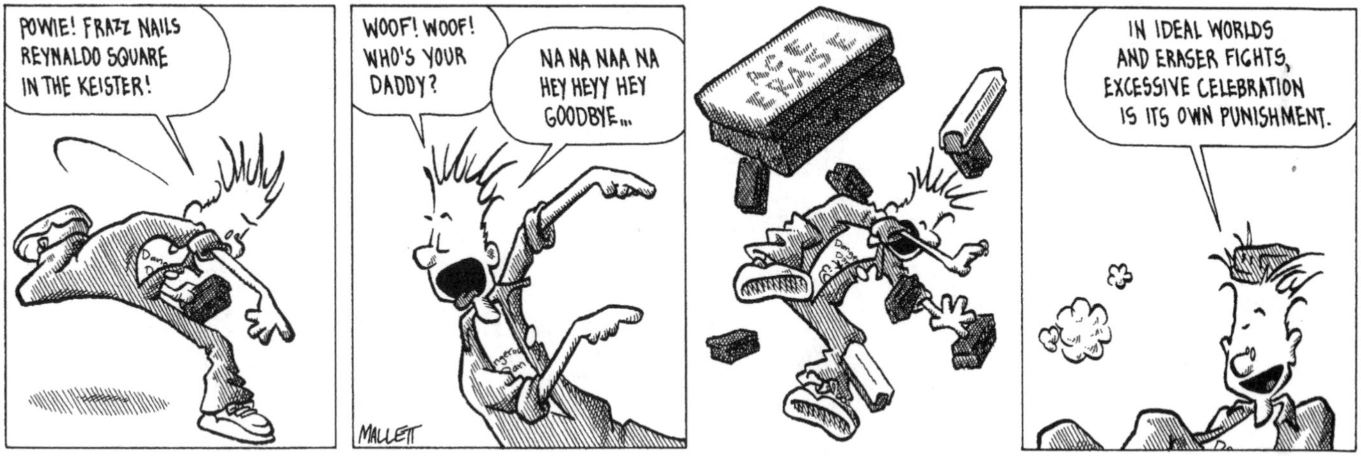
POWIE! FRAZZ NAILS REYNALDO SQUARE IN THE KEISTER!
WOOF! WOOF! WHO'S YOUR DADDY?
NA NA NAA NA HEY HEYY HEY GOODBYE...
MALLETT
IN IDEAL WORLDS AND ERASER FIGHTS, EXCESSIVE CELEBRATION IS ITS OWN PUNISHMENT.

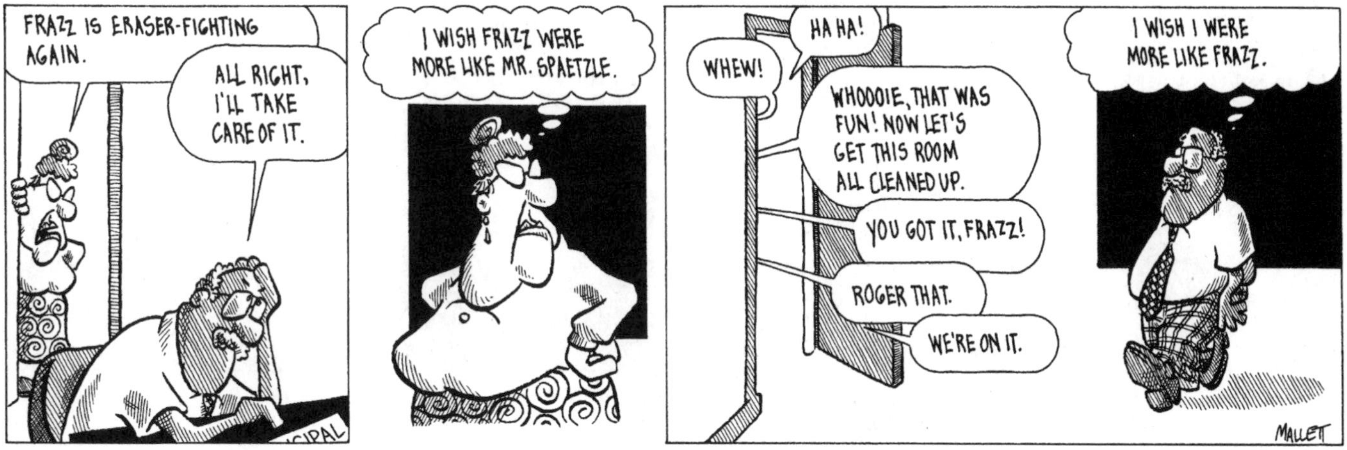
FRAZZ IS ERASER-FIGHTING AGAIN.
ALL RIGHT, I'LL TAKE CARE OF IT.
I WISH FRAZZ WERE MORE LIKE MR. SPAETZLE.
WHEW!
HA HA!
WHOOOIE, THAT WAS FUN! NOW LET'S GET THIS ROOM ALL CLEANED UP.
YOU GOT IT, FRAZZ!
ROGER THAT.
WE'RE ON IT.
I WISH I WERE MORE LIKE FRAZZ.
MALLETT

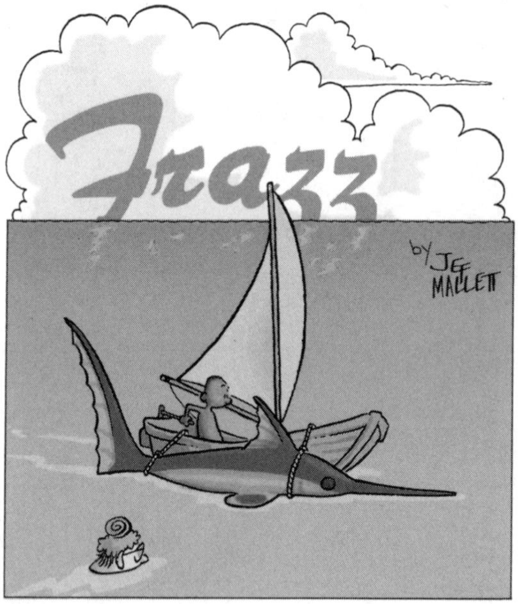
Frazz
by JEFF MALLETT

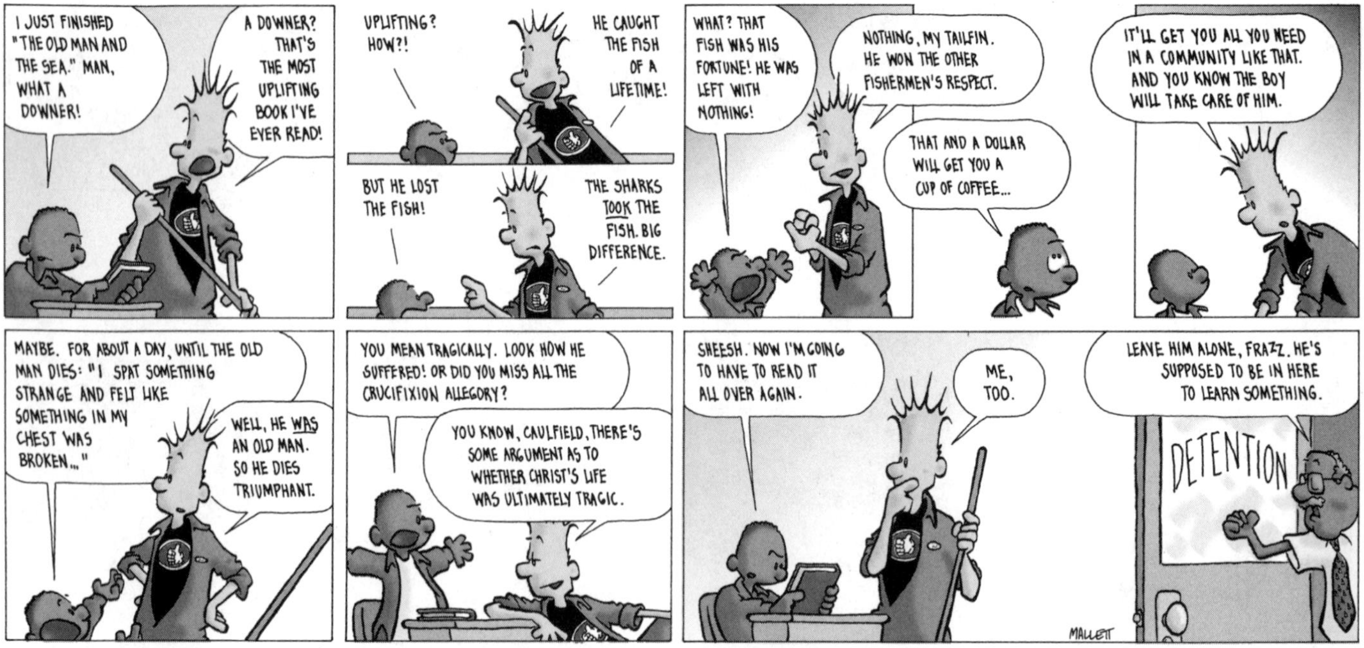
I JUST FINISHED "THE OLD MAN AND THE SEA." MAN, WHAT A DOWNER!
A DOWNER? THAT'S THE MOST UPLIFTING BOOK I'VE EVER READ!
UPLIFTING? HOW?!
HE CAUGHT THE FISH OF A LIFETIME!
BUT HE LOST THE FISH!
THE SHARKS TOOK THE FISH. BIG DIFFERENCE.
WHAT? THAT FISH WAS HIS FORTUNE! HE WAS LEFT WITH NOTHING!
NOTHING, MY TAILFIN. HE WON THE OTHER FISHERMEN'S RESPECT.
THAT AND A DOLLAR WILL GET YOU A CUP OF COFFEE...
IT'LL GET YOU ALL YOU NEED IN A COMMUNITY LIKE THAT. AND YOU KNOW THE BOY WILL TAKE CARE OF HIM.
MAYBE. FOR ABOUT A DAY, UNTIL THE OLD MAN DIES: "I SPAT SOMETHING STRANGE AND FELT LIKE SOMETHING IN MY CHEST WAS BROKEN..."
WELL, HE WAS AN OLD MAN. SO HE DIES TRIUMPHANT.
YOU MEAN TRAGICALLY. LOOK HOW HE SUFFERED! OR DID YOU MISS ALL THE CRUCIFIXION ALLEGORY?
YOU KNOW, CAULFIELD, THERE'S SOME ARGUMENT AS TO WHETHER CHRIST'S LIFE WAS ULTIMATELY TRAGIC.
SHEESH. NOW I'M GOING TO HAVE TO READ IT ALL OVER AGAIN.
ME, TOO.
LEAVE HIM ALONE, FRAZZ. HE'S SUPPOSED TO BE IN HERE TO LEARN SOMETHING.
DETENTION
MALLETT

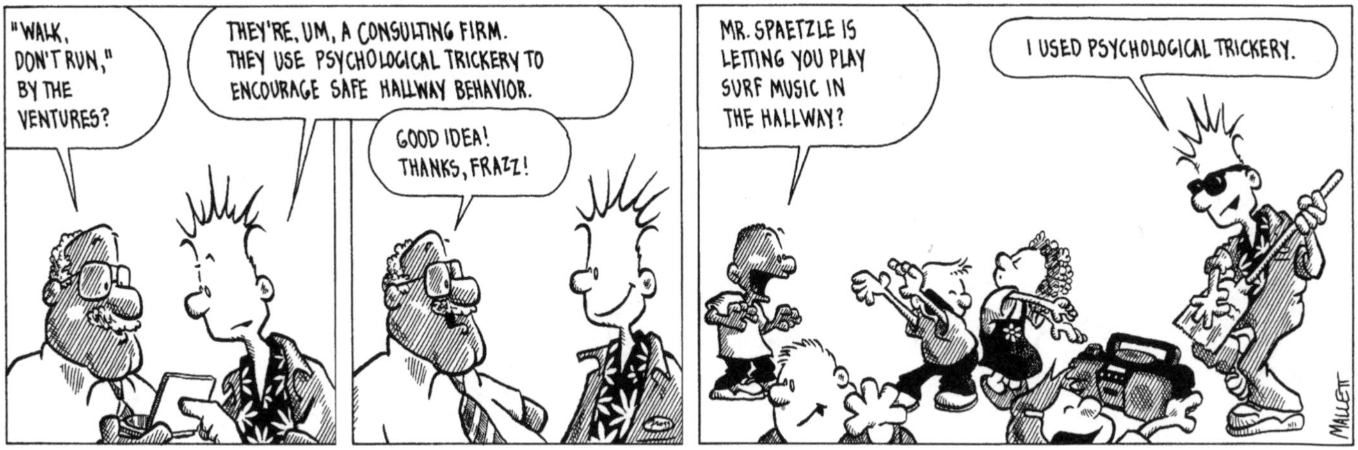
"WALK, DON'T RUN," BY THE VENTURES?
THEY'RE, UM, A CONSULTING FIRM. THEY USE PSYCHOLOGICAL TRICKERY TO ENCOURAGE SAFE HALLWAY BEHAVIOR.
GOOD IDEA! THANKS, FRAZZ!
MR. SPAETZLE IS LETTING YOU PLAY SURF MUSIC IN THE HALLWAY?
I USED PSYCHOLOGICAL TRICKERY.
MALLETT

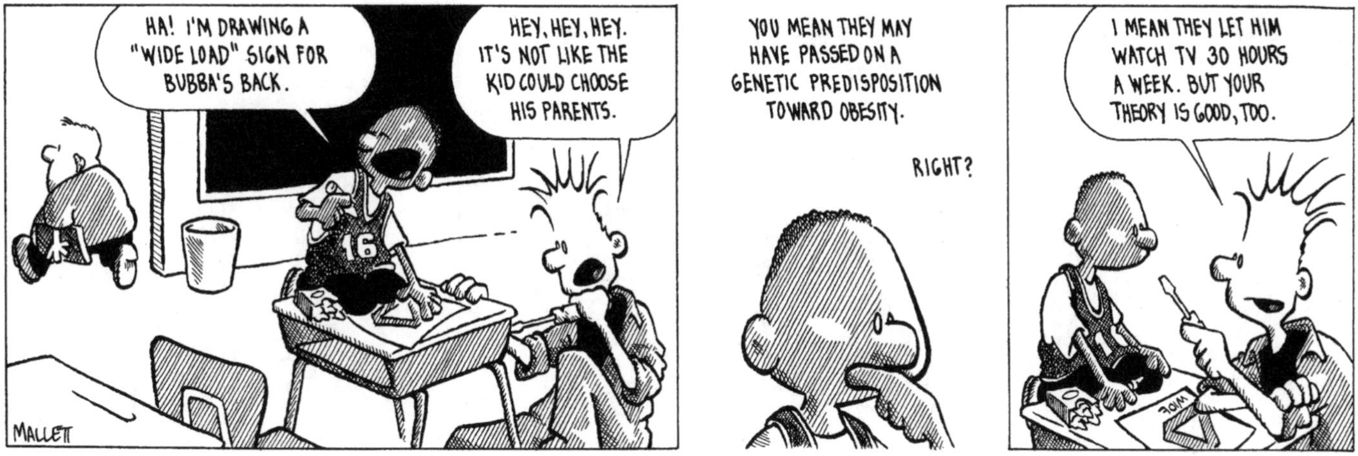
HA! I'M DRAWING A "WIDE LOAD" SIGN FOR BUBBA'S BACK.
HEY, HEY, HEY. IT'S NOT LIKE THE KID COULD CHOOSE HIS PARENTS.
MALLETT
YOU MEAN THEY MAY HAVE PASSED ON A GENETIC PREDISPOSITION TOWARD OBESITY.
RIGHT?
I MEAN THEY LET HIM WATCH TV 30 HOURS A WEEK. BUT YOUR THEORY IS GOOD, TOO.

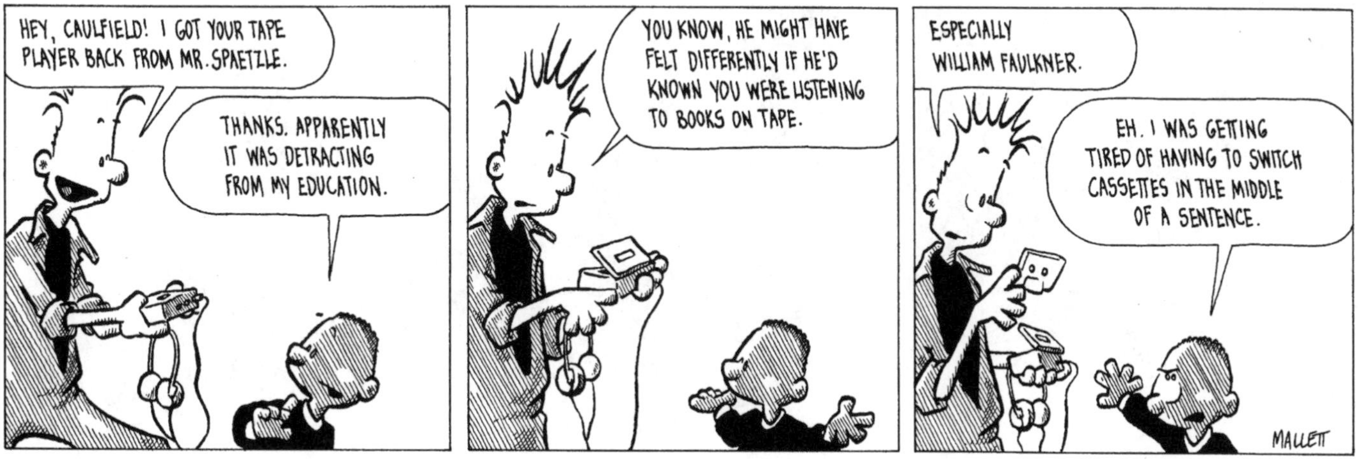
HEY, CAULFIELD! I GOT YOUR TAPE PLAYER BACK FROM MR. SPAETZLE.
THANKS. APPARENTLY IT WAS DETRACTING FROM MY EDUCATION.
YOU KNOW, HE MIGHT HAVE FELT DIFFERENTLY IF HE'D KNOWN YOU WERE LISTENING TO BOOKS ON TAPE.
ESPECIALLY WILLIAM FAULKNER.
EH. I WAS GETTING TIRED OF HAVING TO SWITCH CASSETTES IN THE MIDDLE OF A SENTENCE.
MALLETT

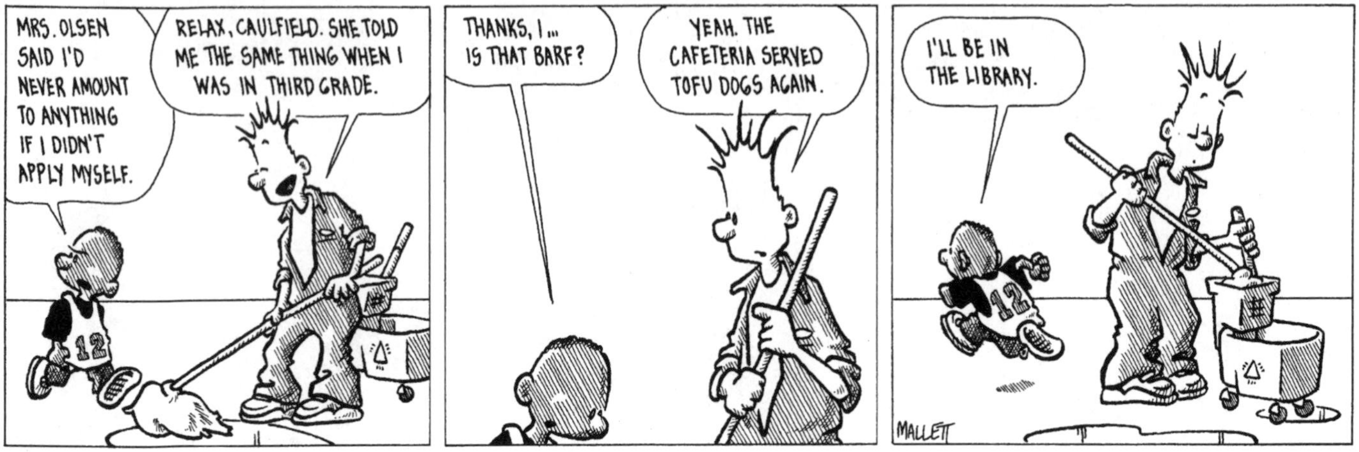
MRS. OLSEN SAID I'D NEVER AMOUNT TO ANYTHING IF I DIDN'T APPLY MYSELF.
RELAX, CAULFIELD. SHE TOLD ME THE SAME THING WHEN I WAS IN THIRD GRADE.
THANKS, I... IS THAT BARF?
YEAH. THE CAFETERIA SERVED TOFU DOGS AGAIN.
I'LL BE IN THE LIBRARY.
MALLETT

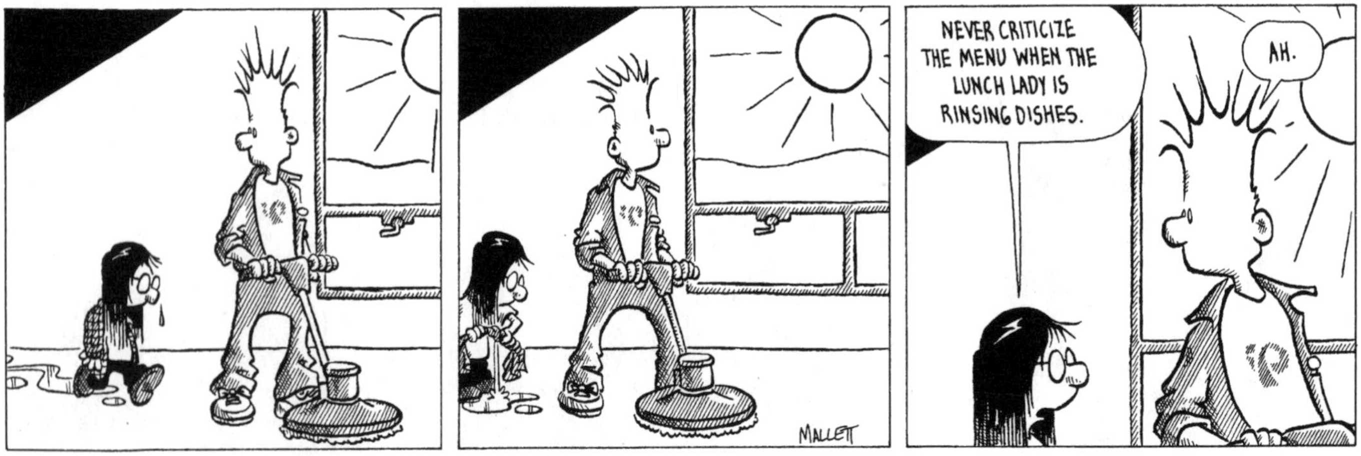
MALLETT
NEVER CRITICIZE THE MENU WHEN THE LUNCH LADY IS RINSING DISHES.
AH.

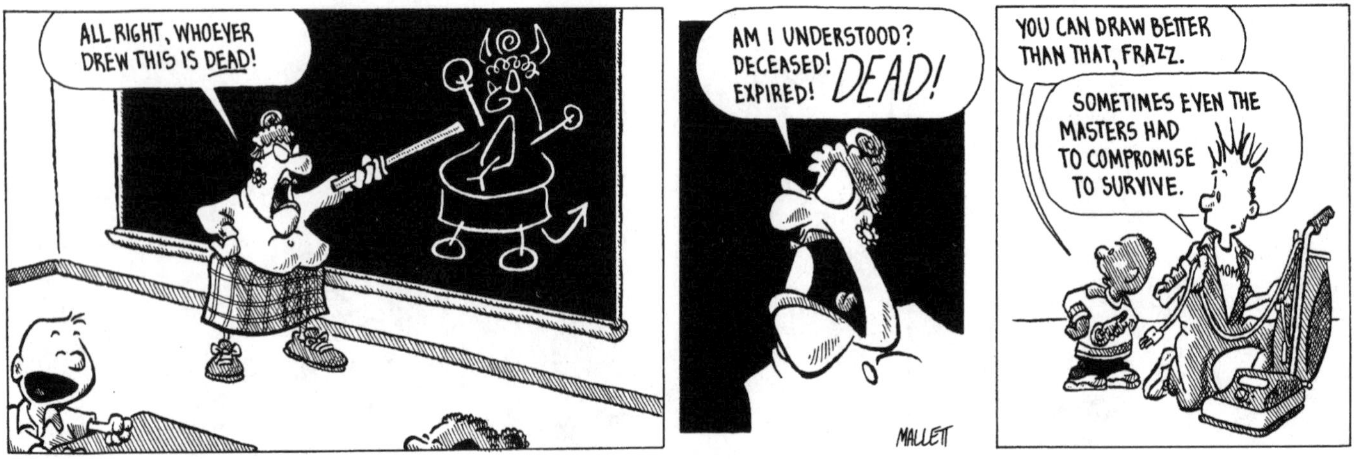
ALL RIGHT, WHOEVER DREW THIS IS DEAD!
AM I UNDERSTOOD? DECEASED! EXPIRED! DEAD!
MALLETT
YOU CAN DRAW BETTER THAN THAT, FRAZZ.
SOMETIMES EVEN THE MASTERS HAD TO COMPROMISE TO SURVIVE.

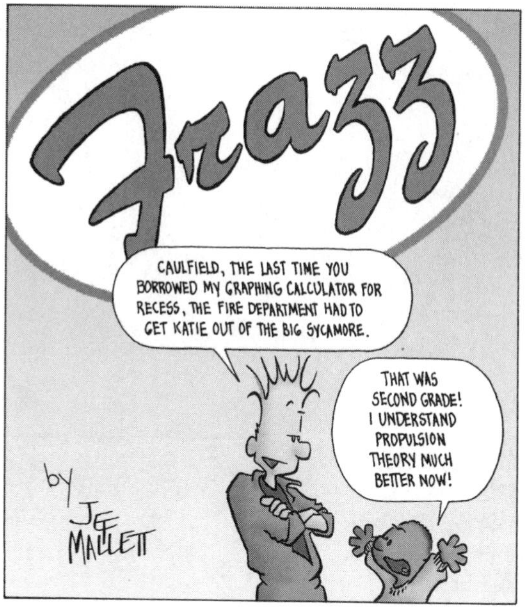
Frazz
CAULFIELD, THE LAST TIME YOU BORROWED MY GRAPHING CALCULATOR FOR RECESS, THE FIRE DEPARTMENT HAD TO GET KATIE OUT OF THE BIG SYCAMORE.
THAT WAS SECOND GRADE! I UNDERSTAND PROPULSION THEORY MUCH BETTER NOW!
by JEF MALLETT

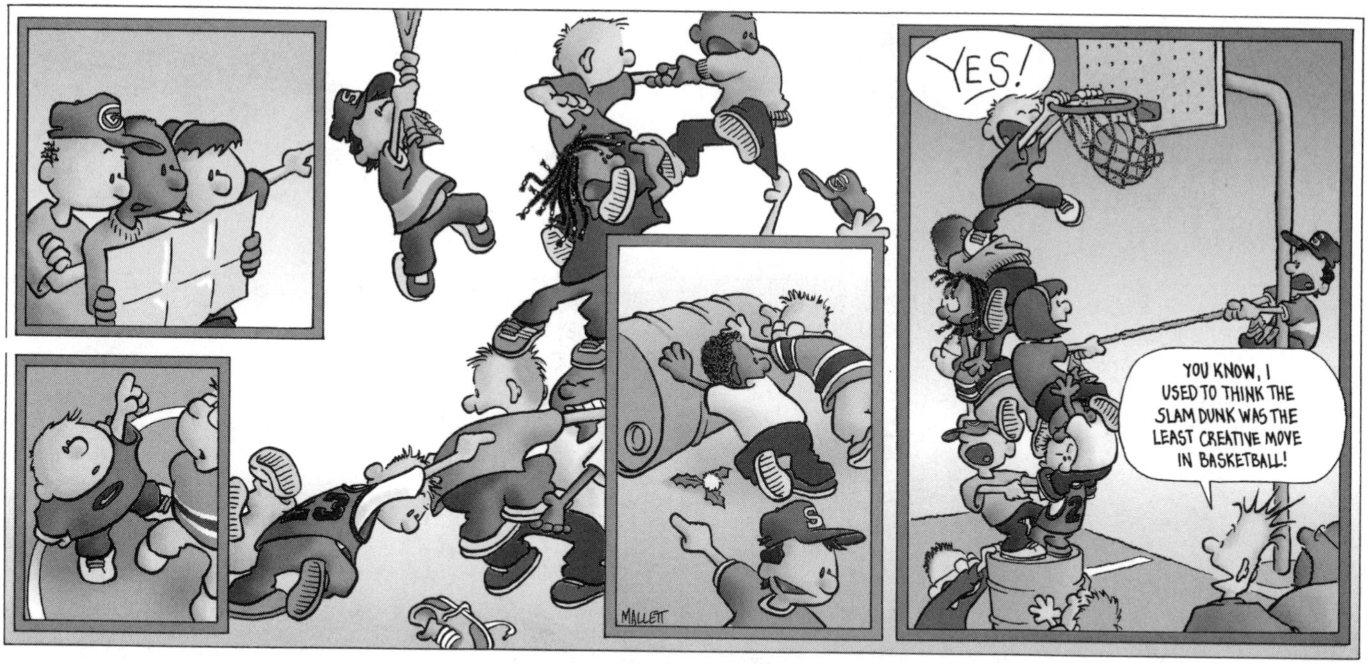
YES!
YOU KNOW, I USED TO THINK THE SLAM DUNK WAS THE LEAST CREATIVE MOVE IN BASKETBALL!
MALLETT

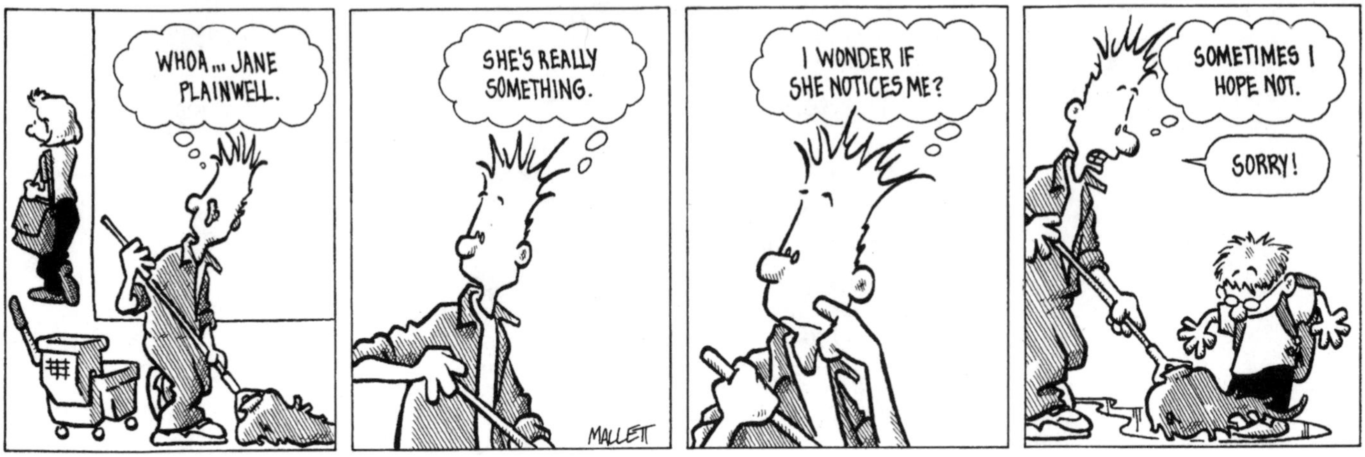
WHOA... JANE PLAINWELL.
SHE'S REALLY SOMETHING.
MALLETT
I WONDER IF SHE NOTICES ME?
SOMETIMES I HOPE NOT.
SORRY!

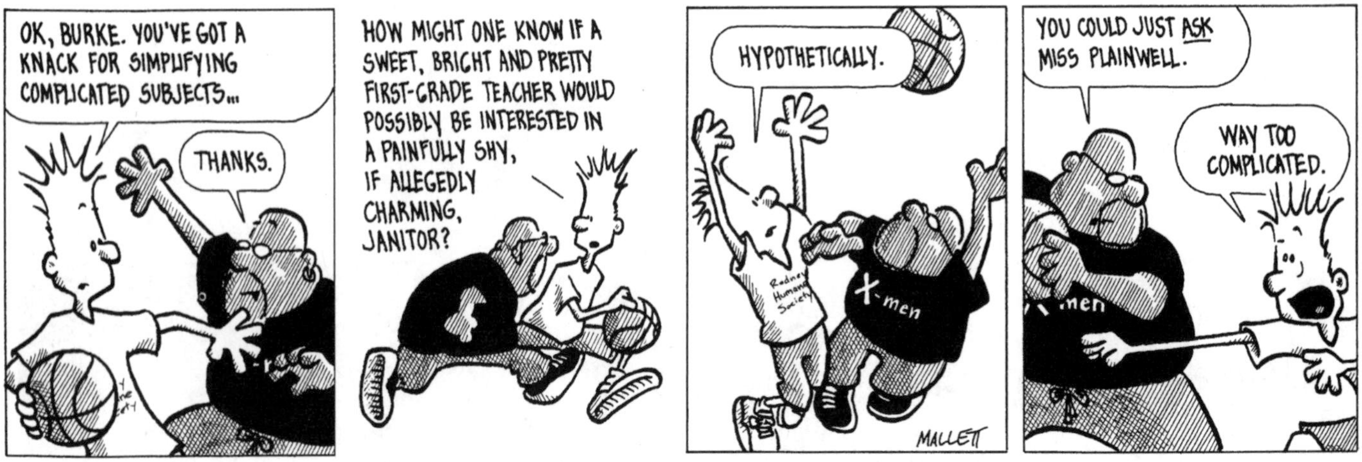
OK, BURKE. YOU'VE GOT A KNACK FOR SIMPLIFYING COMPLICATED SUBJECTS...
THANKS.
HOW MIGHT ONE KNOW IF A SWEET, BRIGHT AND PRETTY FIRST-GRADE TEACHER WOULD POSSIBLY BE INTERESTED IN A PAINFULLY SHY, IF ALLEGEDLY CHARMING, JANITOR?
HYPOTHETICALLY.
X-men
MALLETT
YOU COULD JUST ASK MISS PLAINWELL.
WAY TOO COMPLICATED.

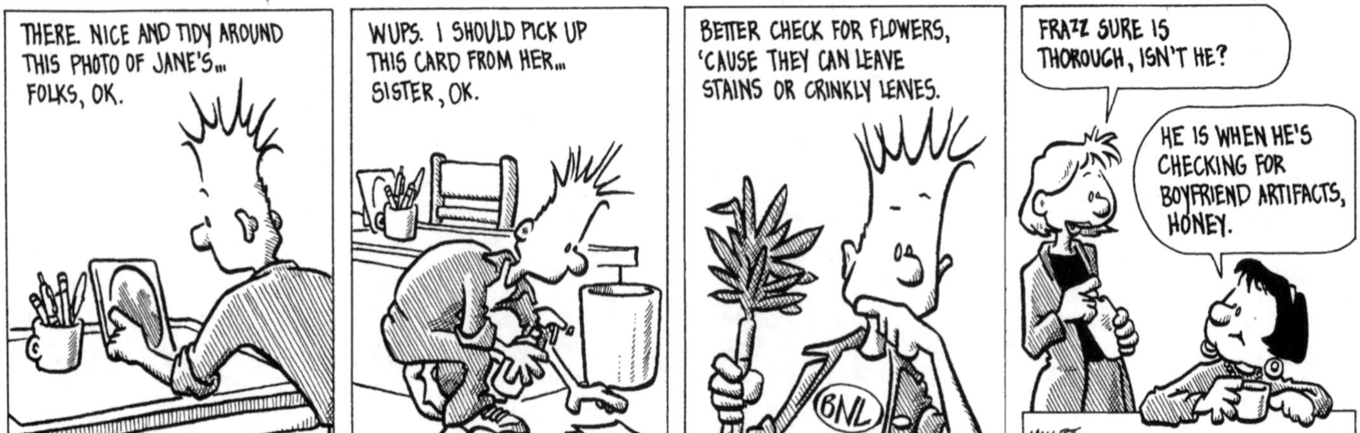
THERE. NICE AND TIDY AROUND THIS PHOTO OF JANE'S... FOLKS, OK.
WUPS. I SHOULD PICK UP THIS CARD FROM HER... SISTER, OK.
BETTER CHECK FOR FLOWERS, 'CAUSE THEY CAN LEAVE STAINS OR CRINKLY LEAVES.
BNL
FRAZZ SURE IS THOROUGH, ISN'T HE?
HE IS WHEN HE'S CHECKING FOR BOYFRIEND ARTIFACTS, HONEY.
MALLETT

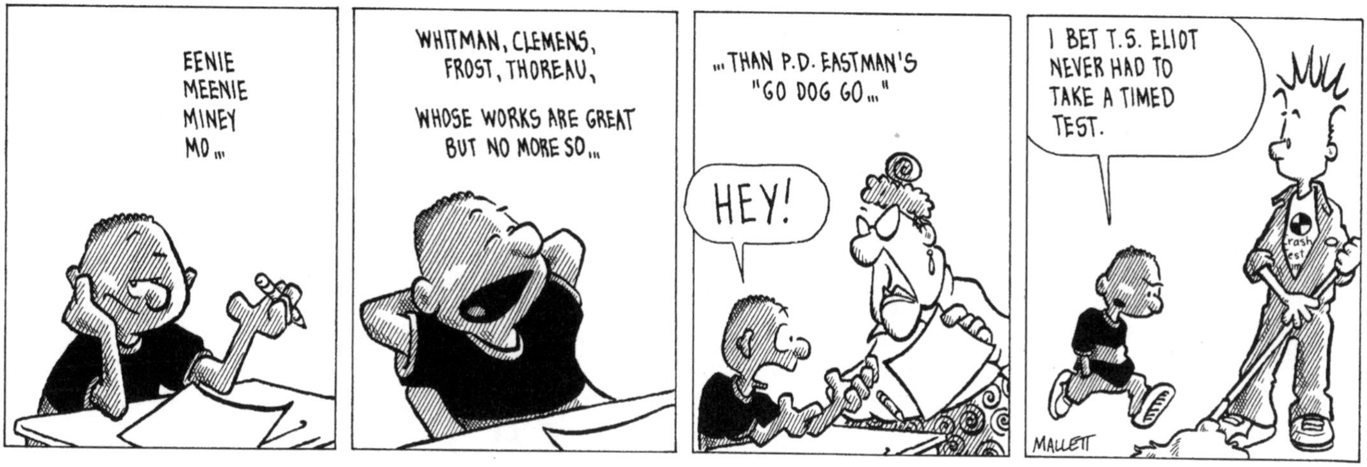
EENIE MEENIE MINEY MO...
WHITMAN, CLEMENS, FROST, THOREAU,
WHOSE WORKS ARE GREAT BUT NO MORE SO...
...THAN P.D. EASTMAN'S "GO DOG GO..."
HEY!
I BET T.S. ELIOT NEVER HAD TO TAKE A TIMED TEST.
MALLETT

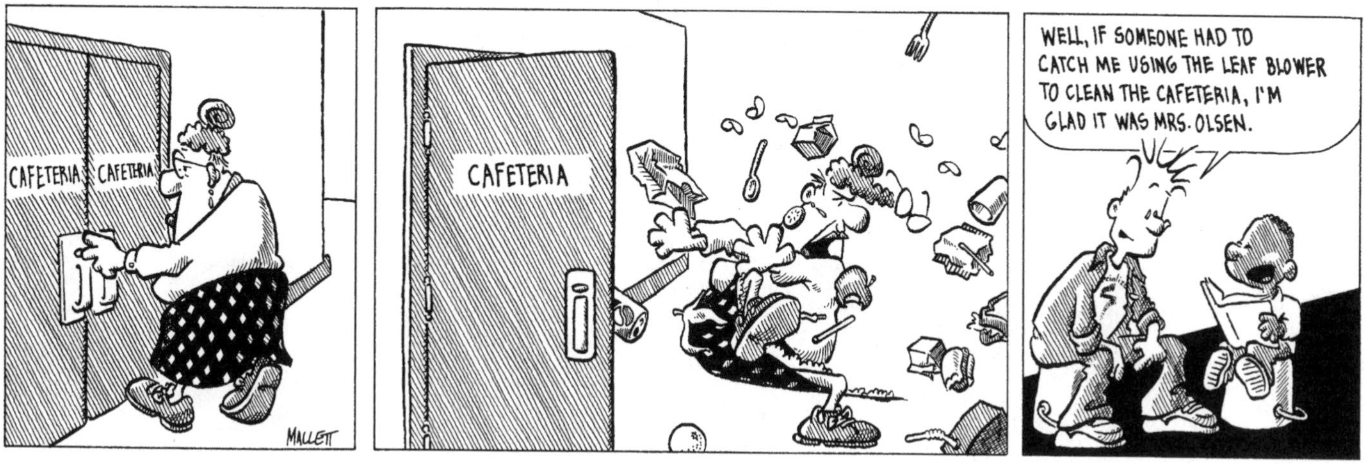
CAFETERIA
CAFETERIA
MALLETT
CAFETERIA
WELL, IF SOMEONE HAD TO CATCH ME USING THE LEAF BLOWER TO CLEAN THE CAFETERIA, I'M GLAD IT WAS MRS. OLSEN.

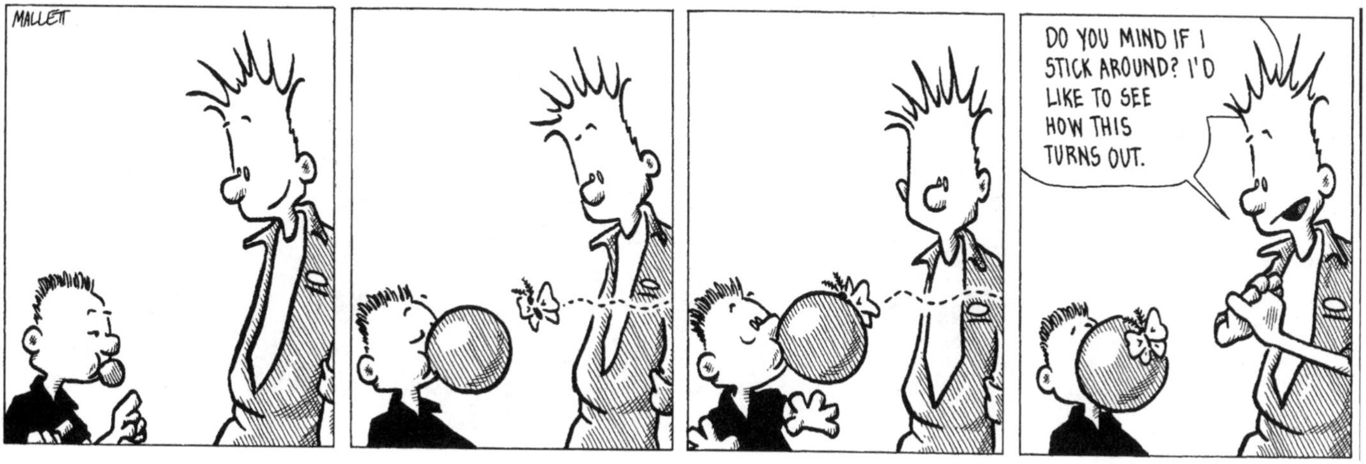
MALLETT
DO YOU MIND IF I STICK AROUND? I'D LIKE TO SEE HOW THIS TURNS OUT.

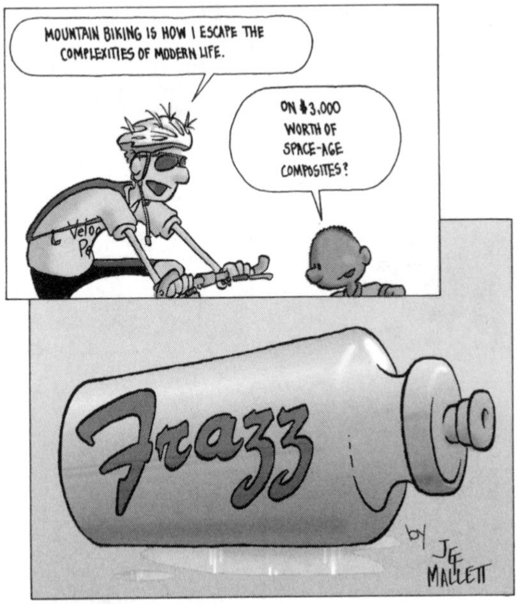
MOUNTAIN BIKING IS HOW I ESCAPE THE COMPLEXITIES OF MODERN LIFE.
ON $3,000 WORTH OF SPACE-AGE COMPOSITES?
Frazz
by JEF MALLETT

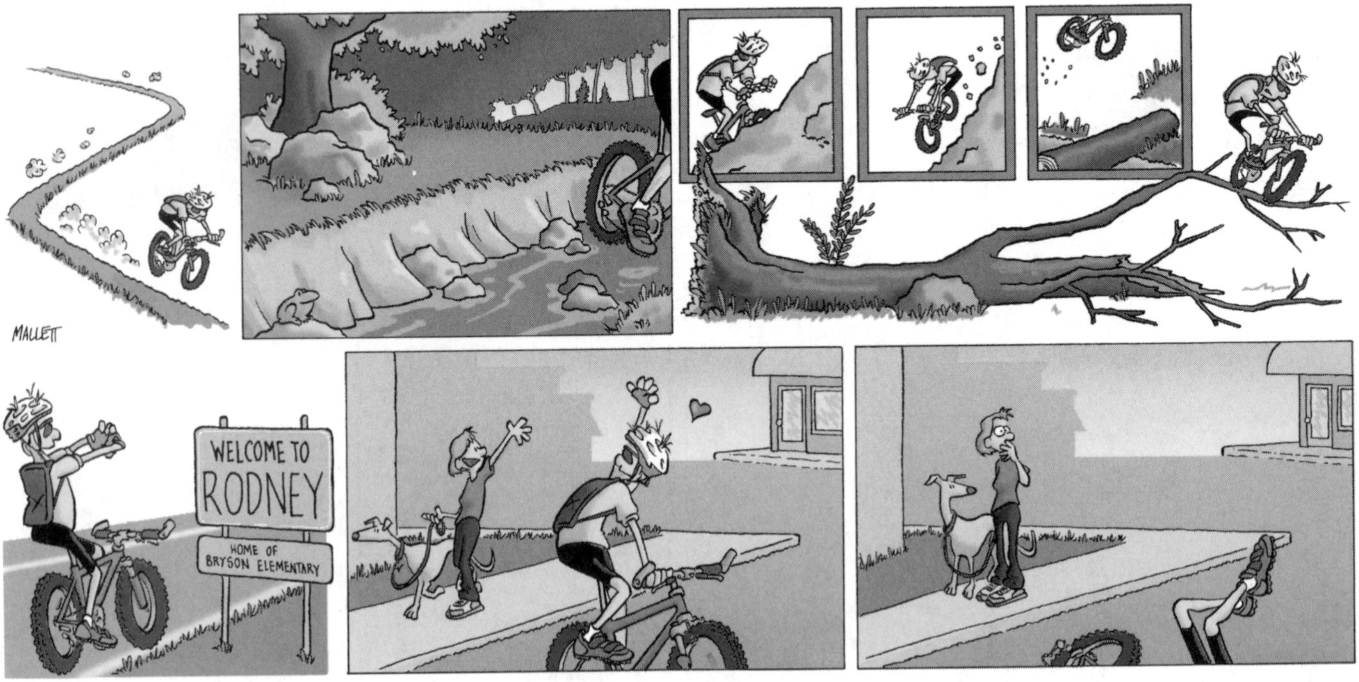
MALLETT
WELCOME TO RODNEY
HOME OF BRYSON ELEMENTARY

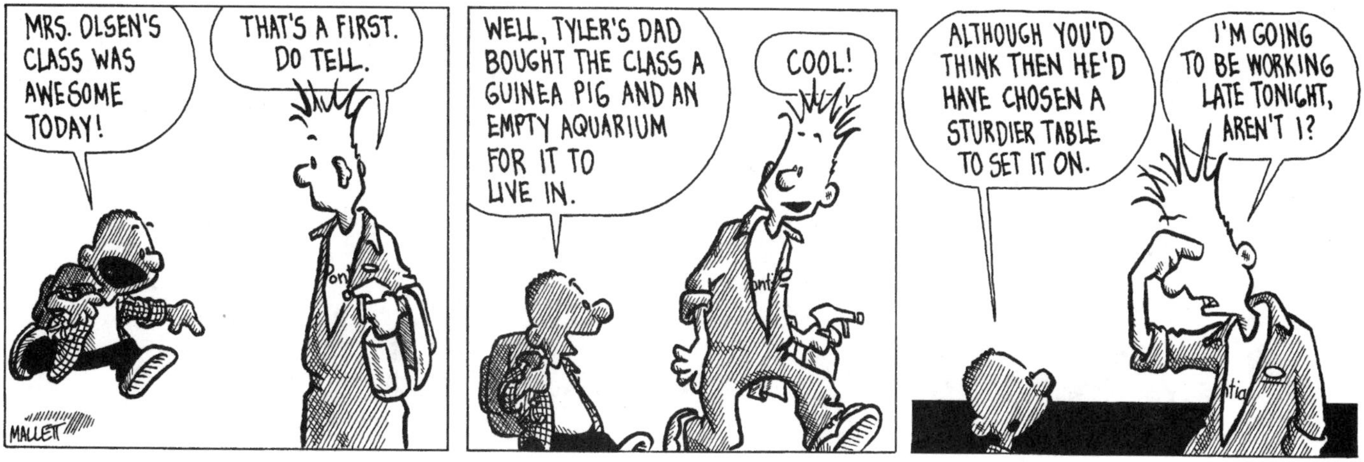
MRS. OLSEN'S CLASS WAS AWESOME TODAY!
THAT'S A FIRST. DO TELL.
WELL, TYLER'S DAD BOUGHT THE CLASS A GUINEA PIG AND AN EMPTY AQUARIUM FOR IT TO LIVE IN.
COOL!
ALTHOUGH YOU'D THINK THEN HE'D HAVE CHOSEN A STURDIER TABLE TO SET IT ON.
I'M GOING TO BE WORKING LATE TONIGHT, AREN'T I?
MALLETT

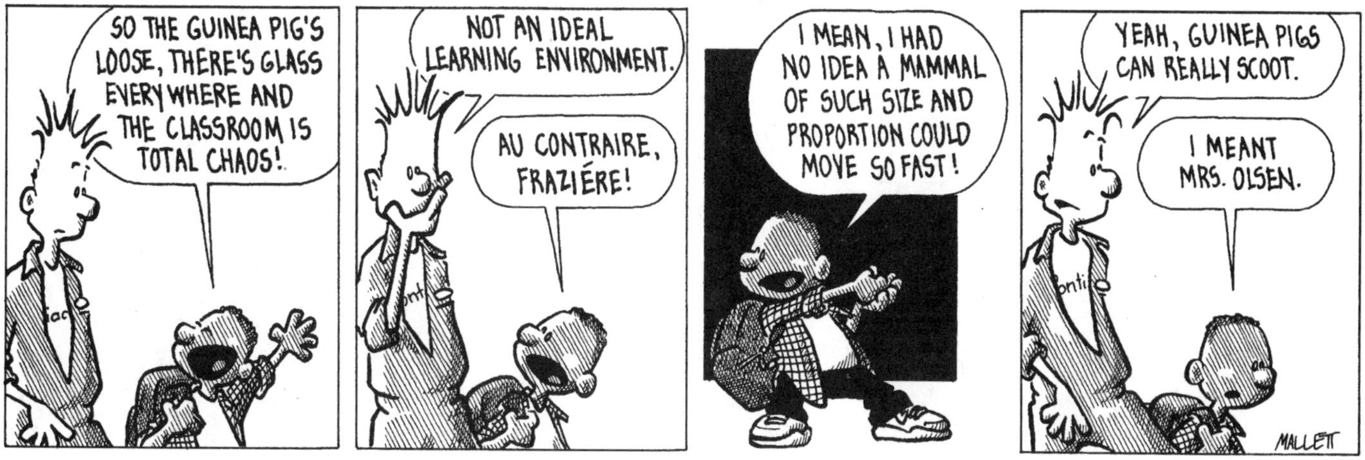
SO THE GUINEA PIG'S LOOSE, THERE'S GLASS EVERYWHERE AND THE CLASSROOM IS TOTAL CHAOS!
NOT AN IDEAL LEARNING ENVIRONMENT.
AU CONTRAIRE, FRAZIÉRE!
I MEAN, I HAD NO IDEA A MAMMAL OF SUCH SIZE AND PROPORTION COULD MOVE SO FAST!
YEAH, GUINEA PIGS CAN REALLY SCOOT.
I MEANT MRS. OLSEN.
MALLETT

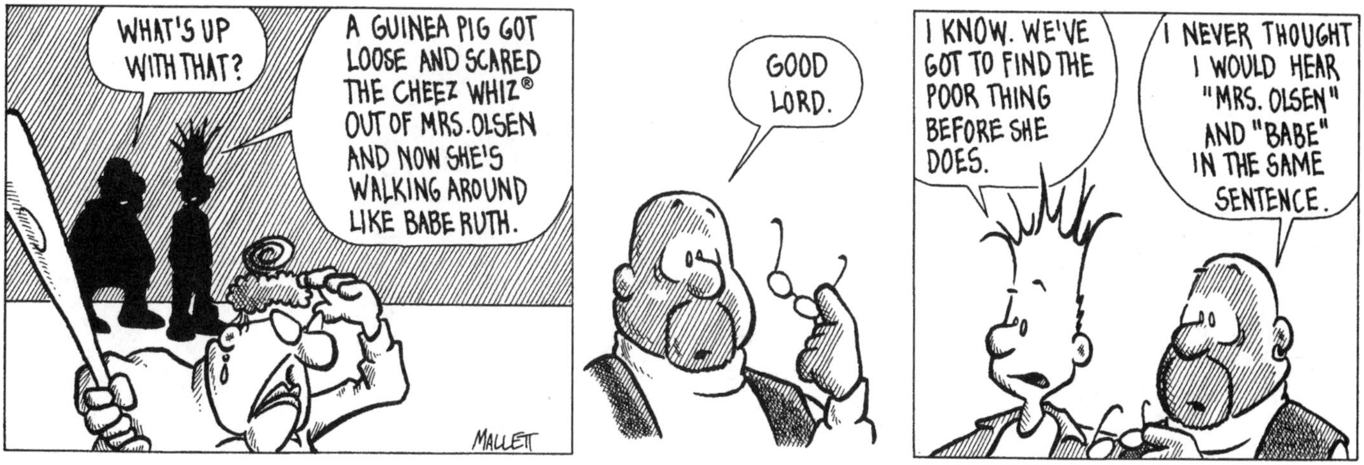
WHAT'S UP WITH THAT?
A GUINEA PIG GOT LOOSE AND SCARED THE CHEEZ WHIZ® OUT OF MRS. OLSEN AND NOW SHE'S WALKING AROUND LIKE BABE RUTH.
MALLETT
GOOD LORD.
I KNOW. WE'VE GOT TO FIND THE POOR THING BEFORE SHE DOES.
I NEVER THOUGHT I WOULD HEAR "MRS. OLSEN" AND "BABE" IN THE SAME SENTENCE.

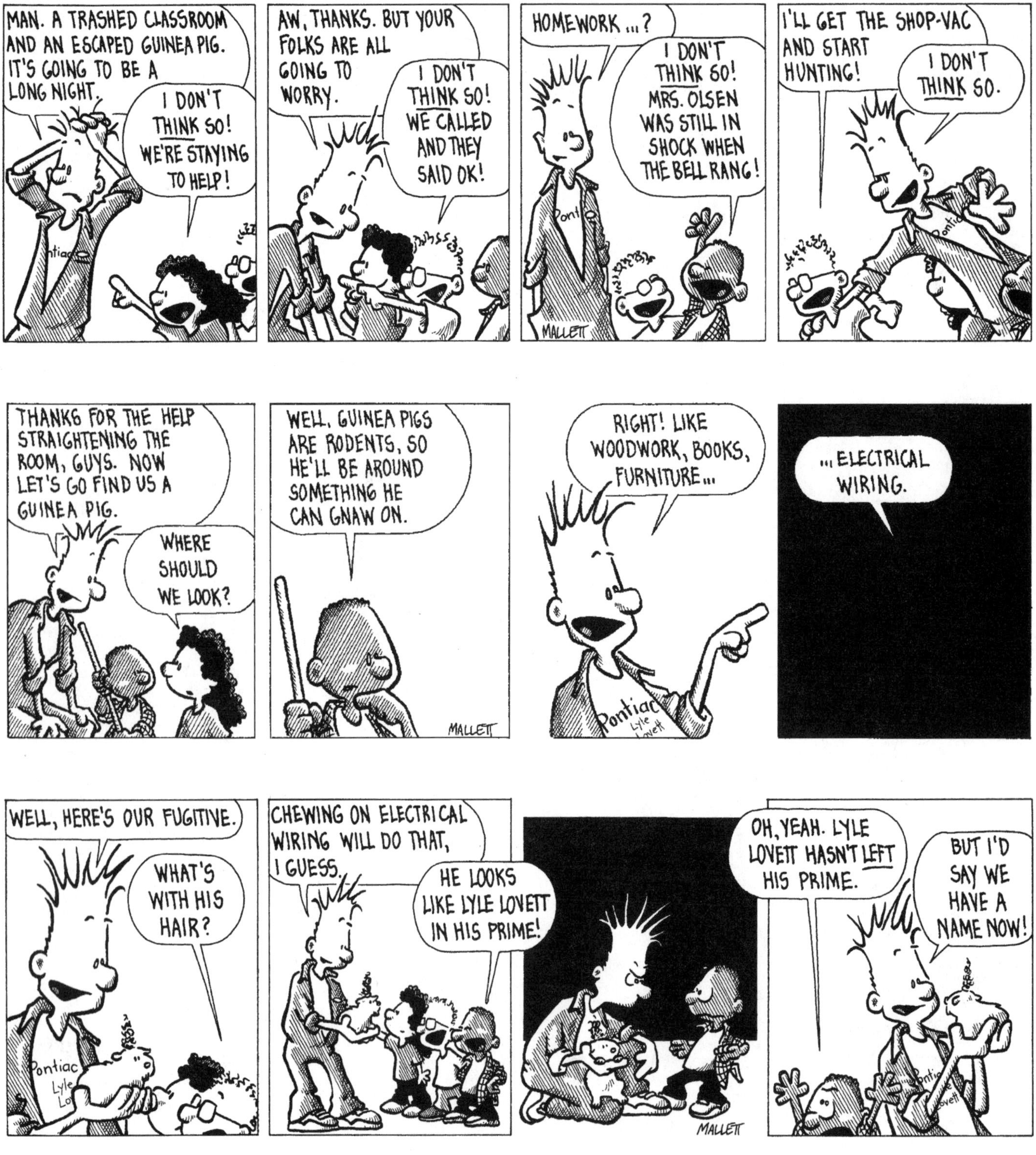
MAN. A TRASHED CLASSROOM AND AN ESCAPED GUINEA PIG. IT'S GOING TO BE A LONG NIGHT.
I DON'T THINK SO! WE'RE STAYING TO HELP!
AW, THANKS. BUT YOUR FOLKS ARE ALL GOING TO WORRY.
I DON'T THINK SO! WE CALLED AND THEY SAID OK!
HOMEWORK ...?
I DON'T THINK SO! MRS. OLSEN WAS STILL IN SHOCK WHEN THE BELL RANG!
MALLETT
I'LL GET THE SHOP-VAC AND START HUNTING!
I DON'T THINK SO.
THANKS FOR THE HELP STRAIGHTENING THE ROOM, GUYS. NOW LET'S GO FIND US A GUINEA PIG.
WHERE SHOULD WE LOOK?
WELL, GUINEA PIGS ARE RODENTS, SO HE'LL BE AROUND SOMETHING HE CAN GNAW ON.
MALLETT
RIGHT! LIKE WOODWORK, BOOKS, FURNITURE...
Pontiac Lyle Lovett
...ELECTRICAL WIRING.
WELL, HERE'S OUR FUGITIVE.
WHAT'S WITH HIS HAIR?
CHEWING ON ELECTRICAL WIRING WILL DO THAT, I GUESS.
HE LOOKS LIKE LYLE LOVETT IN HIS PRIME!
MALLETT
OH, YEAH. LYLE LOVETT HASN'T LEFT HIS PRIME.
BUT I'D SAY WE HAVE A NAME NOW!

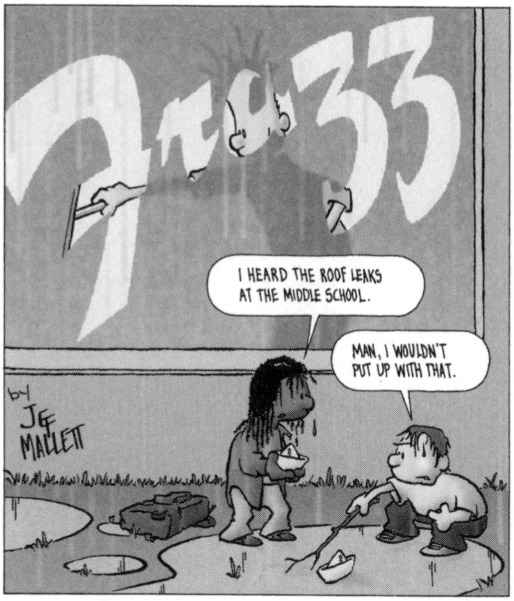
by JEF MALLETT
I HEARD THE ROOF LEAKS AT THE MIDDLE SCHOOL.
MAN, I WOULDN'T PUT UP WITH THAT.

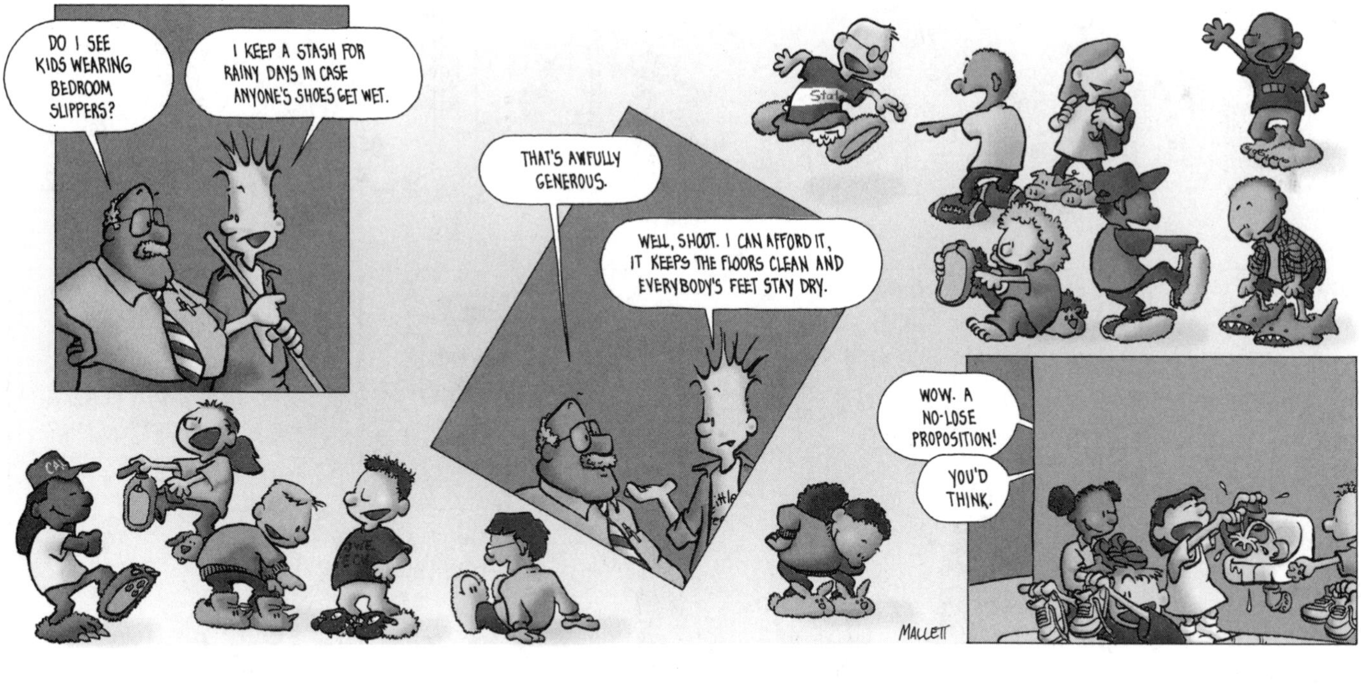
DO I SEE KIDS WEARING BEDROOM SLIPPERS?
I KEEP A STASH FOR RAINY DAYS IN CASE ANYONE'S SHOES GET WET.
THAT'S AWFULLY GENEROUS.
WELL, SHOOT. I CAN AFFORD IT, IT KEEPS THE FLOORS CLEAN AND EVERYBODY'S FEET STAY DRY.
WOW. A NO-LOSE PROPOSITION!
YOU'D THINK.
MALLETT

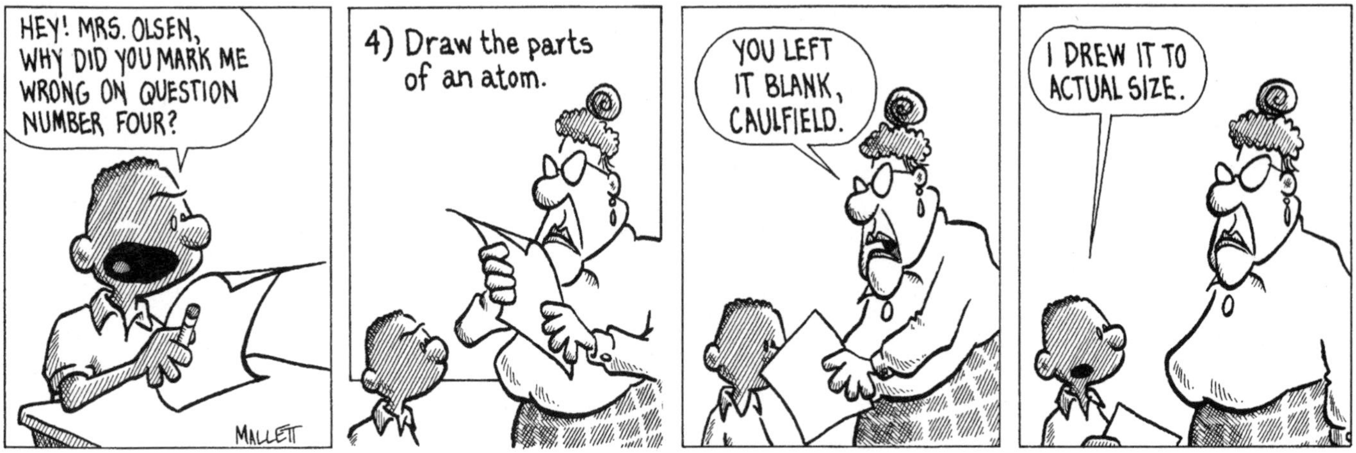
HEY! MRS. OLSEN, WHY DID YOU MARK ME WRONG ON QUESTION NUMBER FOUR?
4) Draw the parts of an atom.
YOU LEFT IT BLANK, CAULFIELD.
I DREW IT TO ACTUAL SIZE.
MALLETT

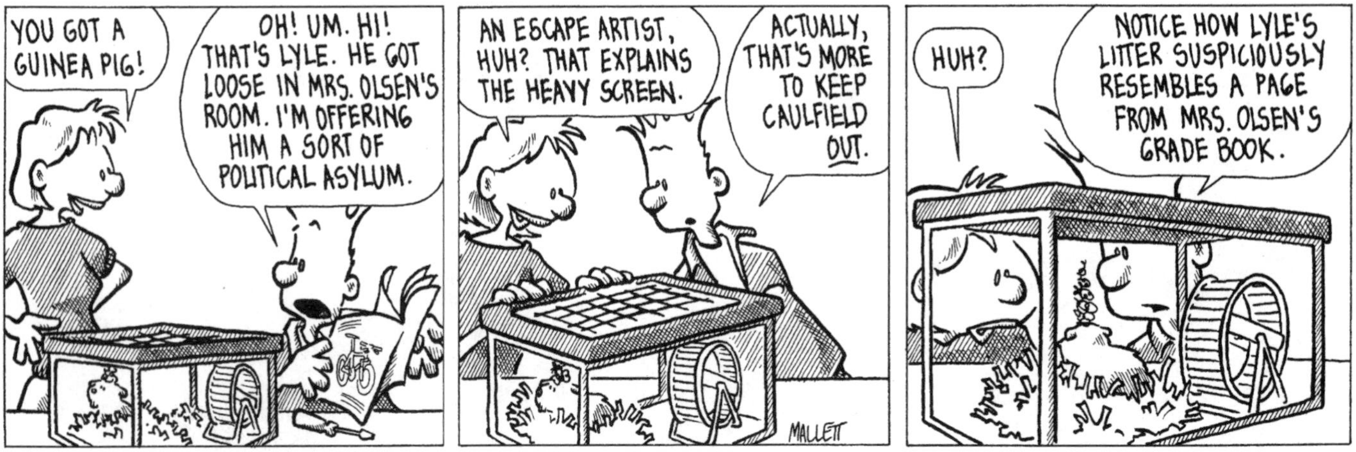
YOU GOT A GUINEA PIG!
OH! UM. HI! THAT'S LYLE. HE GOT LOOSE IN MRS. OLSEN'S ROOM. I'M OFFERING HIM A SORT OF POLITICAL ASYLUM.
AN ESCAPE ARTIST, HUH? THAT EXPLAINS THE HEAVY SCREEN.
ACTUALLY, THAT'S MORE TO KEEP CAULFIELD OUT.
HUH?
NOTICE HOW LYLE'S LITTER SUSPICIOUSLY RESEMBLES A PAGE FROM MRS. OLSEN'S GRADE BOOK.
MALLETT

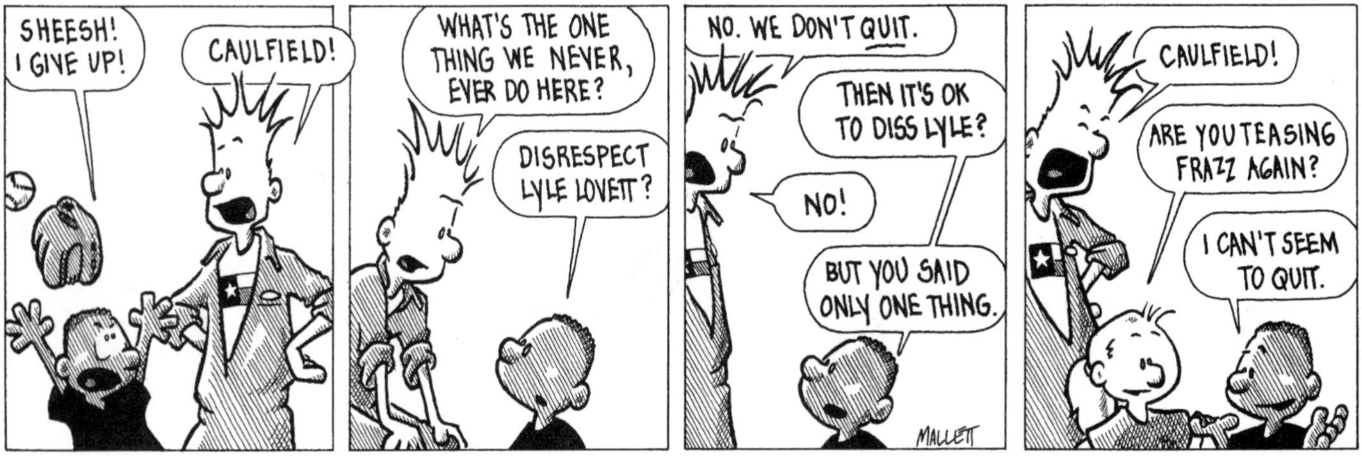
SHEESH! I GIVE UP!
CAULFIELD!
WHAT'S THE ONE THING WE NEVER, EVER DO HERE?
DISRESPECT LYLE LOVETT?
NO. WE DON'T QUIT.
THEN IT'S OK TO DISS LYLE?
NO!
BUT YOU SAID ONLY ONE THING.
CAULFIELD!
ARE YOU TEASING FRAZZ AGAIN?
I CAN'T SEEM TO QUIT.
MALLETT

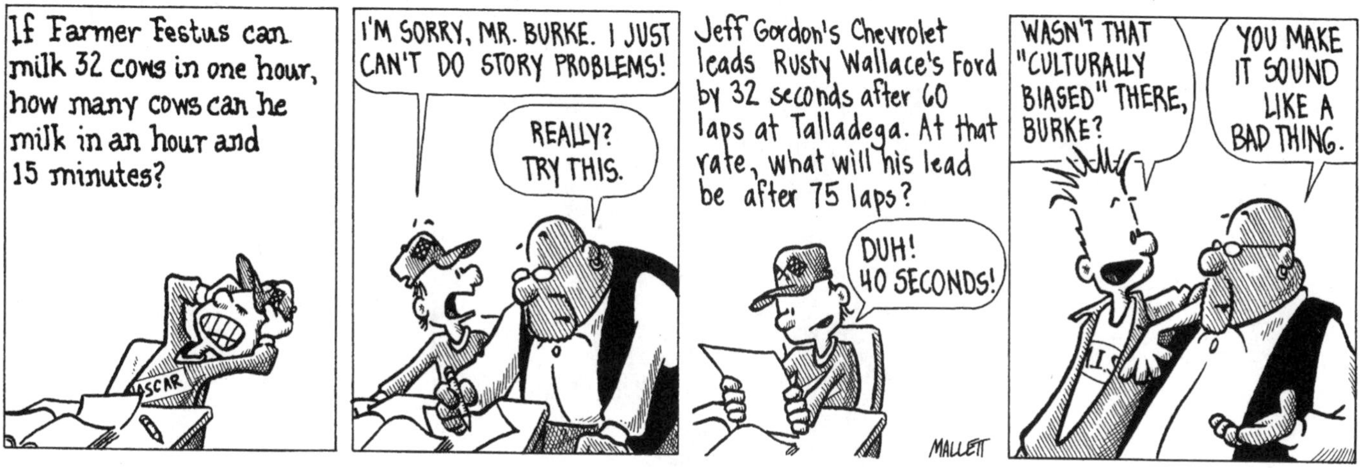
If Farmer Festus can milk 32 cows in one hour, how many cows can he milk in an hour and 15 minutes?
ASCAR
I'M SORRY, MR. BURKE. I JUST CAN'T DO STORY PROBLEMS!
REALLY? TRY THIS.
Jeff Gordon's Chevrolet leads Rusty Wallace's Ford by 32 seconds after 60 laps at Talladega. At that rate, what will his lead be after 75 laps?
DUH! 40 SECONDS!
WASN'T THAT "CULTURALLY BIASED" THERE, BURKE?
YOU MAKE IT SOUND LIKE A BAD THING.
MALLETT

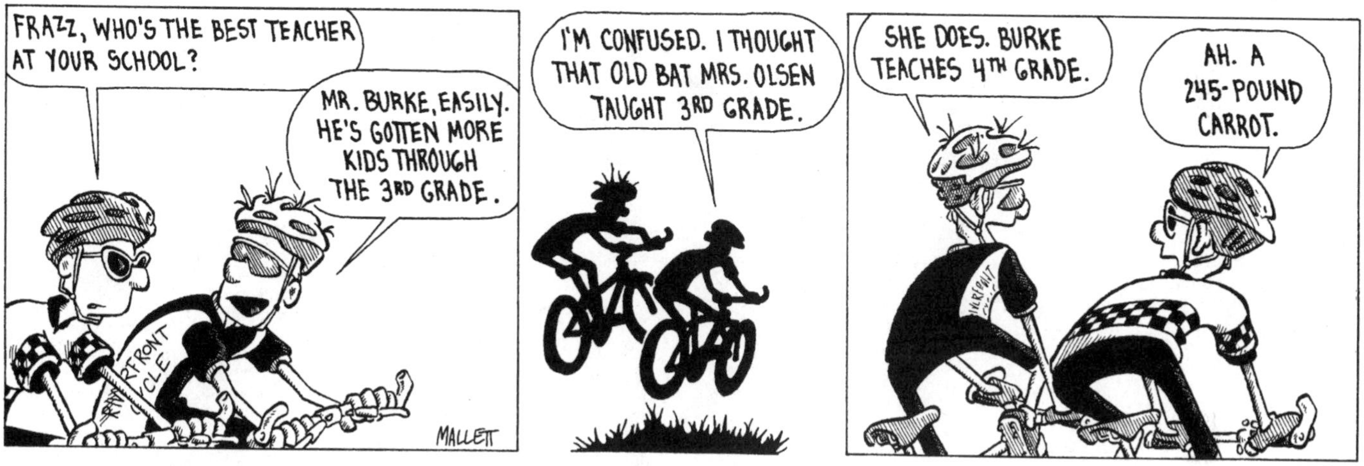
FRAZZ, WHO'S THE BEST TEACHER AT YOUR SCHOOL?
MR. BURKE, EASILY. HE'S GOTTEN MORE KIDS THROUGH THE 3RD GRADE.
RIVERFRONT CYCLE
MALLETT
I'M CONFUSED. I THOUGHT THAT OLD BAT MRS. OLSEN TAUGHT 3RD GRADE.
SHE DOES. BURKE TEACHES 4TH GRADE.
AH. A 245-POUND CARROT.

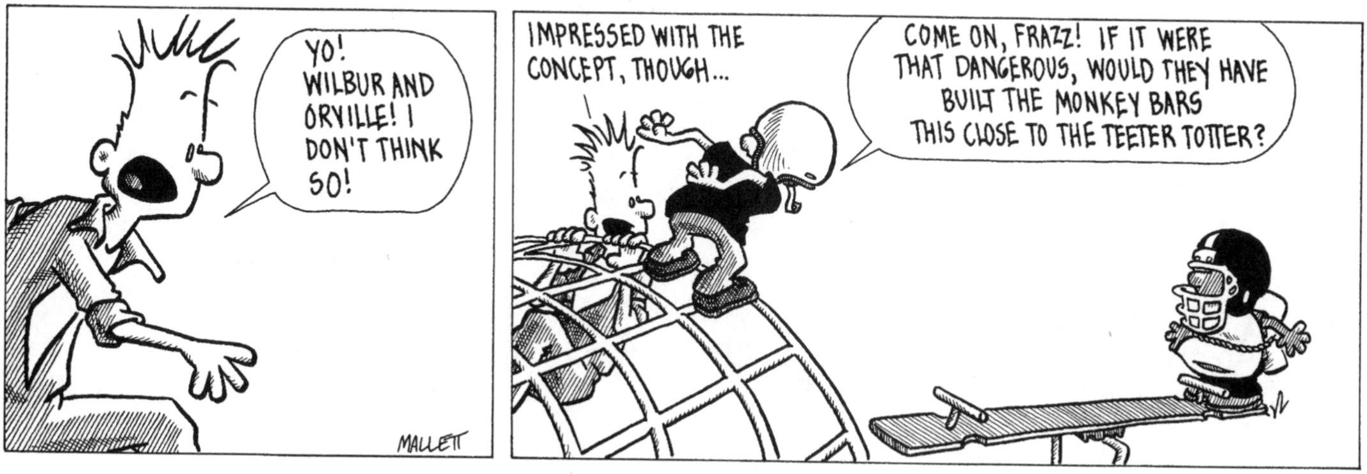
YO! WILBUR AND ORVILLE! I DON'T THINK SO!
MALLETT
IMPRESSED WITH THE CONCEPT, THOUGH...
COME ON, FRAZZ! IF IT WERE THAT DANGEROUS, WOULD THEY HAVE BUILT THE MONKEY BARS THIS CLOSE TO THE TEETER TOTTER?

WALL STREET JOUR
Frazz
by Jef Mallett
YOU READ THAT RAG? IT DOESN'T EVEN HAVE COMICS.
WELL, THIS ISSUE NOW HAS A CARTOON OF ALAN GREENSPAN IN A FRILLY PINK COCKTAIL DRESS.

SO IF FARMER FESTUS HAS 28 DELICIOUS APPLES AND SELLS HALF OF THEM, HOW MANY DOES HE HAVE LEFT?
HARD TO SAY.
IF HE SELLS THEM ON THE FUTURES MARKET AND TIMES IT RIGHT, HE COULD END UP WITH MORE THAN HE STARTED WITH.
OR HE COULD BE BUCKING FOR A SUBSIDY. 28 APPLES IS A PRETTY WEAK CROP.
SUSPICIOUSLY SO.
AS IF I'D TRUST ANYBODY WHO MARKETS THE MEALIEST VARIETY OF APPLE AS "DELICIOUS."
SO, IT DEPENDS.
IT DEPENDS.
THAT'S WHAT I PUT ON MY TEST, AND MRS. OLSEN GAVE ME AN "E."
REALLY? THAT'S WHAT MY FRIEND JIM PUT IN HIS DISSERTATION, AND THEY GAVE HIM A DOCTORATE.
MALLETT

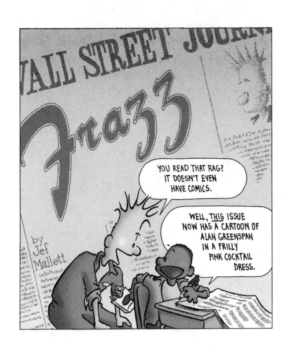

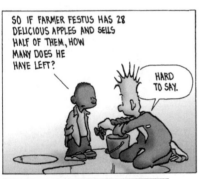

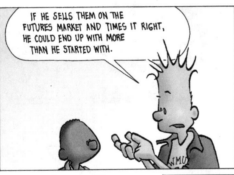

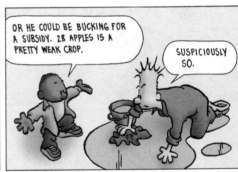

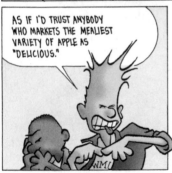

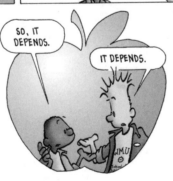

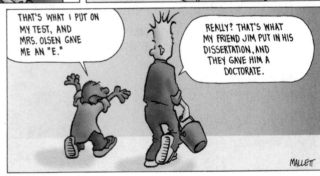

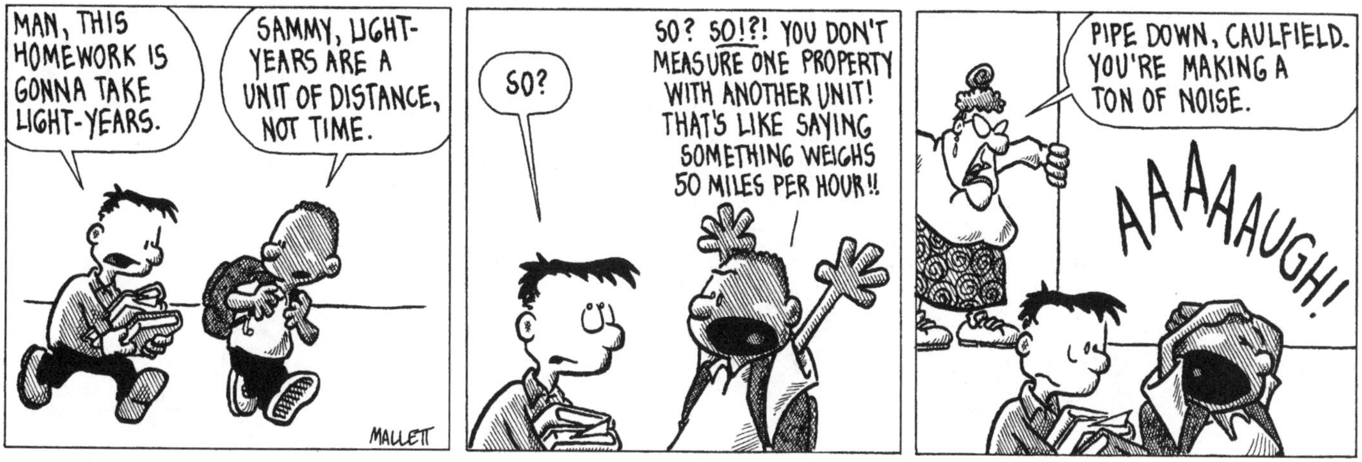
MAN, THIS HOMEWORK IS GONNA TAKE LIGHT-YEARS.
SAMMY, LIGHT-YEARS ARE A UNIT OF DISTANCE, NOT TIME.
MALLETT
SO?
SO? SO!?! YOU DON'T MEASURE ONE PROPERTY WITH ANOTHER UNIT! THAT'S LIKE SAYING SOMETHING WEIGHS 50 MILES PER HOUR!!
PIPE DOWN, CAULFIELD. YOU'RE MAKING A TON OF NOISE.
AAAAAUGH!

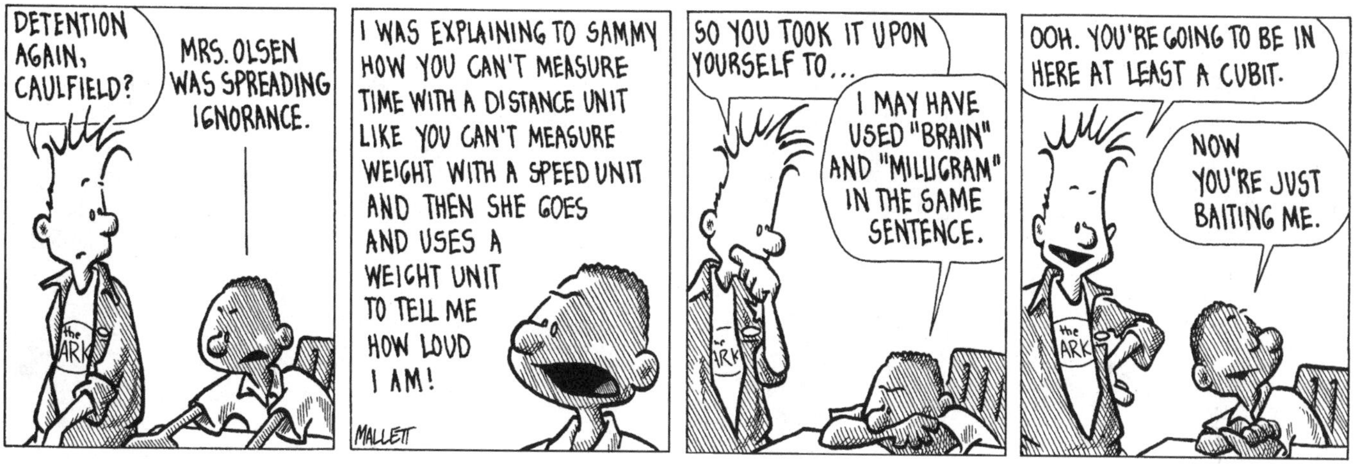
DETENTION AGAIN, CAULFIELD?
MRS. OLSEN WAS SPREADING IGNORANCE.
I WAS EXPLAINING TO SAMMY HOW YOU CAN'T MEASURE TIME WITH A DISTANCE UNIT LIKE YOU CAN'T MEASURE WEIGHT WITH A SPEED UNIT AND THEN SHE GOES AND USES A WEIGHT UNIT TO TELL ME HOW LOUD I AM!
MALLETT
SO YOU TOOK IT UPON YOURSELF TO...
I MAY HAVE USED "BRAIN" AND "MILLIGRAM" IN THE SAME SENTENCE.
OOH. YOU'RE GOING TO BE IN HERE AT LEAST A CUBIT.
NOW YOU'RE JUST BAITING ME.

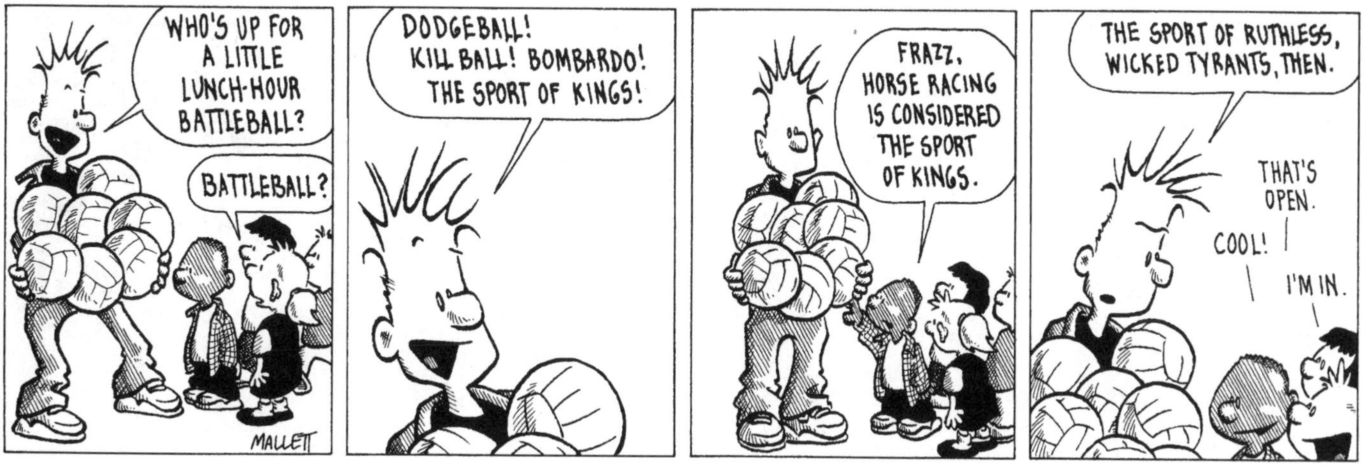
WHO'S UP FOR A LITTLE LUNCH-HOUR BATTLEBALL?
BATTLEBALL?
MALLETT
DODGEBALL! KILL BALL! BOMBARDO! THE SPORT OF KINGS!
FRAZZ, HORSE RACING IS CONSIDERED THE SPORT OF KINGS.
THE SPORT OF RUTHLESS, WICKED TYRANTS, THEN.
THAT'S OPEN.
COOL!
I'M IN.

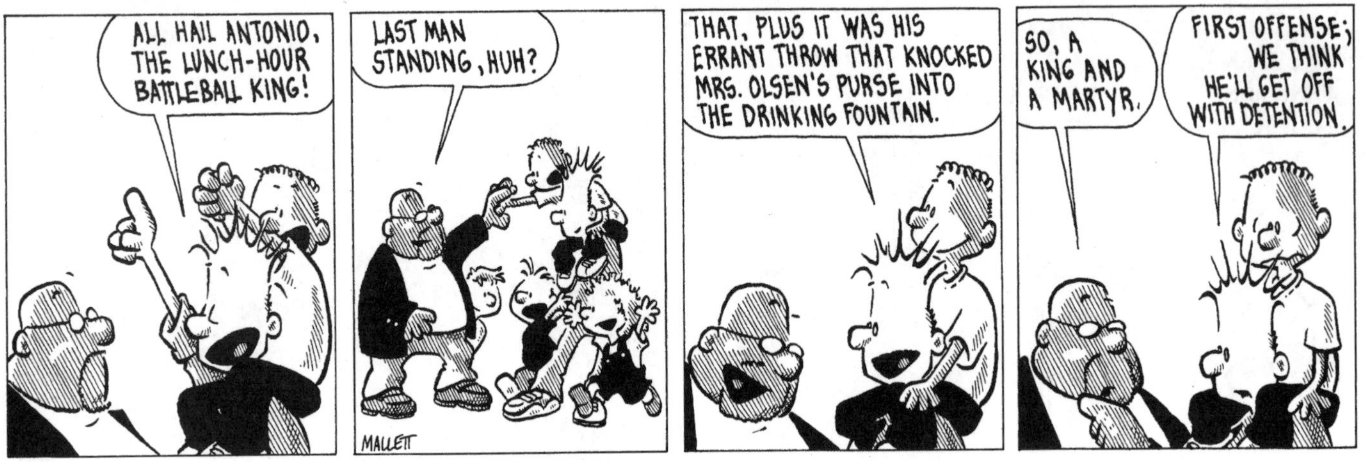
ALL HAIL ANTONIO, THE LUNCH-HOUR BATTLEBALL KING!
LAST MAN STANDING, HUH?
MALLETT
THAT, PLUS IT WAS HIS ERRANT THROW THAT KNOCKED MRS. OLSEN'S PURSE INTO THE DRINKING FOUNTAIN.
SO, A KING AND A MARTYR.
FIRST OFFENSE; WE THINK HE'LL GET OFF WITH DETENTION.

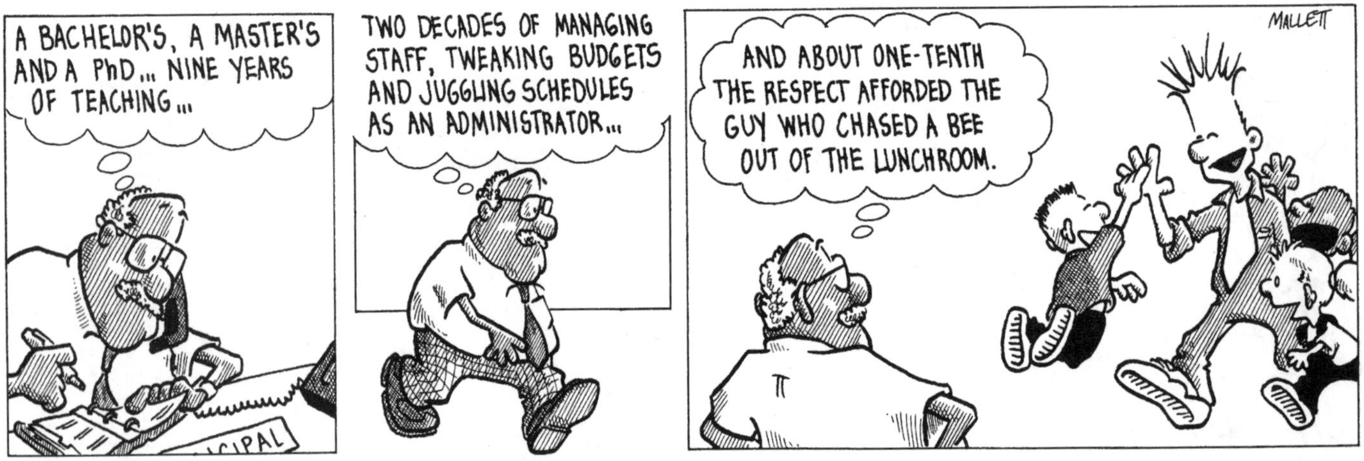
A BACHELOR'S, A MASTER'S AND A PhD... NINE YEARS OF TEACHING...
TWO DECADES OF MANAGING STAFF, TWEAKING BUDGETS AND JUGGLING SCHEDULES AS AN ADMINISTRATOR...
MALLETT
AND ABOUT ONE-TENTH THE RESPECT AFFORDED THE GUY WHO CHASED A BEE OUT OF THE LUNCHROOM.

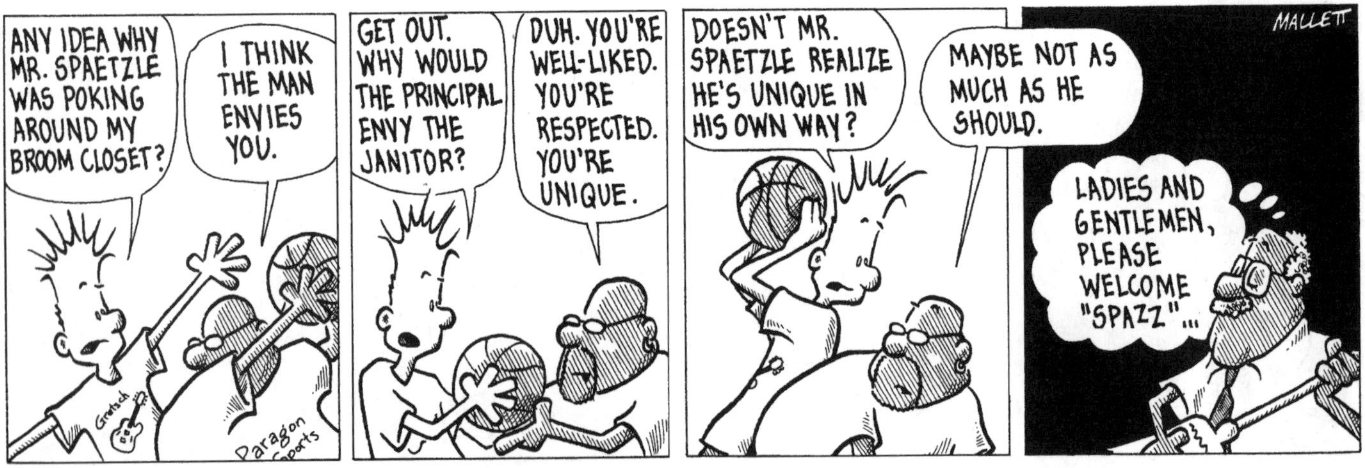
ANY IDEA WHY MR. SPAETZLE WAS POKING AROUND MY BROOM CLOSET?
I THINK THE MAN ENVIES YOU.
Gretsch
Paragon Sports
GET OUT. WHY WOULD THE PRINCIPAL ENVY THE JANITOR?
DUH. YOU'RE WELL-LIKED. YOU'RE RESPECTED. YOU'RE UNIQUE.
DOESN'T MR. SPAETZLE REALIZE HE'S UNIQUE IN HIS OWN WAY?
MAYBE NOT AS MUCH AS HE SHOULD.
MALLETT
LADIES AND GENTLEMEN, PLEASE WELCOME "SPAZZ"...

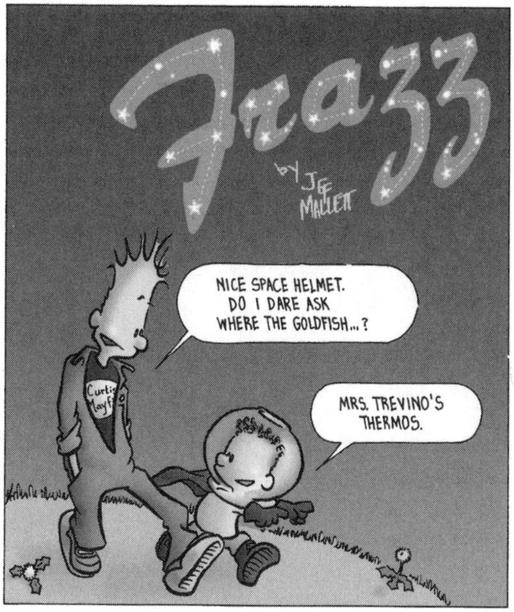
Frazz
by Jef Mallett
NICE SPACE HELMET. DO I DARE ASK WHERE THE GOLDFISH...?
MRS. TREVINO'S THERMOS.
Curtis Mayfield

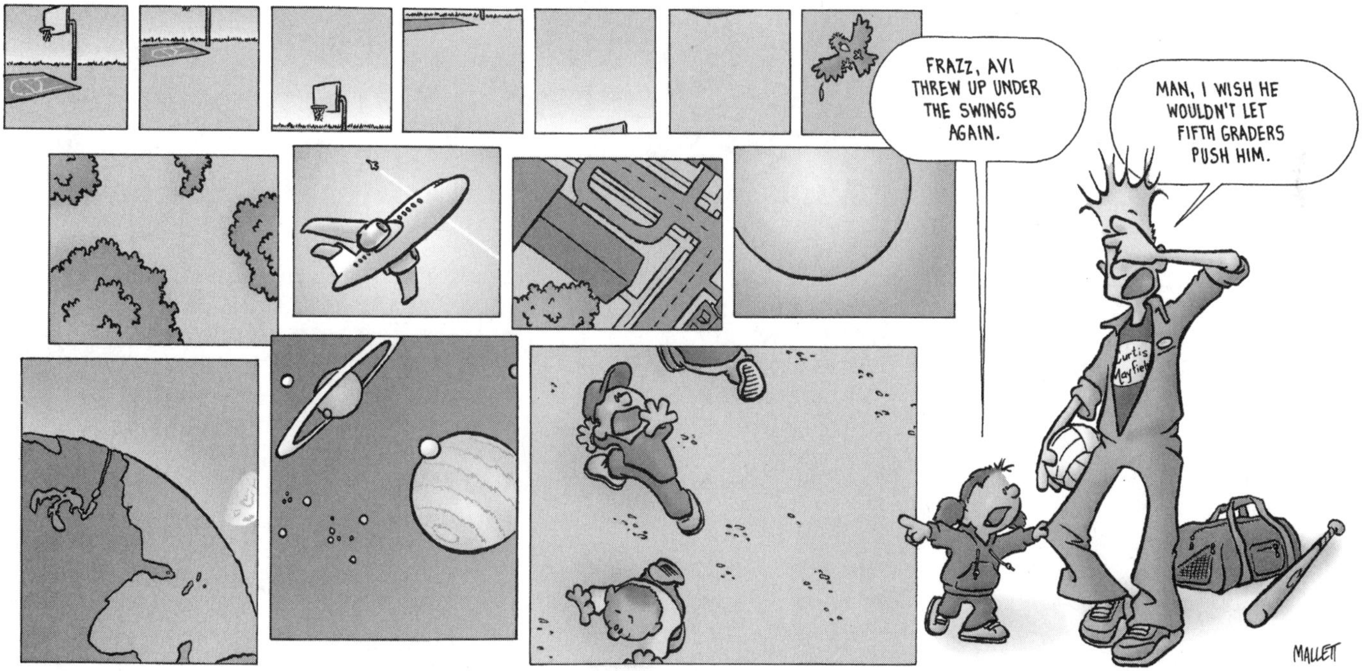
FRAZZ, AVI THREW UP UNDER THE SWINGS AGAIN.
MAN, I WISH HE WOULDN'T LET FIFTH GRADERS PUSH HIM.
Curtis Mayfield
MALLETT

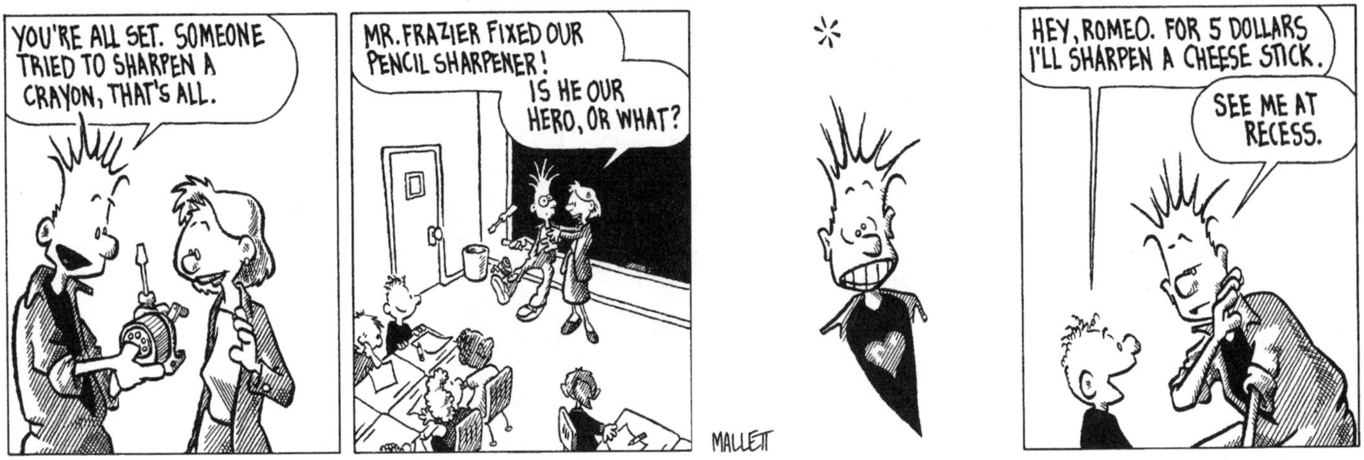
YOU'RE ALL SET. SOMEONE TRIED TO SHARPEN A CRAYON, THAT'S ALL.
MR. FRAZIER FIXED OUR PENCIL SHARPENER!
IS HE OUR HERO, OR WHAT?
MALLETT
HEY, ROMEO. FOR 5 DOLLARS I'LL SHARPEN A CHEESE STICK.
SEE ME AT RECESS.

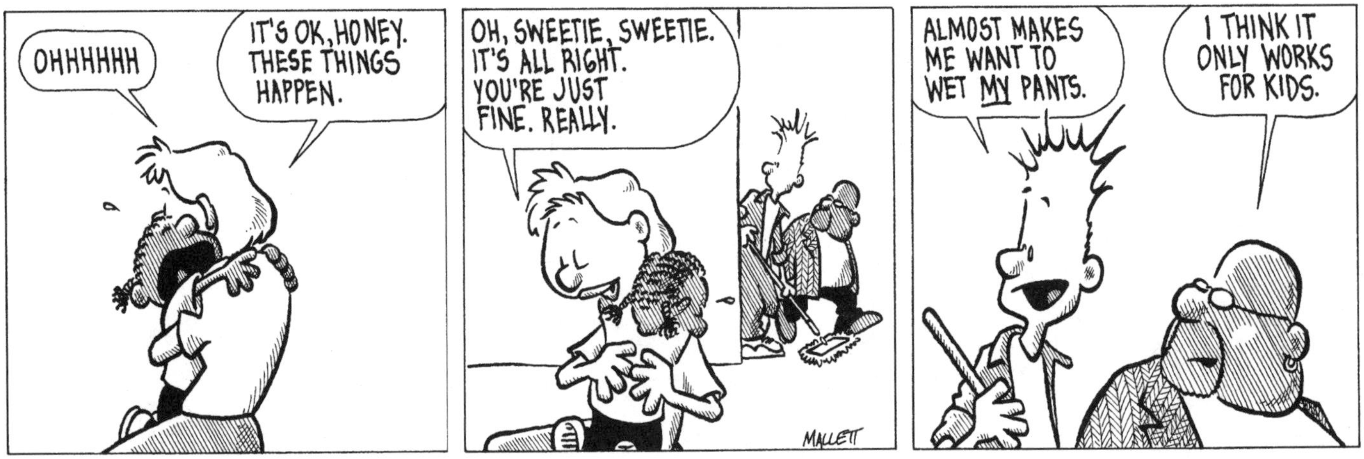
OHHHHHH
IT'S OK, HONEY. THESE THINGS HAPPEN.
OH, SWEETIE, SWEETIE. IT'S ALL RIGHT. YOU'RE JUST FINE. REALLY.
MALLETT
ALMOST MAKES ME WANT TO WET MY PANTS.
I THINK IT ONLY WORKS FOR KIDS.

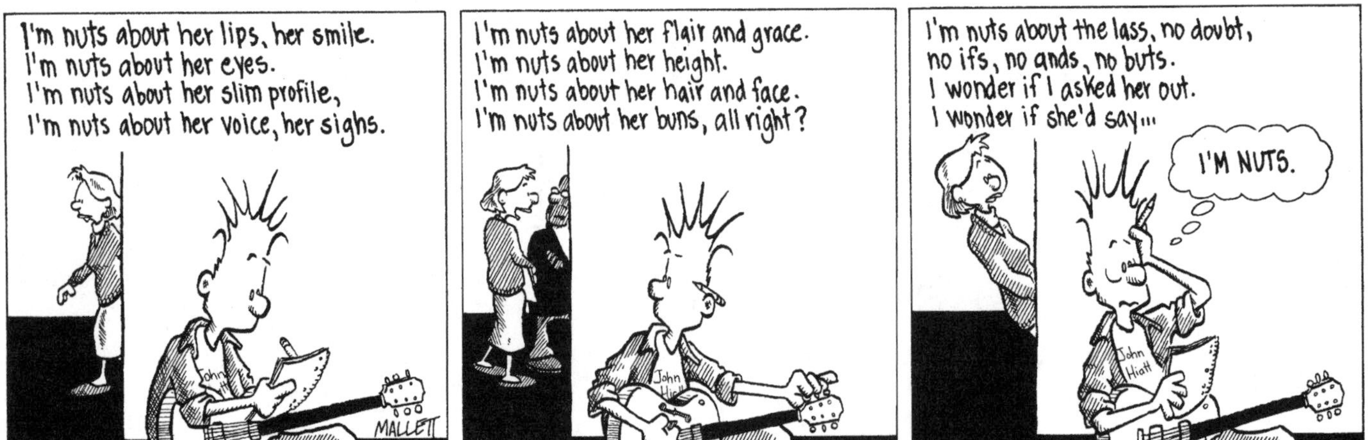
I'm nuts about her lips, her smile.
I'm nuts about her eyes.
I'm nuts about her slim profile,
I'm nuts about her voice, her sighs.
MALLETT
I'm nuts about her flair and grace.
I'm nuts about her height.
I'm nuts about her hair and face.
I'm nuts about her buns, all right?
I'm nuts about the lass, no doubt,
no ifs, no ands, no buts.
I wonder if I asked her out.
I wonder if she'd say...
I'M NUTS.

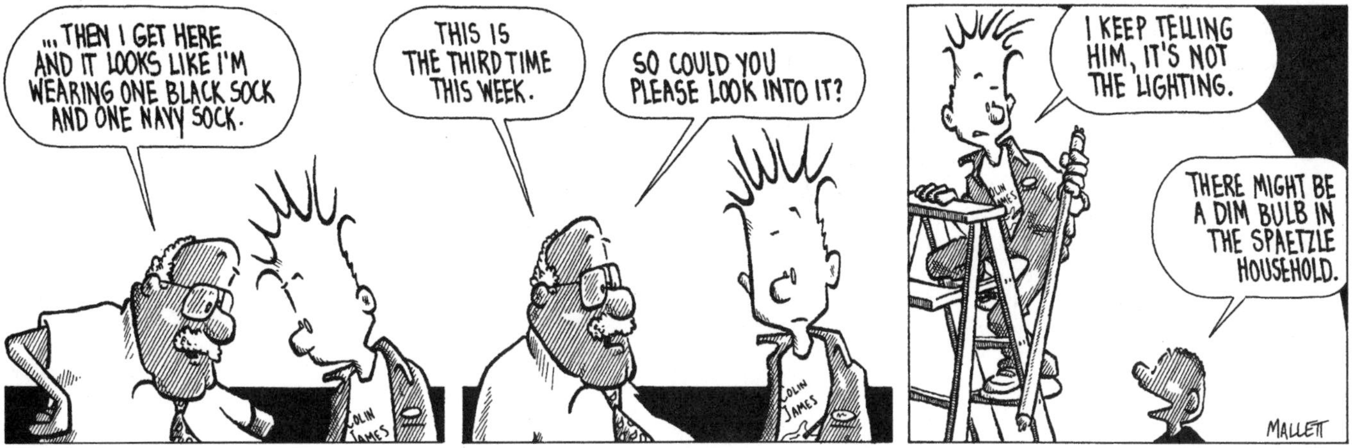
...THEN I GET HERE AND IT LOOKS LIKE I'M WEARING ONE BLACK SOCK AND ONE NAVY SOCK.
COLIN JAMES
THIS IS THE THIRD TIME THIS WEEK.
SO COULD YOU PLEASE LOOK INTO IT?
COLIN JAMES
I KEEP TELLING HIM, IT'S NOT THE LIGHTING.
THERE MIGHT BE A DIM BULB IN THE SPAETZLE HOUSEHOLD.
MALLETT

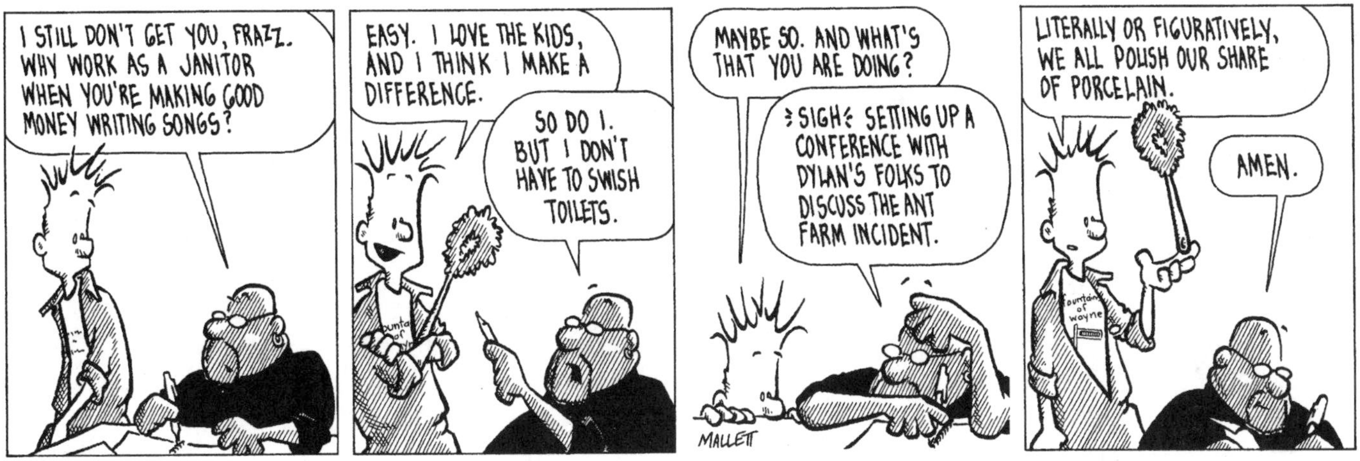
I STILL DON'T GET YOU, FRAZZ. WHY WORK AS A JANITOR WHEN YOU'RE MAKING GOOD MONEY WRITING SONGS?
EASY. I LOVE THE KIDS, AND I THINK I MAKE A DIFFERENCE.
SO DO I. BUT I DON'T HAVE TO SWISH TOILETS.
MAYBE SO. AND WHAT'S THAT YOU ARE DOING?
SIGH SETTING UP A CONFERENCE WITH DYLAN'S FOLKS TO DISCUSS THE ANT FARM INCIDENT.
MALLETT
LITERALLY OR FIGURATIVELY, WE ALL POLISH OUR SHARE OF PORCELAIN.
AMEN.

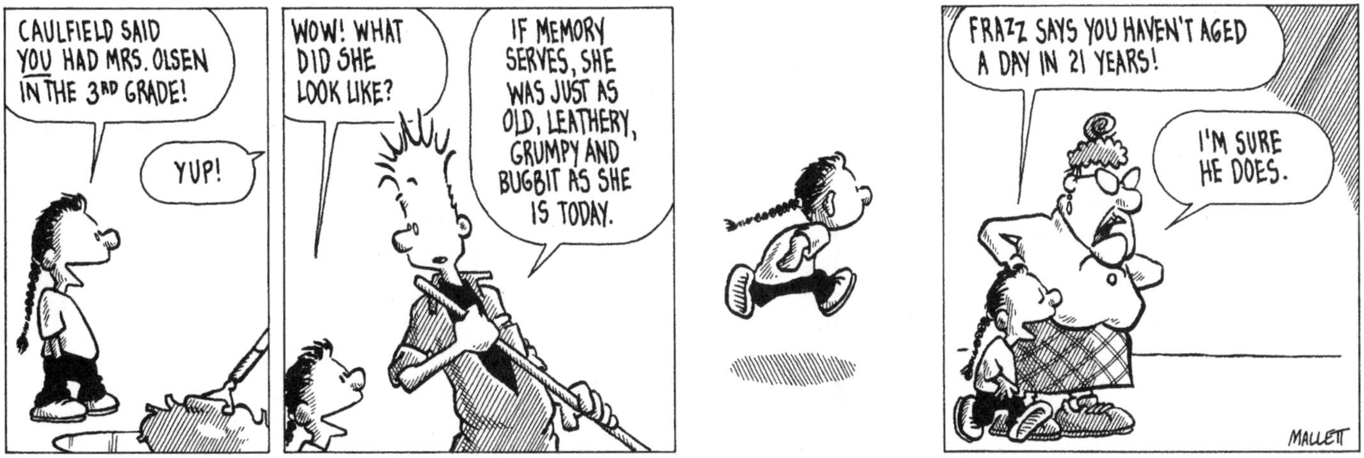
CAULFIELD SAID YOU HAD MRS. OLSEN IN THE 3RD GRADE!
YUP!
WOW! WHAT DID SHE LOOK LIKE?
IF MEMORY SERVES, SHE WAS JUST AS OLD, LEATHERY, GRUMPY AND BUGBIT AS SHE IS TODAY.
FRAZZ SAYS YOU HAVEN'T AGED A DAY IN 21 YEARS!
I'M SURE HE DOES.
MALLETT

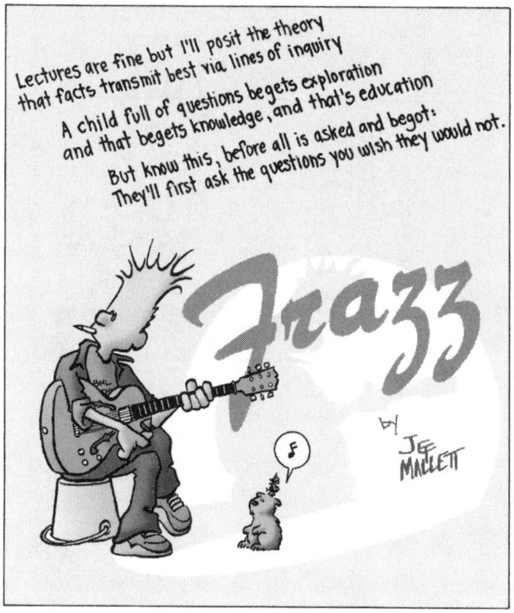
Lectures are fine but I'll posit the theory
that facts transmit best via lines of inquiry
A child full of questions begets exploration
and that begets knowledge, and that's education
But know this, before all is asked and begot:
They'll first ask the questions you wish they would not.
Frazz
by Jef Mallett

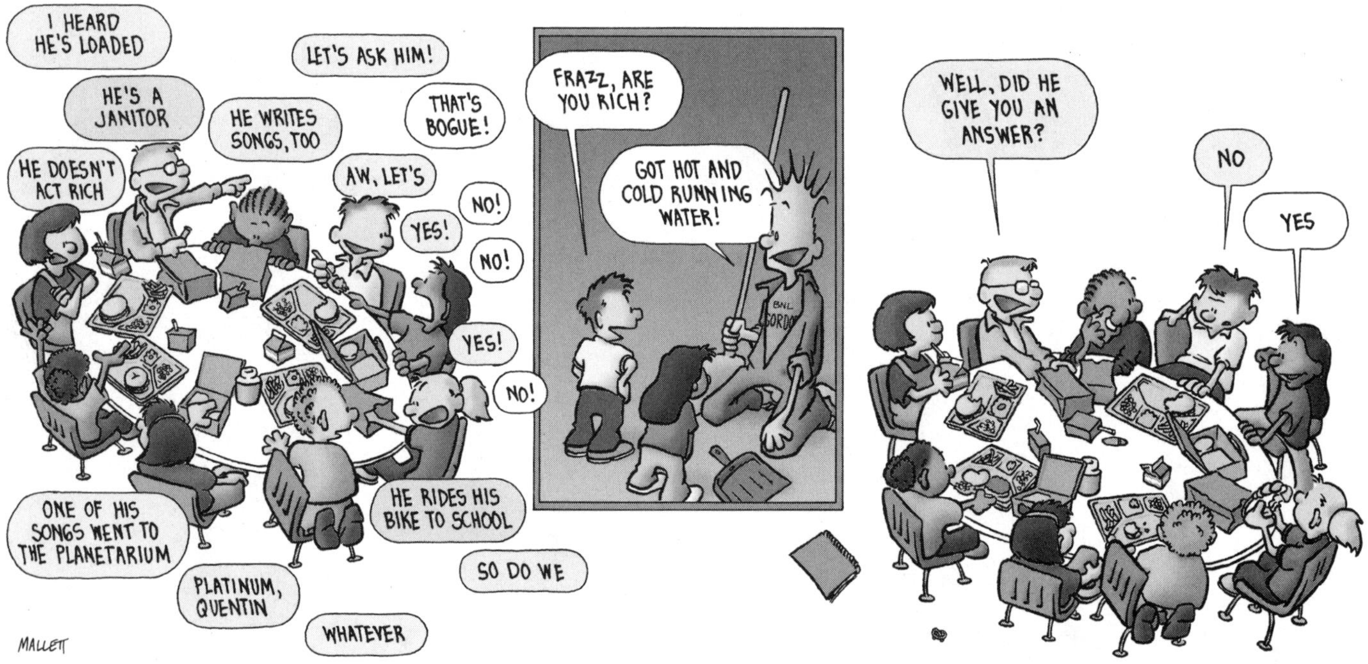
I HEARD HE'S LOADED
LET'S ASK HIM!
HE'S A JANITOR
HE WRITES SONGS, TOO
THAT'S BOGUE!
HE DOESN'T ACT RICH
AW, LET'S
NO!
YES!
NO!
YES!
NO!
ONE OF HIS SONGS WENT TO THE PLANETARIUM
HE RIDES HIS BIKE TO SCHOOL
SO DO WE
PLATINUM, QUENTIN
WHATEVER
MALLETT
FRAZZ, ARE YOU RICH?
GOT HOT AND COLD RUNNING WATER!
WELL, DID HE GIVE YOU AN ANSWER?
NO
YES

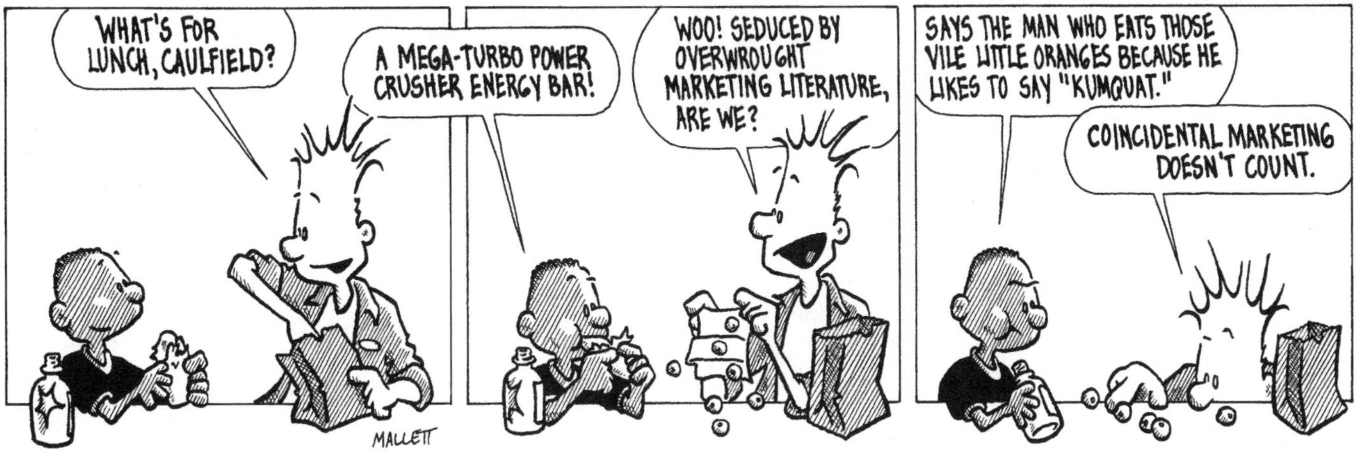
WHAT'S FOR LUNCH, CAULFIELD?
A MEGA-TURBO POWER CRUSHER ENERGY BAR!
WOO! SEDUCED BY OVERWROUGHT MARKETING LITERATURE, ARE WE?
SAYS THE MAN WHO EATS THOSE VILE LITTLE ORANGES BECAUSE HE LIKES TO SAY "KUMQUAT."
COINCIDENTAL MARKETING DOESN'T COUNT.
MALLETT

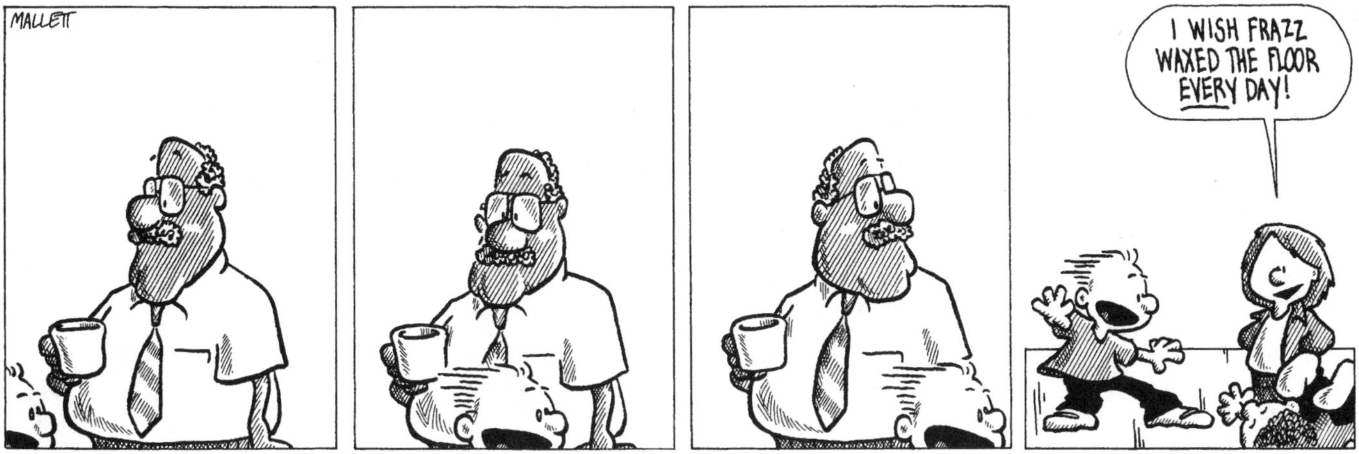
MALLETT
I WISH FRAZZ WAXED THE FLOOR EVERY DAY!

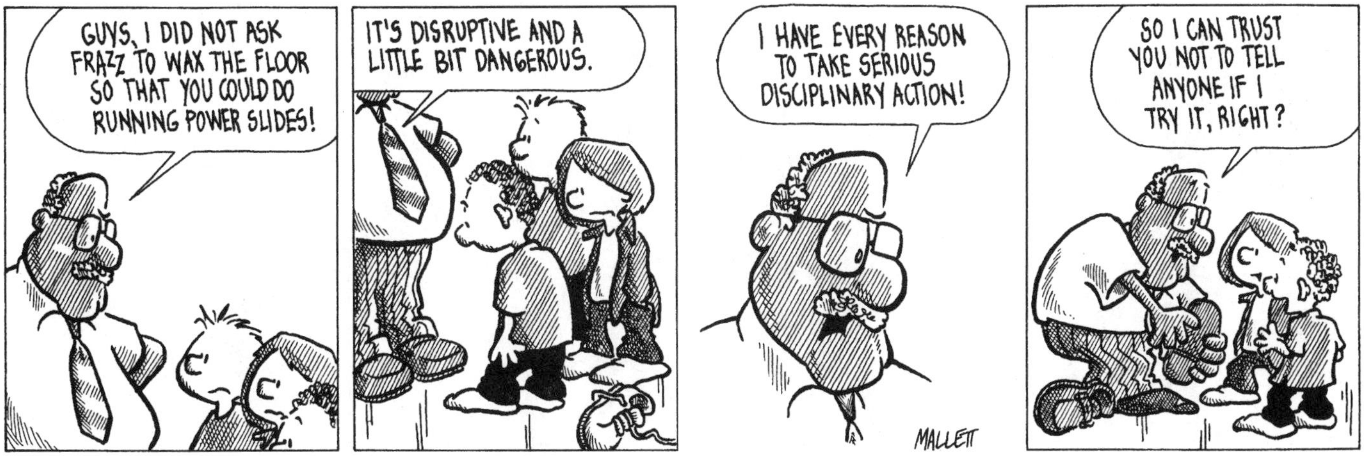
GUYS, I DID NOT ASK FRAZZ TO WAX THE FLOOR SO THAT YOU COULD DO RUNNING POWER SLIDES!
IT'S DISRUPTIVE AND A LITTLE BIT DANGEROUS.
I HAVE EVERY REASON TO TAKE SERIOUS DISCIPLINARY ACTION!
MALLETT
SO I CAN TRUST YOU NOT TO TELL ANYONE IF I TRY IT, RIGHT?

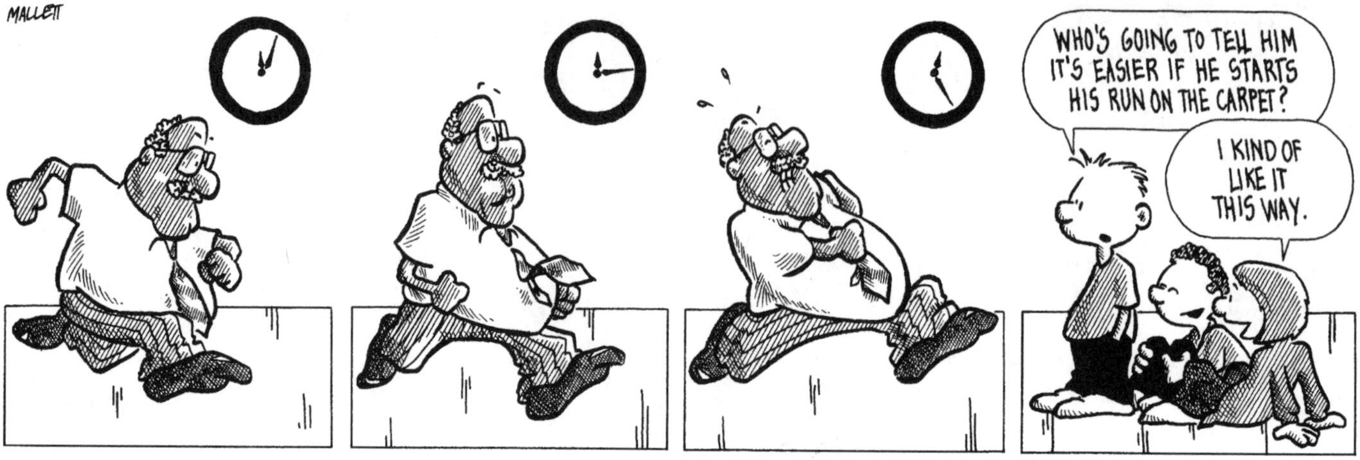
MALLETT
WHO'S GOING TO TELL HIM IT'S EASIER IF HE STARTS HIS RUN ON THE CARPET?
I KIND OF LIKE IT THIS WAY.

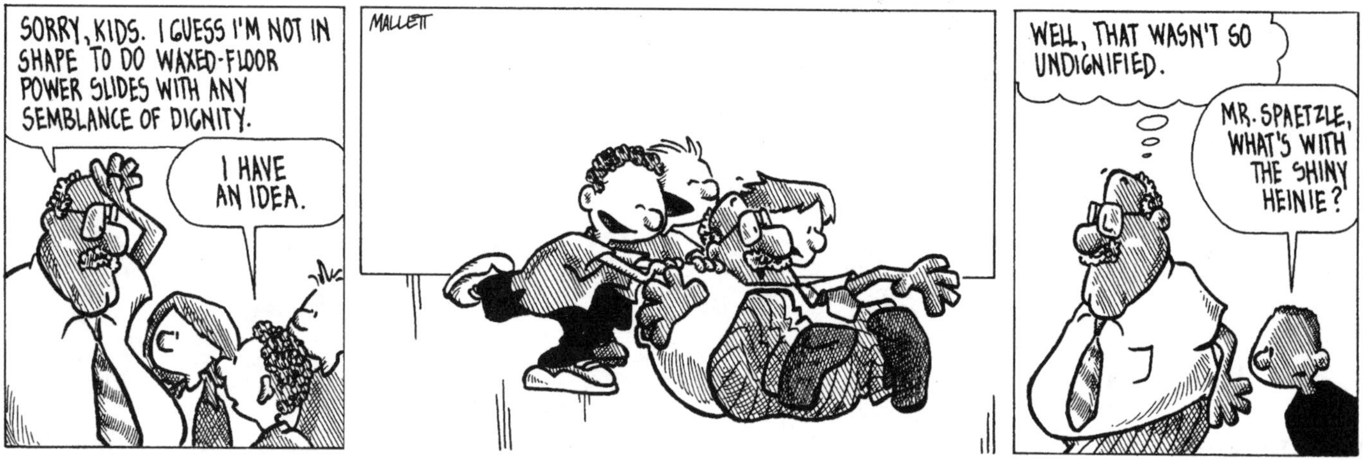
SORRY, KIDS. I GUESS I'M NOT IN SHAPE TO DO WAXED-FLOOR POWER SLIDES WITH ANY SEMBLANCE OF DIGNITY.
I HAVE AN IDEA.
MALLETT
WELL, THAT WASN'T SO UNDIGNIFIED.
MR. SPAETZLE, WHAT'S WITH THE SHINY HEINIE?

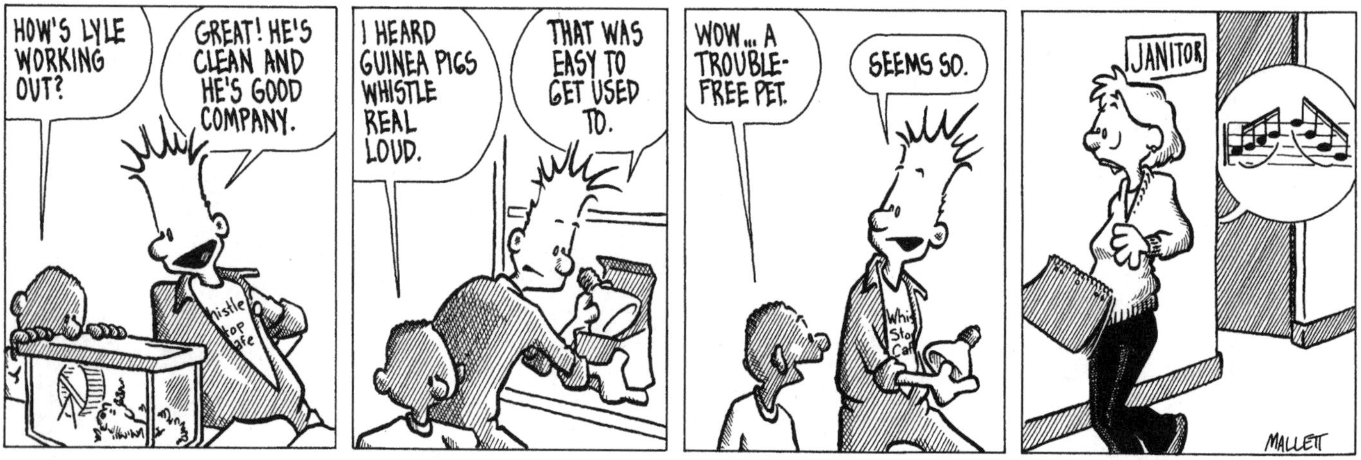
HOW'S LYLE WORKING OUT?
GREAT! HE'S CLEAN AND HE'S GOOD COMPANY.
I HEARD GUINEA PIGS WHISTLE REAL LOUD.
THAT WAS EASY TO GET USED TO.
WOW... A TROUBLE-FREE PET.
SEEMS SO.
JANITOR
MALLETT

Frazz
JEF MALLETT
SO, WHAT IS IAMBIC PENTAMETER?
AN ANCIENT FORM OF VERSE, I'M PRETTY SURE.
HO HUM. DOES THIS AFFECT MY LIFE TODAY?
I GUESS IT DOESN'T; THEN AGAIN, IT MAY.

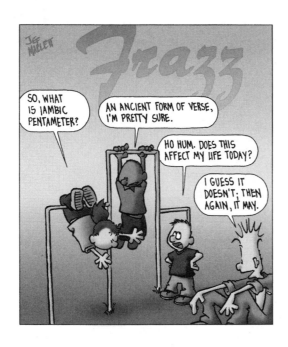

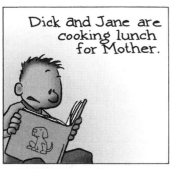

Dick and Jane are cooking lunch for Mother.
Oh, look! Here comes Spot! Spot would like to help.
Sniff! Sniff! Oh, my, that cheese sure smells good to Spot.
No, no, Spot! That cheese is for Mother's sandwich.
Out, damned spot! Out, I say!
What need we fear who... knows... it
MALLETT
SO, YEAH. NEVER TRY TO SMUGGLE IN SHAKESPEARE ON READ-ALOUD DAY.
I'LL REMEMBER THAT.

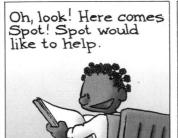

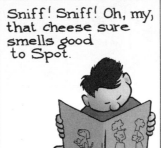

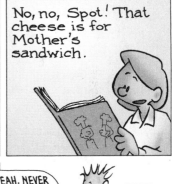

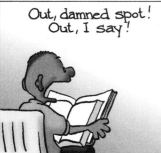

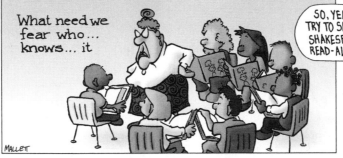

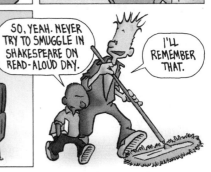

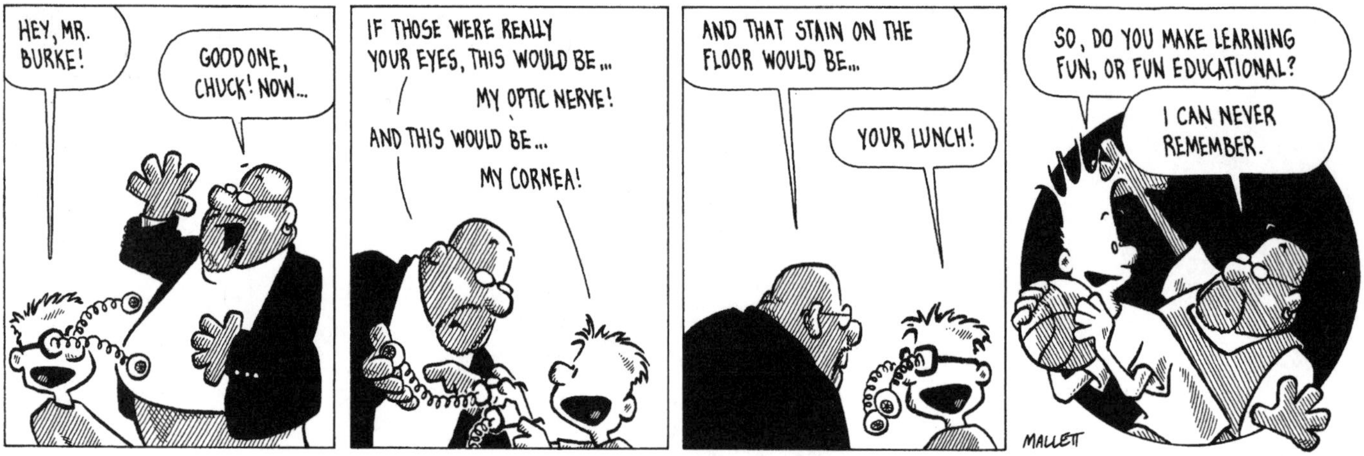
HEY, MR. BURKE!
GOOD ONE, CHUCK! NOW...
IF THOSE WERE REALLY YOUR EYES, THIS WOULD BE...
MY OPTIC NERVE!
AND THIS WOULD BE...
MY CORNEA!
AND THAT STAIN ON THE FLOOR WOULD BE...
YOUR LUNCH!
SO, DO YOU MAKE LEARNING FUN, OR FUN EDUCATIONAL?
I CAN NEVER REMEMBER.
MALLETT

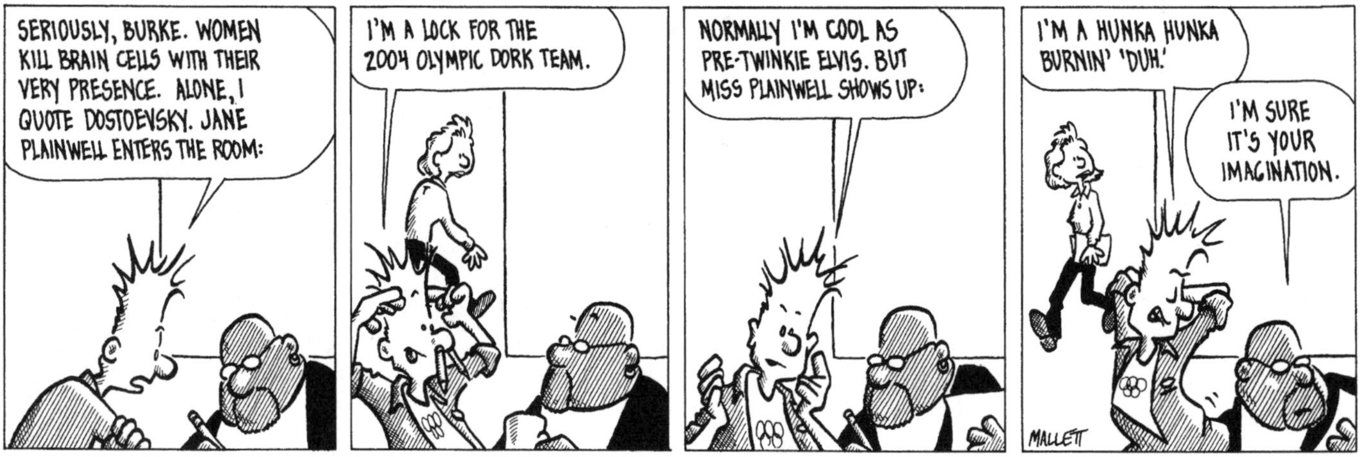
SERIOUSLY, BURKE. WOMEN KILL BRAIN CELLS WITH THEIR VERY PRESENCE. ALONE, I QUOTE DOSTOEVSKY. JANE PLAINWELL ENTERS THE ROOM:
I'M A LOCK FOR THE 2004 OLYMPIC DORK TEAM.
NORMALLY I'M COOL AS PRE-TWINKIE ELVIS. BUT MISS PLAINWELL SHOWS UP:
I'M A HUNKA HUNKA BURNIN' 'DUH.'
I'M SURE IT'S YOUR IMAGINATION.
MALLETT

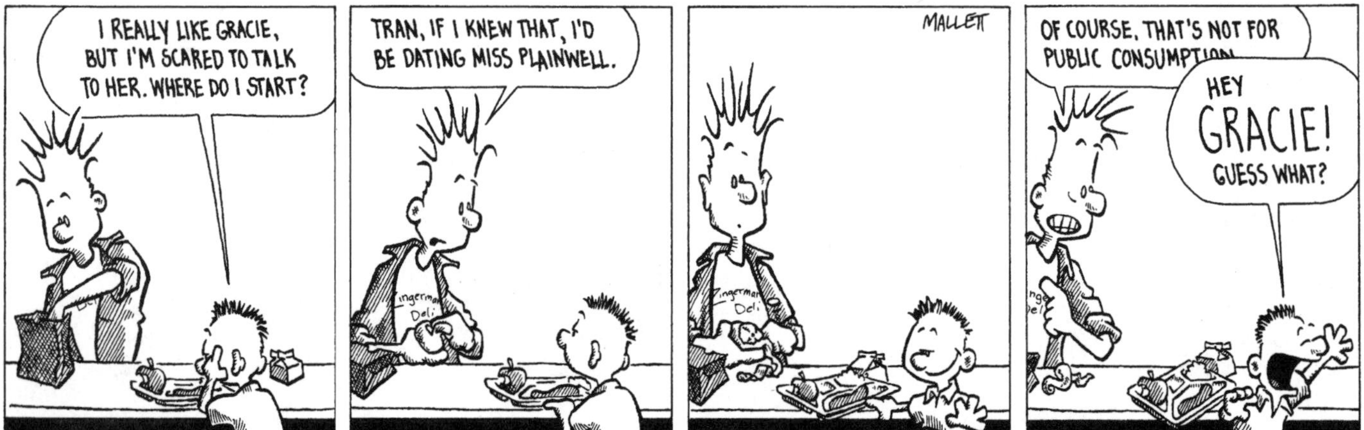
I REALLY LIKE GRACIE, BUT I'M SCARED TO TALK TO HER. WHERE DO I START?
TRAN, IF I KNEW THAT, I'D BE DATING MISS PLAINWELL.
MALLETT
OF COURSE, THAT'S NOT FOR PUBLIC CONSUMPT
HEY GRACIE! GUESS WHAT?

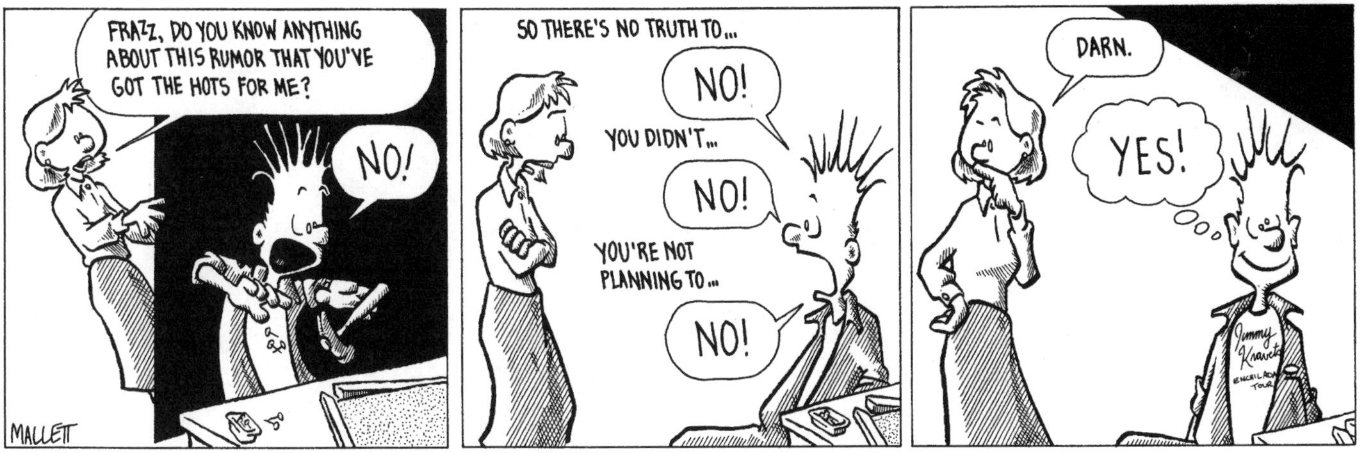
FRAZZ, DO YOU KNOW ANYTHING ABOUT THIS RUMOR THAT YOU'VE GOT THE HOTS FOR ME?
NO!
MALLETT
SO THERE'S NO TRUTH TO...
NO!
YOU DIDN'T...
NO!
YOU'RE NOT PLANNING TO...
NO!
DARN.
YES!

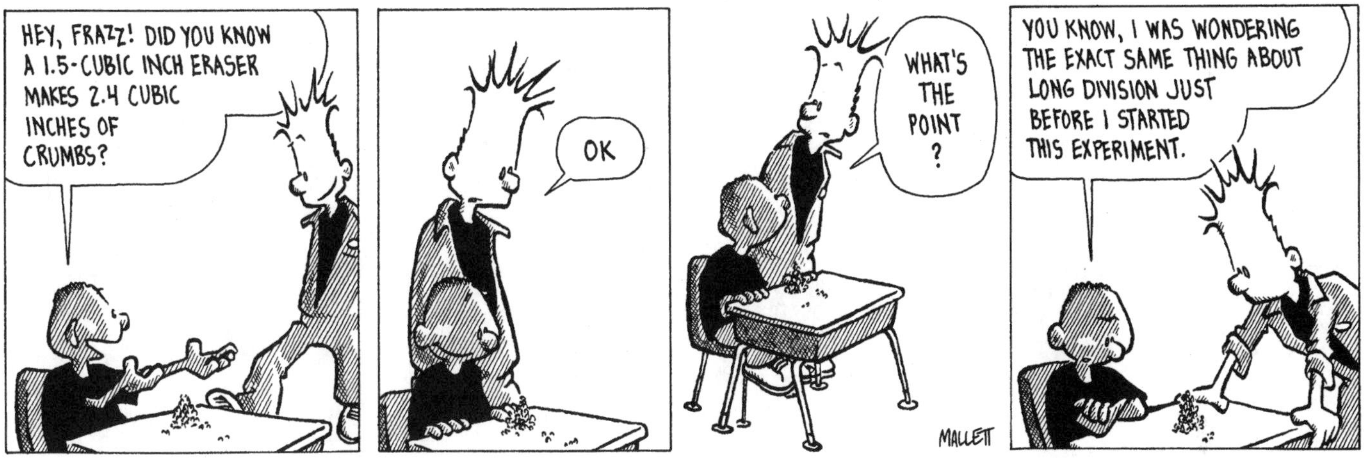
HEY, FRAZZ! DID YOU KNOW A 1.5-CUBIC INCH ERASER MAKES 2.4 CUBIC INCHES OF CRUMBS?
OK
WHAT'S THE POINT ?
MALLETT
YOU KNOW, I WAS WONDERING THE EXACT SAME THING ABOUT LONG DIVISION JUST BEFORE I STARTED THIS EXPERIMENT.

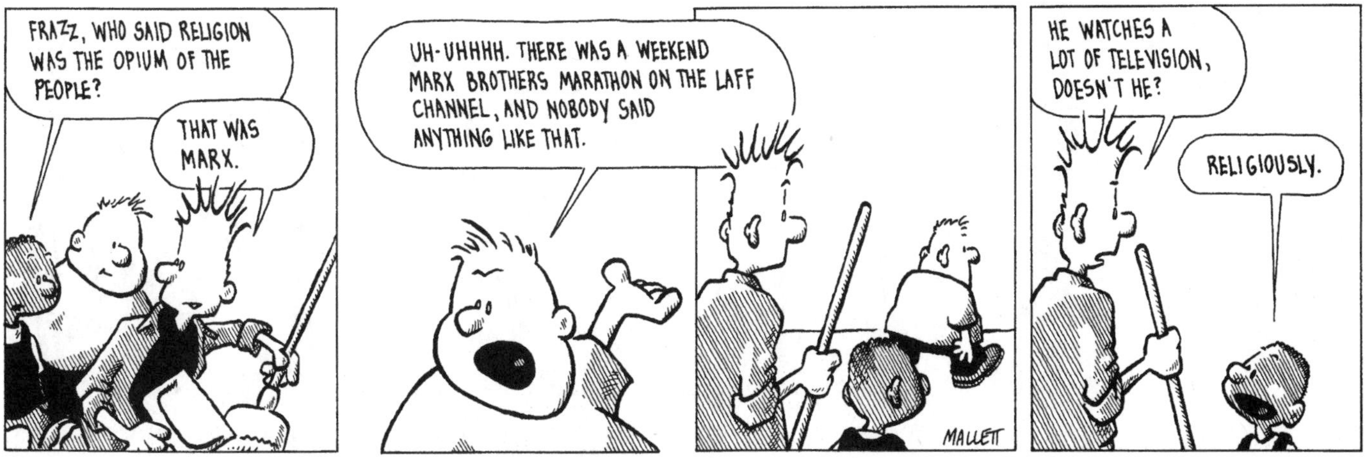
FRAZZ, WHO SAID RELIGION WAS THE OPIUM OF THE PEOPLE?
THAT WAS MARX.
UH-UHHHH. THERE WAS A WEEKEND MARX BROTHERS MARATHON ON THE LAFF CHANNEL, AND NOBODY SAID ANYTHING LIKE THAT.
MALLETT
HE WATCHES A LOT OF TELEVISION, DOESN'T HE?
RELIGIOUSLY.

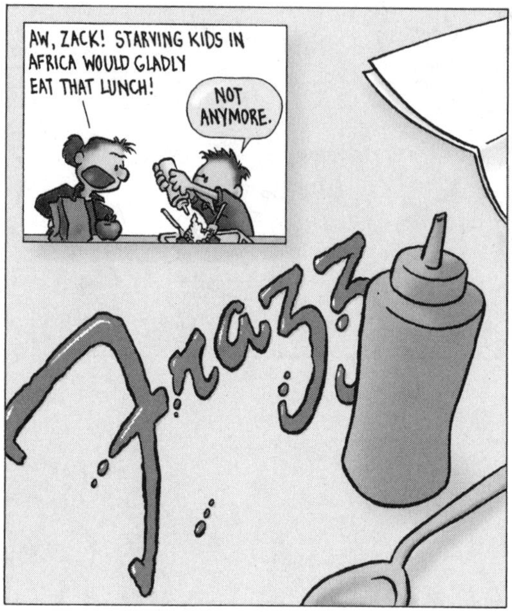
AW, ZACK! STARVING KIDS IN AFRICA WOULD GLADLY EAT THAT LUNCH!
NOT ANYMORE.
Frazz

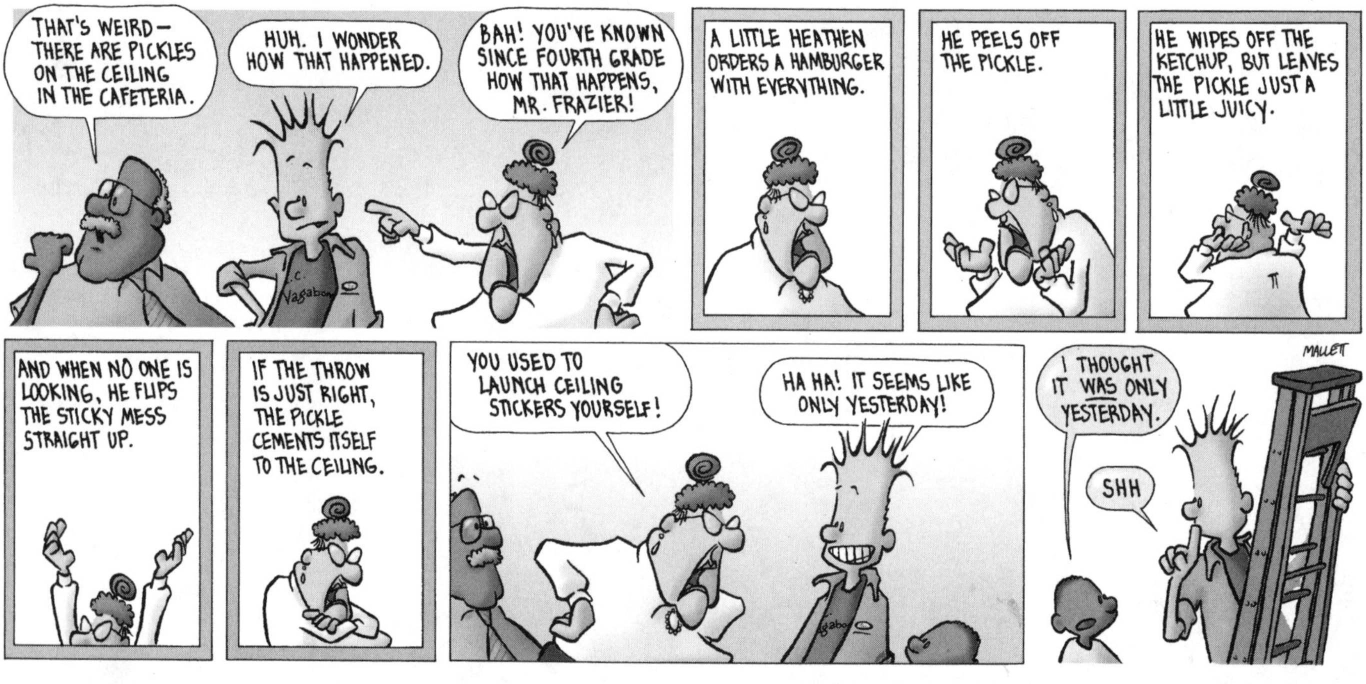
THAT'S WEIRD — THERE ARE PICKLES ON THE CEILING IN THE CAFETERIA.
HUH. I WONDER HOW THAT HAPPENED.
BAH! YOU'VE KNOWN SINCE FOURTH GRADE HOW THAT HAPPENS, MR. FRAZIER!
A LITTLE HEATHEN ORDERS A HAMBURGER WITH EVERYTHING.
HE PEELS OFF THE PICKLE.
HE WIPES OFF THE KETCHUP, BUT LEAVES THE PICKLE JUST A LITTLE JUICY.
AND WHEN NO ONE IS LOOKING, HE FLIPS THE STICKY MESS STRAIGHT UP.
IF THE THROW IS JUST RIGHT, THE PICKLE CEMENTS ITSELF TO THE CEILING.
YOU USED TO LAUNCH CEILING STICKERS YOURSELF!
HA HA! IT SEEMS LIKE ONLY YESTERDAY!
I THOUGHT IT WAS ONLY YESTERDAY.
SHH
MALLETT

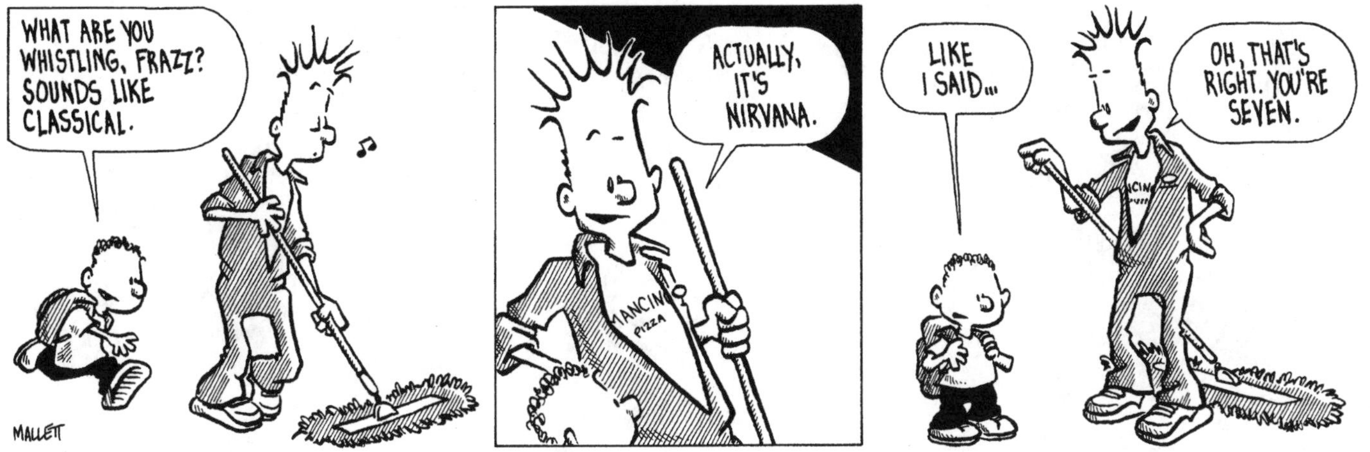
WHAT ARE YOU WHISTLING, FRAZZ? SOUNDS LIKE CLASSICAL.
ACTUALLY, IT'S NIRVANA.
LIKE I SAID...
OH, THAT'S RIGHT. YOU'RE SEVEN.
MALLETT

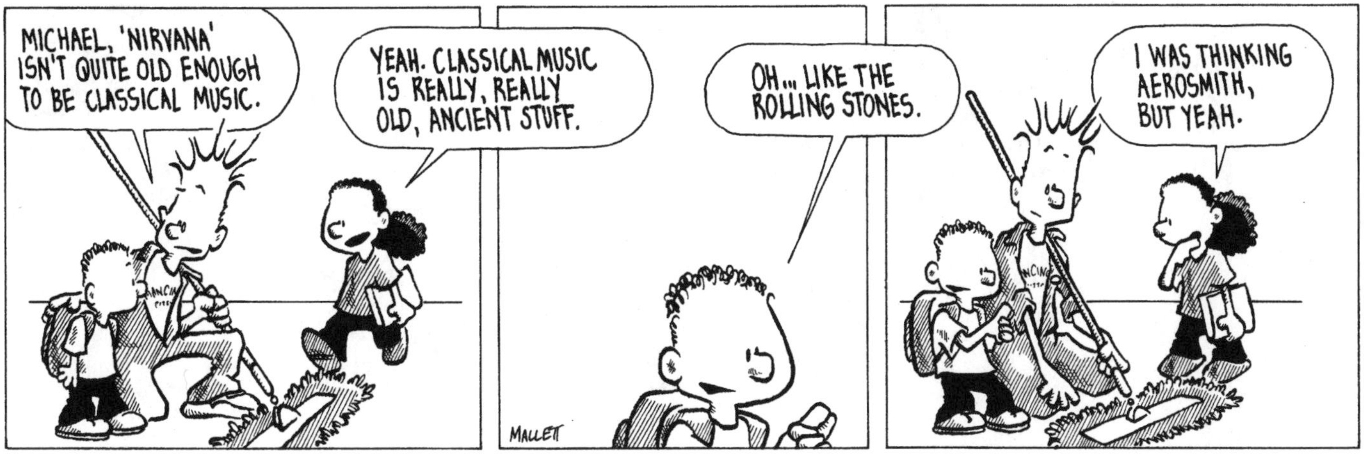
MICHAEL, 'NIRVANA' ISN'T QUITE OLD ENOUGH TO BE CLASSICAL MUSIC.
YEAH. CLASSICAL MUSIC IS REALLY, REALLY OLD, ANCIENT STUFF.
OH... LIKE THE ROLLING STONES.
I WAS THINKING AEROSMITH, BUT YEAH.
MALLETT

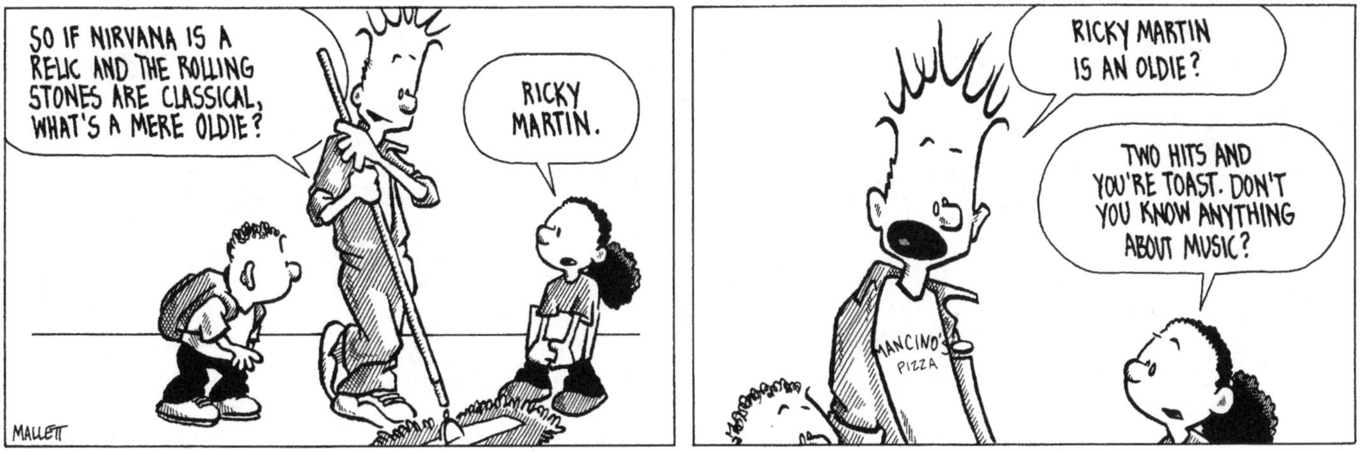
SO IF NIRVANA IS A RELIC AND THE ROLLING STONES ARE CLASSICAL, WHAT'S A MERE OLDIE?
RICKY MARTIN.
RICKY MARTIN IS AN OLDIE?
TWO HITS AND YOU'RE TOAST. DON'T YOU KNOW ANYTHING ABOUT MUSIC?
MALLETT

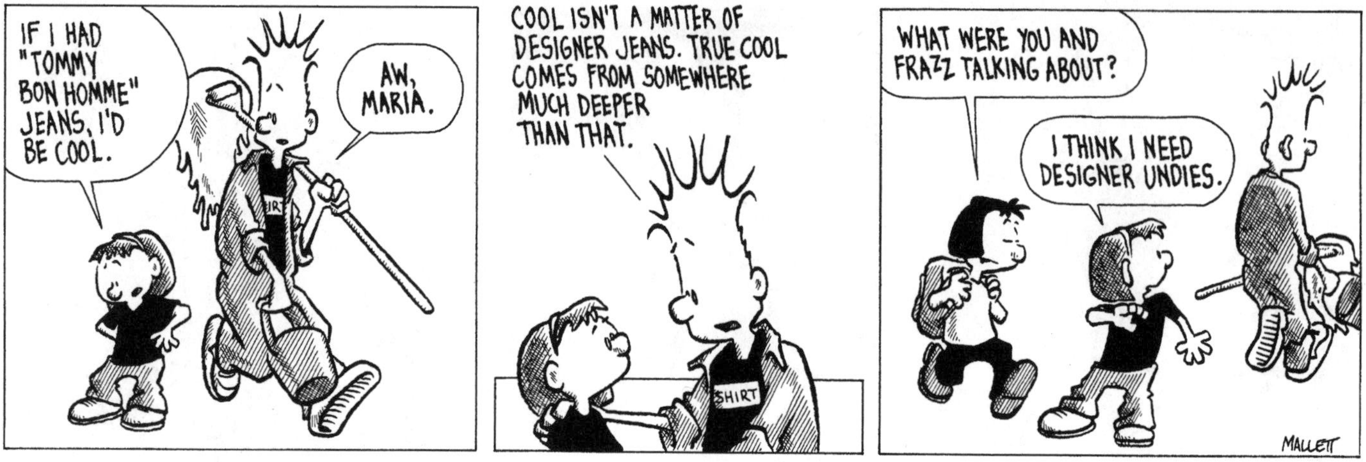
IF I HAD "TOMMY BON HOMME" JEANS, I'D BE COOL.
AW, MARIA.
COOL ISN'T A MATTER OF DESIGNER JEANS. TRUE COOL COMES FROM SOMEWHERE MUCH DEEPER THAN THAT.
SHIRT
WHAT WERE YOU AND FRAZZ TALKING ABOUT?
I THINK I NEED DESIGNER UNDIES.
MALLETT

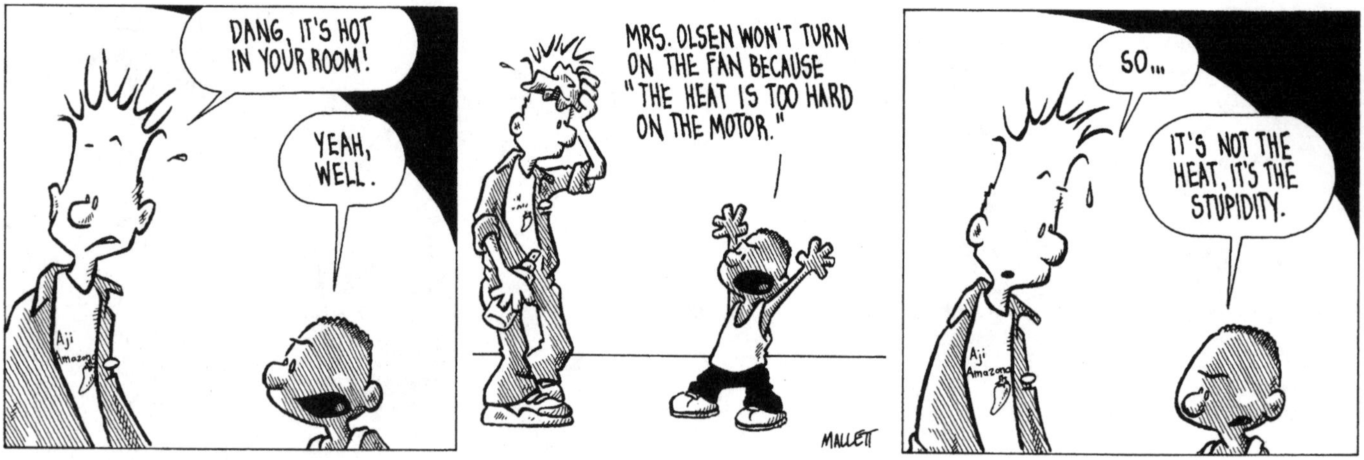
DANG, IT'S HOT IN YOUR ROOM!
YEAH, WELL.
MRS. OLSEN WON'T TURN ON THE FAN BECAUSE "THE HEAT IS TOO HARD ON THE MOTOR."
MALLETT
SO...
IT'S NOT THE HEAT, IT'S THE STUPIDITY.

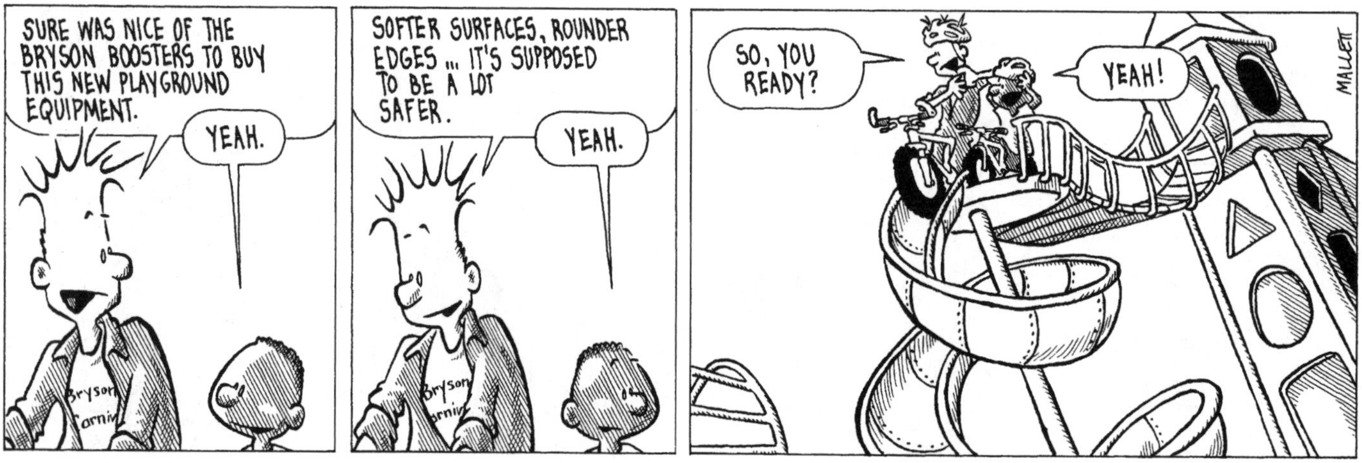
SURE WAS NICE OF THE BRYSON BOOSTERS TO BUY THIS NEW PLAYGROUND EQUIPMENT.
YEAH.
SOFTER SURFACES, ROUNDER EDGES ... IT'S SUPPOSED TO BE A LOT SAFER.
YEAH.
SO, YOU READY?
YEAH!
MALLETT

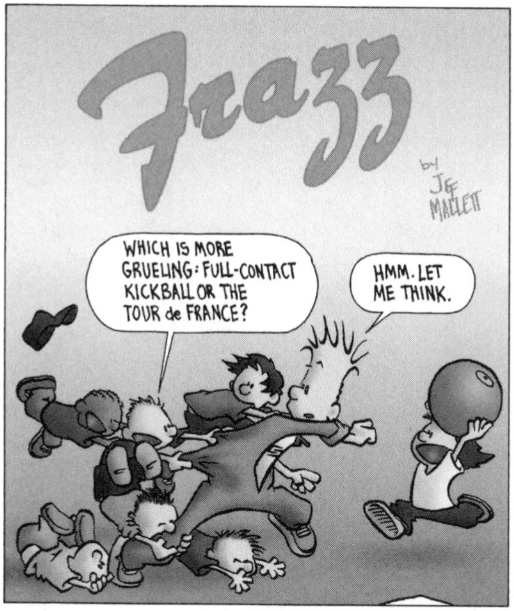
Frazz
by JEF MALLETT
WHICH IS MORE GRUELING: FULL-CONTACT KICKBALL OR THE TOUR de FRANCE?
HMM. LET ME THINK.

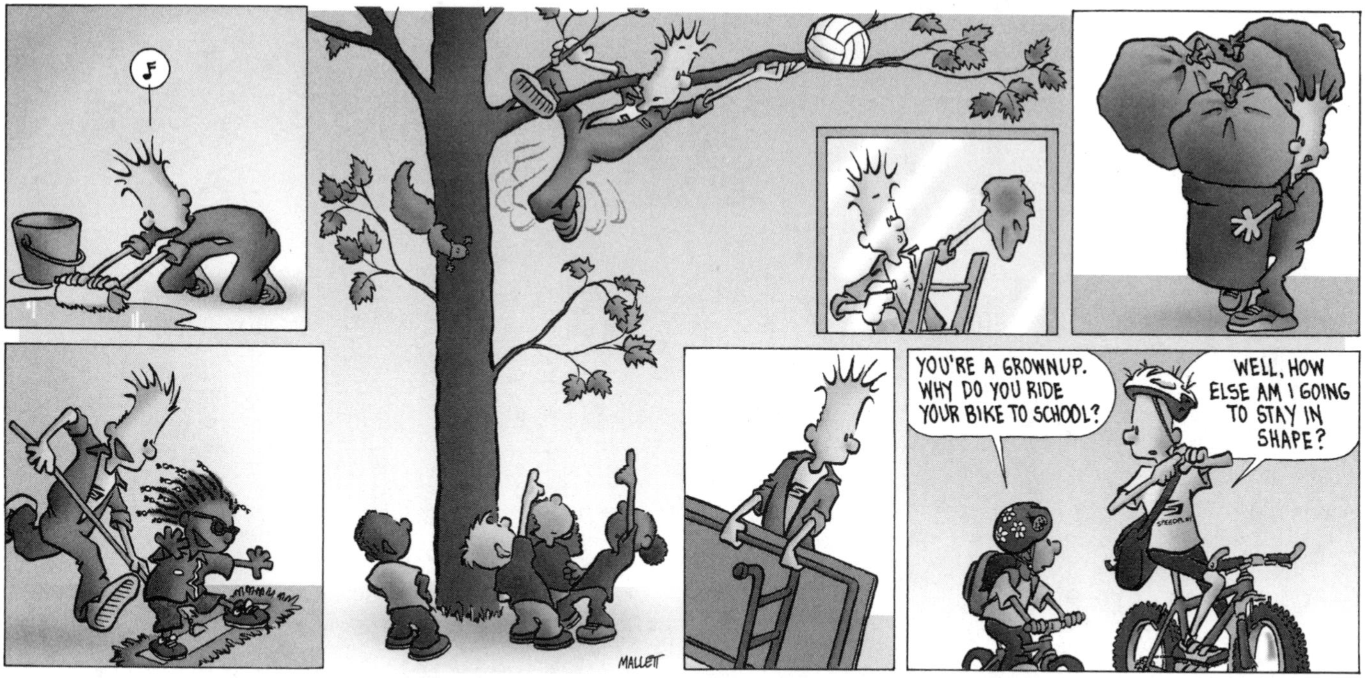
MALLETT
YOU'RE A GROWNUP. WHY DO YOU RIDE YOUR BIKE TO SCHOOL?
WELL, HOW ELSE AM I GOING TO STAY IN SHAPE?

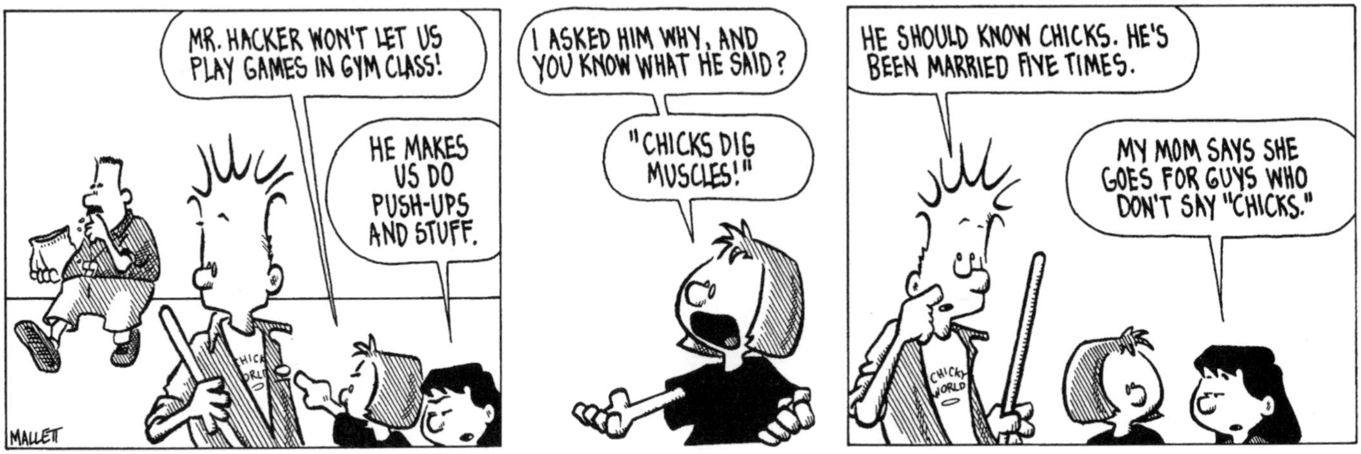
MR. HACKER WON'T LET US PLAY GAMES IN GYM CLASS!
HE MAKES US DO PUSH-UPS AND STUFF.
I ASKED HIM WHY, AND YOU KNOW WHAT HE SAID?
"CHICKS DIG MUSCLES!"
HE SHOULD KNOW CHICKS. HE'S BEEN MARRIED FIVE TIMES.
MY MOM SAYS SHE GOES FOR GUYS WHO DON'T SAY "CHICKS."
MALLETT

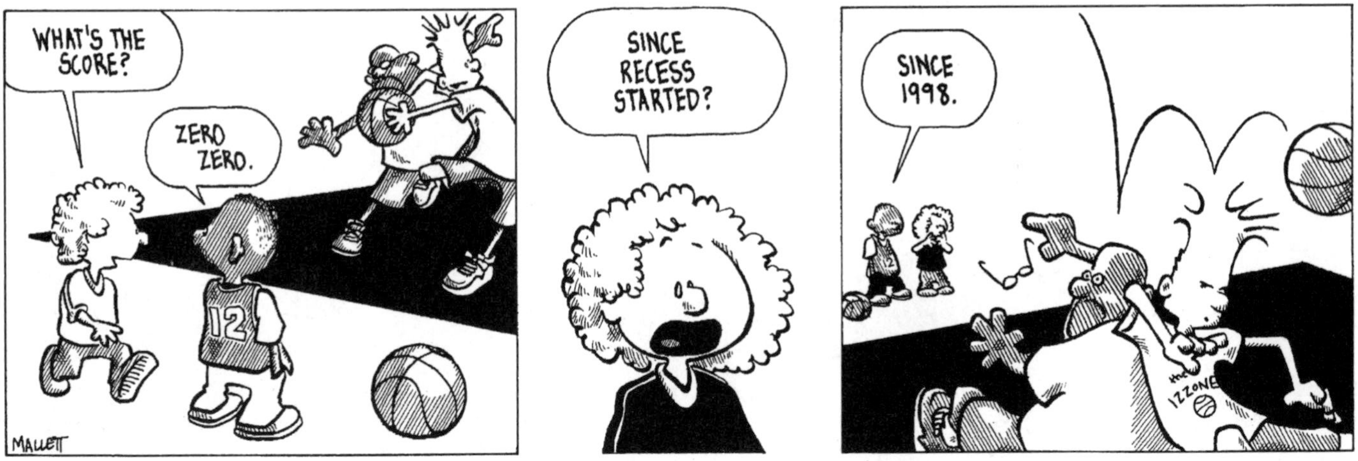
WHAT'S THE SCORE?
ZERO ZERO.
SINCE RECESS STARTED?
SINCE 1998.
MALLETT

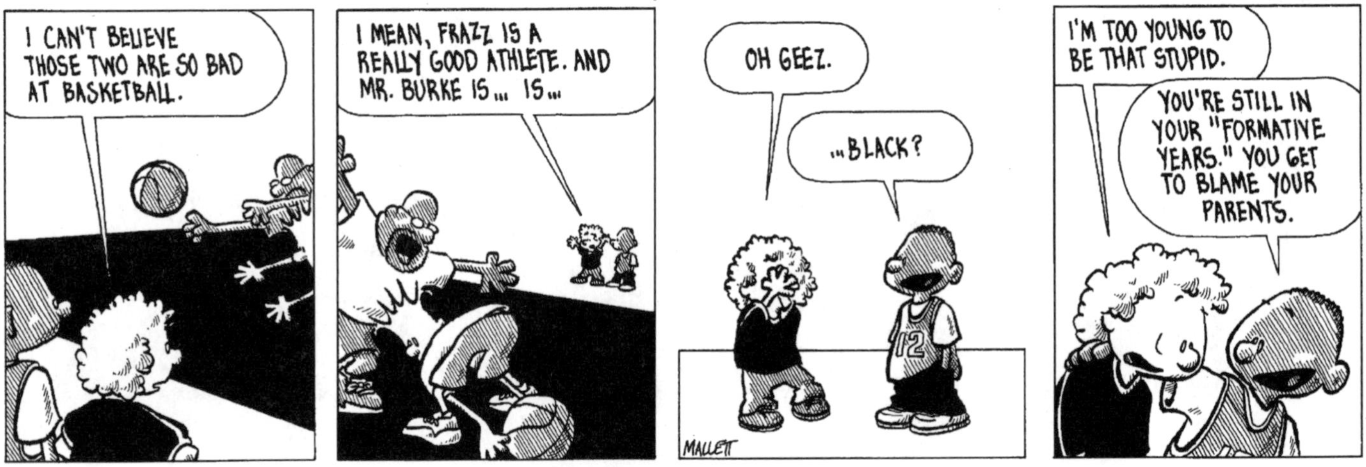
I CAN'T BELIEVE THOSE TWO ARE SO BAD AT BASKETBALL.
I MEAN, FRAZZ IS A REALLY GOOD ATHLETE. AND MR. BURKE IS... IS...
OH GEEZ.
...BLACK?
I'M TOO YOUNG TO BE THAT STUPID.
YOU'RE STILL IN YOUR "FORMATIVE YEARS." YOU GET TO BLAME YOUR PARENTS.
MALLETT

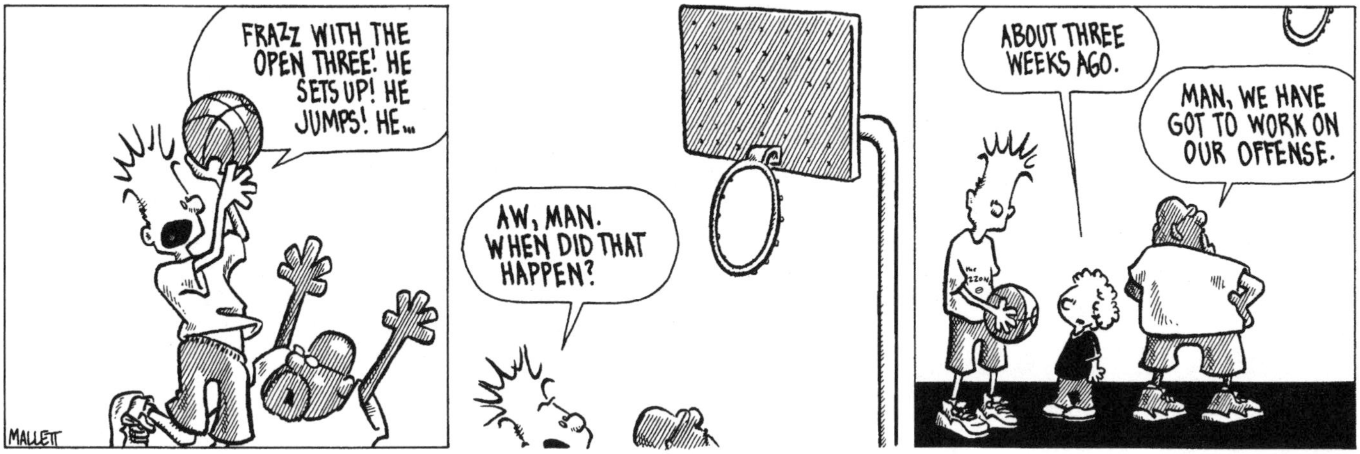
MALLETT
FRAZZ WITH THE OPEN THREE! HE SETS UP! HE JUMPS! HE...
AW, MAN. WHEN DID THAT HAPPEN?
ABOUT THREE WEEKS AGO.
MAN, WE HAVE GOT TO WORK ON OUR OFFENSE.

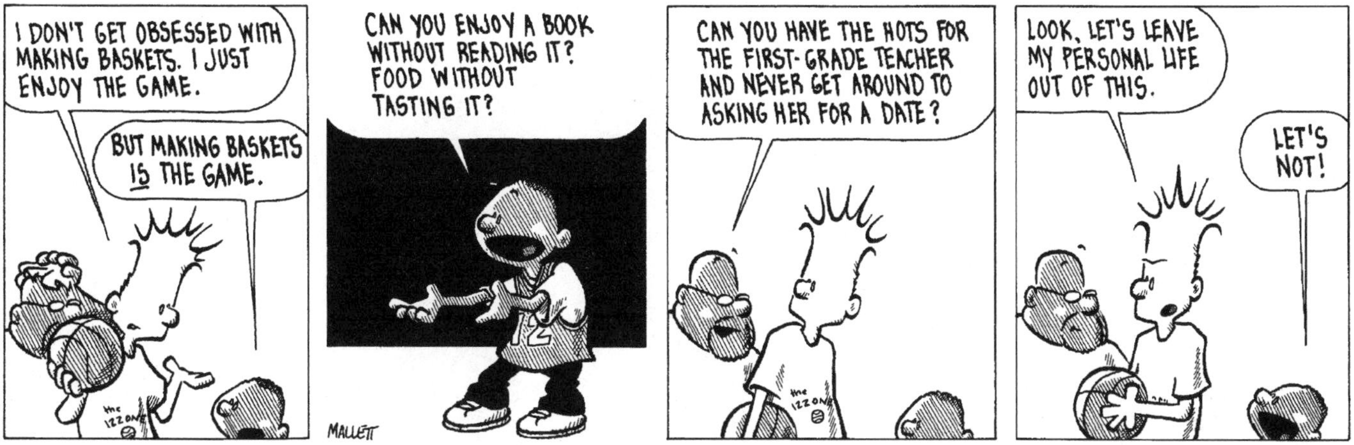
I DON'T GET OBSESSED WITH MAKING BASKETS. I JUST ENJOY THE GAME.
BUT MAKING BASKETS IS THE GAME.
CAN YOU ENJOY A BOOK WITHOUT READING IT? FOOD WITHOUT TASTING IT?
MALLETT
CAN YOU HAVE THE HOTS FOR THE FIRST-GRADE TEACHER AND NEVER GET AROUND TO ASKING HER FOR A DATE?
LOOK, LET'S LEAVE MY PERSONAL LIFE OUT OF THIS.
LET'S NOT!

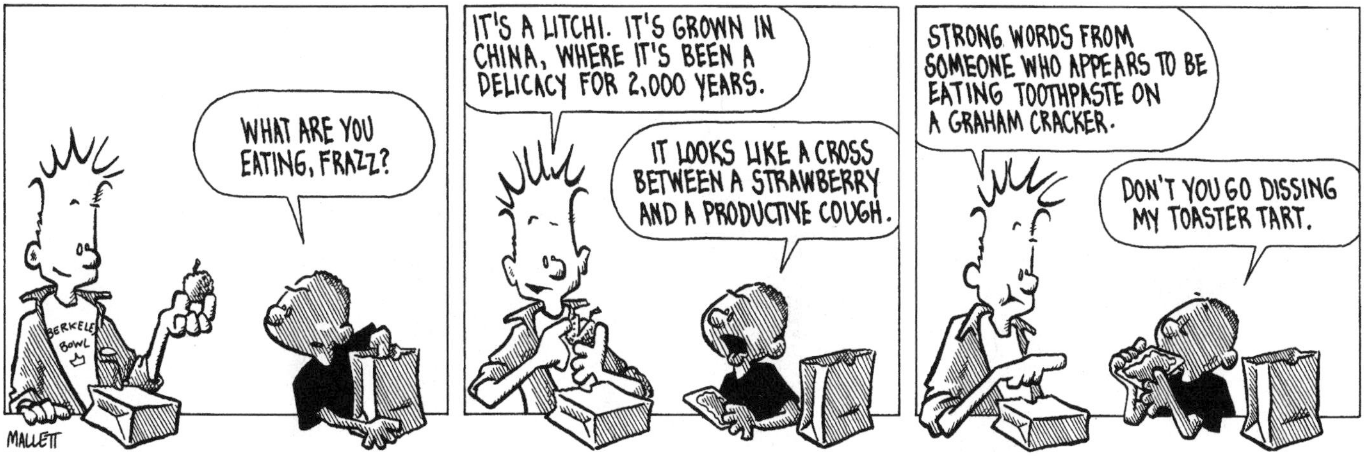
WHAT ARE YOU EATING, FRAZZ?
BERKELEY BOWL
MALLETT
IT'S A LITCHI. IT'S GROWN IN CHINA, WHERE IT'S BEEN A DELICACY FOR 2,000 YEARS.
IT LOOKS LIKE A CROSS BETWEEN A STRAWBERRY AND A PRODUCTIVE COUGH.
STRONG WORDS FROM SOMEONE WHO APPEARS TO BE EATING TOOTHPASTE ON A GRAHAM CRACKER.
DON'T YOU GO DISSING MY TOASTER TART.

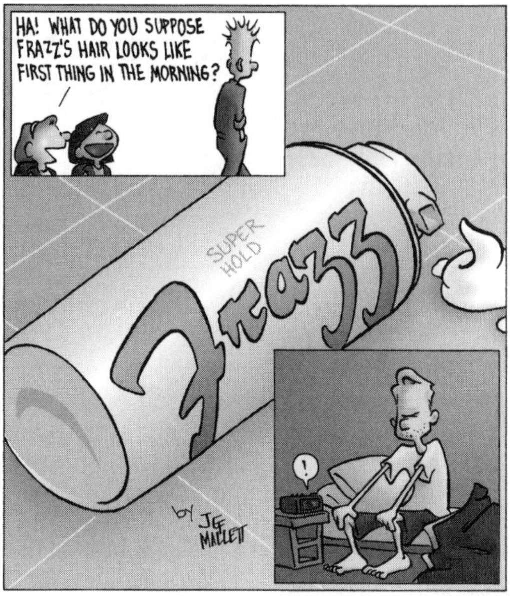
HA! WHAT DO YOU SUPPOSE FRAZZ'S HAIR LOOKS LIKE FIRST THING IN THE MORNING?
SUPER HOLD
Frazz
!
by JEF MALLETT

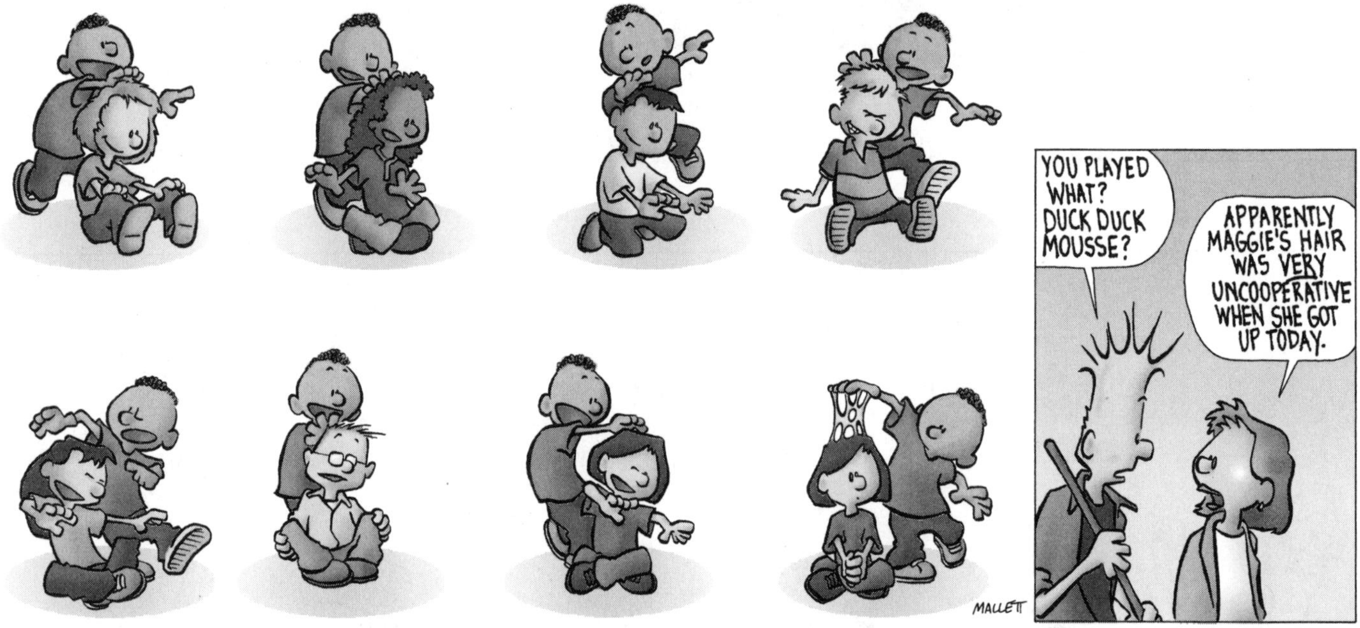
YOU PLAYED WHAT? DUCK DUCK MOUSSE?
APPARENTLY MAGGIE'S HAIR WAS VERY UNCOOPERATIVE WHEN SHE GOT UP TODAY.
MALLETT

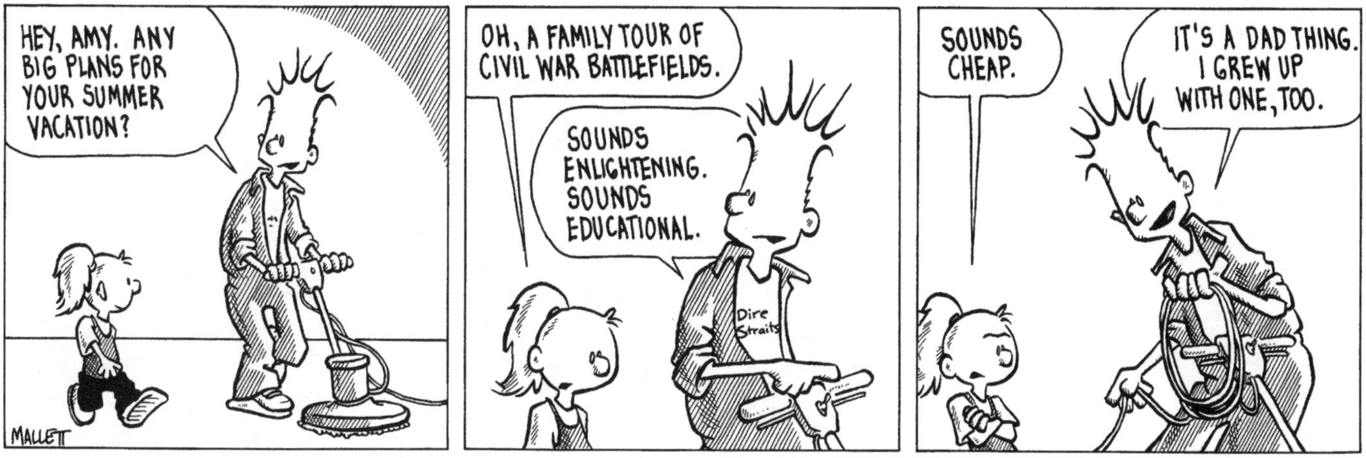
HEY, AMY. ANY BIG PLANS FOR YOUR SUMMER VACATION?
MALLETT
OH, A FAMILY TOUR OF CIVIL WAR BATTLEFIELDS.
SOUNDS ENLIGHTENING. SOUNDS EDUCATIONAL.
Dire Straits
SOUNDS CHEAP.
IT'S A DAD THING. I GREW UP WITH ONE, TOO.

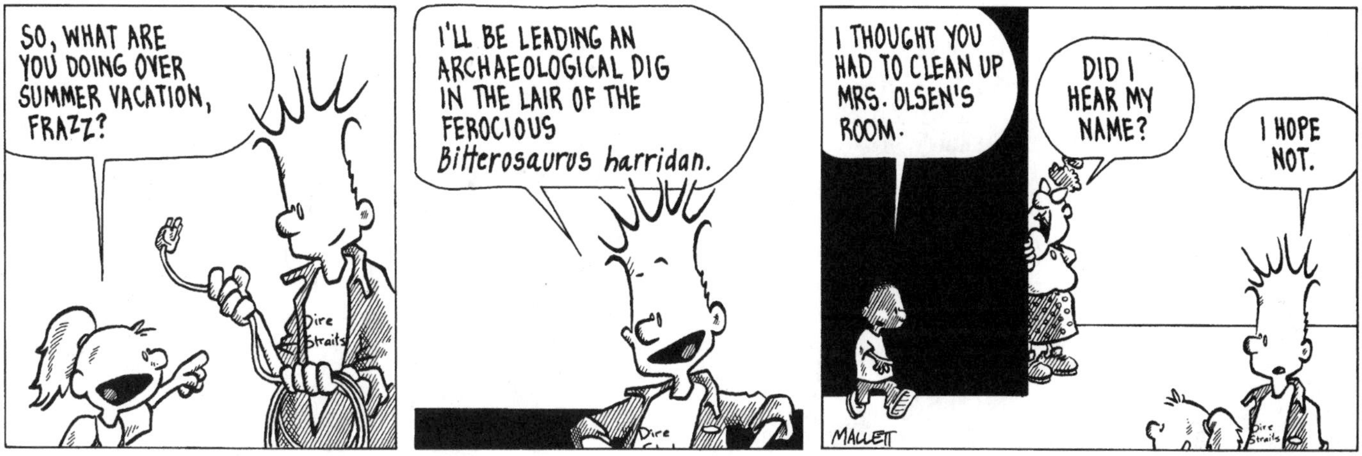
SO, WHAT ARE YOU DOING OVER SUMMER VACATION, FRAZZ?
Dire Straits
I'LL BE LEADING AN ARCHAEOLOGICAL DIG IN THE LAIR OF THE FEROCIOUS *Bitterosaurus harridan*.
I THOUGHT YOU HAD TO CLEAN UP MRS. OLSEN'S ROOM.
DID I HEAR MY NAME?
I HOPE NOT.
Dire Straits
MALLETT

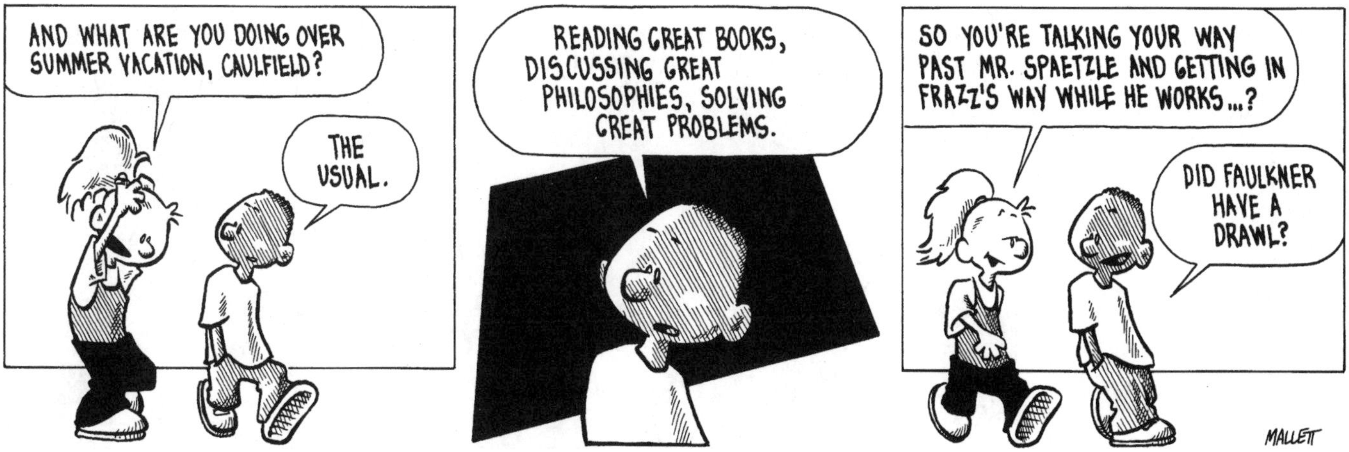
AND WHAT ARE YOU DOING OVER SUMMER VACATION, CAULFIELD?
THE USUAL.
READING GREAT BOOKS, DISCUSSING GREAT PHILOSOPHIES, SOLVING GREAT PROBLEMS.
SO YOU'RE TALKING YOUR WAY PAST MR. SPAETZLE AND GETTING IN FRAZZ'S WAY WHILE HE WORKS...?
DID FAULKNER HAVE A DRAWL?
MALLETT

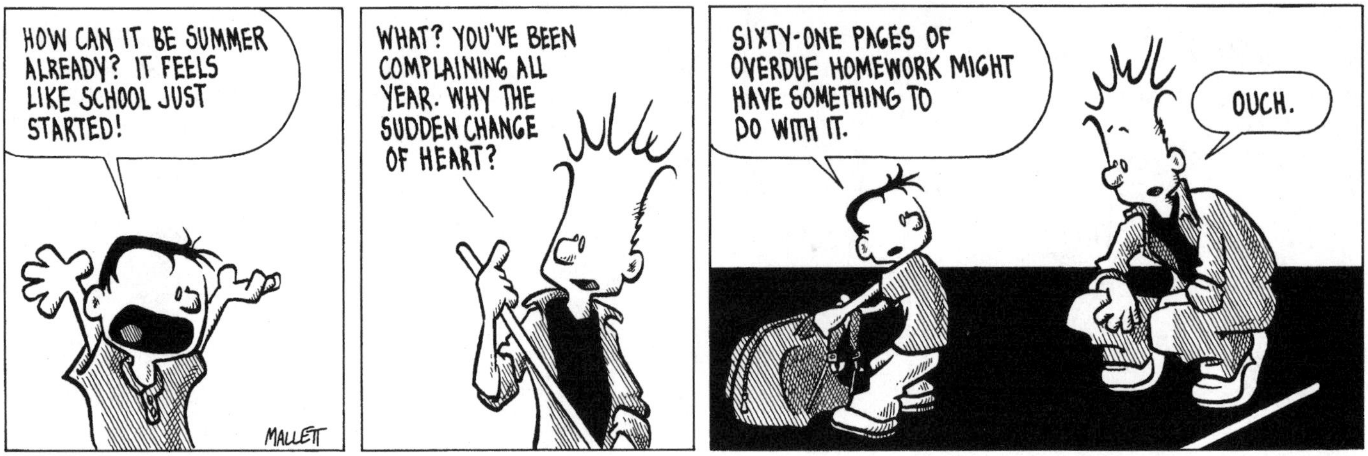
HOW CAN IT BE SUMMER ALREADY? IT FEELS LIKE SCHOOL JUST STARTED!
MALLETT
WHAT? YOU'VE BEEN COMPLAINING ALL YEAR. WHY THE SUDDEN CHANGE OF HEART?
SIXTY-ONE PAGES OF OVERDUE HOMEWORK MIGHT HAVE SOMETHING TO DO WITH IT.
OUCH.

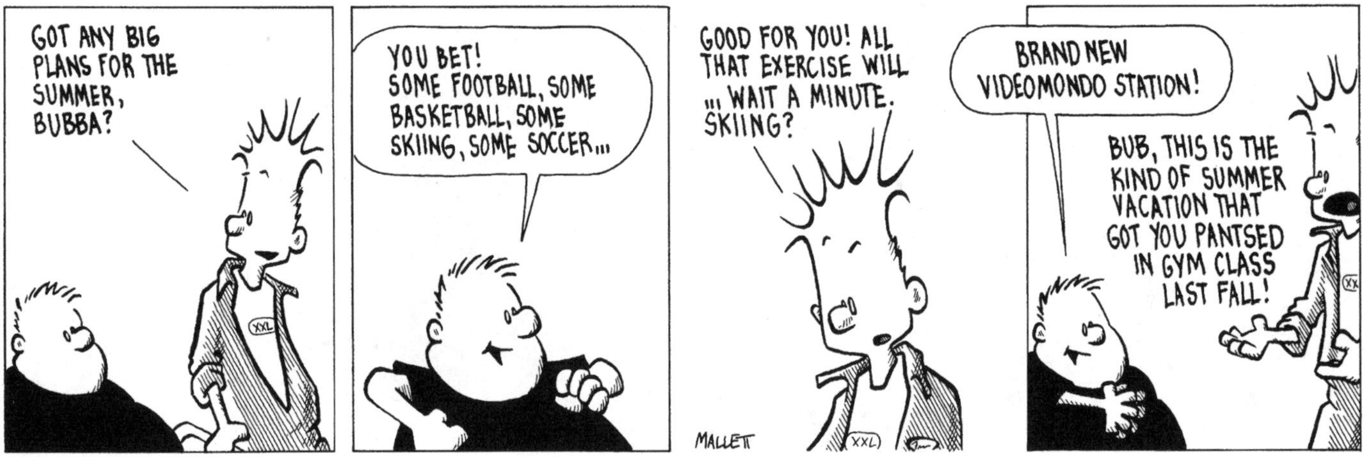
GOT ANY BIG PLANS FOR THE SUMMER, BUBBA?
XXL
YOU BET! SOME FOOTBALL, SOME BASKETBALL, SOME SKIING, SOME SOCCER...
GOOD FOR YOU! ALL THAT EXERCISE WILL ... WAIT A MINUTE. SKIING?
MALLETT
BRAND NEW VIDEOMONDO STATION!
BUB, THIS IS THE KIND OF SUMMER VACATION THAT GOT YOU PANTSED IN GYM CLASS LAST FALL!

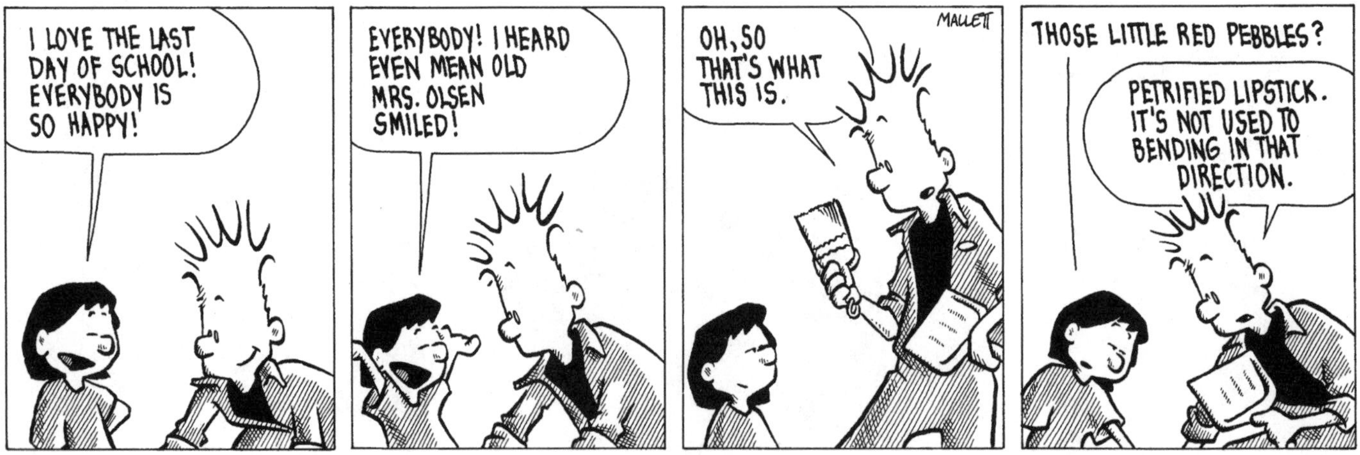
I LOVE THE LAST DAY OF SCHOOL! EVERYBODY IS SO HAPPY!
EVERYBODY! I HEARD EVEN MEAN OLD MRS. OLSEN SMILED!
MALLETT
OH, SO THAT'S WHAT THIS IS.
THOSE LITTLE RED PEBBLES?
PETRIFIED LIPSTICK. IT'S NOT USED TO BENDING IN THAT DIRECTION.

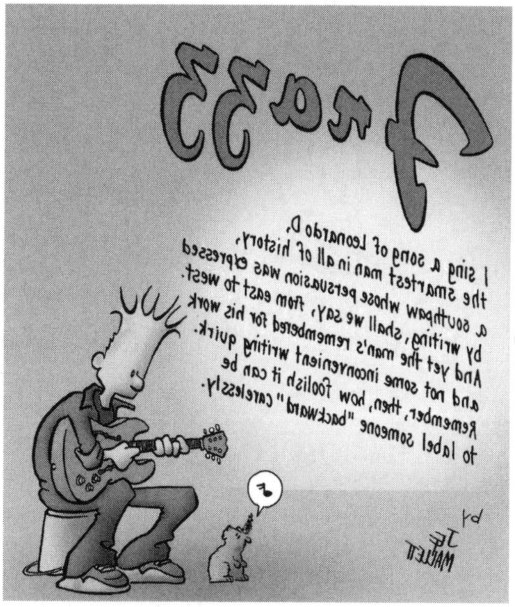

Frazz
I sing a song of Leonardo D,
the smartest man in all of history,
a southpaw whose persuasion was expressed
by writing, shall we say, from east to west.
And yet the man's remembered for his work
and not some inconvenient writing quirk.
Remember, then, how foolish it can be
to label someone "backward" carelessly.
by JEF MALLETT

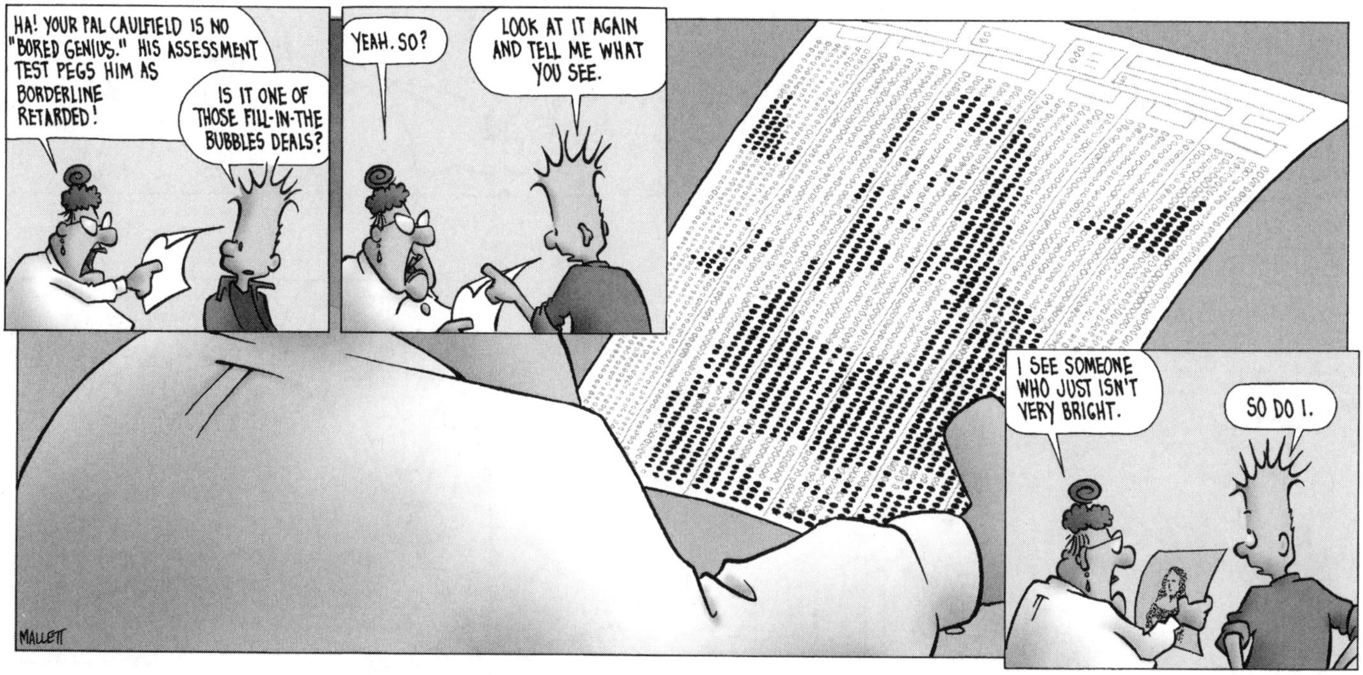

HA! YOUR PAL CAULFIELD IS NO "BORED GENIUS." HIS ASSESSMENT TEST PEGS HIM AS BORDERLINE RETARDED!
IS IT ONE OF THOSE FILL-IN-THE BUBBLES DEALS?
YEAH. SO?
LOOK AT IT AGAIN AND TELL ME WHAT YOU SEE.
I SEE SOMEONE WHO JUST ISN'T VERY BRIGHT.
SO DO I.
MALLETT

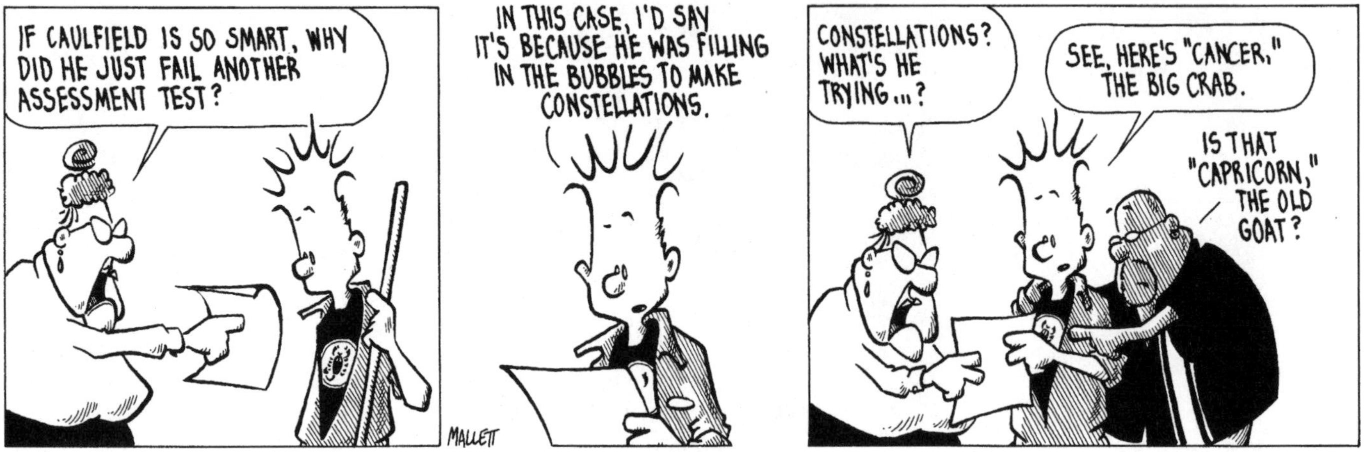
IF CAULFIELD IS SO SMART, WHY DID HE JUST FAIL ANOTHER ASSESSMENT TEST?
IN THIS CASE, I'D SAY IT'S BECAUSE HE WAS FILLING IN THE BUBBLES TO MAKE CONSTELLATIONS.
CONSTELLATIONS? WHAT'S HE TRYING...?
SEE, HERE'S "CANCER," THE BIG CRAB.
IS THAT "CAPRICORN," THE OLD GOAT?
MALLETT

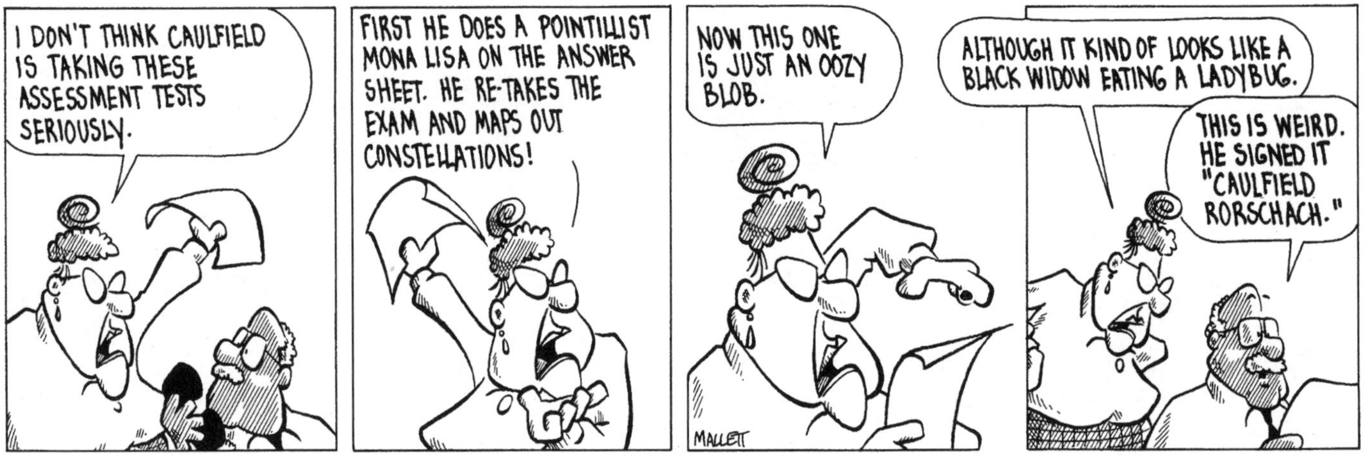
I DON'T THINK CAULFIELD IS TAKING THESE ASSESSMENT TESTS SERIOUSLY.
FIRST HE DOES A POINTILLIST MONA LISA ON THE ANSWER SHEET. HE RE-TAKES THE EXAM AND MAPS OUT CONSTELLATIONS!
NOW THIS ONE IS JUST AN OOZY BLOB.
MALLETT
ALTHOUGH IT KIND OF LOOKS LIKE A BLACK WIDOW EATING A LADYBUG.
THIS IS WEIRD. HE SIGNED IT "CAULFIELD RORSCHACH."

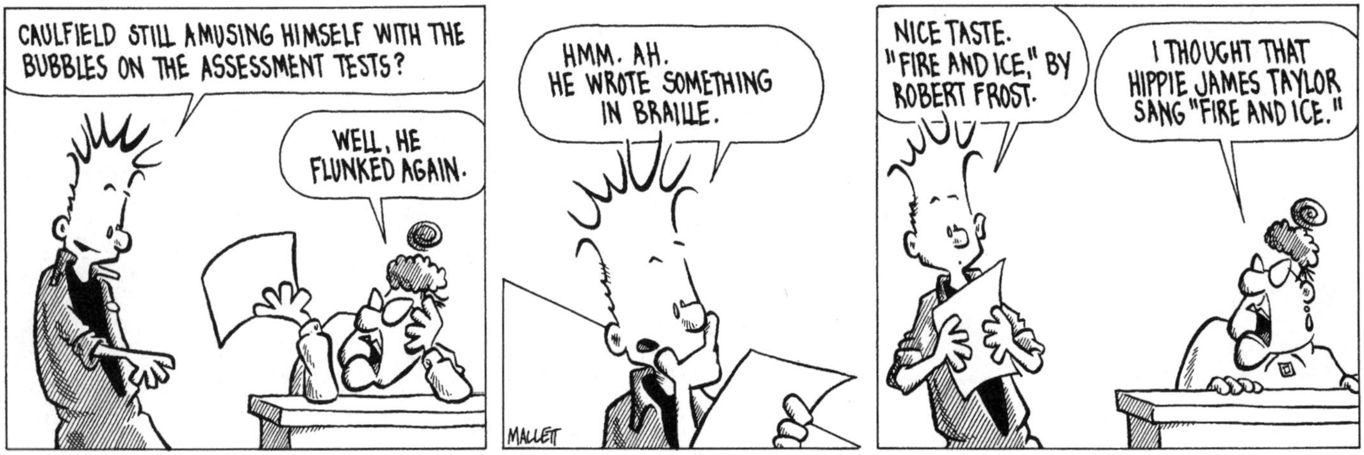
CAULFIELD STILL AMUSING HIMSELF WITH THE BUBBLES ON THE ASSESSMENT TESTS?
WELL, HE FLUNKED AGAIN.
HMM. AH. HE WROTE SOMETHING IN BRAILLE.
MALLETT
NICE TASTE. "FIRE AND ICE," BY ROBERT FROST.
I THOUGHT THAT HIPPIE JAMES TAYLOR SANG "FIRE AND ICE."

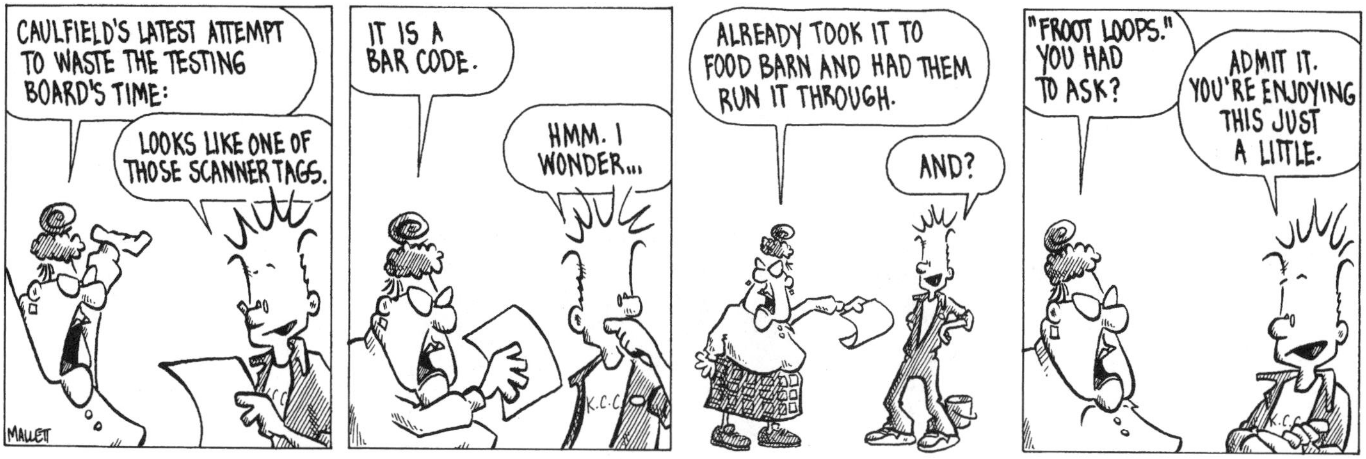
CAULFIELD'S LATEST ATTEMPT TO WASTE THE TESTING BOARD'S TIME:
LOOKS LIKE ONE OF THOSE SCANNER TAGS.
IT IS A BAR CODE.
HMM. I WONDER...
ALREADY TOOK IT TO FOOD BARN AND HAD THEM RUN IT THROUGH.
AND?
"FROOT LOOPS." YOU HAD TO ASK?
ADMIT IT. YOU'RE ENJOYING THIS JUST A LITTLE.
MALLETT

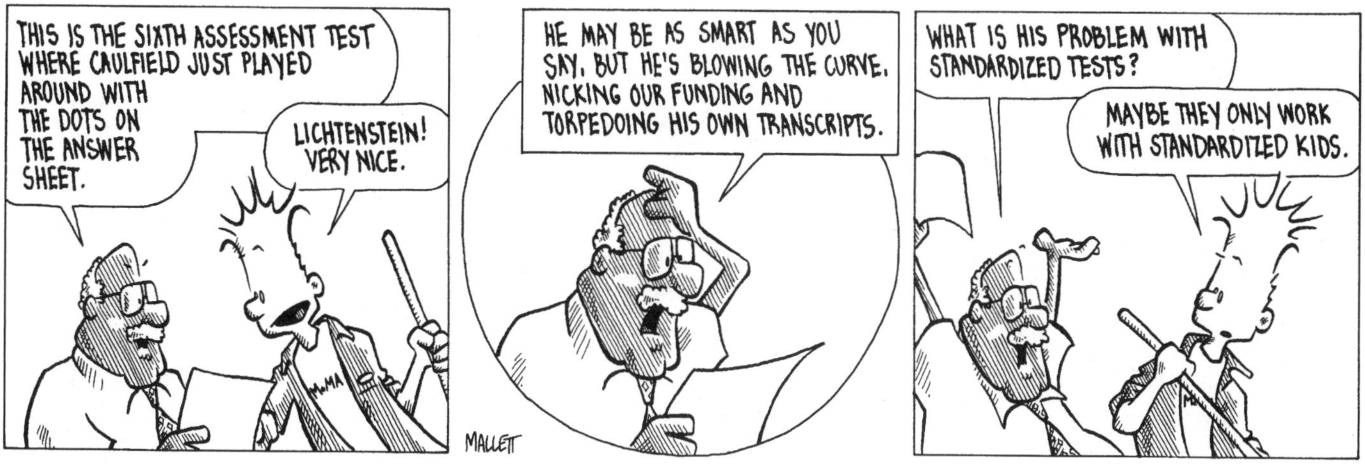
THIS IS THE SIXTH ASSESSMENT TEST WHERE CAULFIELD JUST PLAYED AROUND WITH THE DOTS ON THE ANSWER SHEET.
LICHTENSTEIN! VERY NICE.
HE MAY BE AS SMART AS YOU SAY, BUT HE'S BLOWING THE CURVE, NICKING OUR FUNDING AND TORPEDOING HIS OWN TRANSCRIPTS.
WHAT IS HIS PROBLEM WITH STANDARDIZED TESTS?
MAYBE THEY ONLY WORK WITH STANDARDIZED KIDS.
MALLETT

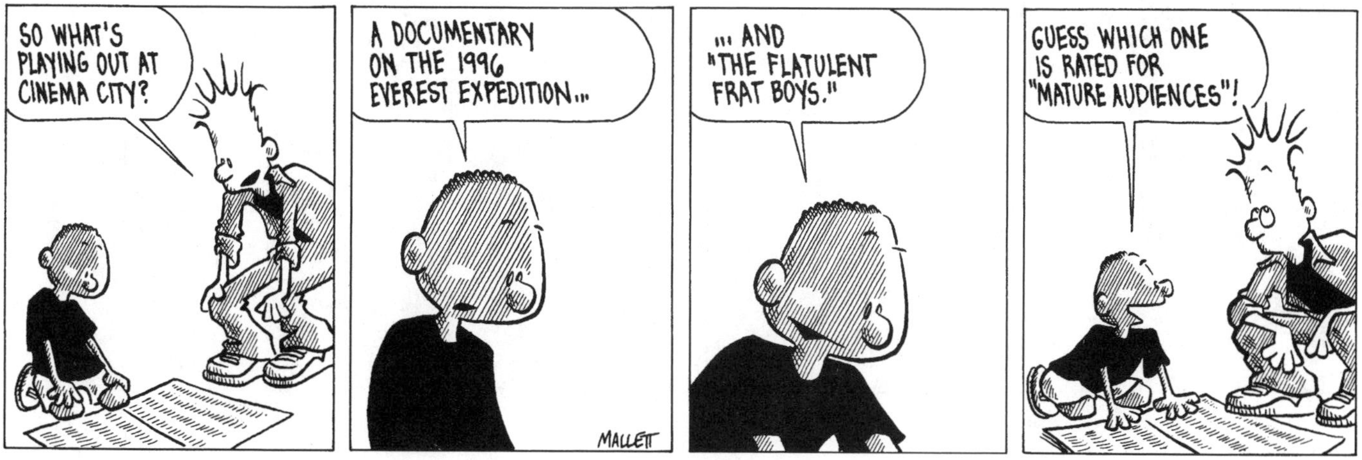
SO WHAT'S PLAYING OUT AT CINEMA CITY?
A DOCUMENTARY ON THE 1996 EVEREST EXPEDITION...
... AND "THE FLATULENT FRAT BOYS."
GUESS WHICH ONE IS RATED FOR "MATURE AUDIENCES"!
MALLETT

Frazz
by Jef Mallett
HOW'S LYLE?
BETTER THAN ELVIS, MOZART AND THE RAMONES!
YOUR GUINEA PIG LYLE, NOT LYLE LOVETT.
HIM, TOO.
Soda
I'M AMAZED GUINEA PIGS CAN FIGURE OUT THOSE UPSIDE-DOWN WATER BOTTLE THINGS.
HOW SO?
WELL, YOU'D THINK IN THE WILD THEY DRANK WATER OFF THE GROUND.
WILD GUINEA PIGS?
SO HOW DOES IT OCCUR TO THEM TO LOOK UPWARD FOR WATER?
OOH, GOOD QUESTION.
MAYBE THEY KNEW TO DRINK FROM WET LEAVES OVERHEAD AFTER A RAIN.
ALSO THERE'S THE NURSING INSTINCT.
IT'S JUST NEAT HOW THIRST IS SUCH A MOTIVATING DRIVE.
TRUE.
EVEN THE TINIEST-BRAINED CREATURES CAN FIGURE OUT HOW TO GET A DRINK.
MALLETT

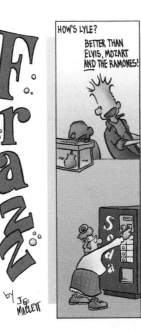

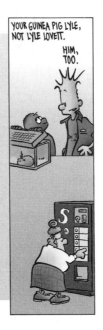

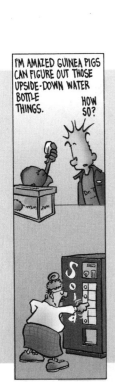

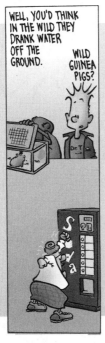

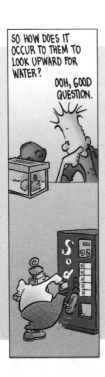

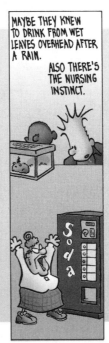

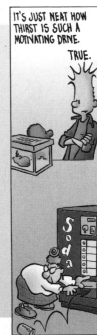

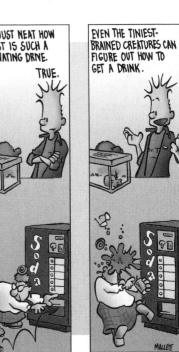

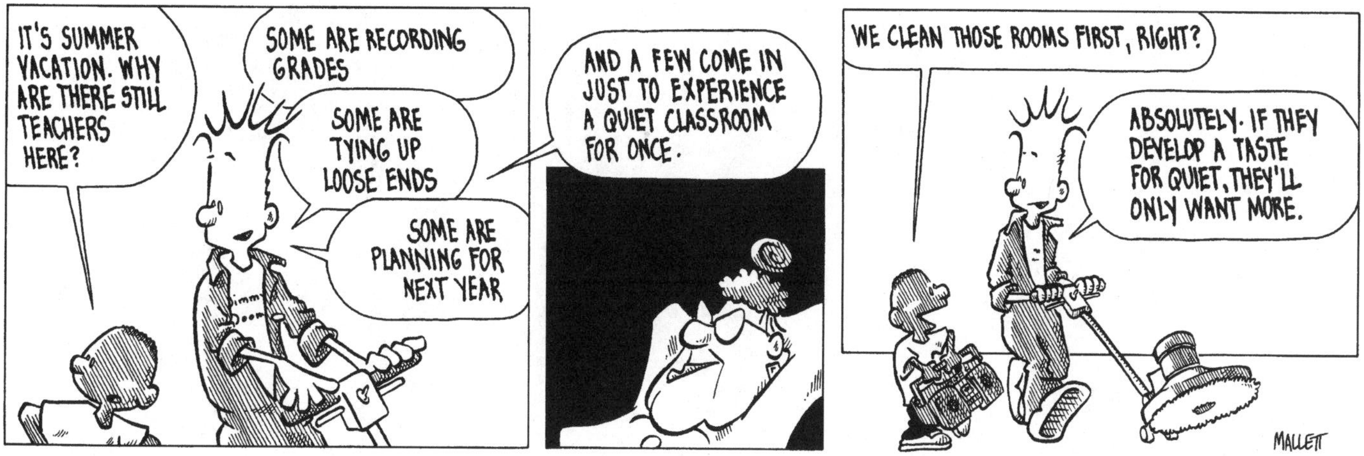
IT'S SUMMER VACATION. WHY ARE THERE STILL TEACHERS HERE?
SOME ARE RECORDING GRADES
SOME ARE TYING UP LOOSE ENDS
SOME ARE PLANNING FOR NEXT YEAR
AND A FEW COME IN JUST TO EXPERIENCE A QUIET CLASSROOM FOR ONCE.
WE CLEAN THOSE ROOMS FIRST, RIGHT?
ABSOLUTELY. IF THEY DEVELOP A TASTE FOR QUIET, THEY'LL ONLY WANT MORE.
MALLETT

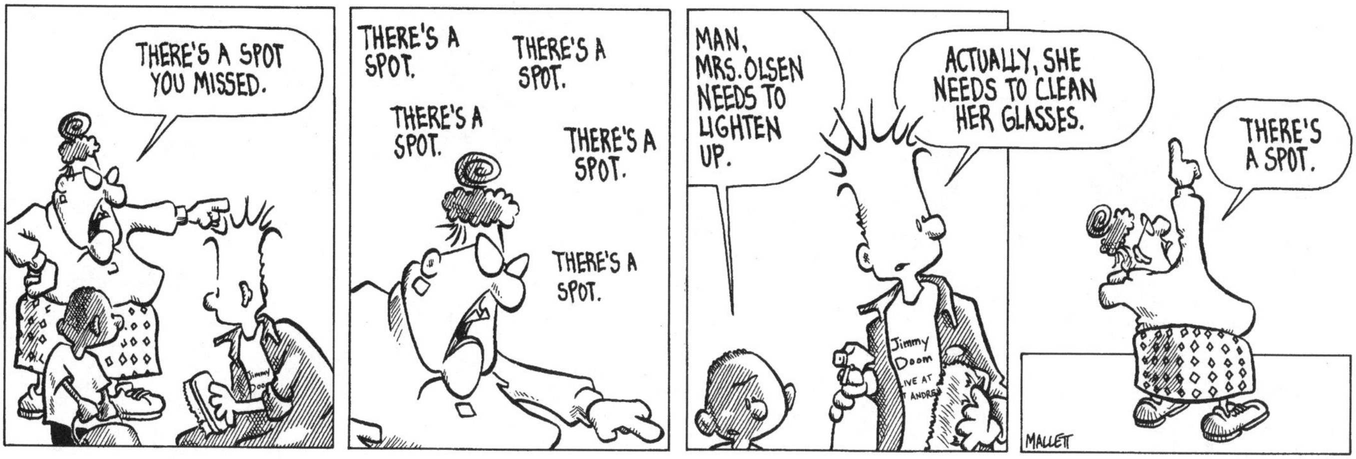
THERE'S A SPOT YOU MISSED.
THERE'S A SPOT.
THERE'S A SPOT.
THERE'S A SPOT.
THERE'S A SPOT.
THERE'S A SPOT.
MAN, MRS. OLSEN NEEDS TO LIGHTEN UP.
ACTUALLY, SHE NEEDS TO CLEAN HER GLASSES.
THERE'S A SPOT.
MALLETT

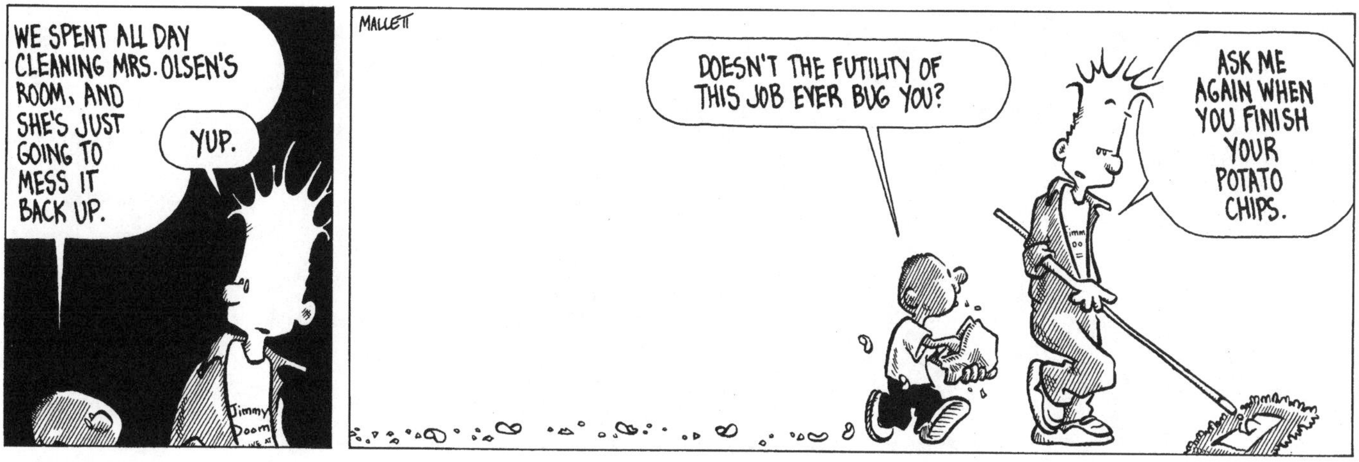
WE SPENT ALL DAY CLEANING MRS. OLSEN'S ROOM, AND SHE'S JUST GOING TO MESS IT BACK UP.
YUP.
MALLETT
DOESN'T THE FUTILITY OF THIS JOB EVER BUG YOU?
ASK ME AGAIN WHEN YOU FINISH YOUR POTATO CHIPS.

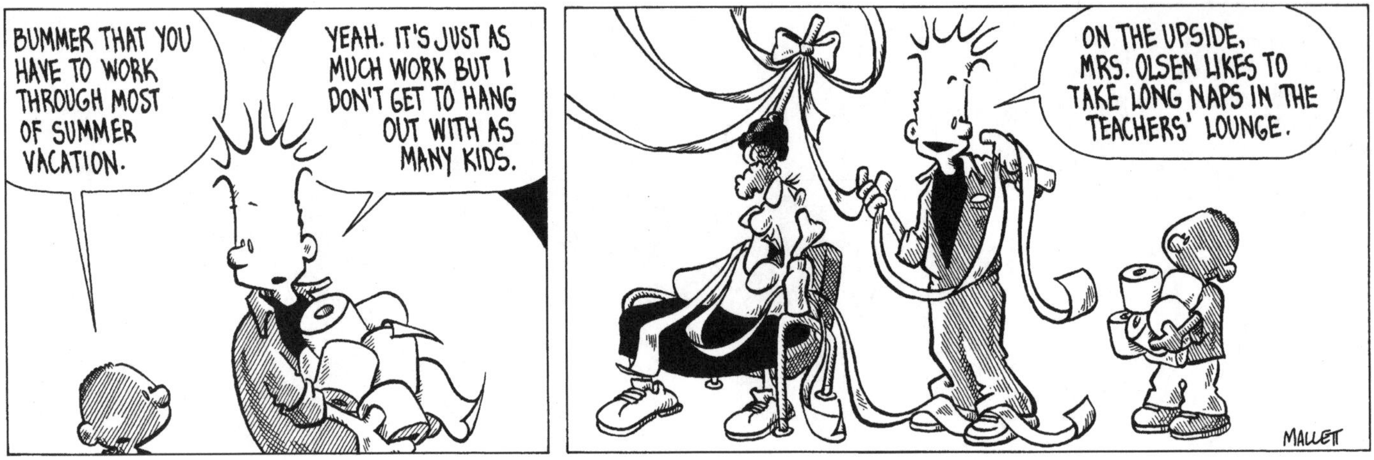
BUMMER THAT YOU HAVE TO WORK THROUGH MOST OF SUMMER VACATION.
YEAH. IT'S JUST AS MUCH WORK BUT I DON'T GET TO HANG OUT WITH AS MANY KIDS.
ON THE UPSIDE, MRS. OLSEN LIKES TO TAKE LONG NAPS IN THE TEACHERS' LOUNGE.
MALLETT

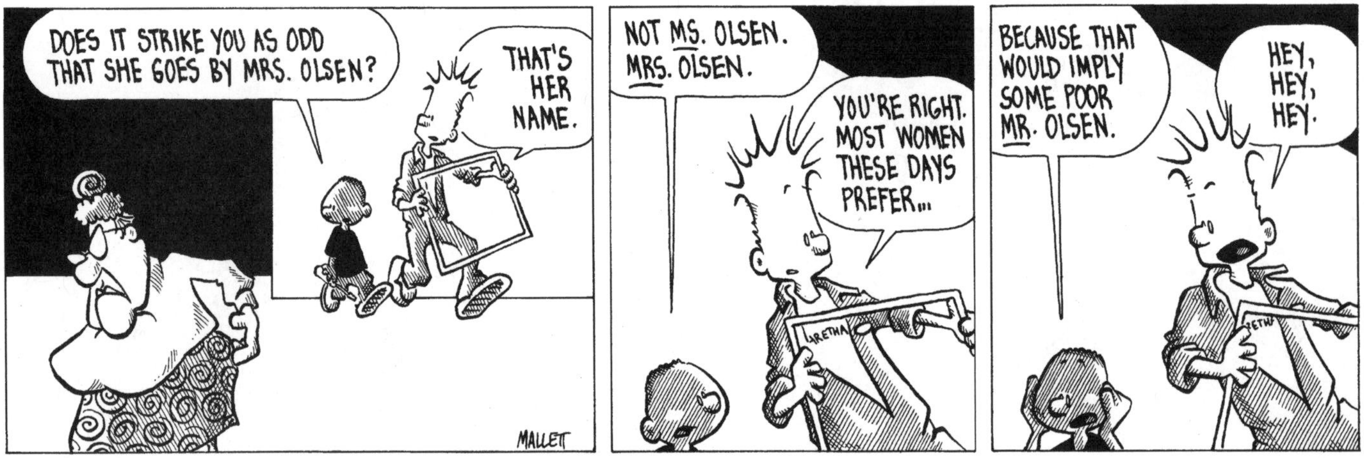
DOES IT STRIKE YOU AS ODD THAT SHE GOES BY MRS. OLSEN?
THAT'S HER NAME.
MALLETT
NOT MS. OLSEN. MRS. OLSEN.
YOU'RE RIGHT. MOST WOMEN THESE DAYS PREFER...
ARETHA
BECAUSE THAT WOULD IMPLY SOME POOR MR. OLSEN.
HEY, HEY, HEY.

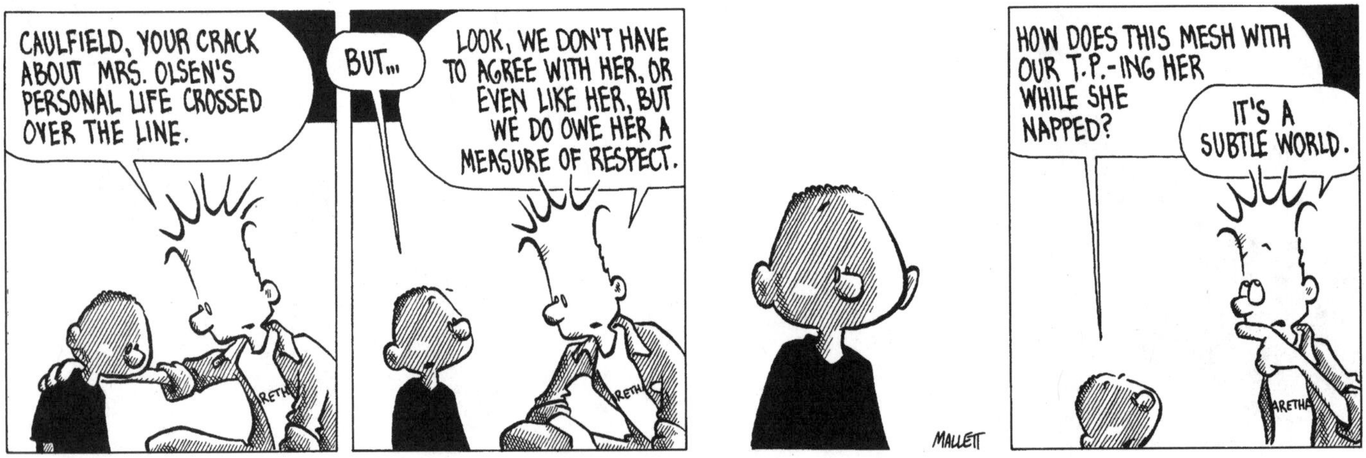
CAULFIELD, YOUR CRACK ABOUT MRS. OLSEN'S PERSONAL LIFE CROSSED OVER THE LINE.
BUT...
LOOK, WE DON'T HAVE TO AGREE WITH HER, OR EVEN LIKE HER, BUT WE DO OWE HER A MEASURE OF RESPECT.
MALLETT
HOW DOES THIS MESH WITH OUR T.P.-ING HER WHILE SHE NAPPED?
IT'S A SUBTLE WORLD.
ARETHA

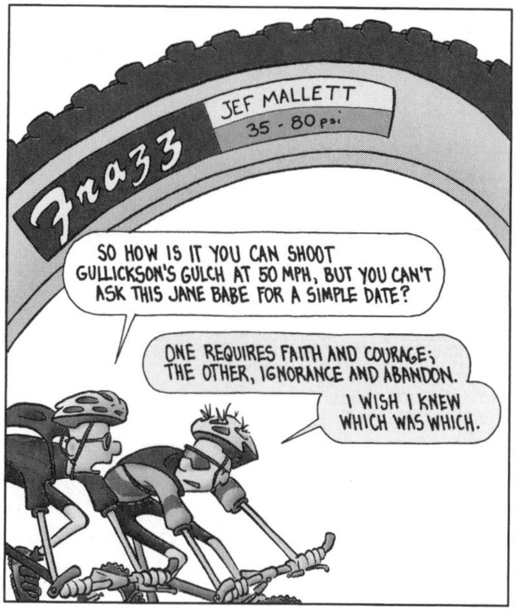
JEF MALLETT
35 - 80 psi
Frazz
SO HOW IS IT YOU CAN SHOOT GULLICKSON'S GULCH AT 50 MPH, BUT YOU CAN'T ASK THIS JANE BABE FOR A SIMPLE DATE?
ONE REQUIRES FAITH AND COURAGE; THE OTHER, IGNORANCE AND ABANDON.
I WISH I KNEW WHICH WAS WHICH.

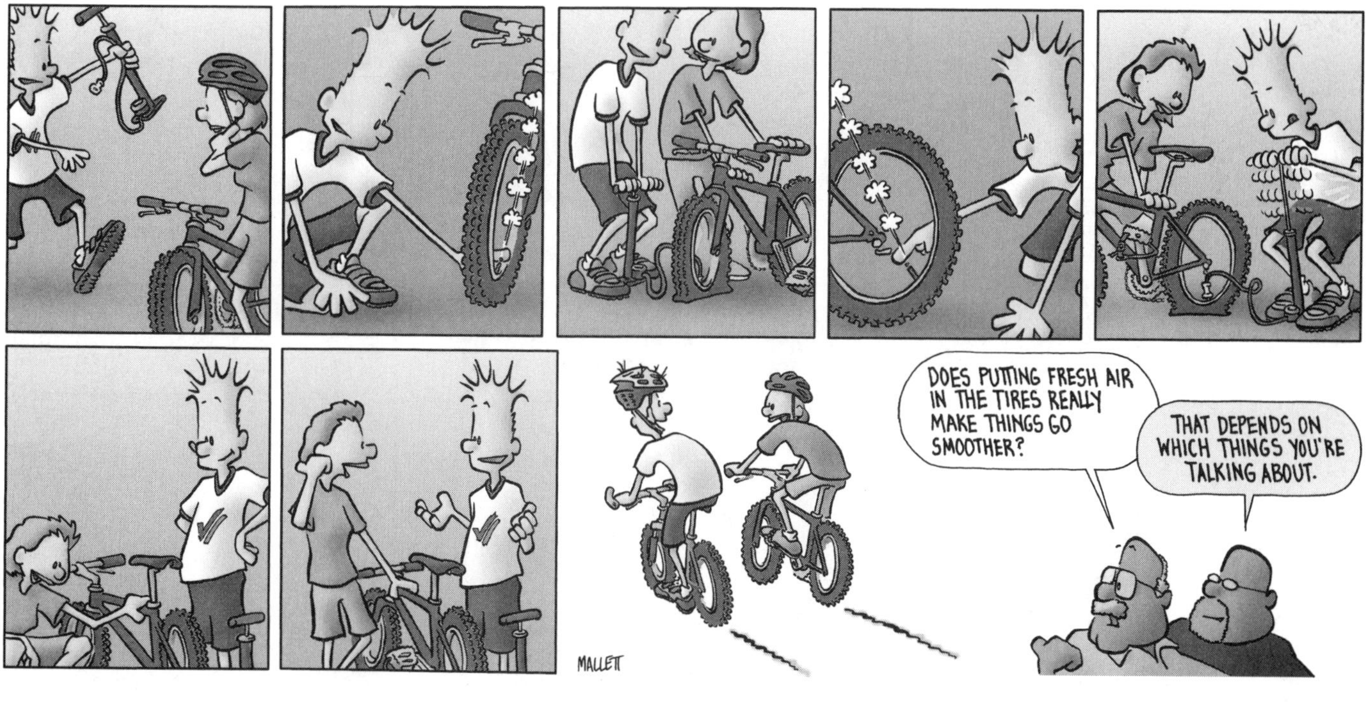
MALLETT
DOES PUTTING FRESH AIR IN THE TIRES REALLY MAKE THINGS GO SMOOTHER?
THAT DEPENDS ON WHICH THINGS YOU'RE TALKING ABOUT.

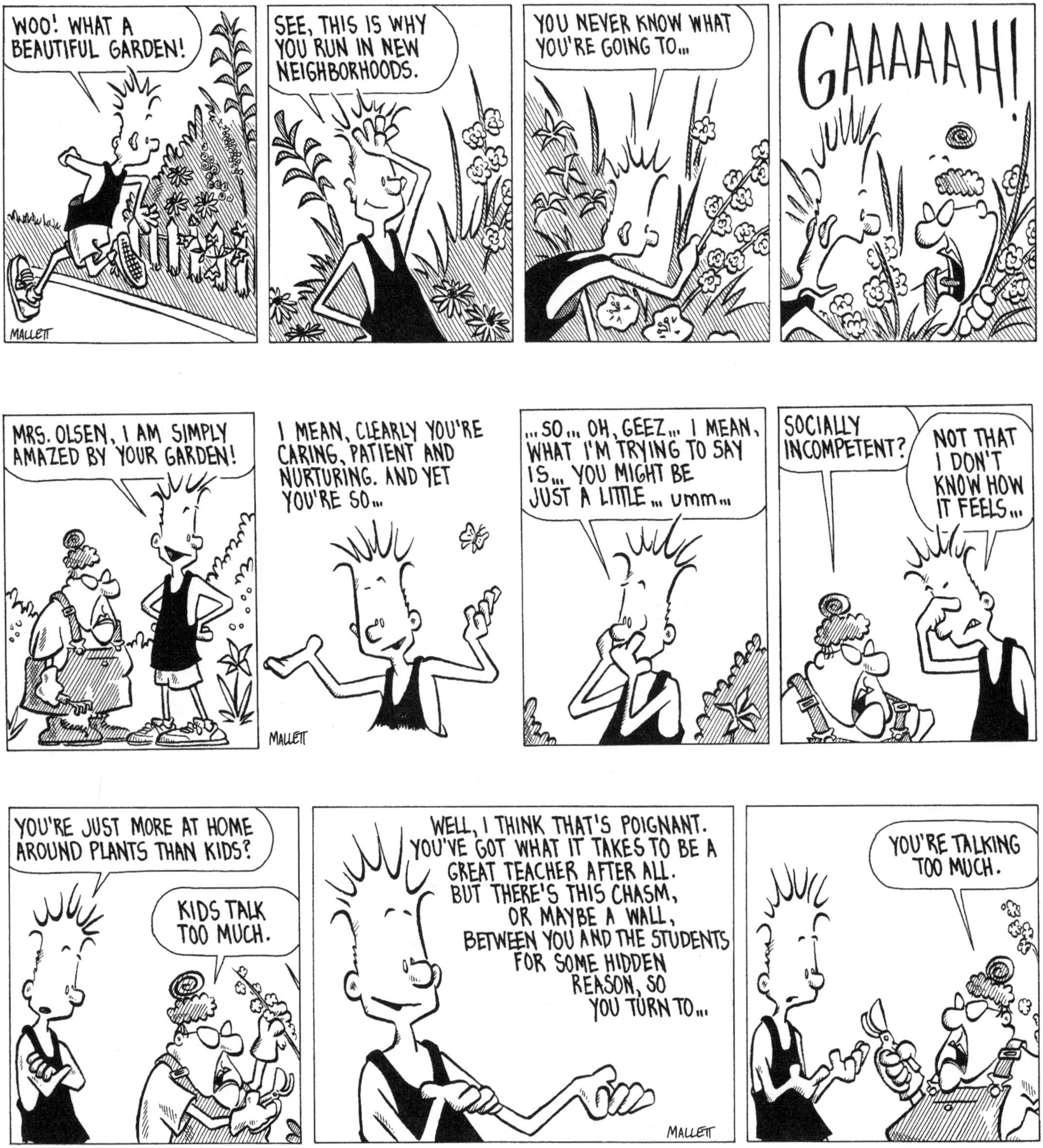
WOO! WHAT A BEAUTIFUL GARDEN!
MALLETT
SEE, THIS IS WHY YOU RUN IN NEW NEIGHBORHOODS.
YOU NEVER KNOW WHAT YOU'RE GOING TO...
GAAAAAH!
MRS. OLSEN, I AM SIMPLY AMAZED BY YOUR GARDEN!
I MEAN, CLEARLY YOU'RE CARING, PATIENT AND NURTURING. AND YET YOU'RE SO...
MALLETT
...SO... OH, GEEZ... I MEAN, WHAT I'M TRYING TO SAY IS... YOU MIGHT BE JUST A LITTLE ... umm...
SOCIALLY INCOMPETENT?
NOT THAT I DON'T KNOW HOW IT FEELS...
YOU'RE JUST MORE AT HOME AROUND PLANTS THAN KIDS?
KIDS TALK TOO MUCH.
WELL, I THINK THAT'S POIGNANT. YOU'VE GOT WHAT IT TAKES TO BE A GREAT TEACHER AFTER ALL. BUT THERE'S THIS CHASM, OR MAYBE A WALL, BETWEEN YOU AND THE STUDENTS FOR SOME HIDDEN REASON, SO YOU TURN TO...
MALLETT
YOU'RE TALKING TOO MUCH.

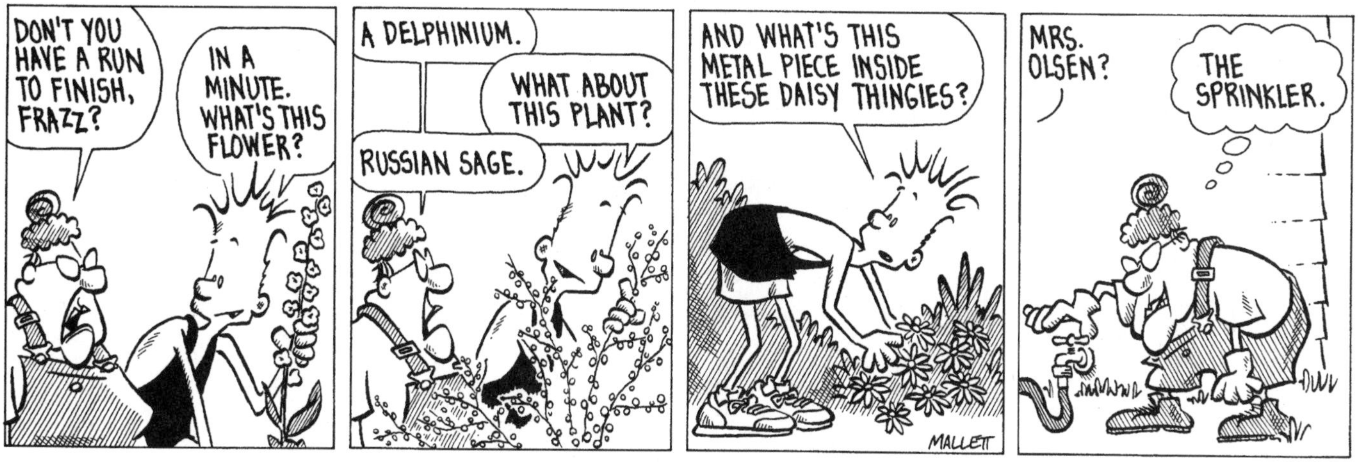
DON'T YOU HAVE A RUN TO FINISH, FRAZZ?
IN A MINUTE. WHAT'S THIS FLOWER?
A DELPHINIUM.
WHAT ABOUT THIS PLANT?
RUSSIAN SAGE.
AND WHAT'S THIS METAL PIECE INSIDE THESE DAISY THINGIES?
MALLETT
MRS. OLSEN?
THE SPRINKLER.

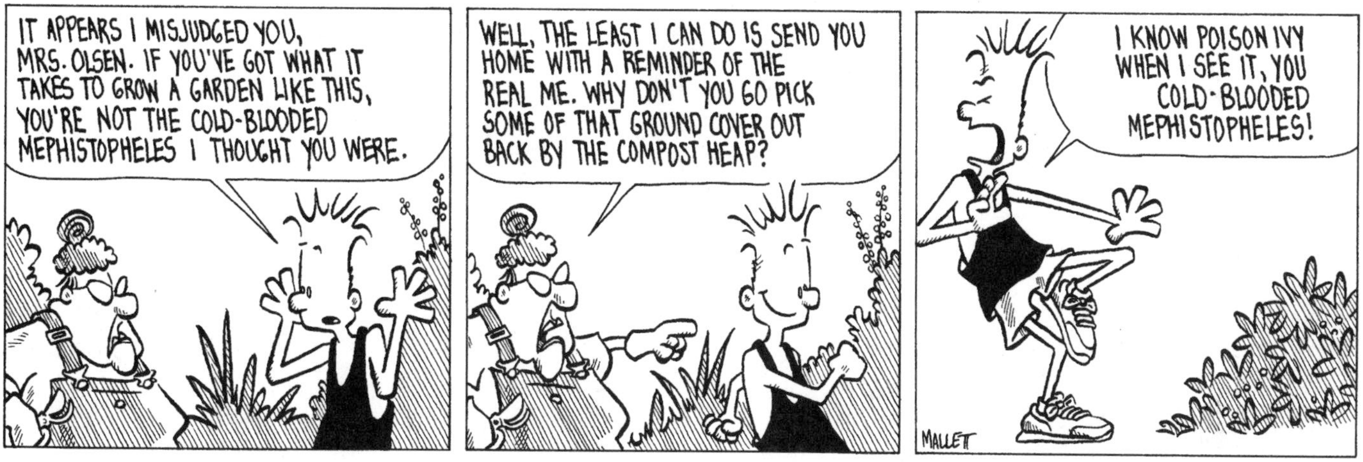
IT APPEARS I MISJUDGED YOU, MRS. OLSEN. IF YOU'VE GOT WHAT IT TAKES TO GROW A GARDEN LIKE THIS, YOU'RE NOT THE COLD-BLOODED MEPHISTOPHELES I THOUGHT YOU WERE.
WELL, THE LEAST I CAN DO IS SEND YOU HOME WITH A REMINDER OF THE REAL ME. WHY DON'T YOU GO PICK SOME OF THAT GROUND COVER OUT BACK BY THE COMPOST HEAP?
I KNOW POISON IVY WHEN I SEE IT, YOU COLD-BLOODED MEPHISTOPHELES!
MALLETT

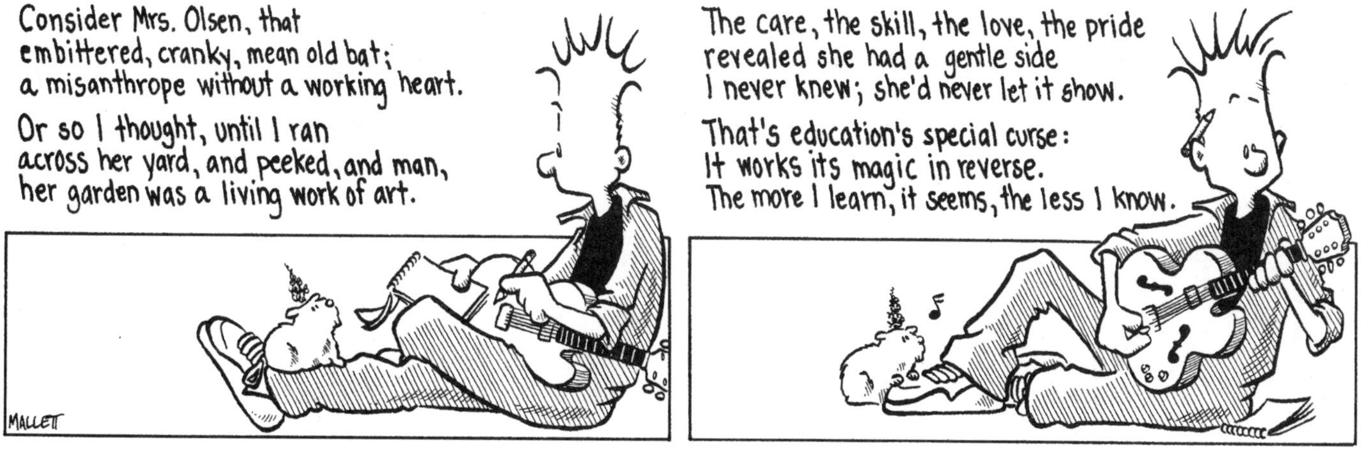
Consider Mrs. Olsen, that
embittered, cranky, mean old bat;
a misanthrope without a working heart.
Or so I thought, until I ran
across her yard, and peeked, and man,
her garden was a living work of art.
MALLETT
The care, the skill, the love, the pride
revealed she had a gentle side
I never knew; she'd never let it show.
That's education's special curse:
It works its magic in reverse.
The more I learn, it seems, the less I know.

Frazz
IT'S SO HARD TO PICTURE AN ENDLESS UNIVERSE. YET IT WAS SO EASY TO PICTURE AN ENDLESS SCHOOL YEAR.
I ALWAYS HAVE TROUBLE WITH THE TIME-SPACE CONTINUUM, TOO.
by JEF MALLETT

MR. SPAETZLE HAS BEEN AT HIS DESK ALL DAY WITHOUT A BREAK. THAT CAN'T BE GOOD FOR HIS HEALTH.
COME WITH ME.
HOLY COW! YOU'RE SLOWING THE AGING PROCESS BY ACCELERATING TIME!
WELL, IT WAS EINSTEIN'S IDEA, BUT I'M THE ONE WITH ACCESS TO THE BUILDING'S MASTER CLOCK.
MALLETT

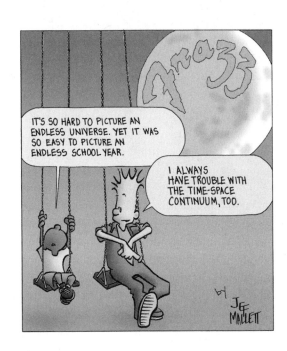

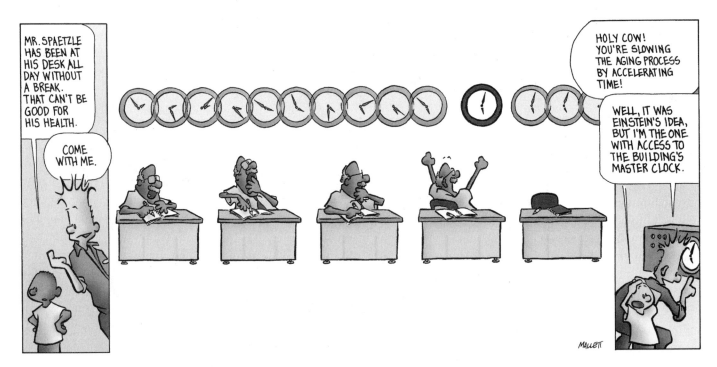

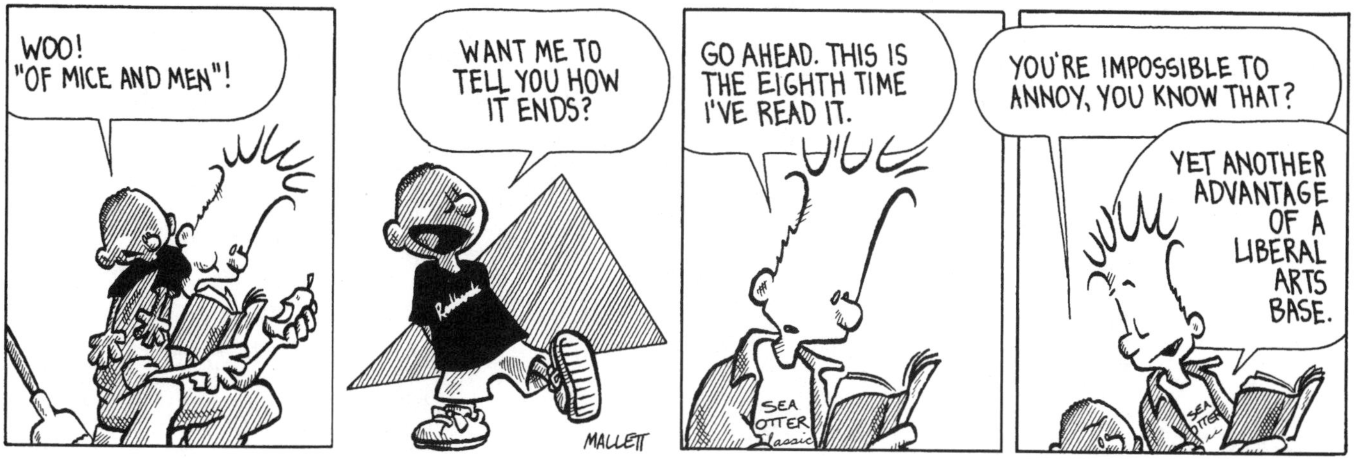
WOO! "OF MICE AND MEN"!
WANT ME TO TELL YOU HOW IT ENDS?
MALLETT
GO AHEAD. THIS IS THE EIGHTH TIME I'VE READ IT.
SEA OTTER Classic
YOU'RE IMPOSSIBLE TO ANNOY, YOU KNOW THAT?
YET ANOTHER ADVANTAGE OF A LIBERAL ARTS BASE.

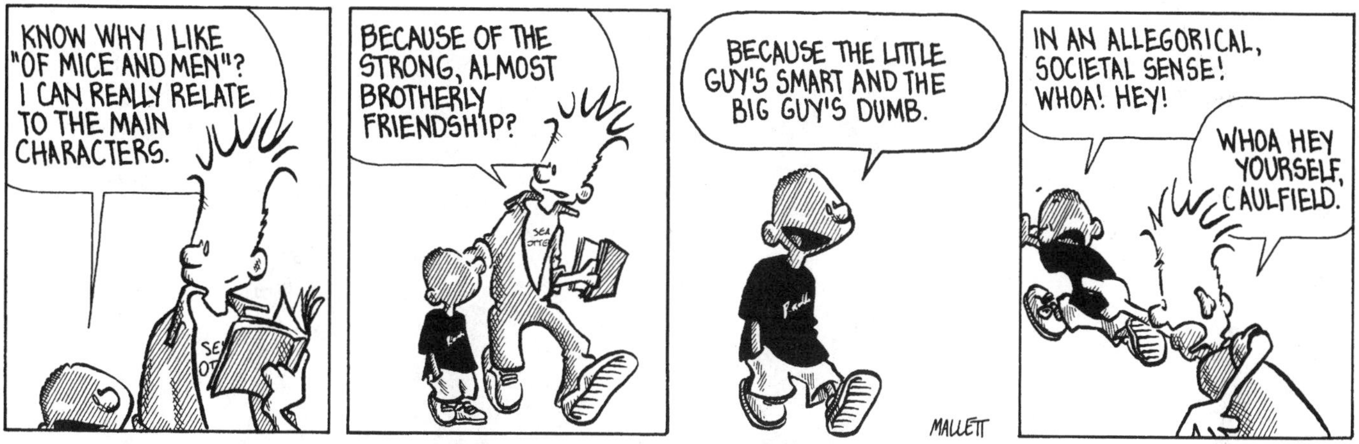
KNOW WHY I LIKE "OF MICE AND MEN"? I CAN REALLY RELATE TO THE MAIN CHARACTERS.
BECAUSE OF THE STRONG, ALMOST BROTHERLY FRIENDSHIP?
BECAUSE THE LITTLE GUY'S SMART AND THE BIG GUY'S DUMB.
MALLETT
IN AN ALLEGORICAL, SOCIETAL SENSE! WHOA! HEY!
WHOA HEY YOURSELF, CAULFIELD.

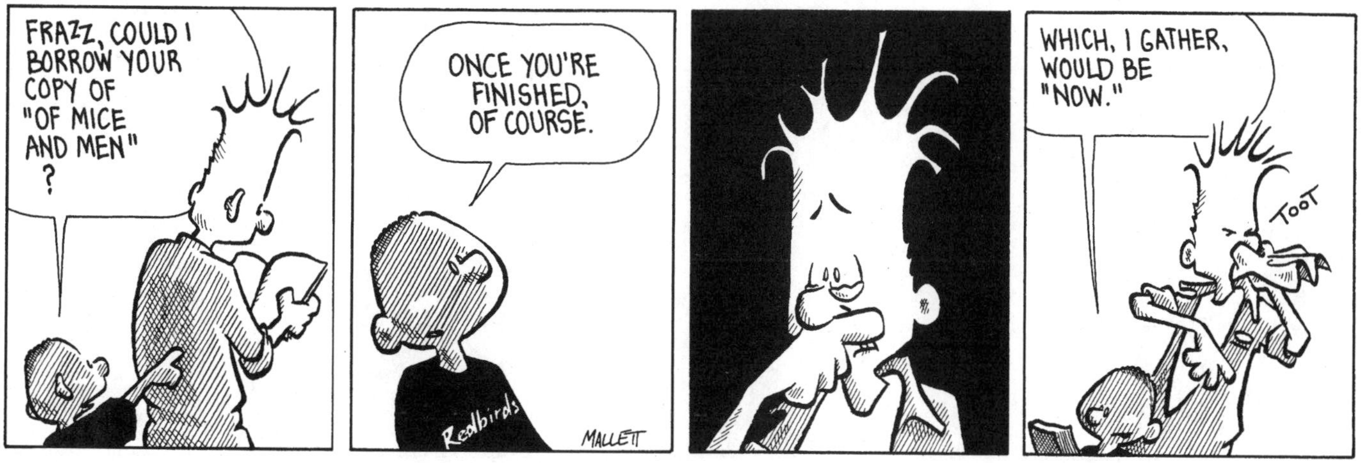
FRAZZ, COULD I BORROW YOUR COPY OF "OF MICE AND MEN" ?
ONCE YOU'RE FINISHED, OF COURSE.
Redbirds
MALLETT
WHICH, I GATHER, WOULD BE "NOW."
TOOT

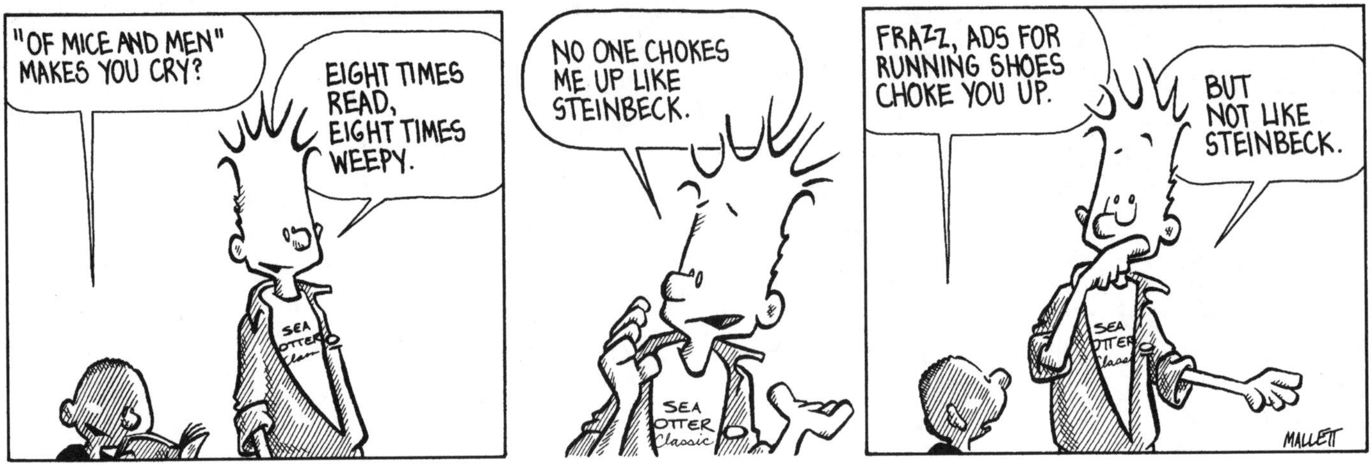
"OF MICE AND MEN" MAKES YOU CRY?
EIGHT TIMES READ, EIGHT TIMES WEEPY.
NO ONE CHOKES ME UP LIKE STEINBECK.
FRAZZ, ADS FOR RUNNING SHOES CHOKE YOU UP.
BUT NOT LIKE STEINBECK.
MALLETT

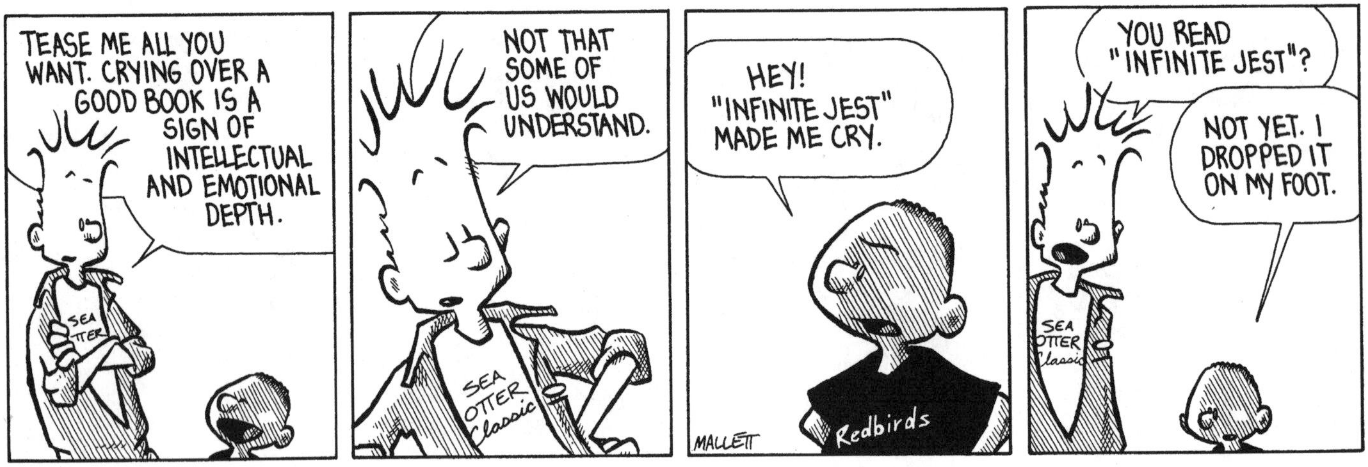
TEASE ME ALL YOU WANT. CRYING OVER A GOOD BOOK IS A SIGN OF INTELLECTUAL AND EMOTIONAL DEPTH.
NOT THAT SOME OF US WOULD UNDERSTAND.
HEY! "INFINITE JEST" MADE ME CRY.
MALLETT
Redbirds
YOU READ "INFINITE JEST"?
NOT YET. I DROPPED IT ON MY FOOT.

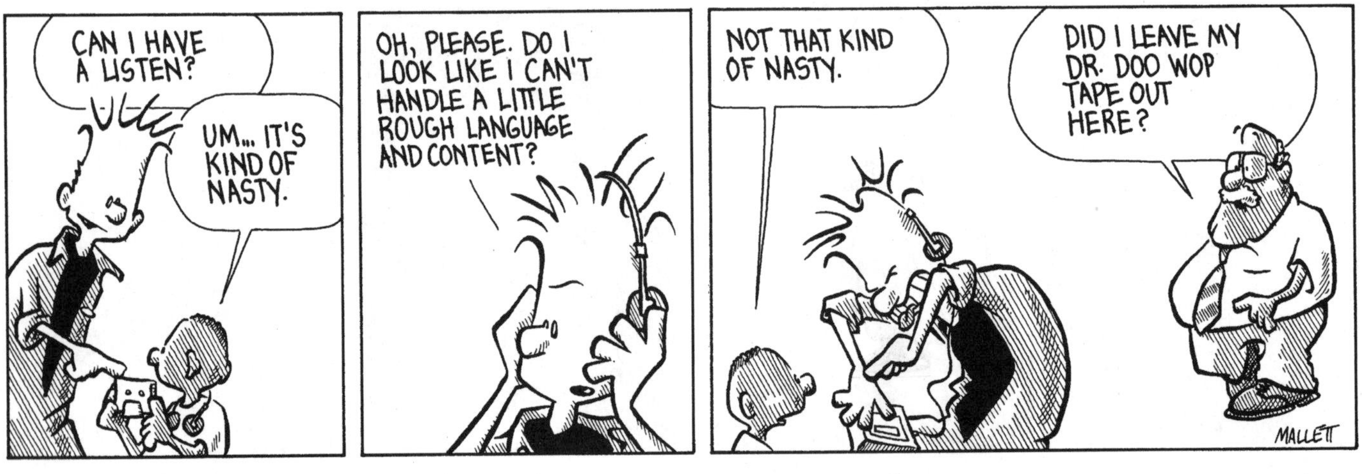
CAN I HAVE A LISTEN?
UM... IT'S KIND OF NASTY.
OH, PLEASE. DO I LOOK LIKE I CAN'T HANDLE A LITTLE ROUGH LANGUAGE AND CONTENT?
NOT THAT KIND OF NASTY.
DID I LEAVE MY DR. DOO WOP TAPE OUT HERE?
MALLETT

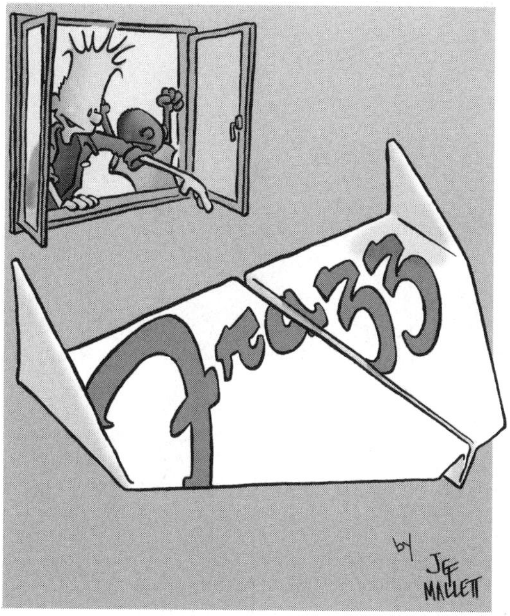
Frazz
by JEF MALLETT

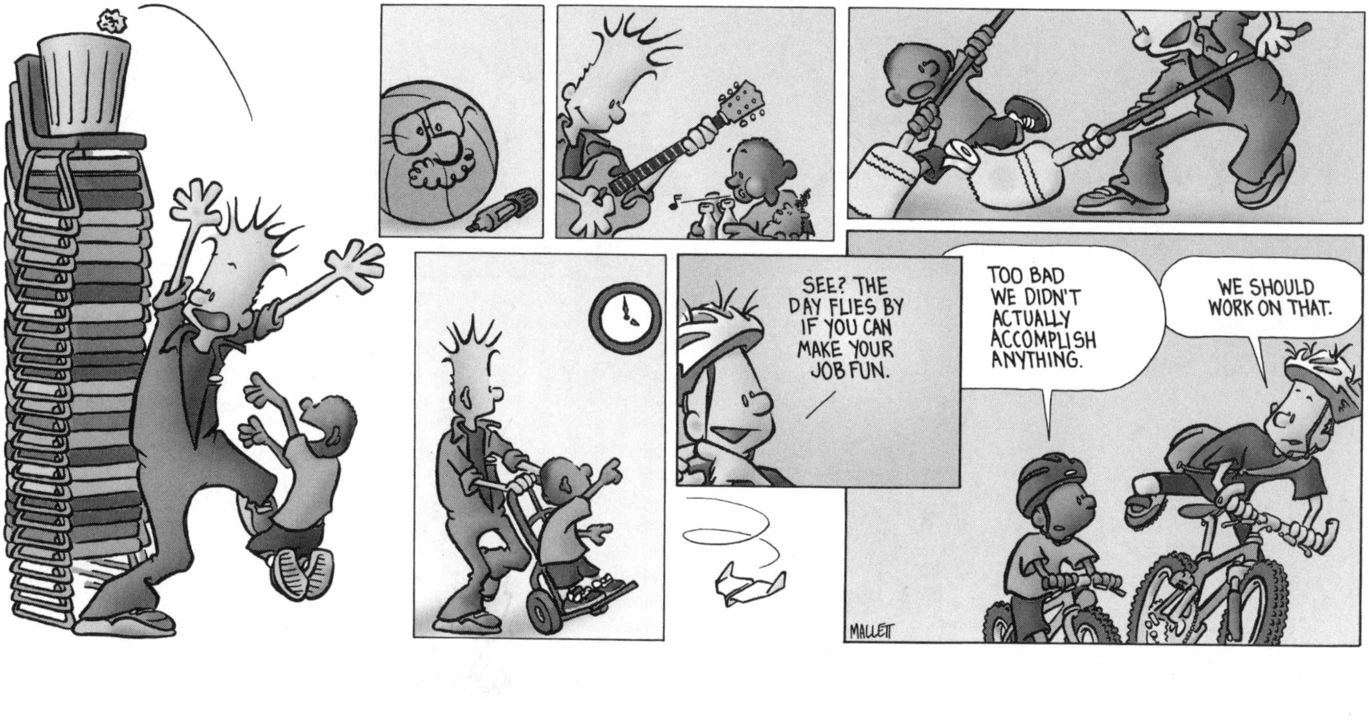
SEE? THE DAY FLIES BY IF YOU CAN MAKE YOUR JOB FUN.
TOO BAD WE DIDN'T ACTUALLY ACCOMPLISH ANYTHING.
WE SHOULD WORK ON THAT.
MALLETT

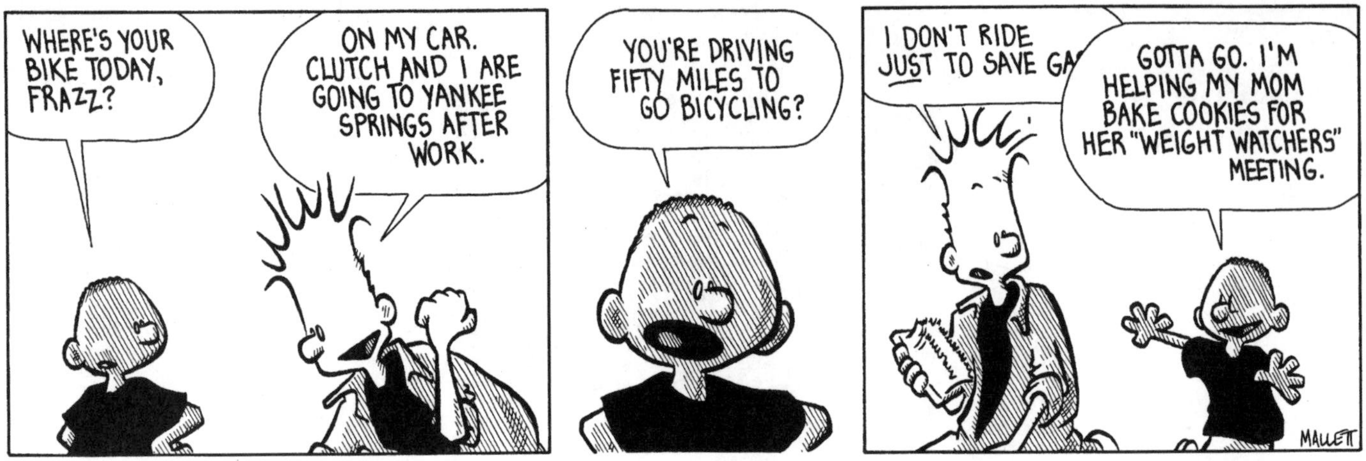
WHERE'S YOUR BIKE TODAY, FRAZZ?
ON MY CAR. CLUTCH AND I ARE GOING TO YANKEE SPRINGS AFTER WORK.
YOU'RE DRIVING FIFTY MILES TO GO BICYCLING?
I DON'T RIDE JUST TO SAVE GA
GOTTA GO. I'M HELPING MY MOM BAKE COOKIES FOR HER "WEIGHT WATCHERS" MEETING.
MALLETT

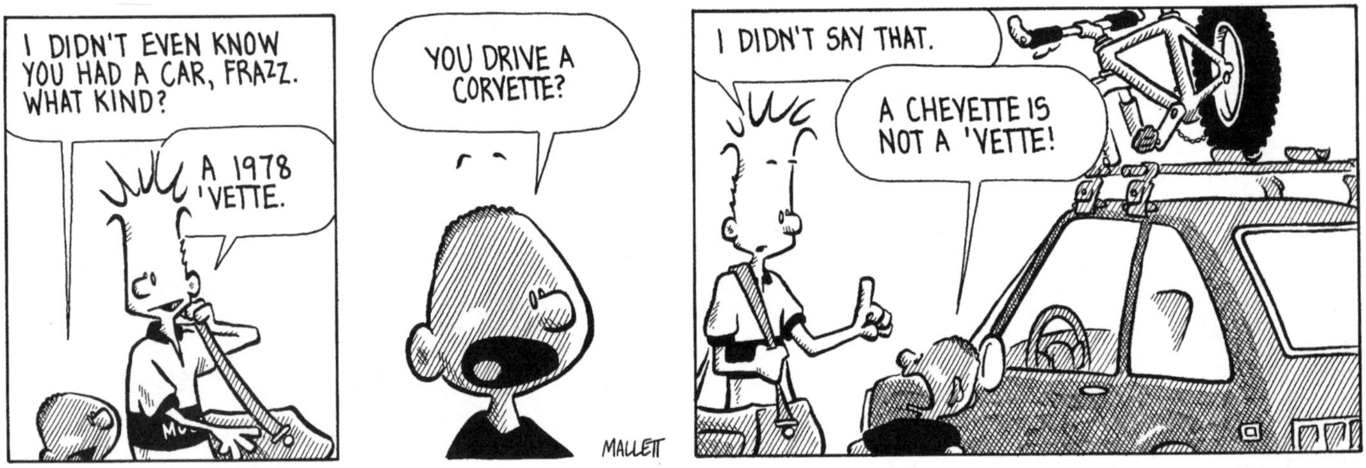
I DIDN'T EVEN KNOW YOU HAD A CAR, FRAZZ. WHAT KIND?
A 1978 'VETTE.
YOU DRIVE A CORVETTE?
MALLETT
I DIDN'T SAY THAT.
A CHEYETTE IS NOT A 'VETTE!

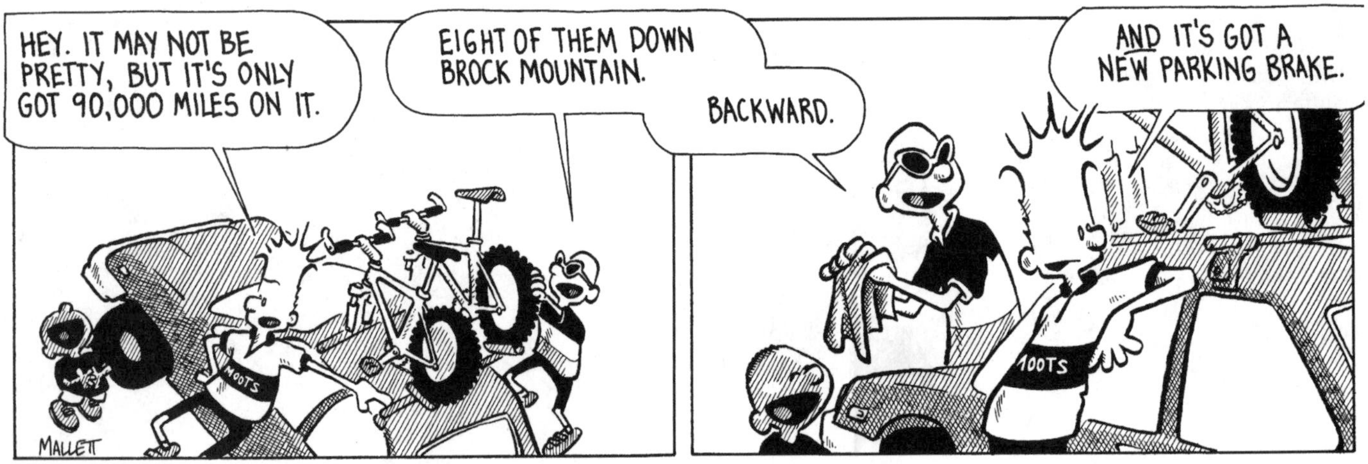
HEY. IT MAY NOT BE PRETTY, BUT IT'S ONLY GOT 90,000 MILES ON IT.
EIGHT OF THEM DOWN BROCK MOUNTAIN.
BACKWARD.
MALLETT
AND IT'S GOT A NEW PARKING BRAKE.

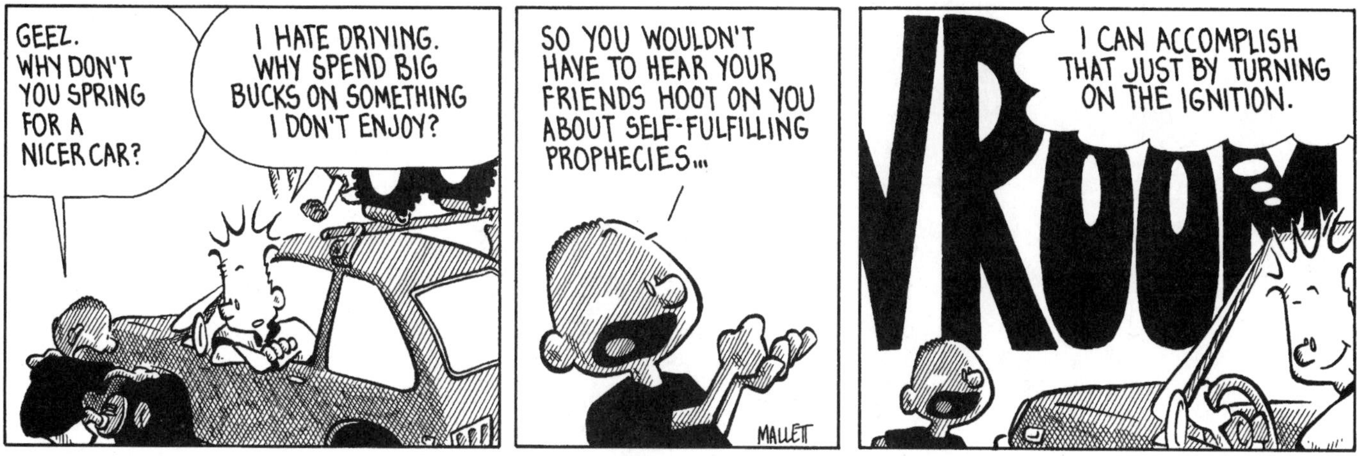
GEEZ. WHY DON'T YOU SPRING FOR A NICER CAR?
I HATE DRIVING. WHY SPEND BIG BUCKS ON SOMETHING I DON'T ENJOY?
SO YOU WOULDN'T HAVE TO HEAR YOUR FRIENDS HOOT ON YOU ABOUT SELF-FULFILLING PROPHECIES...
VROOM
I CAN ACCOMPLISH THAT JUST BY TURNING ON THE IGNITION.
MALLETT

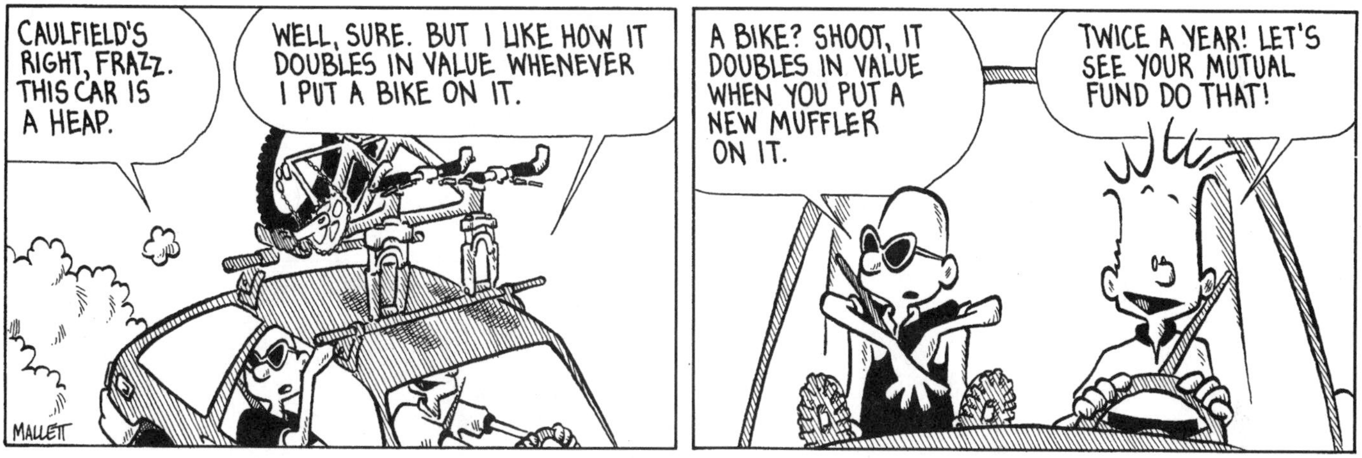
CAULFIELD'S RIGHT, FRAZZ. THIS CAR IS A HEAP.
WELL, SURE. BUT I LIKE HOW IT DOUBLES IN VALUE WHENEVER I PUT A BIKE ON IT.
MALLETT
A BIKE? SHOOT, IT DOUBLES IN VALUE WHEN YOU PUT A NEW MUFFLER ON IT.
TWICE A YEAR! LET'S SEE YOUR MUTUAL FUND DO THAT!

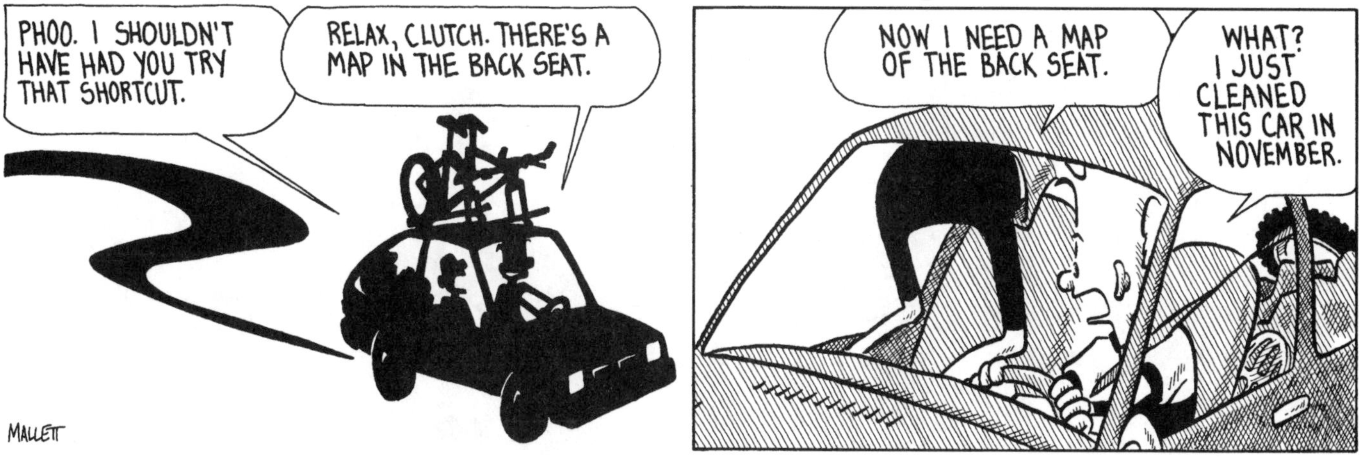
PHOO. I SHOULDN'T HAVE HAD YOU TRY THAT SHORTCUT.
RELAX, CLUTCH. THERE'S A MAP IN THE BACK SEAT.
MALLETT
NOW I NEED A MAP OF THE BACK SEAT.
WHAT? I JUST CLEANED THIS CAR IN NOVEMBER.

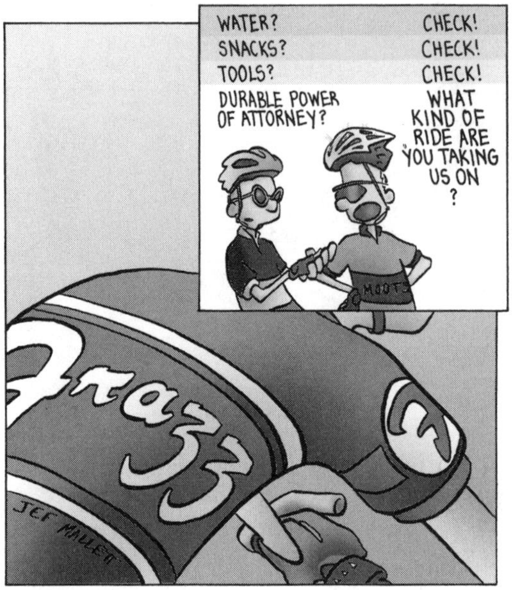
WATER? CHECK!
SNACKS? CHECK!
TOOLS? CHECK!
DURABLE POWER OF ATTORNEY?
WHAT KIND OF RIDE ARE YOU TAKING US ON?
MOOTS
Frazz
JEF MALLETT

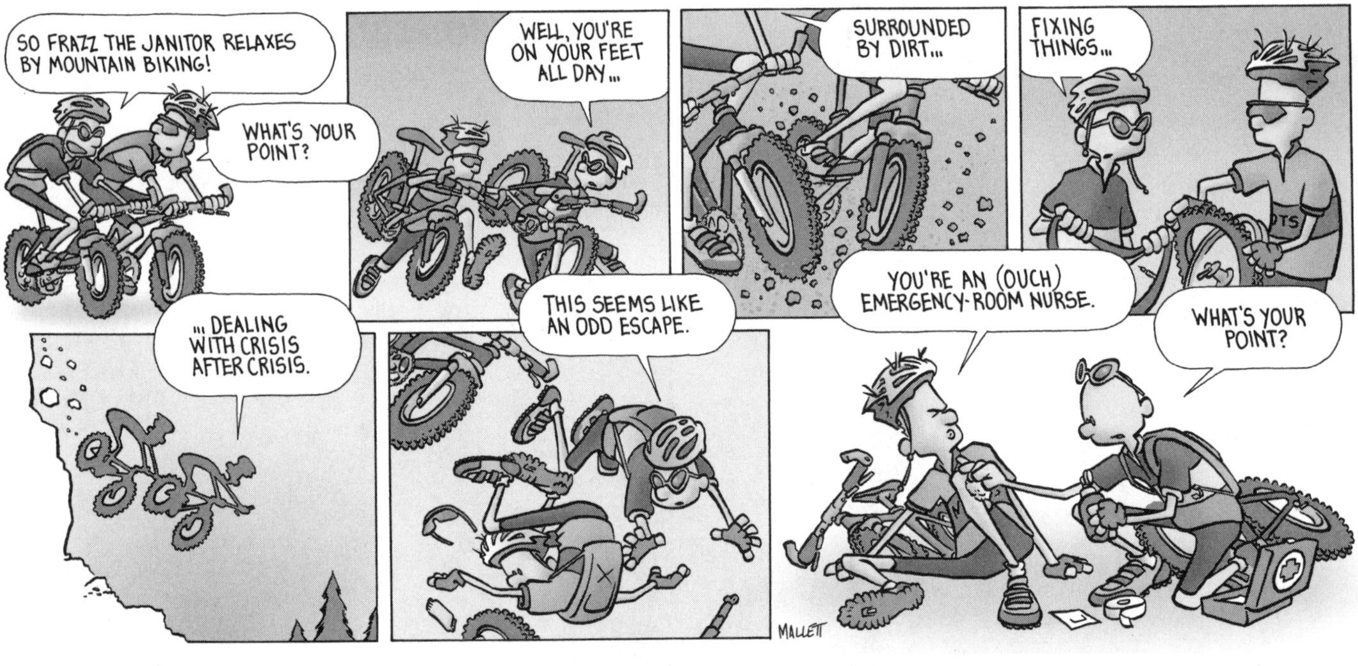
SO FRAZZ THE JANITOR RELAXES BY MOUNTAIN BIKING!
WHAT'S YOUR POINT?
WELL, YOU'RE ON YOUR FEET ALL DAY...
SURROUNDED BY DIRT...
FIXING THINGS...
...DEALING WITH CRISIS AFTER CRISIS.
THIS SEEMS LIKE AN ODD ESCAPE.
YOU'RE AN (OUCH) EMERGENCY-ROOM NURSE.
WHAT'S YOUR POINT?
MALLETT

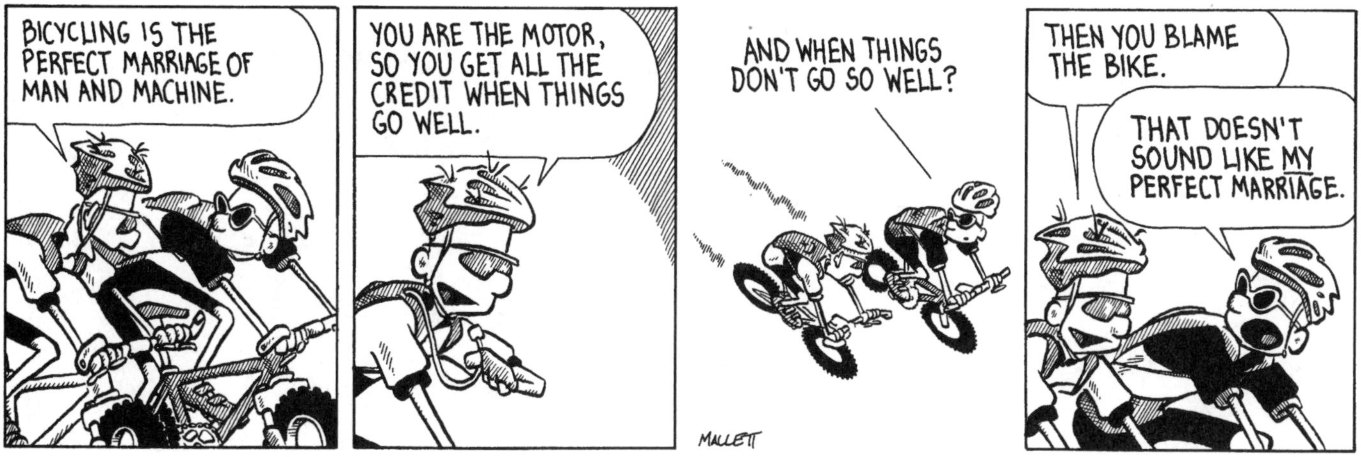
BICYCLING IS THE PERFECT MARRIAGE OF MAN AND MACHINE.
YOU ARE THE MOTOR, SO YOU GET ALL THE CREDIT WHEN THINGS GO WELL.
AND WHEN THINGS DON'T GO SO WELL?
THEN YOU BLAME THE BIKE.
THAT DOESN'T SOUND LIKE MY PERFECT MARRIAGE.
MALLETT

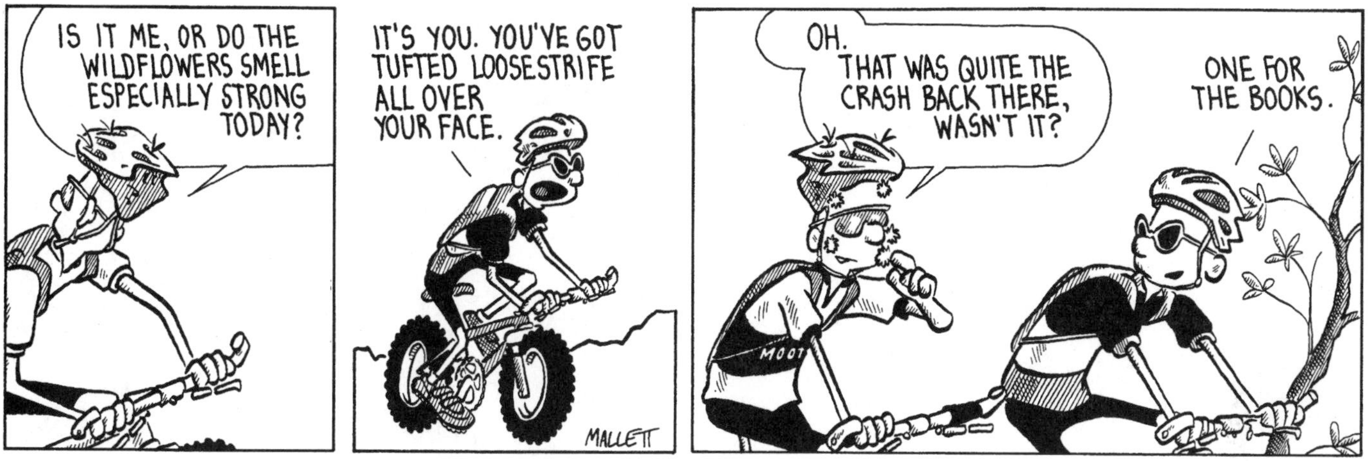
IS IT ME, OR DO THE WILDFLOWERS SMELL ESPECIALLY STRONG TODAY?
IT'S YOU. YOU'VE GOT TUFTED LOOSESTRIFE ALL OVER YOUR FACE.
MALLETT
OH.
THAT WAS QUITE THE CRASH BACK THERE, WASN'T IT?
ONE FOR THE BOOKS.
MOOT

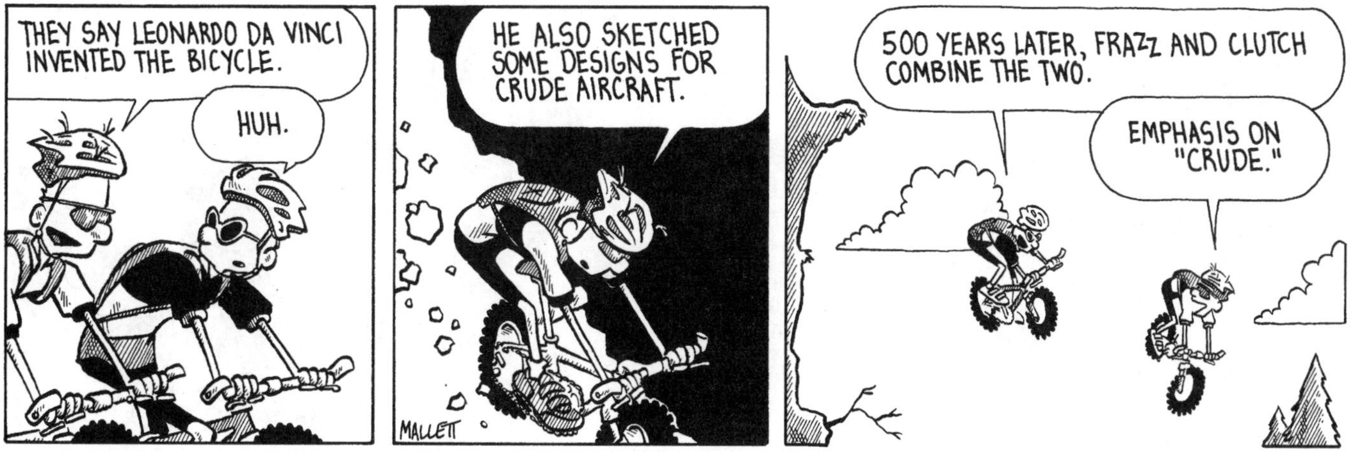
THEY SAY LEONARDO DA VINCI INVENTED THE BICYCLE.
HUH.
HE ALSO SKETCHED SOME DESIGNS FOR CRUDE AIRCRAFT.
MALLETT
500 YEARS LATER, FRAZZ AND CLUTCH COMBINE THE TWO.
EMPHASIS ON "CRUDE."

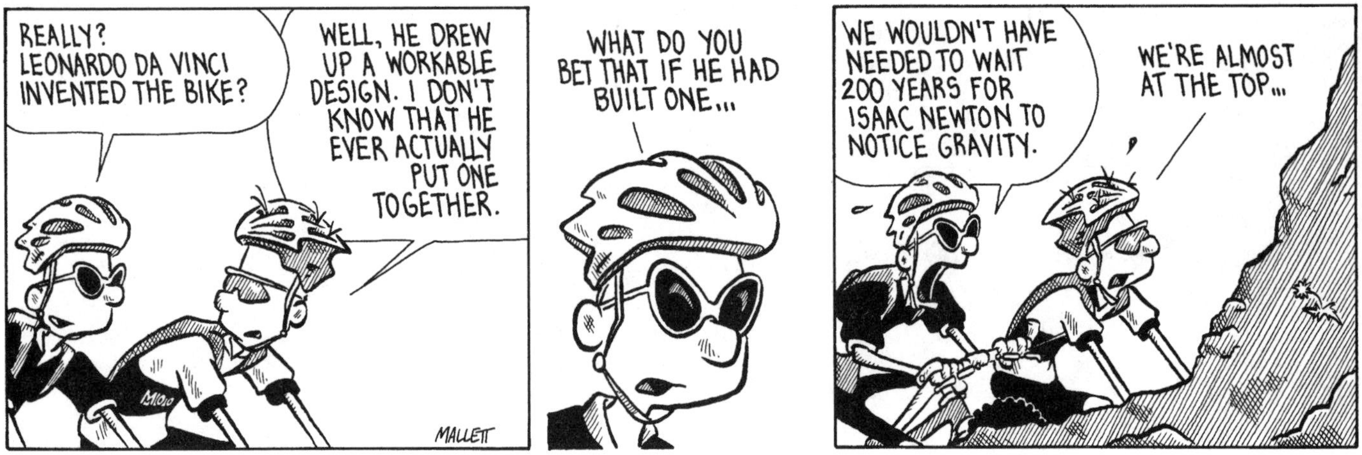
REALLY? LEONARDO DA VINCI INVENTED THE BIKE?
WELL, HE DREW UP A WORKABLE DESIGN. I DON'T KNOW THAT HE EVER ACTUALLY PUT ONE TOGETHER.
MALLETT
WHAT DO YOU BET THAT IF HE HAD BUILT ONE...
WE WOULDN'T HAVE NEEDED TO WAIT 200 YEARS FOR ISAAC NEWTON TO NOTICE GRAVITY.
WE'RE ALMOST AT THE TOP...

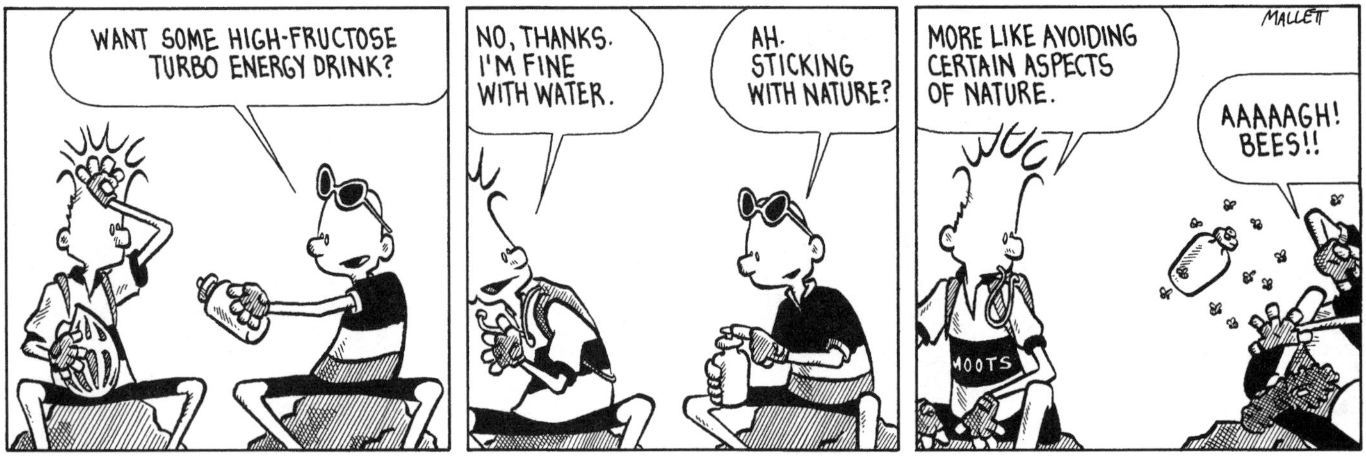
WANT SOME HIGH-FRUCTOSE TURBO ENERGY DRINK?
NO, THANKS. I'M FINE WITH WATER.
AH. STICKING WITH NATURE?
MALLETT
MORE LIKE AVOIDING CERTAIN ASPECTS OF NATURE.
MOOTS
AAAAAGH! BEES!!

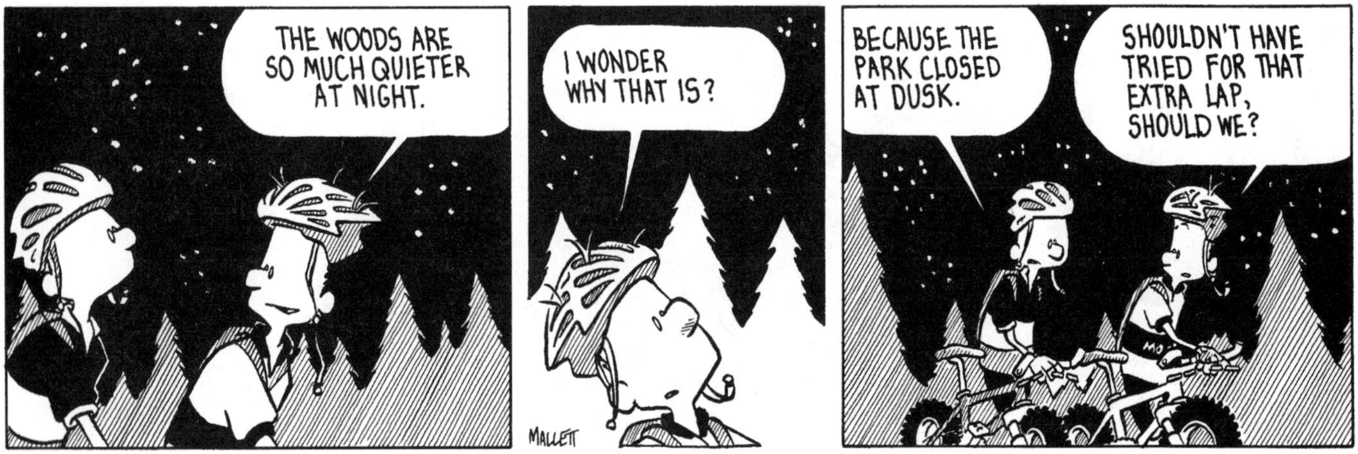
THE WOODS ARE SO MUCH QUIETER AT NIGHT.
I WONDER WHY THAT IS?
MALLETT
BECAUSE THE PARK CLOSED AT DUSK.
SHOULDN'T HAVE TRIED FOR THAT EXTRA LAP, SHOULD WE?

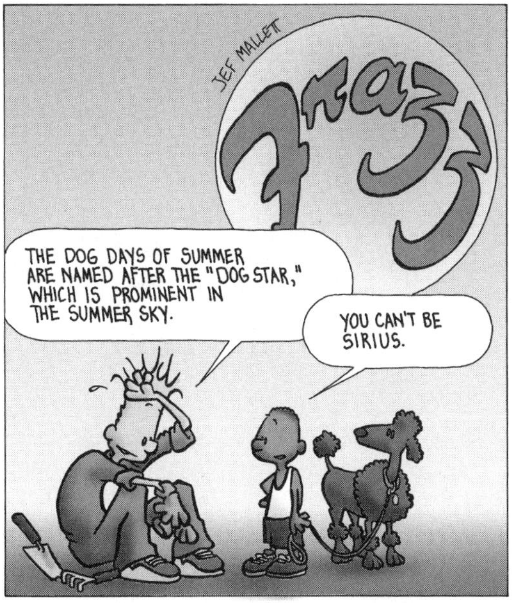
JEF MALLETT
Frazz
THE DOG DAYS OF SUMMER ARE NAMED AFTER THE "DOG STAR," WHICH IS PROMINENT IN THE SUMMER SKY.
YOU CAN'T BE SIRIUS.

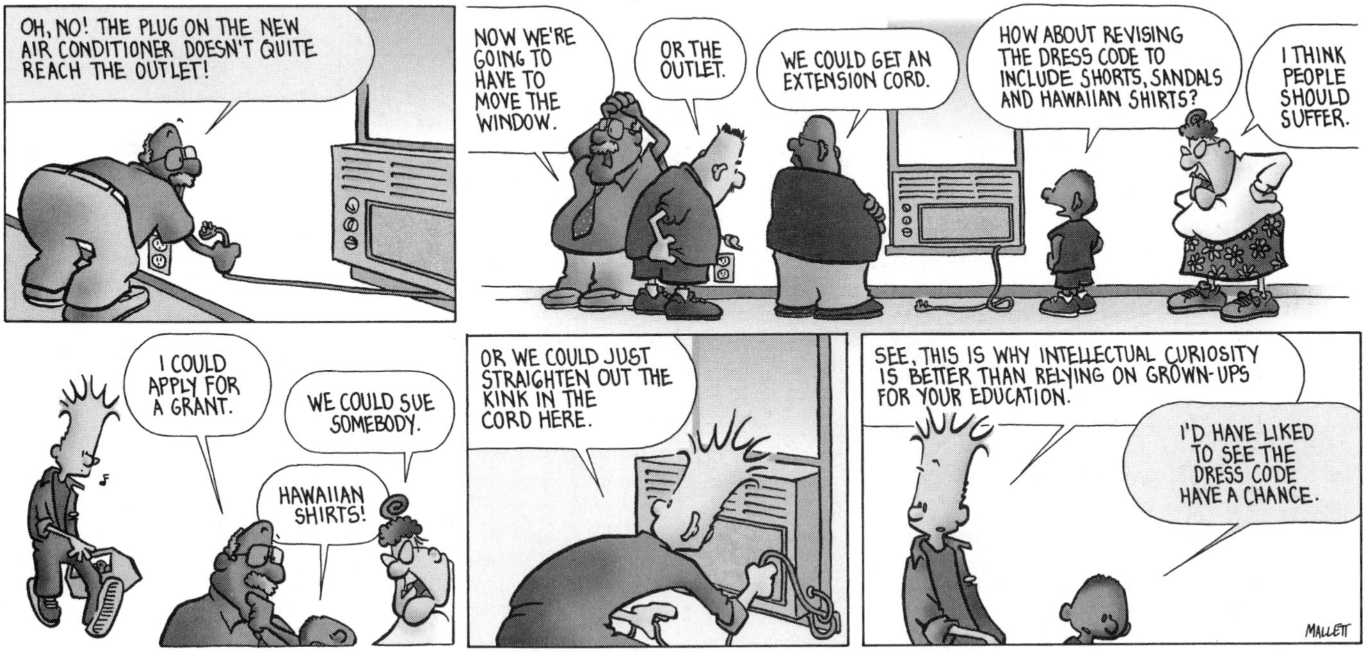
OH, NO! THE PLUG ON THE NEW AIR CONDITIONER DOESN'T QUITE REACH THE OUTLET!
NOW WE'RE GOING TO HAVE TO MOVE THE WINDOW.
OR THE OUTLET.
WE COULD GET AN EXTENSION CORD.
HOW ABOUT REVISING THE DRESS CODE TO INCLUDE SHORTS, SANDALS AND HAWAIIAN SHIRTS?
I THINK PEOPLE SHOULD SUFFER.
I COULD APPLY FOR A GRANT.
WE COULD SUE SOMEBODY.
HAWAIIAN SHIRTS!
OR WE COULD JUST STRAIGHTEN OUT THE KINK IN THE CORD HERE.
SEE, THIS IS WHY INTELLECTUAL CURIOSITY IS BETTER THAN RELYING ON GROWN-UPS FOR YOUR EDUCATION.
I'D HAVE LIKED TO SEE THE DRESS CODE HAVE A CHANCE.
MALLETT

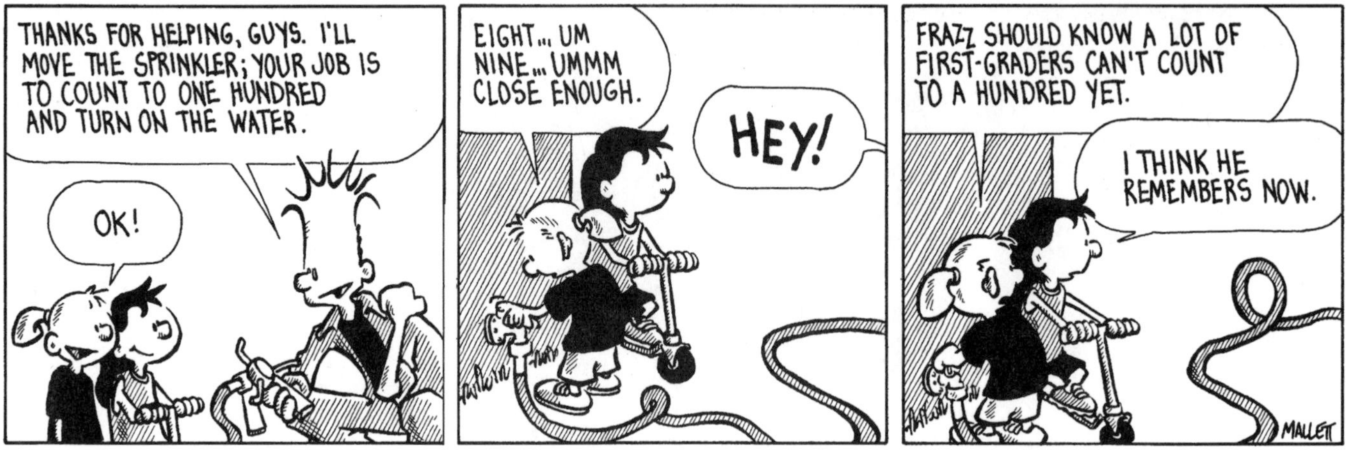
THANKS FOR HELPING, GUYS. I'LL MOVE THE SPRINKLER; YOUR JOB IS TO COUNT TO ONE HUNDRED AND TURN ON THE WATER.
OK!
EIGHT... UM NINE... UMMM CLOSE ENOUGH.
HEY!
FRAZZ SHOULD KNOW A LOT OF FIRST-GRADERS CAN'T COUNT TO A HUNDRED YET.
I THINK HE REMEMBERS NOW.
MALLETT

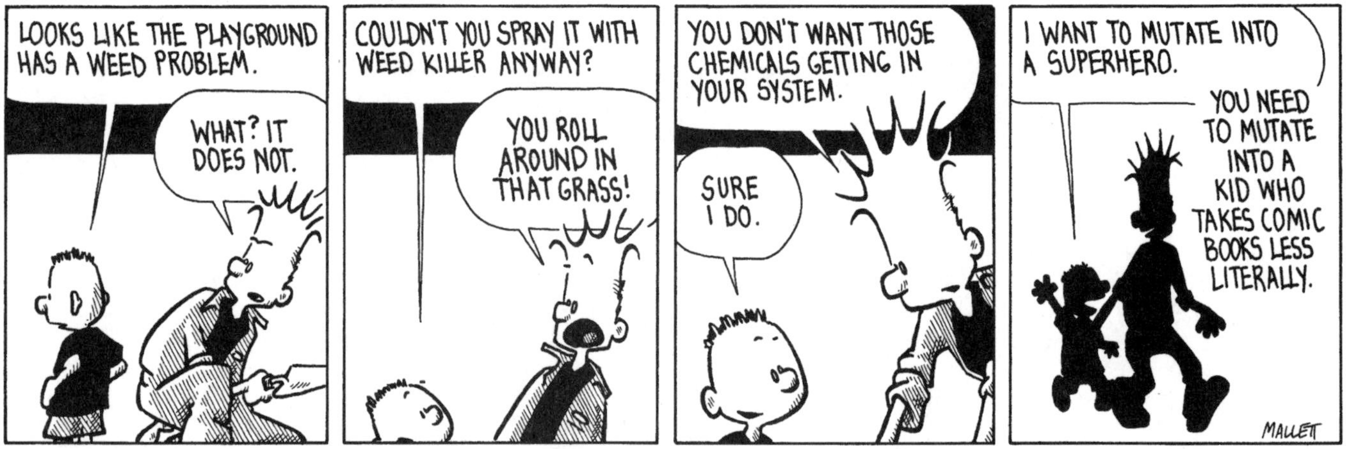
LOOKS LIKE THE PLAYGROUND HAS A WEED PROBLEM.
WHAT? IT DOES NOT.
COULDN'T YOU SPRAY IT WITH WEED KILLER ANYWAY?
YOU ROLL AROUND IN THAT GRASS!
YOU DON'T WANT THOSE CHEMICALS GETTING IN YOUR SYSTEM.
SURE I DO.
I WANT TO MUTATE INTO A SUPERHERO.
YOU NEED TO MUTATE INTO A KID WHO TAKES COMIC BOOKS LESS LITERALLY.
MALLETT

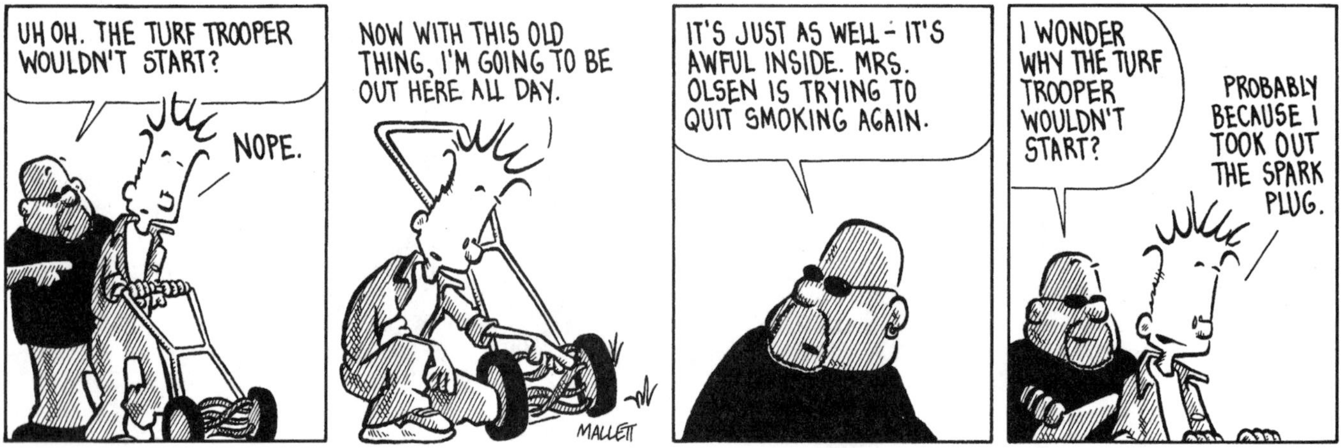
UH OH. THE TURF TROOPER WOULDN'T START?
NOPE.
NOW WITH THIS OLD THING, I'M GOING TO BE OUT HERE ALL DAY.
MALLETT
IT'S JUST AS WELL – IT'S AWFUL INSIDE. MRS. OLSEN IS TRYING TO QUIT SMOKING AGAIN.
I WONDER WHY THE TURF TROOPER WOULDN'T START?
PROBABLY BECAUSE I TOOK OUT THE SPARK PLUG.

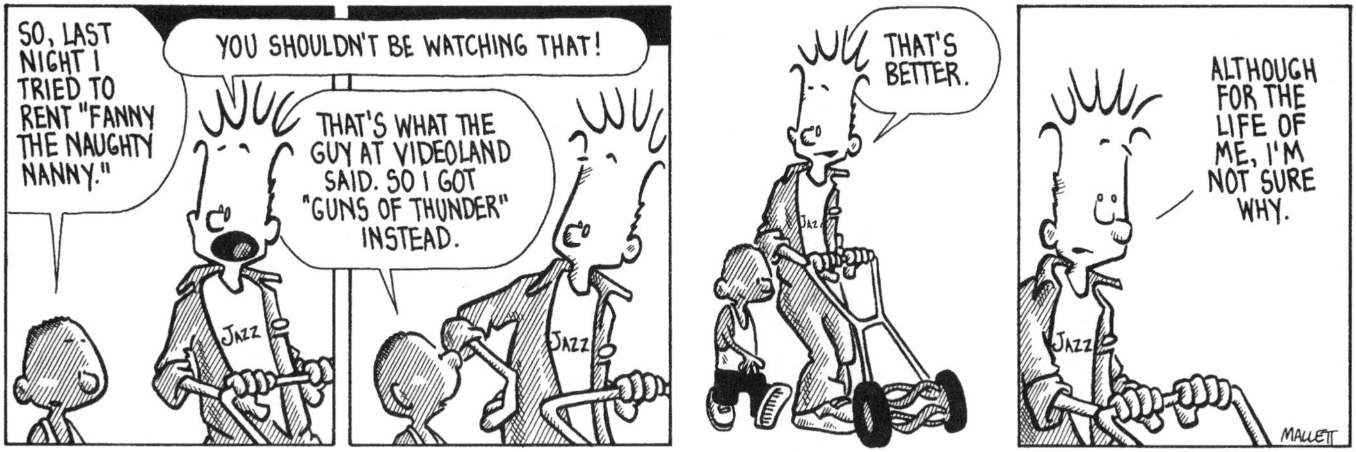
SO, LAST NIGHT I TRIED TO RENT "FANNY THE NAUGHTY NANNY."
YOU SHOULDN'T BE WATCHING THAT!
THAT'S WHAT THE GUY AT VIDEOLAND SAID. SO I GOT "GUNS OF THUNDER" INSTEAD.
JAZZ
THAT'S BETTER.
ALTHOUGH FOR THE LIFE OF ME, I'M NOT SURE WHY.
MALLETT

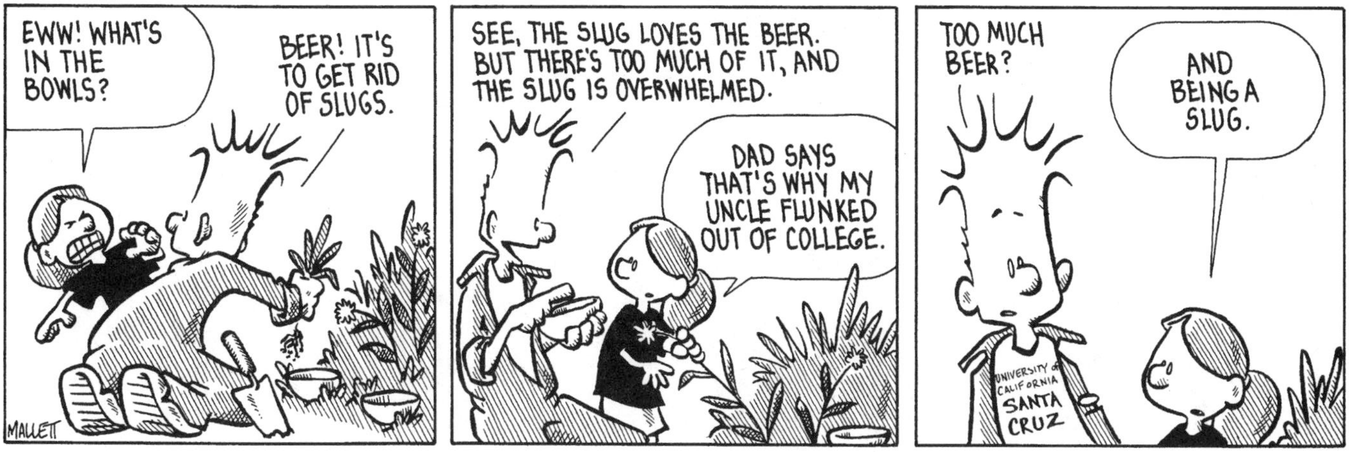
EWW! WHAT'S IN THE BOWLS?
BEER! IT'S TO GET RID OF SLUGS.
MALLETT
SEE, THE SLUG LOVES THE BEER. BUT THERE'S TOO MUCH OF IT, AND THE SLUG IS OVERWHELMED.
DAD SAYS THAT'S WHY MY UNCLE FLUNKED OUT OF COLLEGE.
TOO MUCH BEER?
AND BEING A SLUG.
UNIVERSITY OF CALIFORNIA SANTA CRUZ

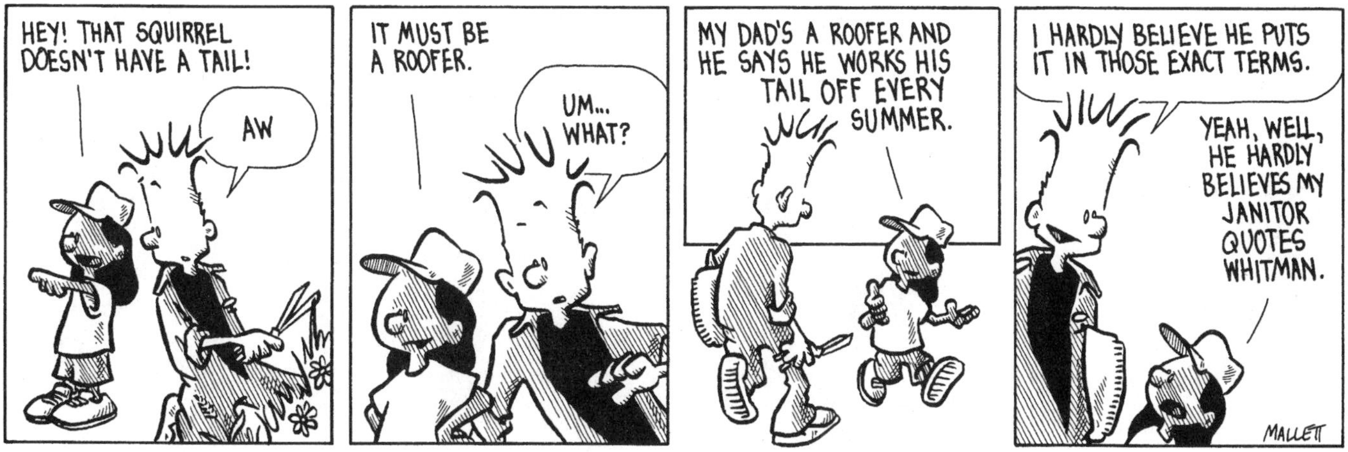
HEY! THAT SQUIRREL DOESN'T HAVE A TAIL!
AW
IT MUST BE A ROOFER.
UM... WHAT?
MY DAD'S A ROOFER AND HE SAYS HE WORKS HIS TAIL OFF EVERY SUMMER.
I HARDLY BELIEVE HE PUTS IT IN THOSE EXACT TERMS.
YEAH, WELL, HE HARDLY BELIEVES MY JANITOR QUOTES WHITMAN.
MALLETT

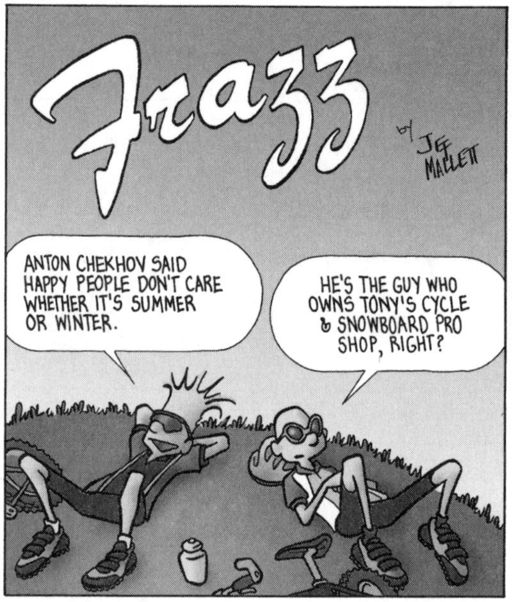
Frazz
by Jeff Mallett
ANTON CHEKHOV SAID HAPPY PEOPLE DON'T CARE WHETHER IT'S SUMMER OR WINTER.
HE'S THE GUY WHO OWNS TONY'S CYCLE & SNOWBOARD PRO SHOP, RIGHT?

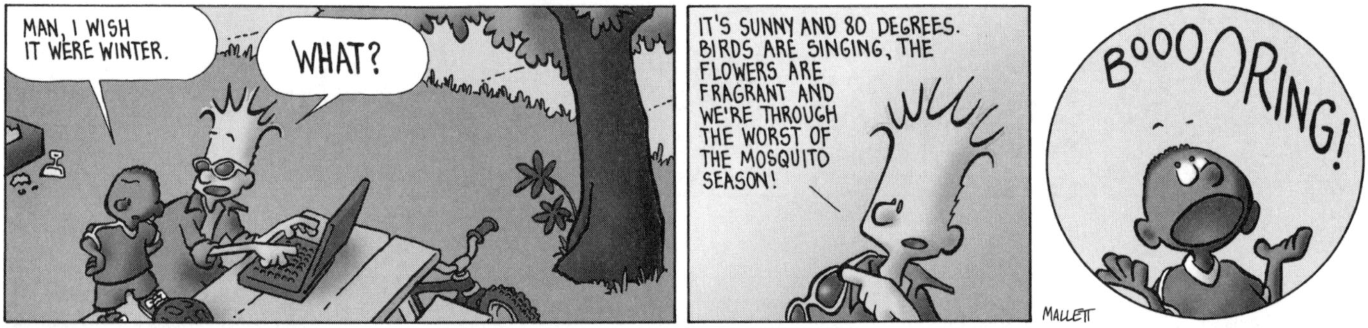
MAN, I WISH IT WERE WINTER.
WHAT?
IT'S SUNNY AND 80 DEGREES. BIRDS ARE SINGING, THE FLOWERS ARE FRAGRANT AND WE'RE THROUGH THE WORST OF THE MOSQUITO SEASON!
BOOOORING!
MALLETT

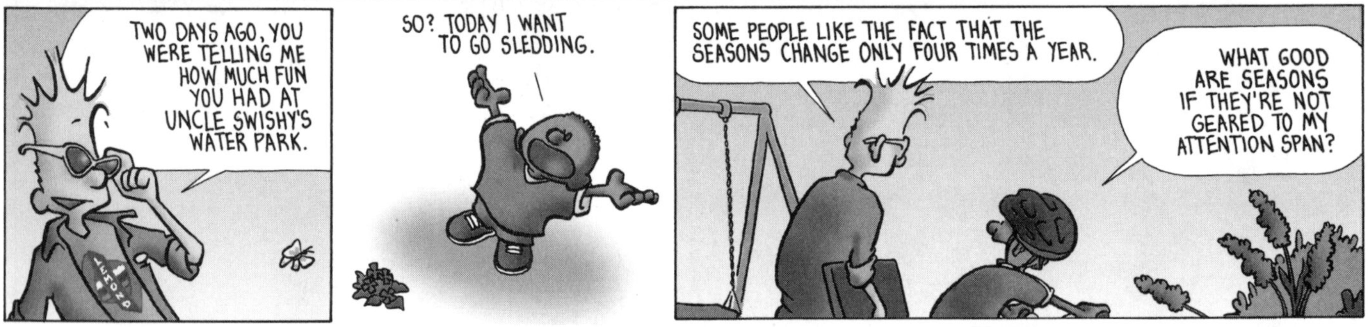
TWO DAYS AGO, YOU WERE TELLING ME HOW MUCH FUN YOU HAD AT UNCLE SWISHY'S WATER PARK.
SO? TODAY I WANT TO GO SLEDDING.
SOME PEOPLE LIKE THE FACT THAT THE SEASONS CHANGE ONLY FOUR TIMES A YEAR.
WHAT GOOD ARE SEASONS IF THEY'RE NOT GEARED TO MY ATTENTION SPAN?

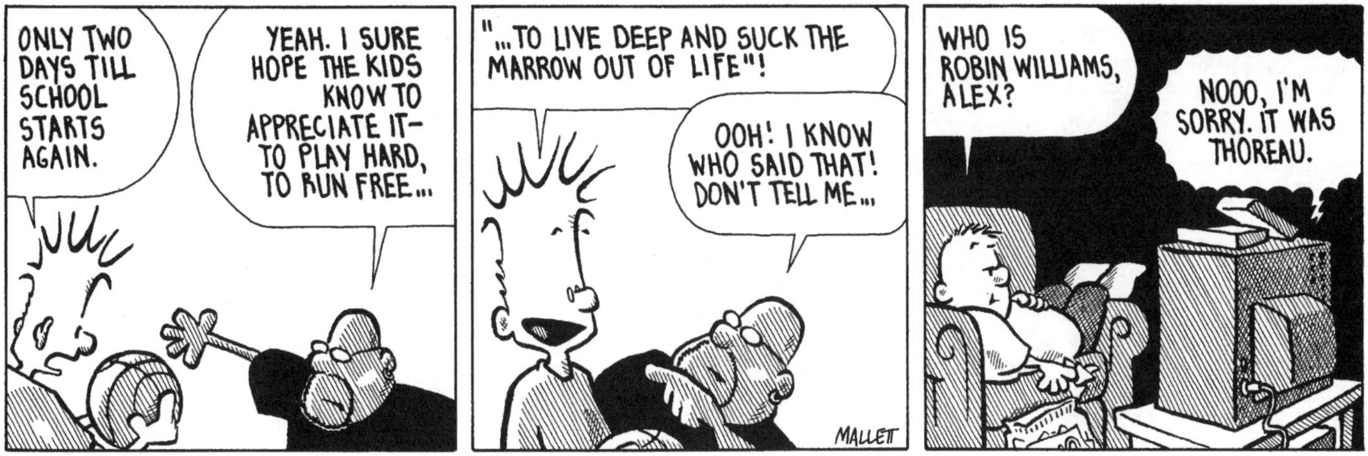
ONLY TWO DAYS TILL SCHOOL STARTS AGAIN.
YEAH. I SURE HOPE THE KIDS KNOW TO APPRECIATE IT– TO PLAY HARD, TO RUN FREE...
"...TO LIVE DEEP AND SUCK THE MARROW OUT OF LIFE"!
OOH! I KNOW WHO SAID THAT! DON'T TELL ME...
WHO IS ROBIN WILLIAMS, ALEX?
NOOO, I'M SORRY. IT WAS THOREAU.
MALLETT

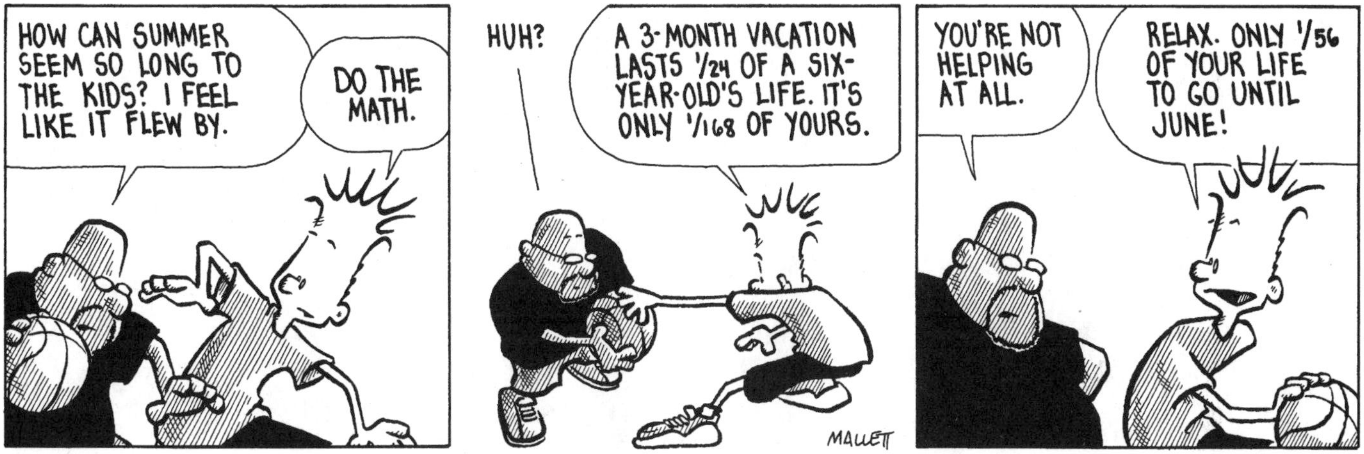
HOW CAN SUMMER SEEM SO LONG TO THE KIDS? I FEEL LIKE IT FLEW BY.
DO THE MATH.
HUH?
A 3-MONTH VACATION LASTS 1/24 OF A SIX-YEAR-OLD'S LIFE. IT'S ONLY 1/168 OF YOURS.
YOU'RE NOT HELPING AT ALL.
RELAX. ONLY 1/56 OF YOUR LIFE TO GO UNTIL JUNE!
MALLETT

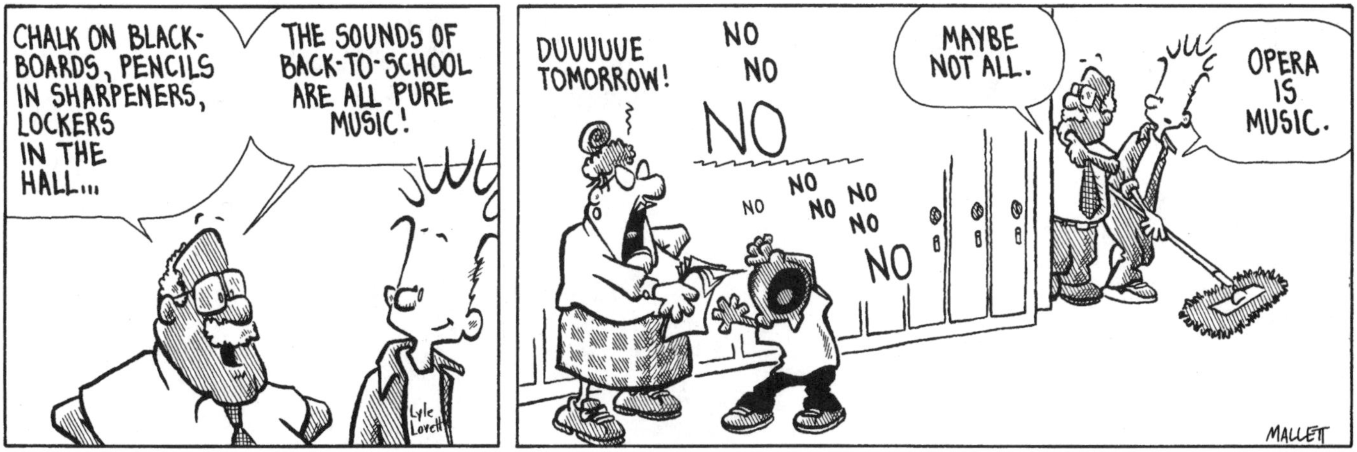
CHALK ON BLACK-BOARDS, PENCILS IN SHARPENERS, LOCKERS IN THE HALL...
THE SOUNDS OF BACK-TO-SCHOOL ARE ALL PURE MUSIC!
Lyle Lovett
DUUUUUE TOMORROW!
NO NO NO
NO NO NO NO NO NO
MAYBE NOT ALL.
OPERA IS MUSIC.
MALLETT

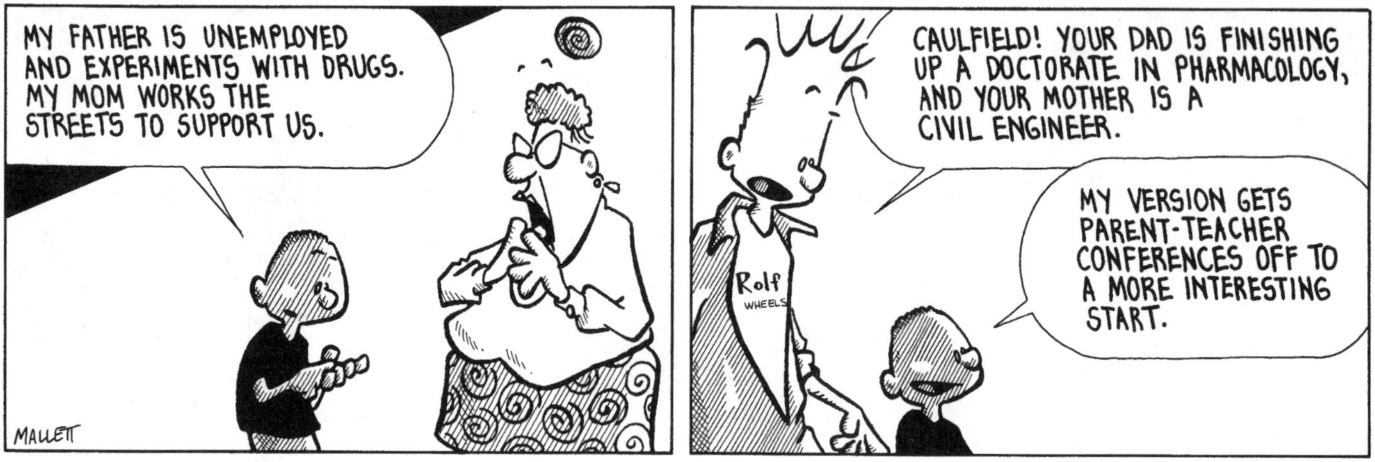
MY FATHER IS UNEMPLOYED AND EXPERIMENTS WITH DRUGS. MY MOM WORKS THE STREETS TO SUPPORT US.
MALLETT
CAULFIELD! YOUR DAD IS FINISHING UP A DOCTORATE IN PHARMACOLOGY, AND YOUR MOTHER IS A CIVIL ENGINEER.
Rolf WHEELS
MY VERSION GETS PARENT-TEACHER CONFERENCES OFF TO A MORE INTERESTING START.

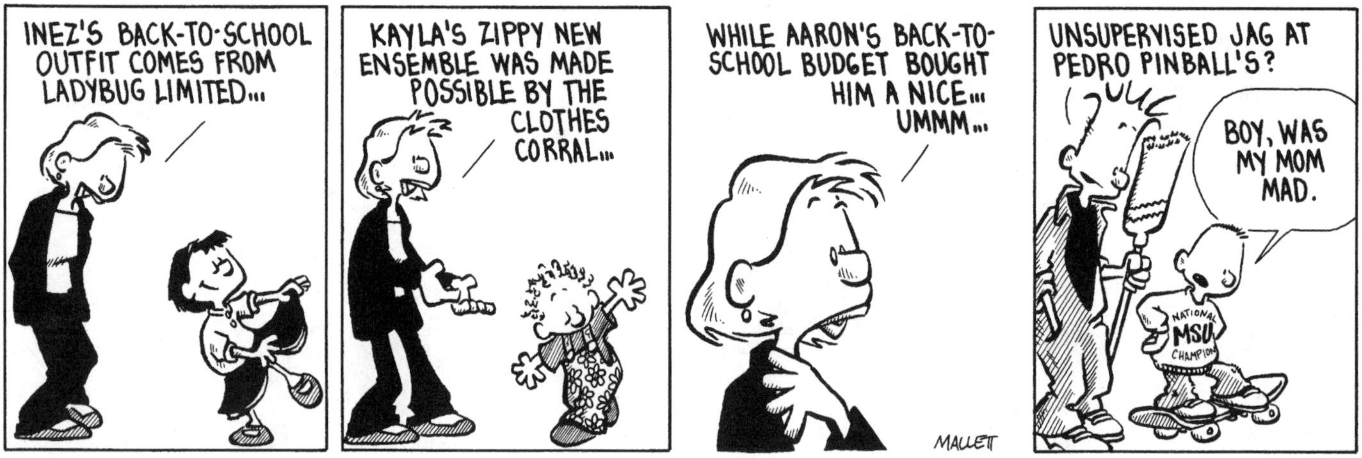
INEZ'S BACK-TO-SCHOOL OUTFIT COMES FROM LADYBUG LIMITED...
KAYLA'S ZIPPY NEW ENSEMBLE WAS MADE POSSIBLE BY THE CLOTHES CORRAL...
WHILE AARON'S BACK-TO-SCHOOL BUDGET BOUGHT HIM A NICE... UMMM...
MALLETT
UNSUPERVISED JAG AT PEDRO PINBALL'S?
BOY, WAS MY MOM MAD.
NATIONAL MSU CHAMPION

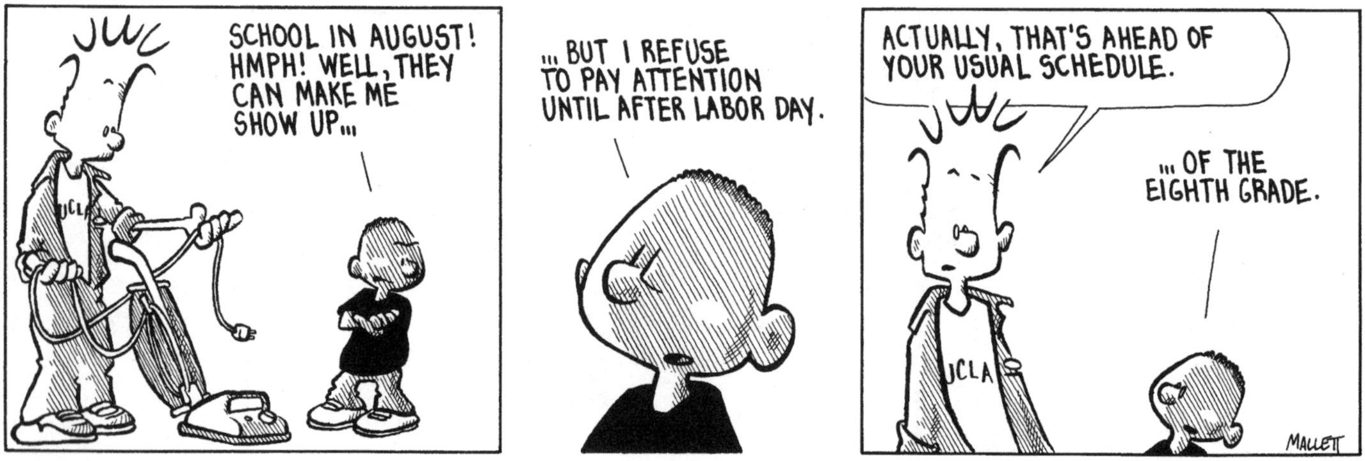
SCHOOL IN AUGUST! HMPH! WELL, THEY CAN MAKE ME SHOW UP...
UCLA
...BUT I REFUSE TO PAY ATTENTION UNTIL AFTER LABOR DAY.
ACTUALLY, THAT'S AHEAD OF YOUR USUAL SCHEDULE.
...OF THE EIGHTH GRADE.
UCLA
MALLETT

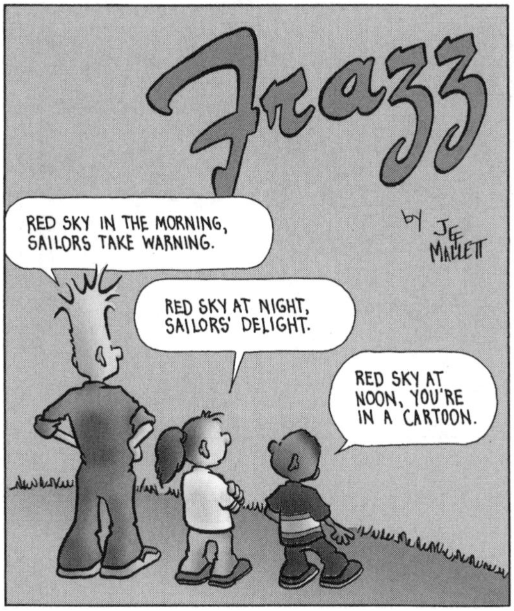
Frazz
by Jef Mallett
RED SKY IN THE MORNING, SAILORS TAKE WARNING.
RED SKY AT NIGHT, SAILORS' DELIGHT.
RED SKY AT NOON, YOU'RE IN A CARTOON.

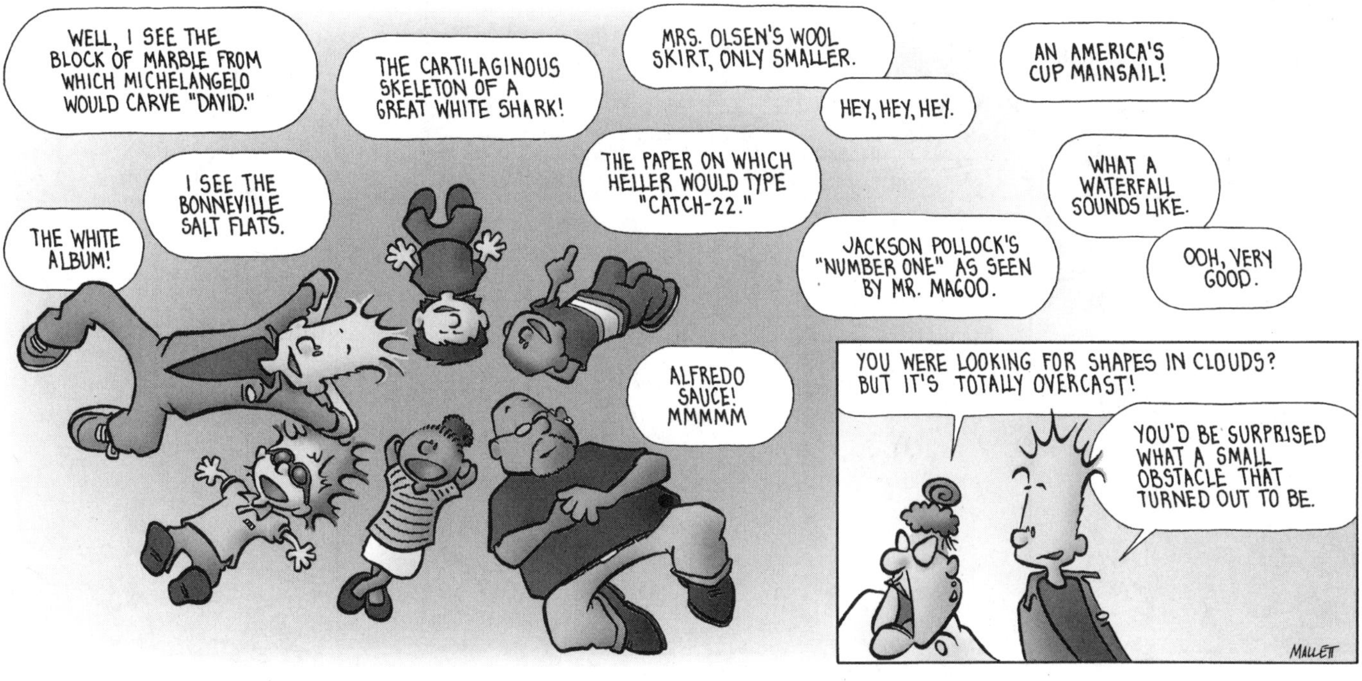
WELL, I SEE THE BLOCK OF MARBLE FROM WHICH MICHELANGELO WOULD CARVE "DAVID."
THE CARTILAGINOUS SKELETON OF A GREAT WHITE SHARK!
MRS. OLSEN'S WOOL SKIRT, ONLY SMALLER.
HEY, HEY, HEY.
AN AMERICA'S CUP MAINSAIL!
I SEE THE BONNEVILLE SALT FLATS.
THE WHITE ALBUM!
THE PAPER ON WHICH HELLER WOULD TYPE "CATCH-22."
WHAT A WATERFALL SOUNDS LIKE.
JACKSON POLLOCK'S "NUMBER ONE" AS SEEN BY MR. MAGOO.
OOH, VERY GOOD.
ALFREDO SAUCE! MMMMM
YOU WERE LOOKING FOR SHAPES IN CLOUDS? BUT IT'S TOTALLY OVERCAST!
YOU'D BE SURPRISED WHAT A SMALL OBSTACLE THAT TURNED OUT TO BE.
MALLETT

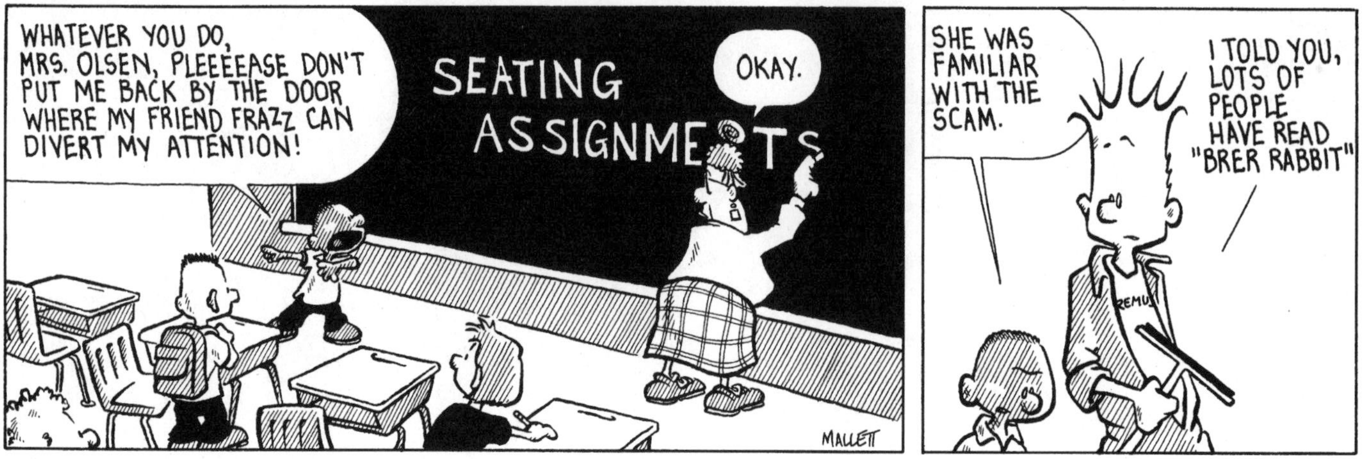
WHATEVER YOU DO, MRS. OLSEN, PLEEEEASE DON'T PUT ME BACK BY THE DOOR WHERE MY FRIEND FRAZZ CAN DIVERT MY ATTENTION!
SEATING
ASSIGNME TS
OKAY.
MALLETT
SHE WAS FAMILIAR WITH THE SCAM.
I TOLD YOU, LOTS OF PEOPLE HAVE READ "BRER RABBIT"
REMUS

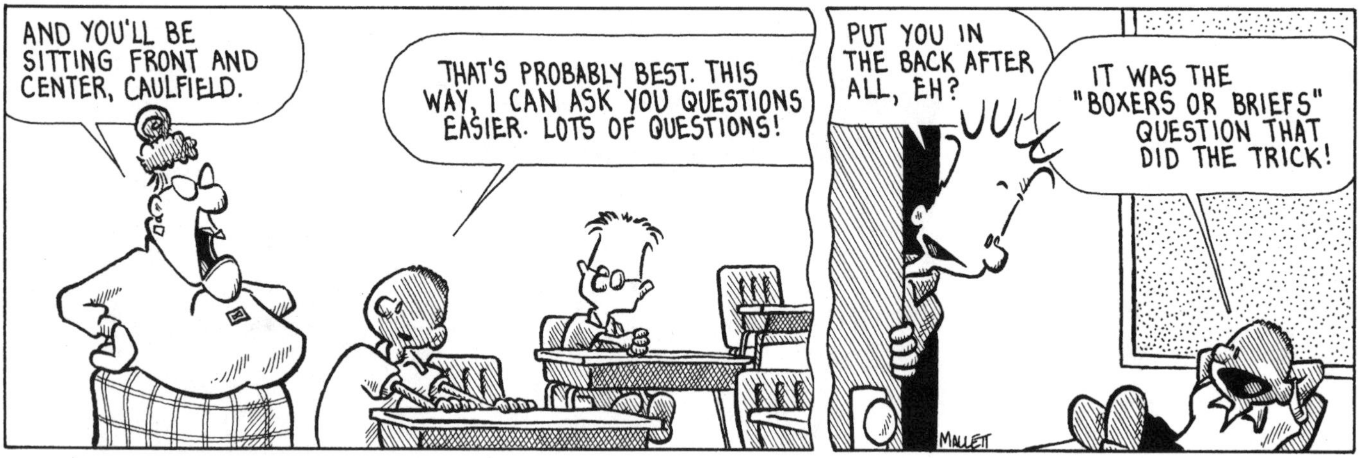
AND YOU'LL BE SITTING FRONT AND CENTER, CAULFIELD.
THAT'S PROBABLY BEST. THIS WAY, I CAN ASK YOU QUESTIONS EASIER. LOTS OF QUESTIONS!
PUT YOU IN THE BACK AFTER ALL, EH?
IT WAS THE "BOXERS OR BRIEFS" QUESTION THAT DID THE TRICK!
MALLETT

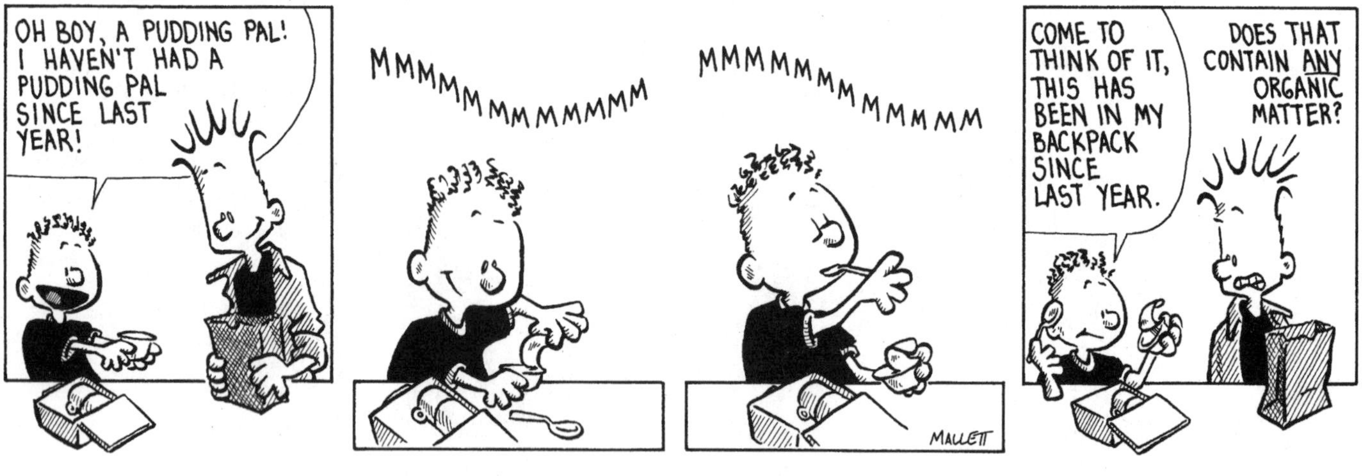
OH BOY, A PUDDING PAL! I HAVEN'T HAD A PUDDING PAL SINCE LAST YEAR!
MMMMMMMMMMMMMM
MMMMMMMMMMMMMMM
MALLETT
COME TO THINK OF IT, THIS HAS BEEN IN MY BACKPACK SINCE LAST YEAR.
DOES THAT CONTAIN ANY ORGANIC MATTER?

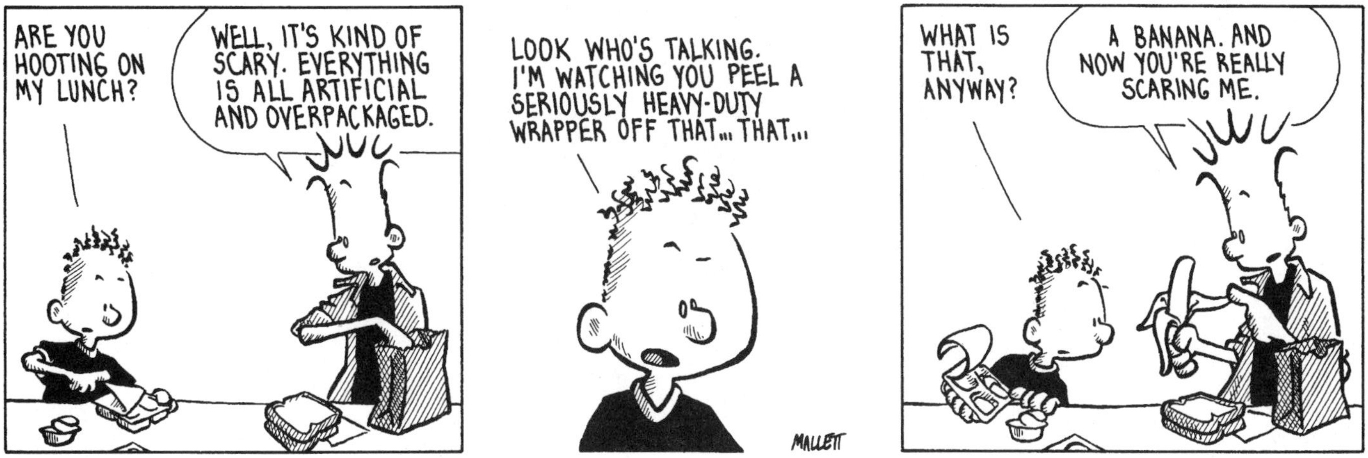
ARE YOU HOOTING ON MY LUNCH?
WELL, IT'S KIND OF SCARY. EVERYTHING IS ALL ARTIFICIAL AND OVERPACKAGED.
LOOK WHO'S TALKING. I'M WATCHING YOU PEEL A SERIOUSLY HEAVY-DUTY WRAPPER OFF THAT... THAT...
MALLETT
WHAT IS THAT, ANYWAY?
A BANANA. AND NOW YOU'RE REALLY SCARING ME.

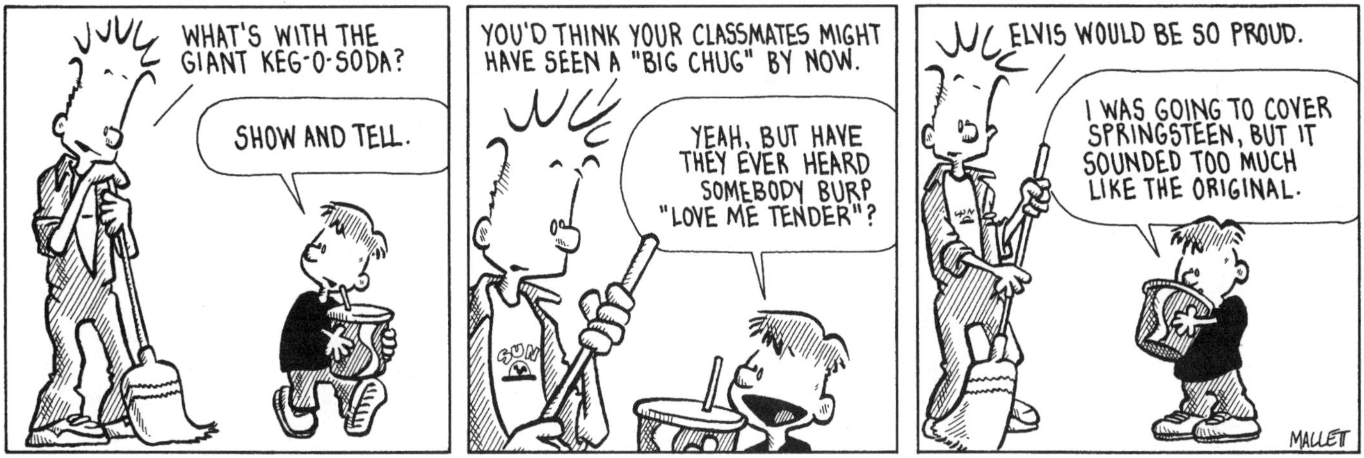
WHAT'S WITH THE GIANT KEG-O-SODA?
SHOW AND TELL.
YOU'D THINK YOUR CLASSMATES MIGHT HAVE SEEN A "BIG CHUG" BY NOW.
YEAH, BUT HAVE THEY EVER HEARD SOMEBODY BURP "LOVE ME TENDER"?
ELVIS WOULD BE SO PROUD.
I WAS GOING TO COVER SPRINGSTEEN, BUT IT SOUNDED TOO MUCH LIKE THE ORIGINAL.
MALLETT

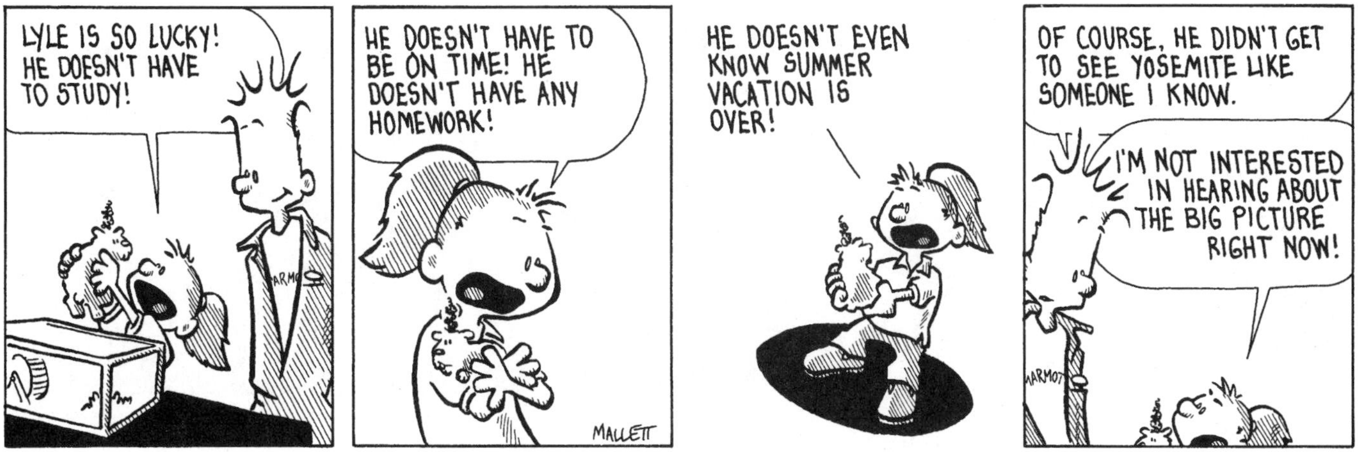
LYLE IS SO LUCKY! HE DOESN'T HAVE TO STUDY!
HE DOESN'T HAVE TO BE ON TIME! HE DOESN'T HAVE ANY HOMEWORK!
MALLETT
HE DOESN'T EVEN KNOW SUMMER VACATION IS OVER!
OF COURSE, HE DIDN'T GET TO SEE YOSEMITE LIKE SOMEONE I KNOW.
I'M NOT INTERESTED IN HEARING ABOUT THE BIG PICTURE RIGHT NOW!

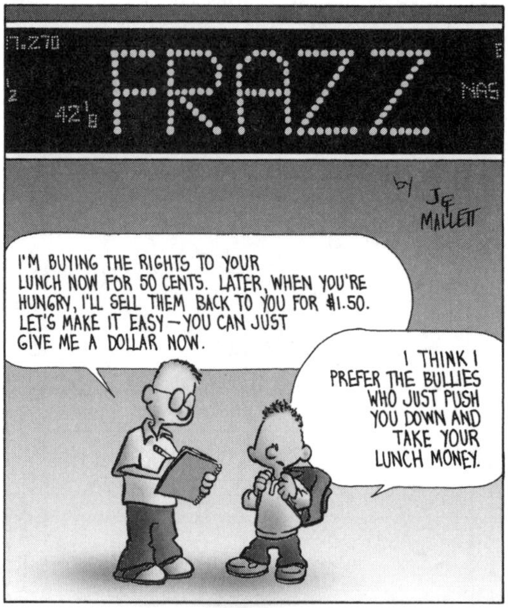
FRAZZ
7,270
42 1/8
NAS
by JEF MALLETT
I'M BUYING THE RIGHTS TO YOUR LUNCH NOW FOR 50 CENTS. LATER, WHEN YOU'RE HUNGRY, I'LL SELL THEM BACK TO YOU FOR $1.50. LET'S MAKE IT EASY — YOU CAN JUST GIVE ME A DOLLAR NOW.
I THINK I PREFER THE BULLIES WHO JUST PUSH YOU DOWN AND TAKE YOUR LUNCH MONEY.

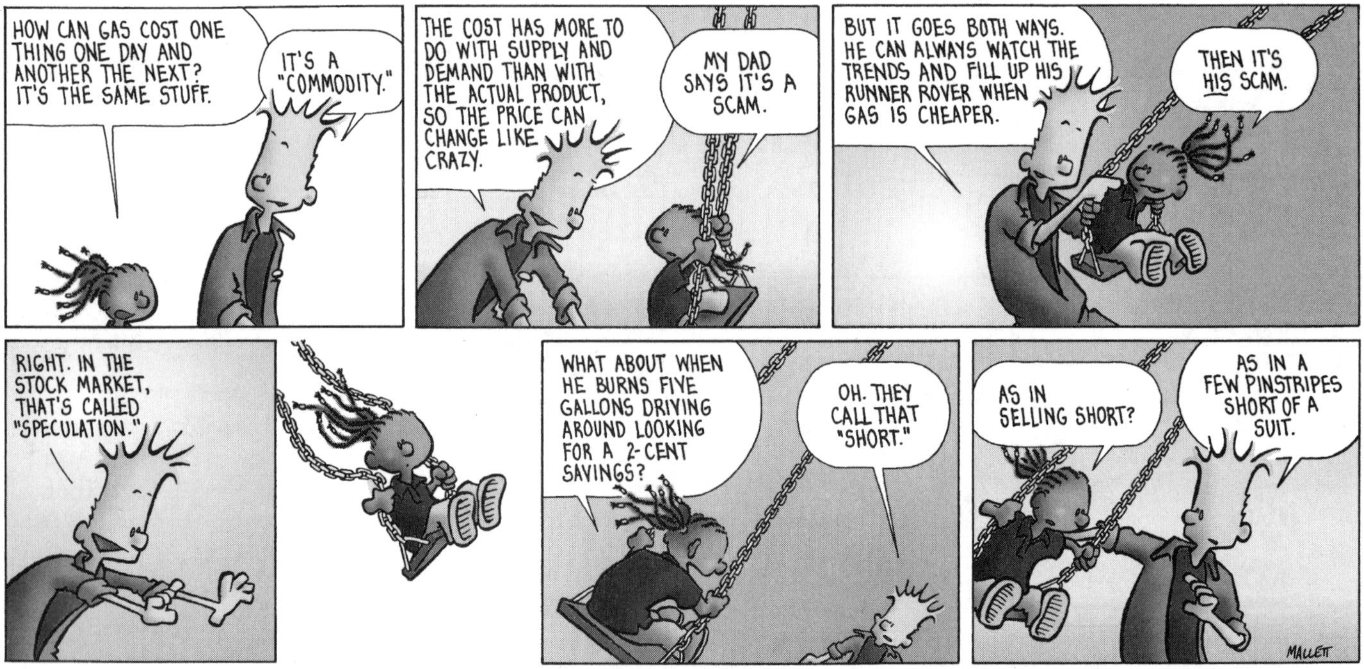
HOW CAN GAS COST ONE THING ONE DAY AND ANOTHER THE NEXT? IT'S THE SAME STUFF.
IT'S A "COMMODITY."
THE COST HAS MORE TO DO WITH SUPPLY AND DEMAND THAN WITH THE ACTUAL PRODUCT, SO THE PRICE CAN CHANGE LIKE CRAZY.
MY DAD SAYS IT'S A SCAM.
BUT IT GOES BOTH WAYS. HE CAN ALWAYS WATCH THE TRENDS AND FILL UP HIS RUNNER ROVER WHEN GAS IS CHEAPER.
THEN IT'S HIS SCAM.
RIGHT. IN THE STOCK MARKET, THAT'S CALLED "SPECULATION."
WHAT ABOUT WHEN HE BURNS FIVE GALLONS DRIVING AROUND LOOKING FOR A 2-CENT SAVINGS?
OH. THEY CALL THAT "SHORT."
AS IN SELLING SHORT?
AS IN A FEW PINSTRIPES SHORT OF A SUIT.
MALLETT

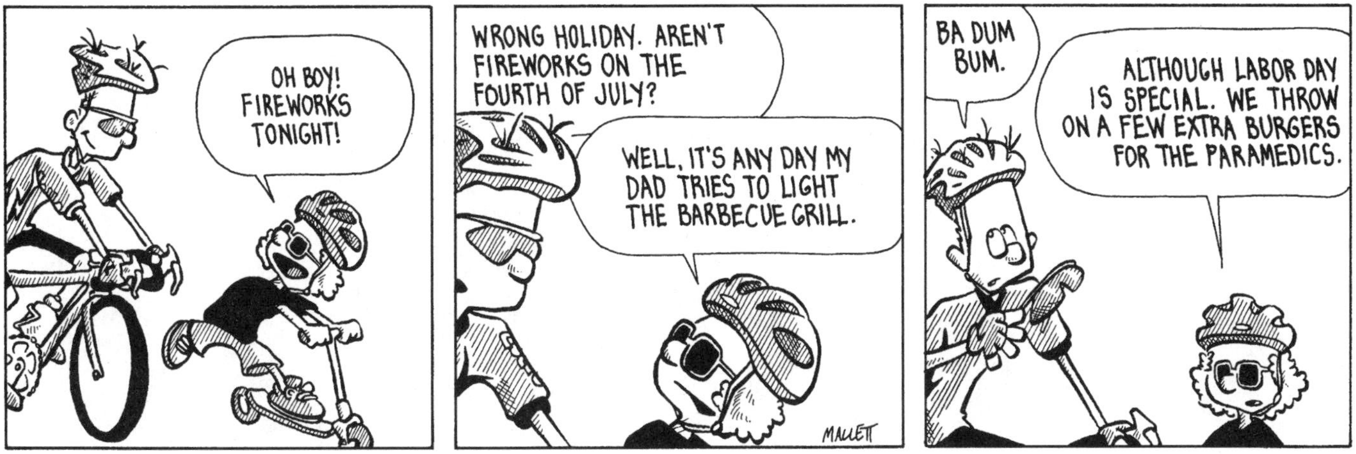
OH BOY! FIREWORKS TONIGHT!
WRONG HOLIDAY. AREN'T FIREWORKS ON THE FOURTH OF JULY?
WELL, IT'S ANY DAY MY DAD TRIES TO LIGHT THE BARBECUE GRILL.
MALLETT
BA DUM BUM.
ALTHOUGH LABOR DAY IS SPECIAL. WE THROW ON A FEW EXTRA BURGERS FOR THE PARAMEDICS.

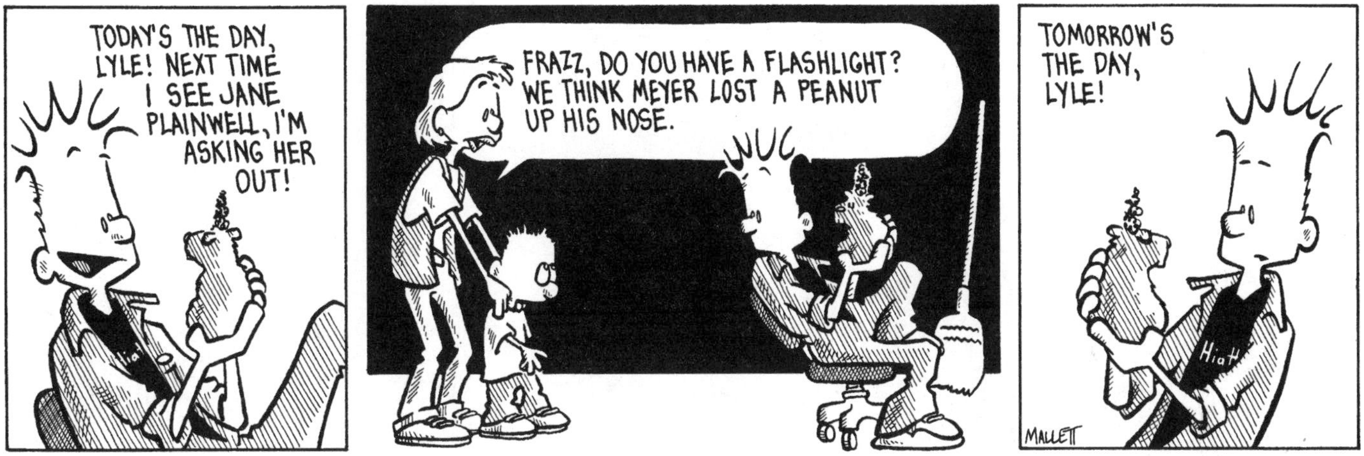
TODAY'S THE DAY, LYLE! NEXT TIME I SEE JANE PLAINWELL, I'M ASKING HER OUT!
FRAZZ, DO YOU HAVE A FLASHLIGHT? WE THINK MEYER LOST A PEANUT UP HIS NOSE.
TOMORROW'S THE DAY, LYLE!
MALLETT

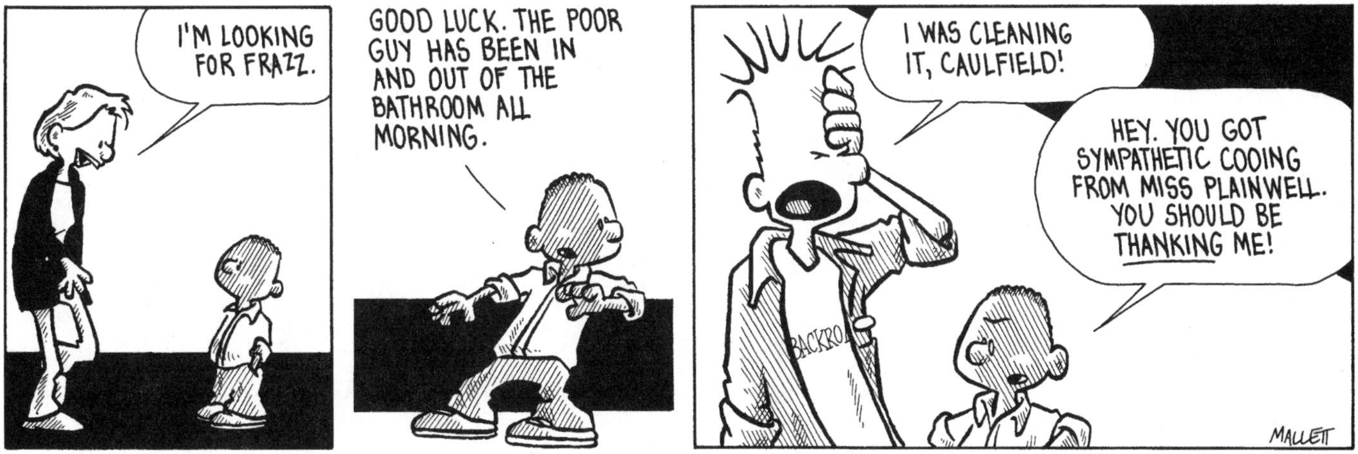
I'M LOOKING FOR FRAZZ.
GOOD LUCK. THE POOR GUY HAS BEEN IN AND OUT OF THE BATHROOM ALL MORNING.
I WAS CLEANING IT, CAULFIELD!
HEY. YOU GOT SYMPATHETIC COOING FROM MISS PLAINWELL. YOU SHOULD BE THANKING ME!
MALLETT

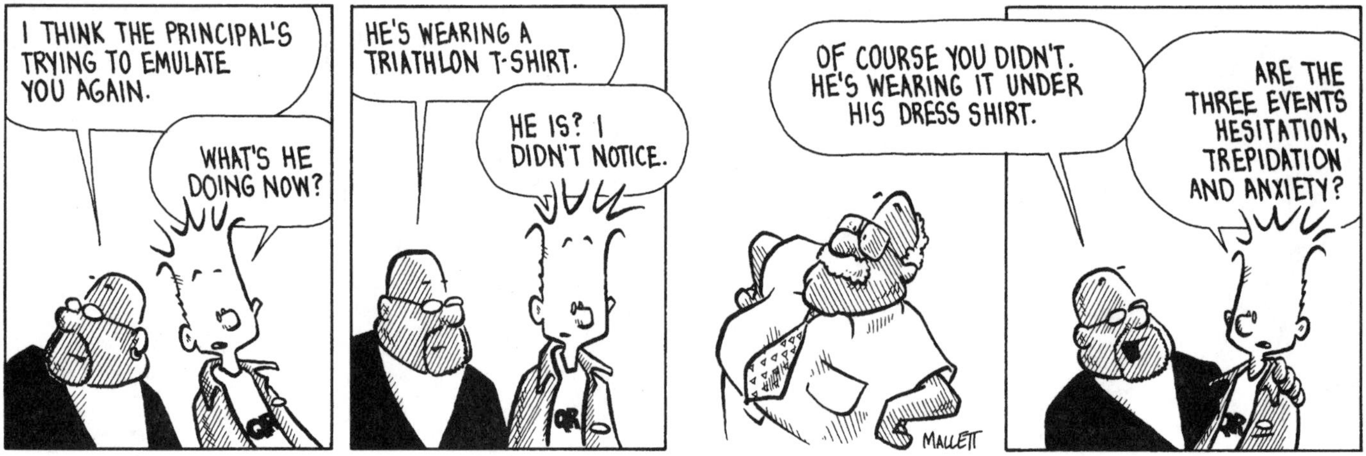
I THINK THE PRINCIPAL'S TRYING TO EMULATE YOU AGAIN.
WHAT'S HE DOING NOW?
HE'S WEARING A TRIATHLON T-SHIRT.
HE IS? I DIDN'T NOTICE.
OF COURSE YOU DIDN'T. HE'S WEARING IT UNDER HIS DRESS SHIRT.
ARE THE THREE EVENTS HESITATION, TREPIDATION AND ANXIETY?
MALLETT

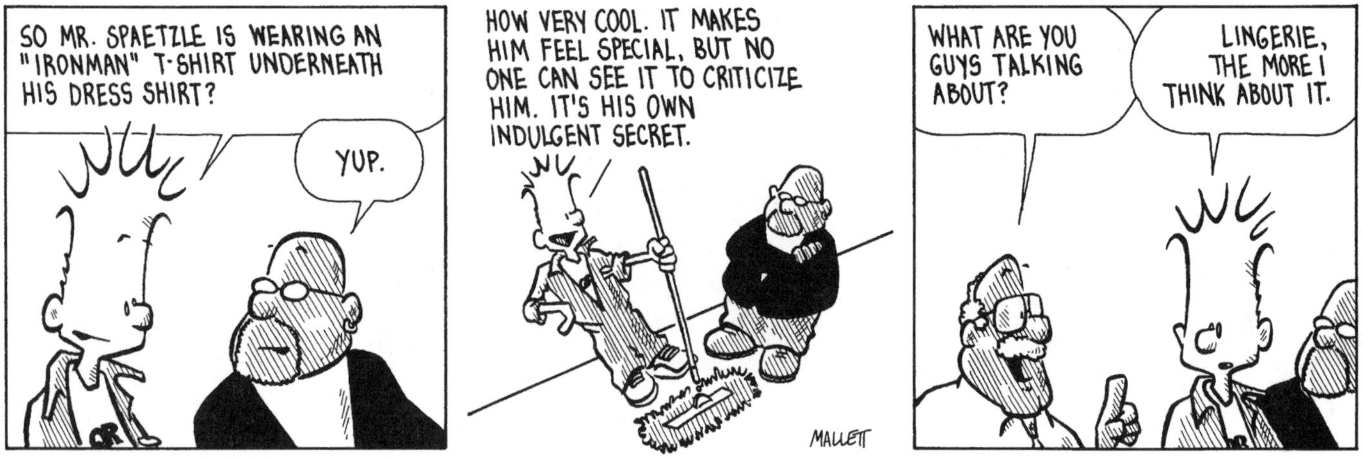
SO MR. SPAETZLE IS WEARING AN "IRONMAN" T-SHIRT UNDERNEATH HIS DRESS SHIRT?
YUP.
HOW VERY COOL. IT MAKES HIM FEEL SPECIAL, BUT NO ONE CAN SEE IT TO CRITICIZE HIM. IT'S HIS OWN INDULGENT SECRET.
MALLETT
WHAT ARE YOU GUYS TALKING ABOUT?
LINGERIE, THE MORE I THINK ABOUT IT.

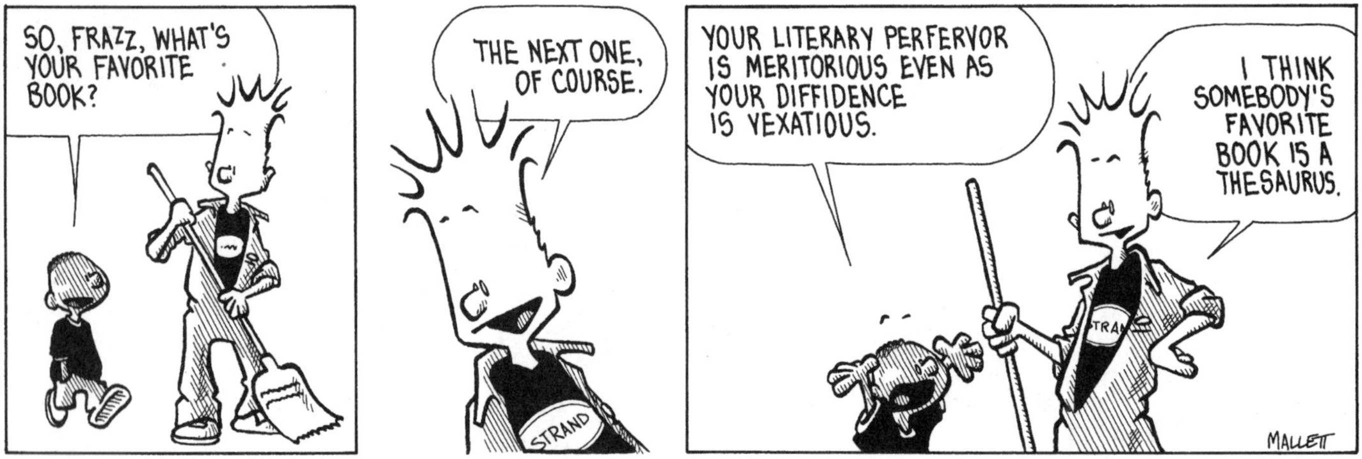
SO, FRAZZ, WHAT'S YOUR FAVORITE BOOK?
THE NEXT ONE, OF COURSE.
STRAND
YOUR LITERARY PERFERVOR IS MERITORIOUS EVEN AS YOUR DIFFIDENCE IS VEXATIOUS.
I THINK SOMEBODY'S FAVORITE BOOK IS A THESAURUS.
MALLETT

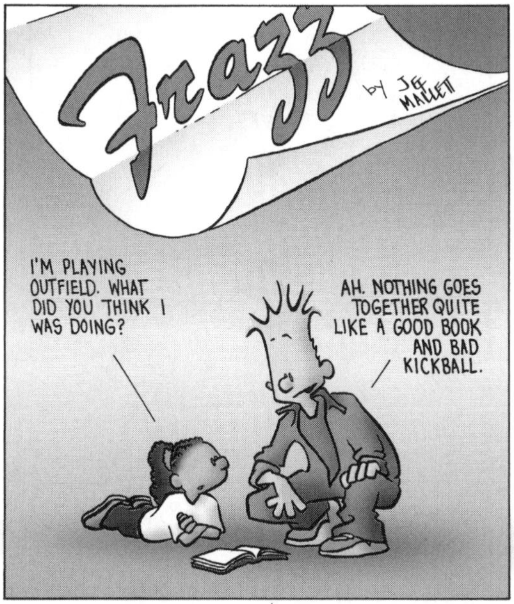
Frazz
by JEF MALLETT
I'M PLAYING OUTFIELD. WHAT DID YOU THINK I WAS DOING?
AH. NOTHING GOES TOGETHER QUITE LIKE A GOOD BOOK AND BAD KICKBALL.

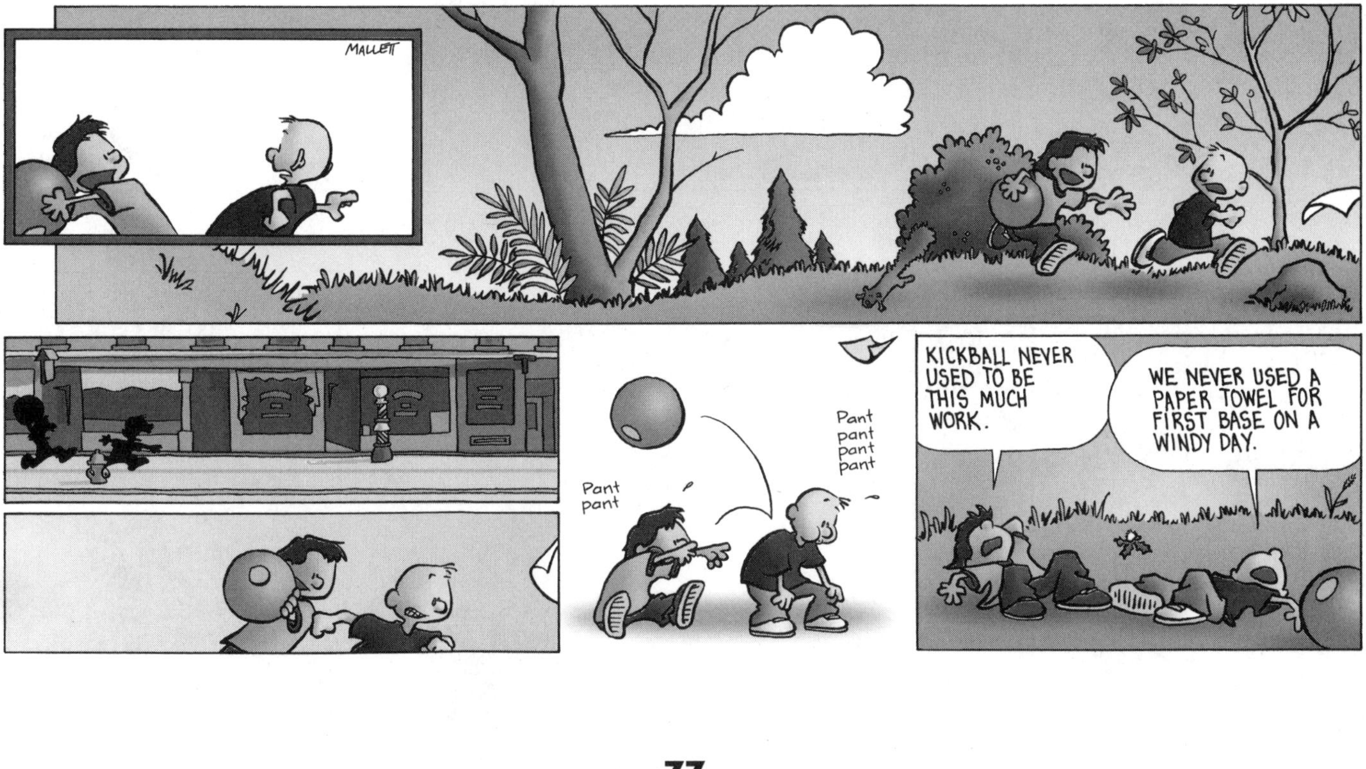
MALLETT
Pant pant
Pant pant pant pant
KICKBALL NEVER USED TO BE THIS MUCH WORK.
WE NEVER USED A PAPER TOWEL FOR FIRST BASE ON A WINDY DAY.

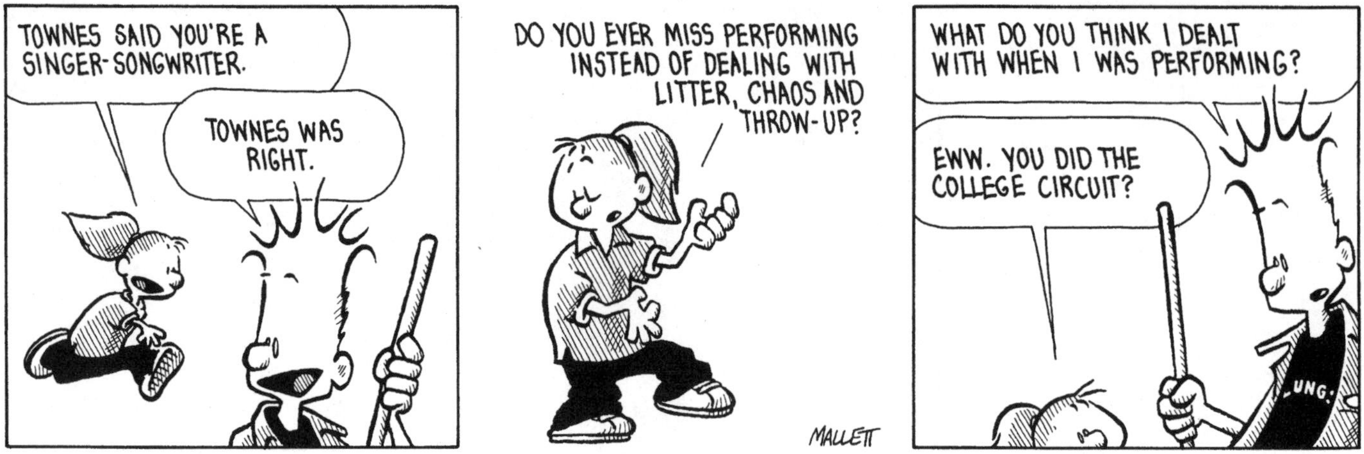
TOWNES SAID YOU'RE A SINGER-SONGWRITER.
TOWNES WAS RIGHT.
DO YOU EVER MISS PERFORMING INSTEAD OF DEALING WITH LITTER, CHAOS AND THROW-UP?
MALLETT
WHAT DO YOU THINK I DEALT WITH WHEN I WAS PERFORMING?
EWW. YOU DID THE COLLEGE CIRCUIT?

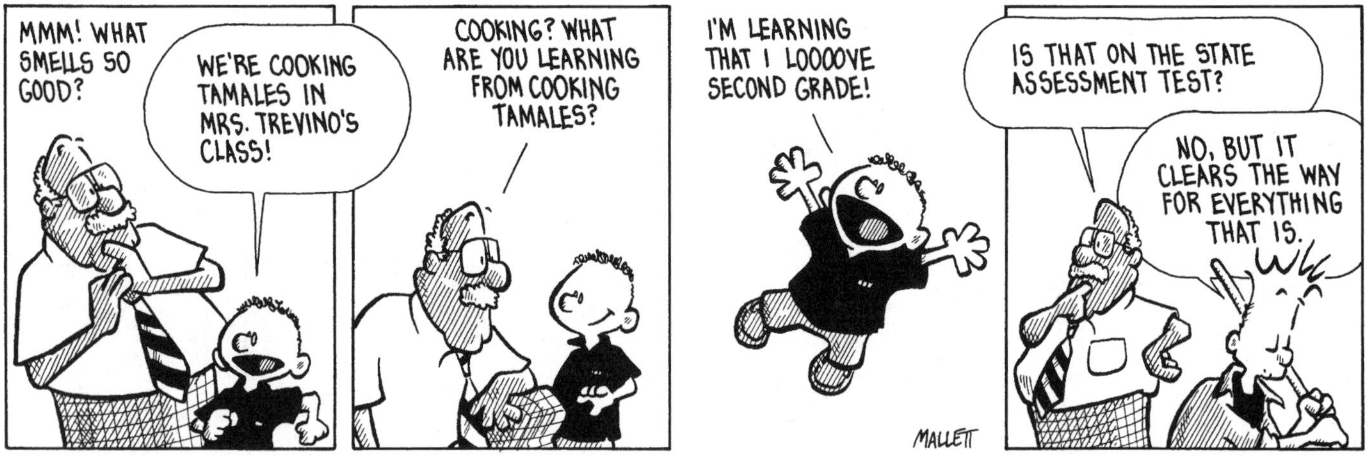
MMM! WHAT SMELLS SO GOOD?
WE'RE COOKING TAMALES IN MRS. TREVINO'S CLASS!
COOKING? WHAT ARE YOU LEARNING FROM COOKING TAMALES?
I'M LEARNING THAT I LOOOOVE SECOND GRADE!
MALLETT
IS THAT ON THE STATE ASSESSMENT TEST?
NO, BUT IT CLEARS THE WAY FOR EVERYTHING THAT IS.

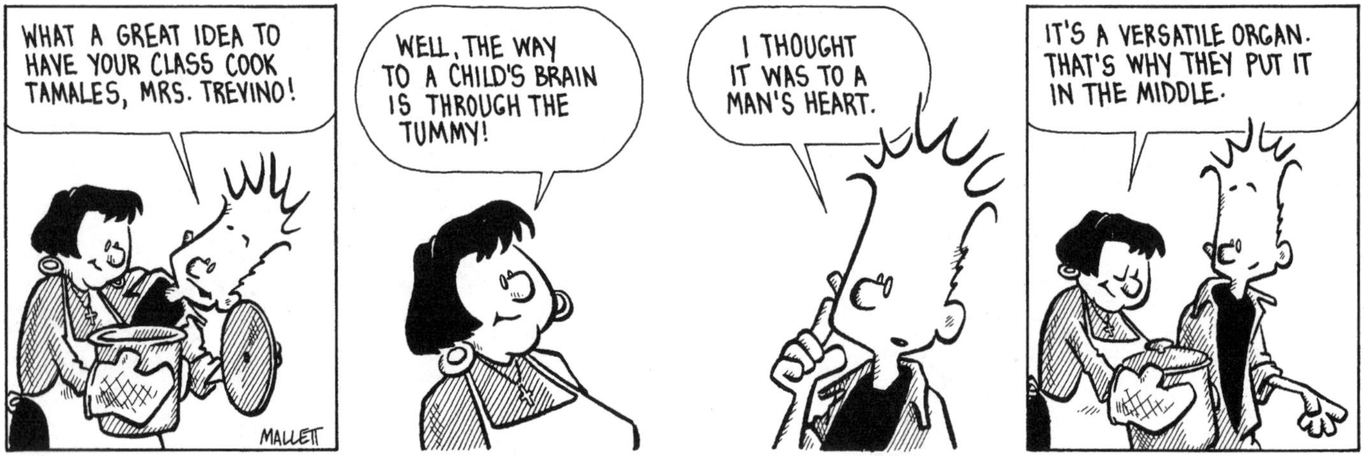
WHAT A GREAT IDEA TO HAVE YOUR CLASS COOK TAMALES, MRS. TREVINO!
MALLETT
WELL, THE WAY TO A CHILD'S BRAIN IS THROUGH THE TUMMY!
I THOUGHT IT WAS TO A MAN'S HEART.
IT'S A VERSATILE ORGAN. THAT'S WHY THEY PUT IT IN THE MIDDLE.

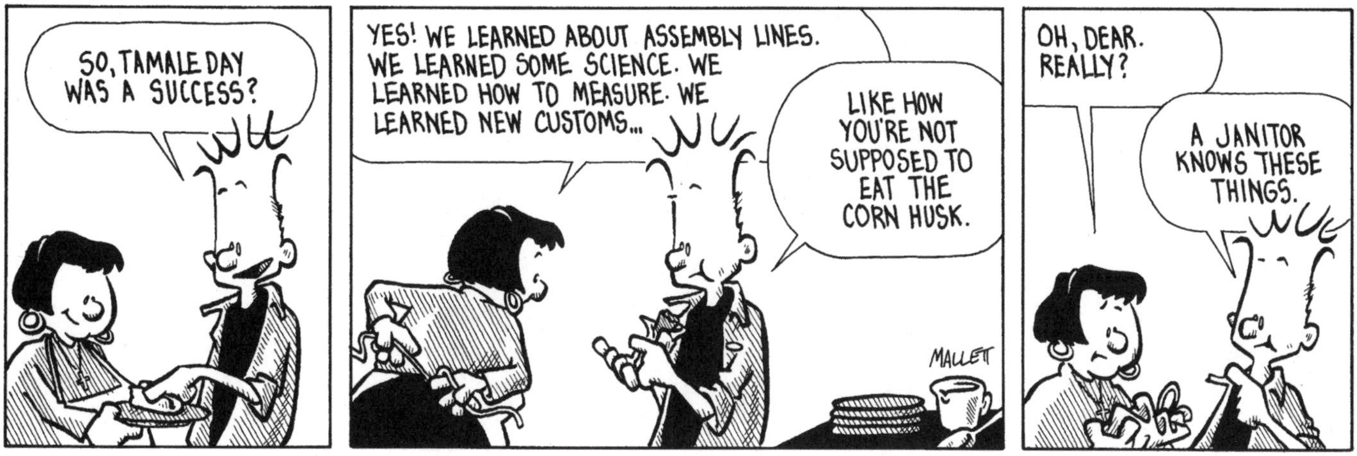
SO, TAMALE DAY WAS A SUCCESS?
YES! WE LEARNED ABOUT ASSEMBLY LINES. WE LEARNED SOME SCIENCE. WE LEARNED HOW TO MEASURE. WE LEARNED NEW CUSTOMS...
LIKE HOW YOU'RE NOT SUPPOSED TO EAT THE CORN HUSK.
MALLETT
OH, DEAR. REALLY?
A JANITOR KNOWS THESE THINGS.

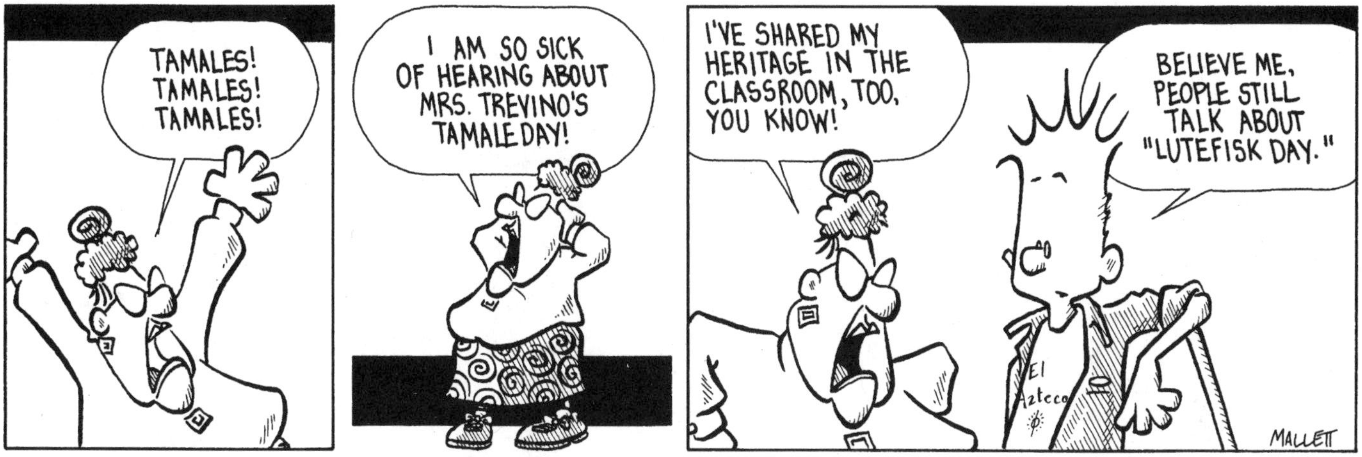
TAMALES! TAMALES! TAMALES!
I AM SO SICK OF HEARING ABOUT MRS. TREVINO'S TAMALE DAY!
I'VE SHARED MY HERITAGE IN THE CLASSROOM, TOO, YOU KNOW!
BELIEVE ME, PEOPLE STILL TALK ABOUT "LUTEFISK DAY."
El Azteca
MALLETT

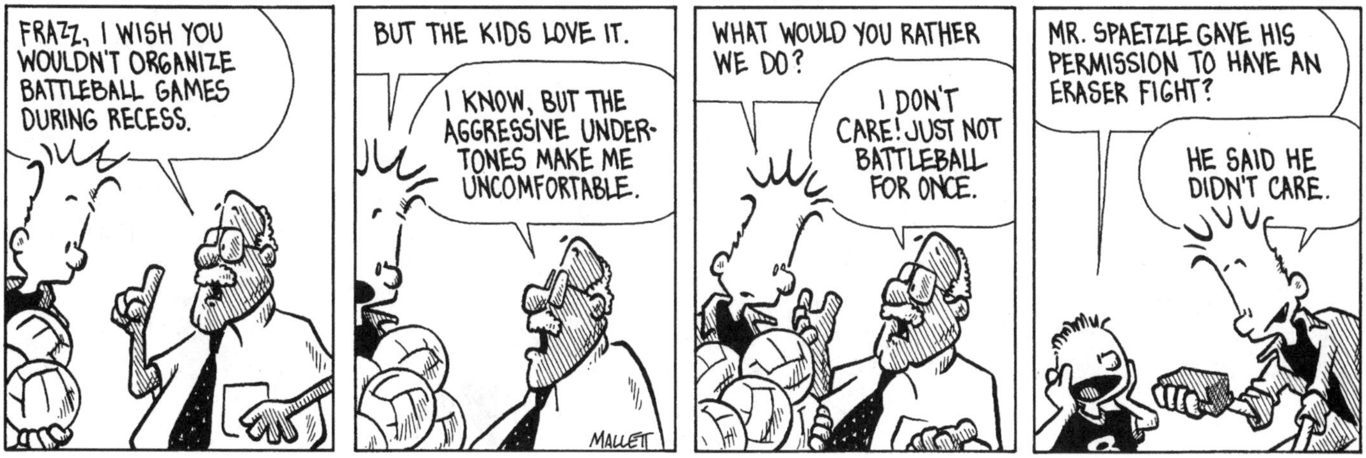
FRAZZ, I WISH YOU WOULDN'T ORGANIZE BATTLEBALL GAMES DURING RECESS.
BUT THE KIDS LOVE IT.
I KNOW, BUT THE AGGRESSIVE UNDERTONES MAKE ME UNCOMFORTABLE.
MALLETT
WHAT WOULD YOU RATHER WE DO?
I DON'T CARE! JUST NOT BATTLEBALL FOR ONCE.
MR. SPAETZLE GAVE HIS PERMISSION TO HAVE AN ERASER FIGHT?
HE SAID HE DIDN'T CARE.

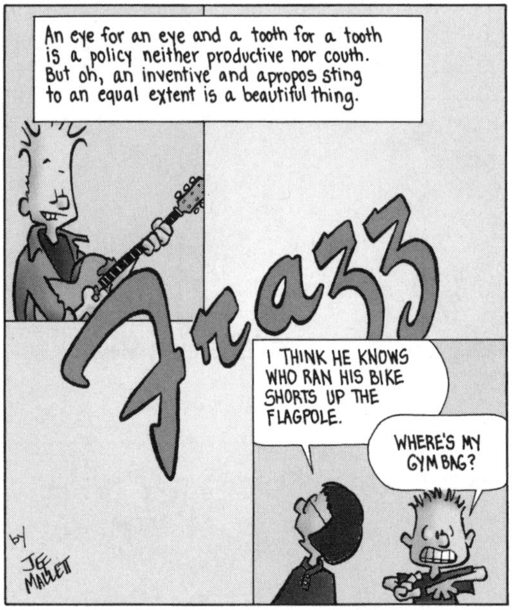
An eye for an eye and a tooth for a tooth
is a policy neither productive nor couth.
But oh, an inventive and apropos sting
to an equal extent is a beautiful thing.
Frazz
I THINK HE KNOWS WHO RAN HIS BIKE SHORTS UP THE FLAGPOLE.
WHERE'S MY GYM BAG?
by JEF MALLETT

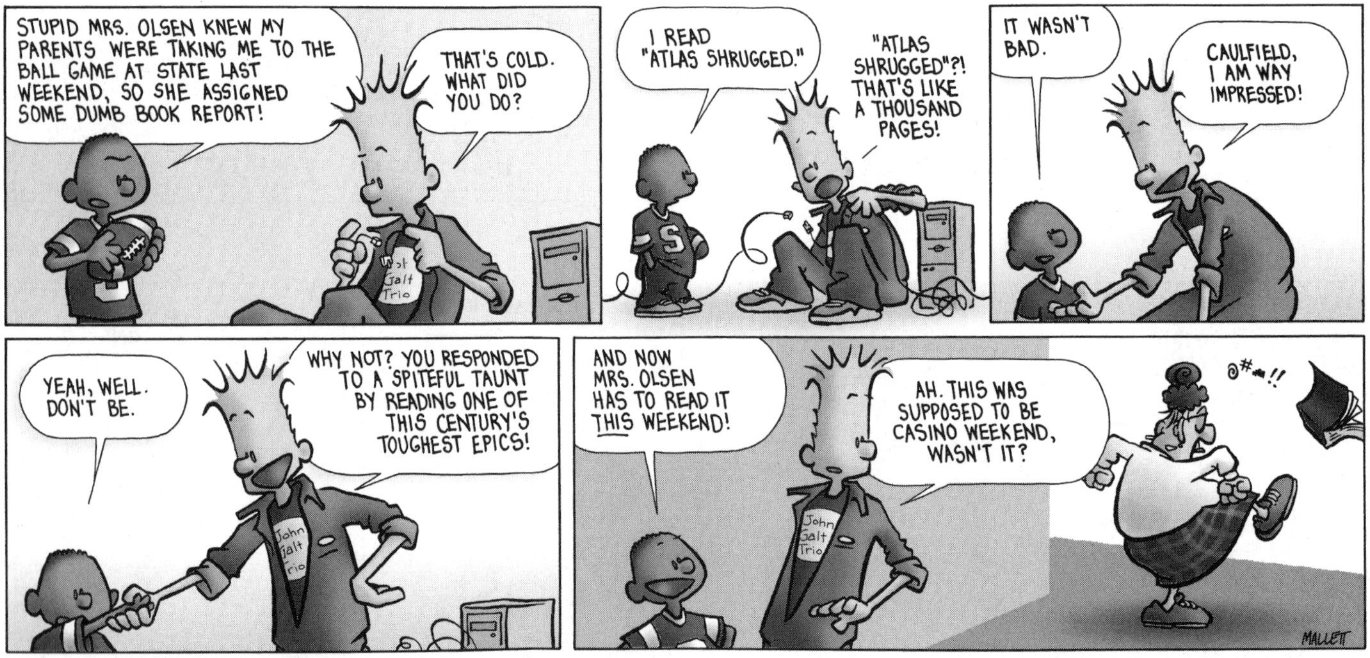
STUPID MRS. OLSEN KNEW MY PARENTS WERE TAKING ME TO THE BALL GAME AT STATE LAST WEEKEND, SO SHE ASSIGNED SOME DUMB BOOK REPORT!
THAT'S COLD. WHAT DID YOU DO?
I READ "ATLAS SHRUGGED."
"ATLAS SHRUGGED"?! THAT'S LIKE A THOUSAND PAGES!
IT WASN'T BAD.
CAULFIELD, I AM WAY IMPRESSED!
YEAH, WELL. DON'T BE.
WHY NOT? YOU RESPONDED TO A SPITEFUL TAUNT BY READING ONE OF THIS CENTURY'S TOUGHEST EPICS!
John Galt Trio
AND NOW MRS. OLSEN HAS TO READ IT THIS WEEKEND!
AH. THIS WAS SUPPOSED TO BE CASINO WEEKEND, WASN'T IT?
MALLETT

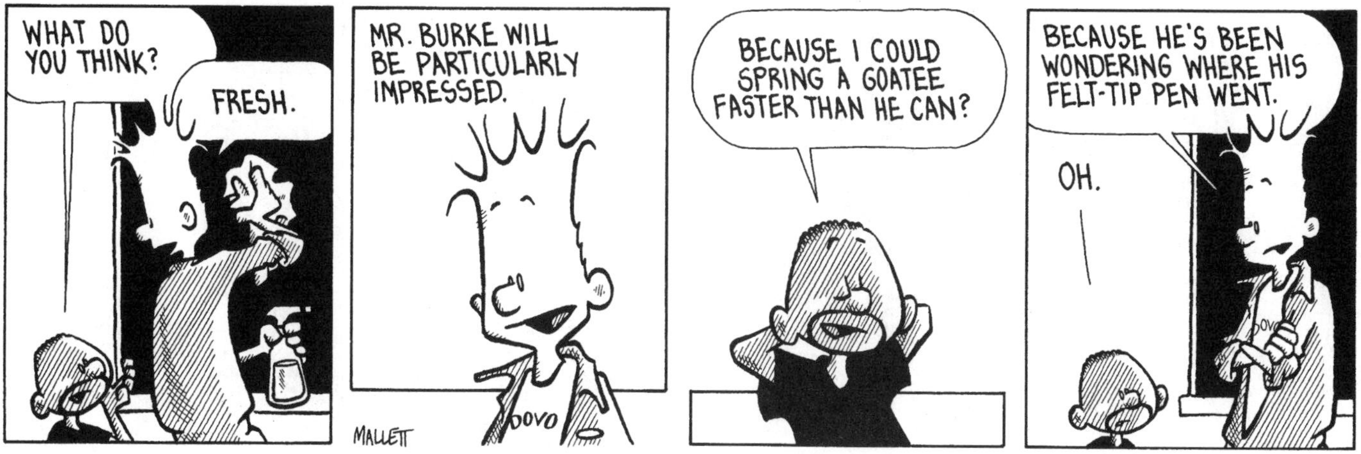
WHAT DO YOU THINK?
FRESH.
MR. BURKE WILL BE PARTICULARLY IMPRESSED.
BECAUSE I COULD SPRING A GOATEE FASTER THAN HE CAN?
BECAUSE HE'S BEEN WONDERING WHERE HIS FELT-TIP PEN WENT.
OH.
MALLETT

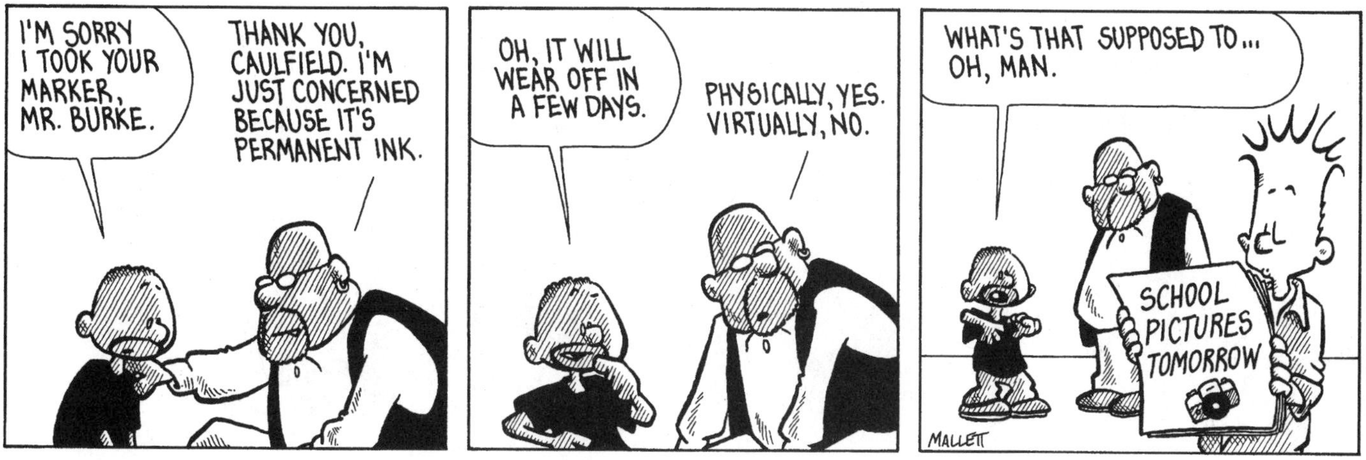
I'M SORRY I TOOK YOUR MARKER, MR. BURKE.
THANK YOU, CAULFIELD. I'M JUST CONCERNED BECAUSE IT'S PERMANENT INK.
OH, IT WILL WEAR OFF IN A FEW DAYS.
PHYSICALLY, YES. VIRTUALLY, NO.
WHAT'S THAT SUPPOSED TO... OH, MAN.
SCHOOL PICTURES TOMORROW
MALLETT

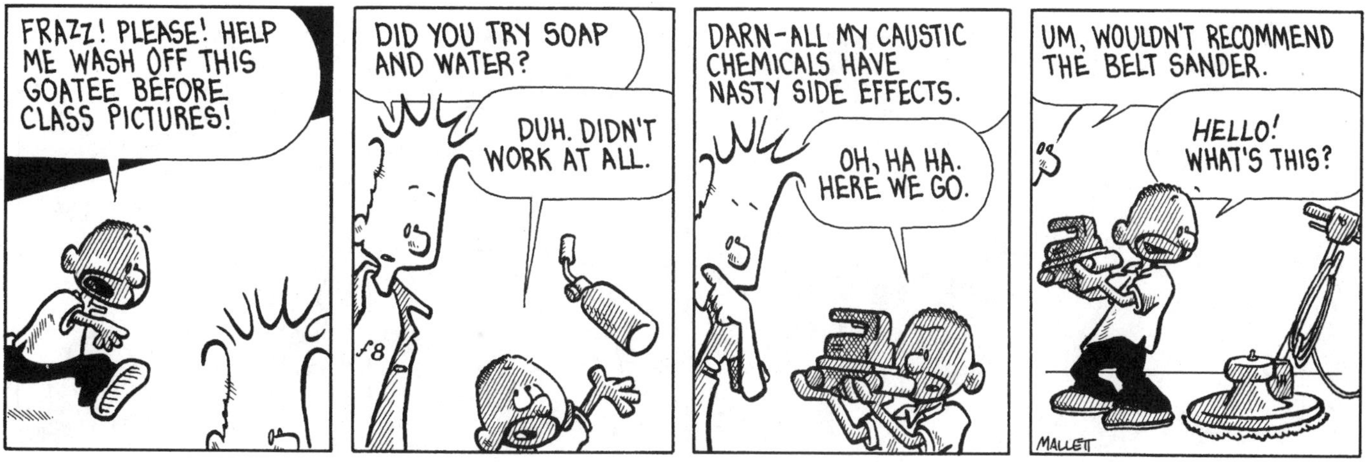
FRAZZ! PLEASE! HELP ME WASH OFF THIS GOATEE BEFORE CLASS PICTURES!
DID YOU TRY SOAP AND WATER?
DUH. DIDN'T WORK AT ALL.
DARN—ALL MY CAUSTIC CHEMICALS HAVE NASTY SIDE EFFECTS.
OH, HA HA. HERE WE GO.
UM, WOULDN'T RECOMMEND THE BELT SANDER.
HELLO! WHAT'S THIS?
MALLETT

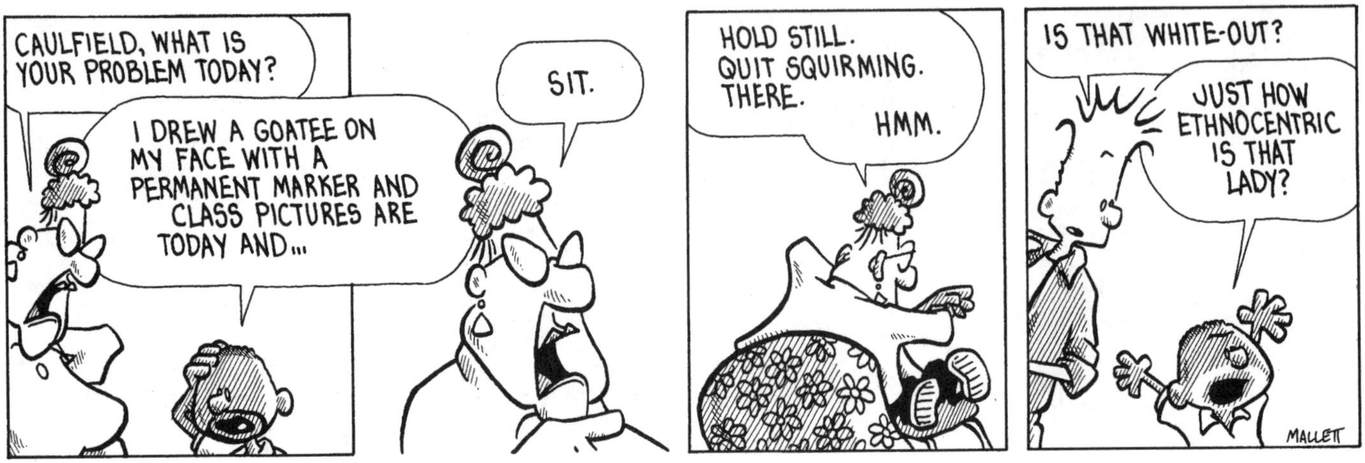
CAULFIELD, WHAT IS YOUR PROBLEM TODAY?
I DREW A GOATEE ON MY FACE WITH A PERMANENT MARKER AND CLASS PICTURES ARE TODAY AND...
SIT.
HOLD STILL. QUIT SQUIRMING. THERE.
HMM.
IS THAT WHITE-OUT?
JUST HOW ETHNOCENTRIC IS THAT LADY?
MALLETT

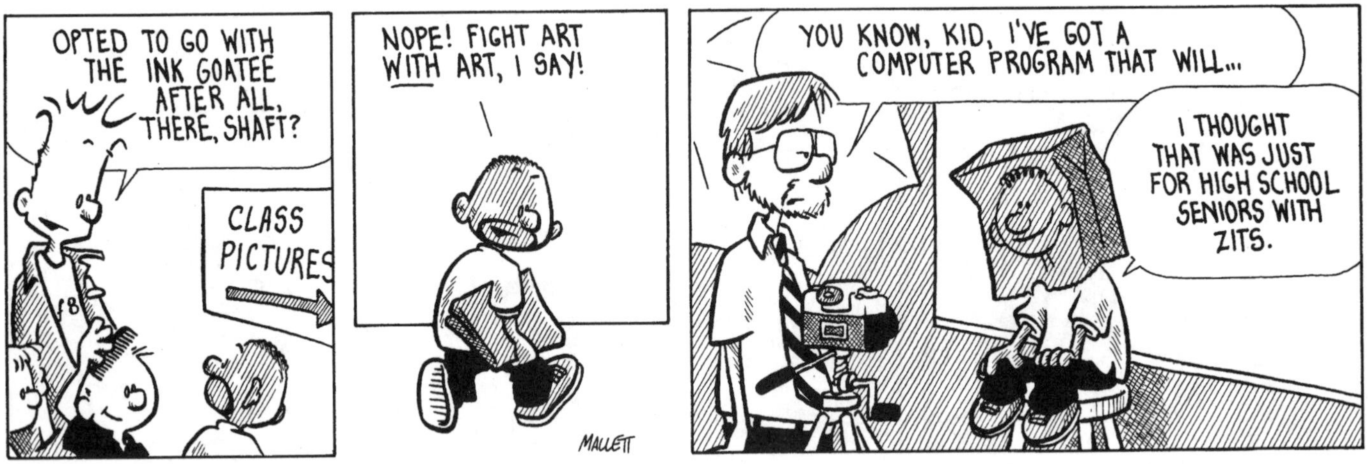
OPTED TO GO WITH THE INK GOATEE AFTER ALL, THERE, SHAFT?
CLASS PICTURES
f8
NOPE! FIGHT ART WITH ART, I SAY!
MALLETT
YOU KNOW, KID, I'VE GOT A COMPUTER PROGRAM THAT WILL...
I THOUGHT THAT WAS JUST FOR HIGH SCHOOL SENIORS WITH ZITS.

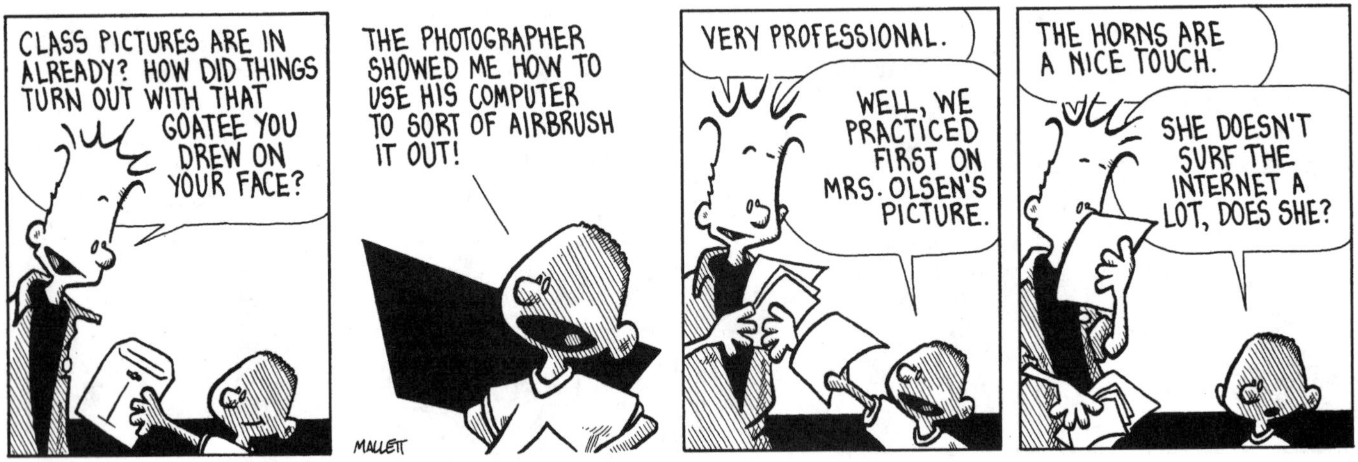
CLASS PICTURES ARE IN ALREADY? HOW DID THINGS TURN OUT WITH THAT GOATEE YOU DREW ON YOUR FACE?
THE PHOTOGRAPHER SHOWED ME HOW TO USE HIS COMPUTER TO SORT OF AIRBRUSH IT OUT!
MALLETT
VERY PROFESSIONAL.
WELL, WE PRACTICED FIRST ON MRS. OLSEN'S PICTURE.
THE HORNS ARE A NICE TOUCH.
SHE DOESN'T SURF THE INTERNET A LOT, DOES SHE?

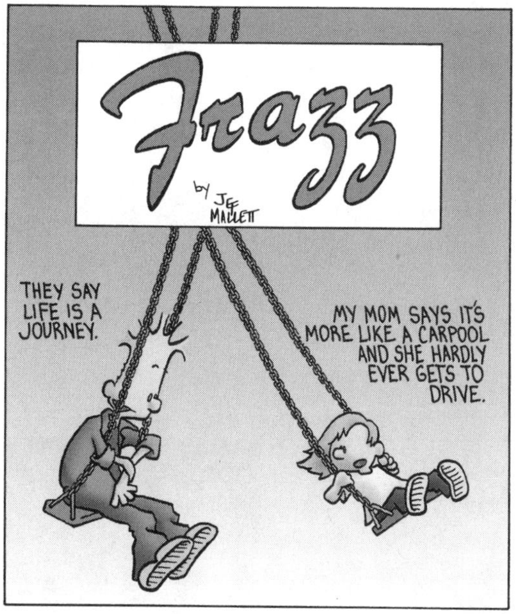
Frazz
by Jef Mallett
THEY SAY LIFE IS A JOURNEY.
MY MOM SAYS IT'S MORE LIKE A CARPOOL AND SHE HARDLY EVER GETS TO DRIVE.

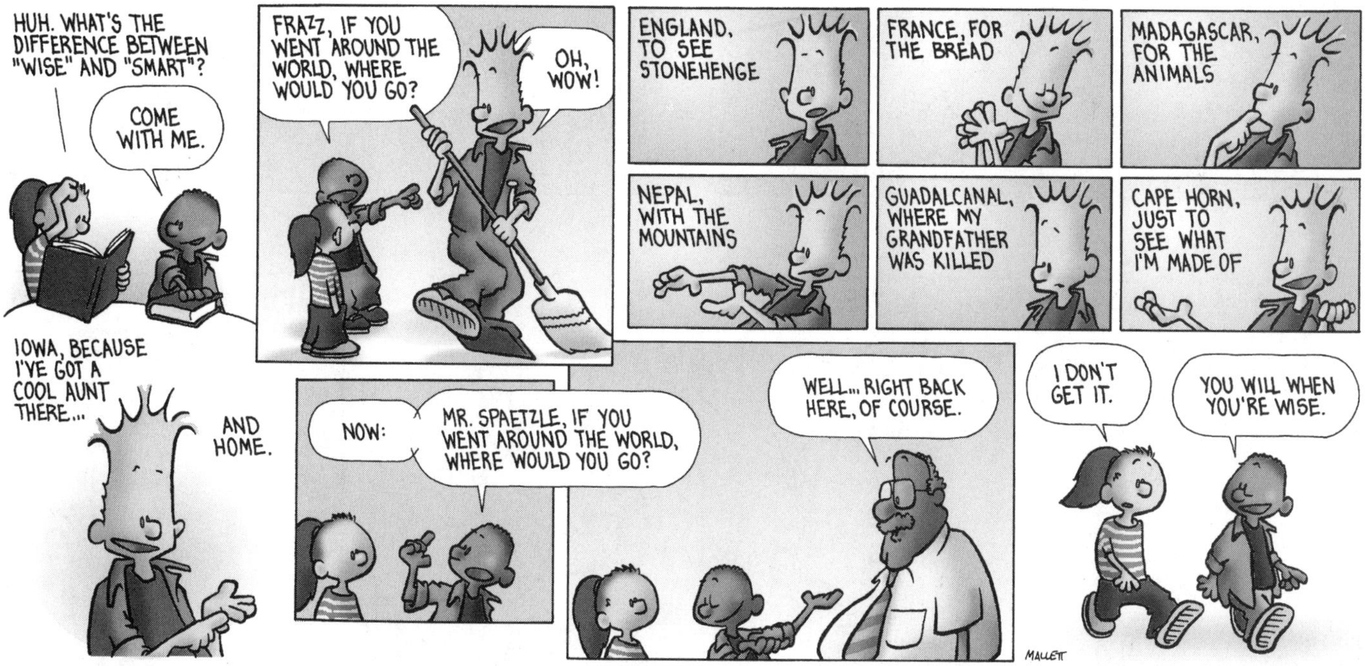
HUH. WHAT'S THE DIFFERENCE BETWEEN "WISE" AND "SMART"?
COME WITH ME.
FRAZZ, IF YOU WENT AROUND THE WORLD, WHERE WOULD YOU GO?
OH, WOW!
ENGLAND, TO SEE STONEHENGE
FRANCE, FOR THE BREAD
MADAGASCAR, FOR THE ANIMALS
NEPAL, WITH THE MOUNTAINS
GUADALCANAL, WHERE MY GRANDFATHER WAS KILLED
CAPE HORN, JUST TO SEE WHAT I'M MADE OF
IOWA, BECAUSE I'VE GOT A COOL AUNT THERE...
AND HOME.
NOW:
MR. SPAETZLE, IF YOU WENT AROUND THE WORLD, WHERE WOULD YOU GO?
WELL... RIGHT BACK HERE, OF COURSE.
I DON'T GET IT.
YOU WILL WHEN YOU'RE WISE.
MALLETT

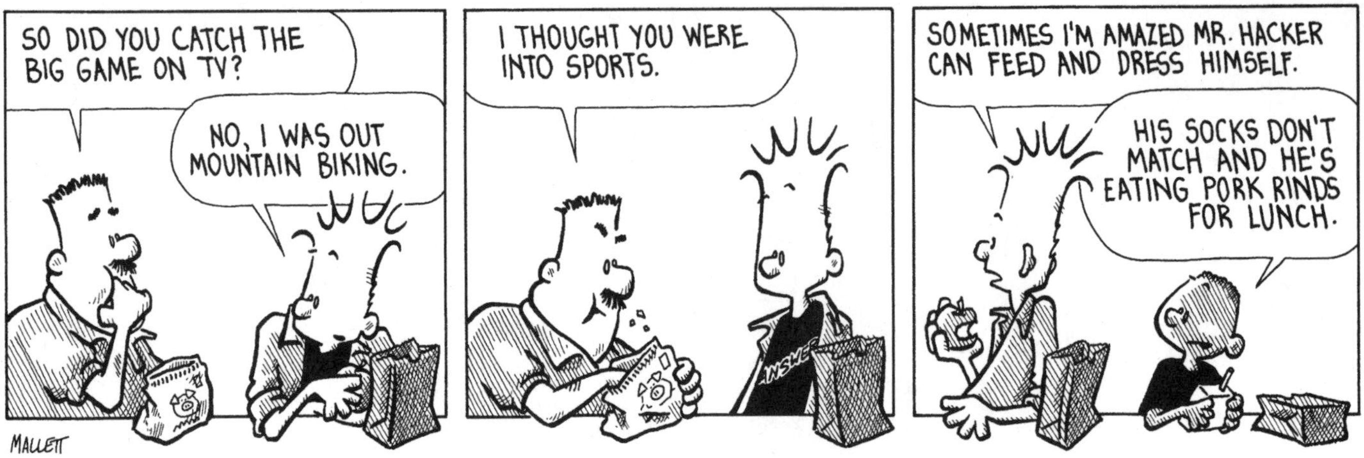
SO DID YOU CATCH THE BIG GAME ON TV?
NO, I WAS OUT MOUNTAIN BIKING.
I THOUGHT YOU WERE INTO SPORTS.
SOMETIMES I'M AMAZED MR. HACKER CAN FEED AND DRESS HIMSELF.
HIS SOCKS DON'T MATCH AND HE'S EATING PORK RINDS FOR LUNCH.
MALLETT

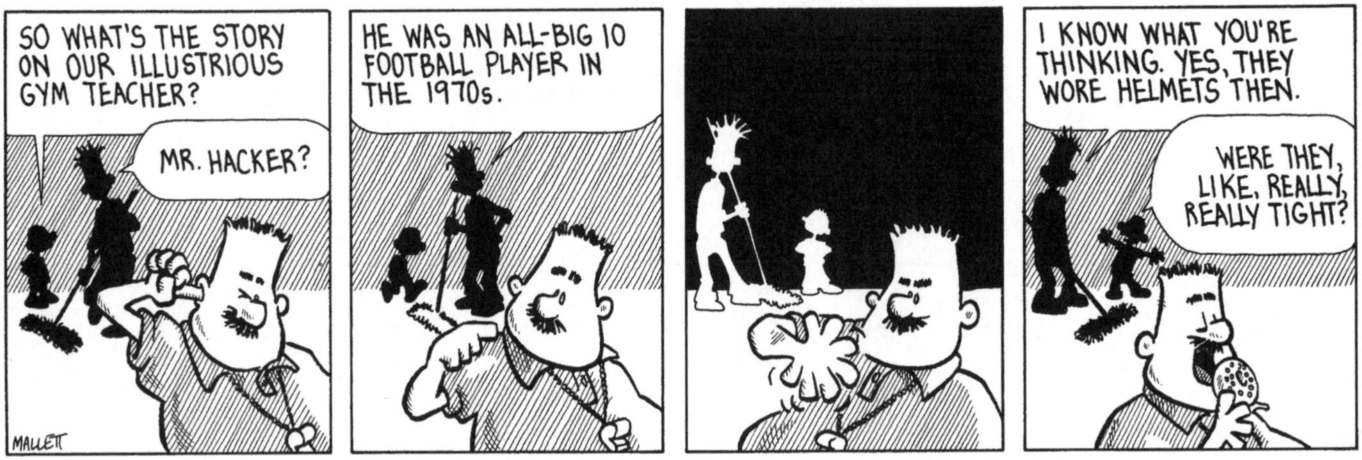
SO WHAT'S THE STORY ON OUR ILLUSTRIOUS GYM TEACHER?
MR. HACKER?
HE WAS AN ALL-BIG 10 FOOTBALL PLAYER IN THE 1970s.
I KNOW WHAT YOU'RE THINKING. YES, THEY WORE HELMETS THEN.
WERE THEY, LIKE, REALLY, REALLY TIGHT?
MALLETT

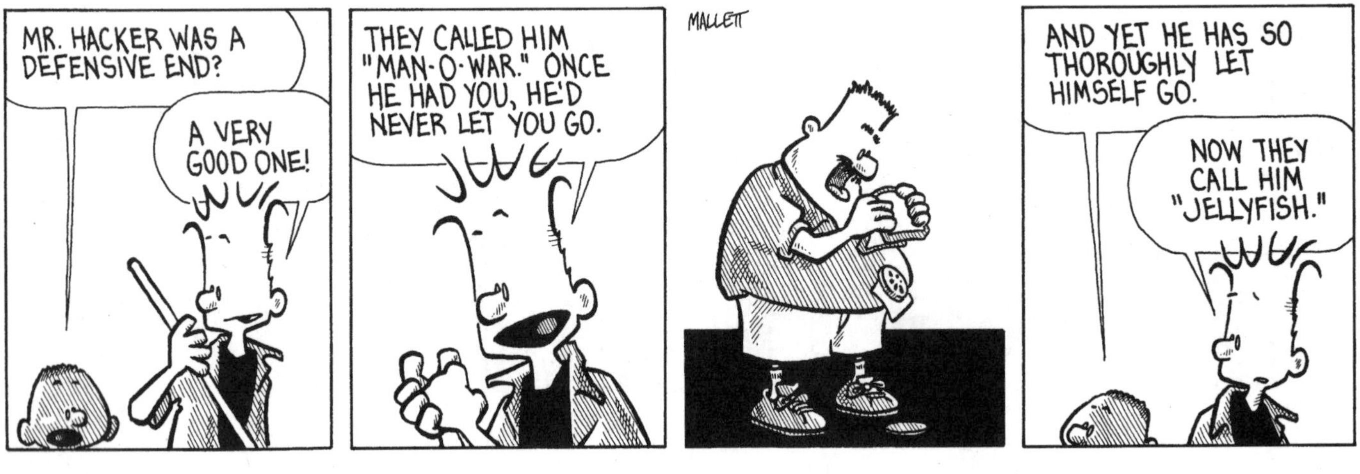
MR. HACKER WAS A DEFENSIVE END?
A VERY GOOD ONE!
THEY CALLED HIM "MAN-O-WAR." ONCE HE HAD YOU, HE'D NEVER LET YOU GO.
MALLETT
AND YET HE HAS SO THOROUGHLY LET HIMSELF GO.
NOW THEY CALL HIM "JELLYFISH."

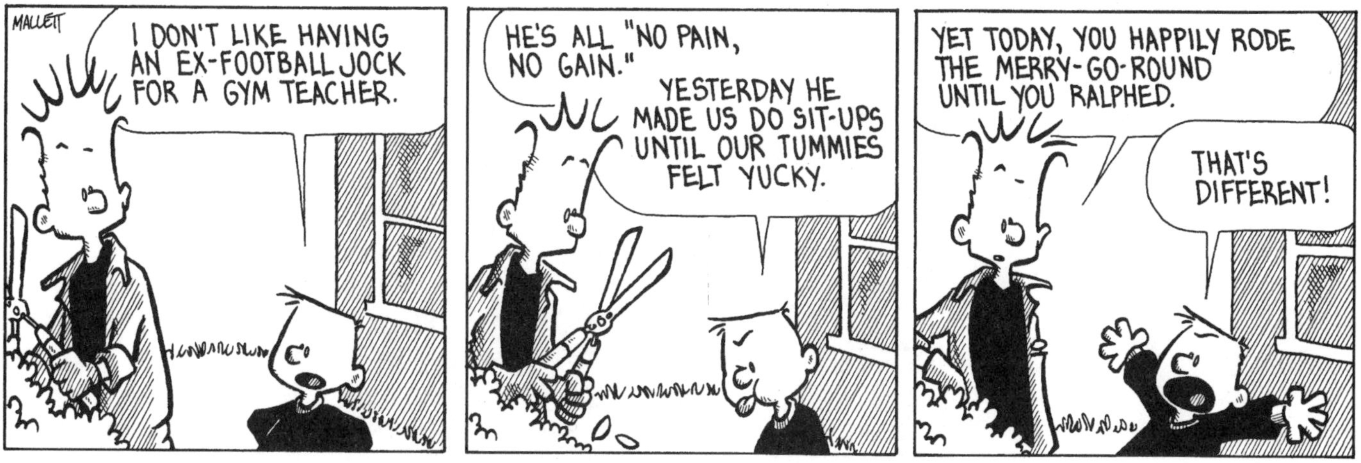
MALLETT
I DON'T LIKE HAVING AN EX-FOOTBALL JOCK FOR A GYM TEACHER.
HE'S ALL "NO PAIN, NO GAIN."
YESTERDAY HE MADE US DO SIT-UPS UNTIL OUR TUMMIES FELT YUCKY.
YET TODAY, YOU HAPPILY RODE THE MERRY-GO-ROUND UNTIL YOU RALPHED.
THAT'S DIFFERENT!

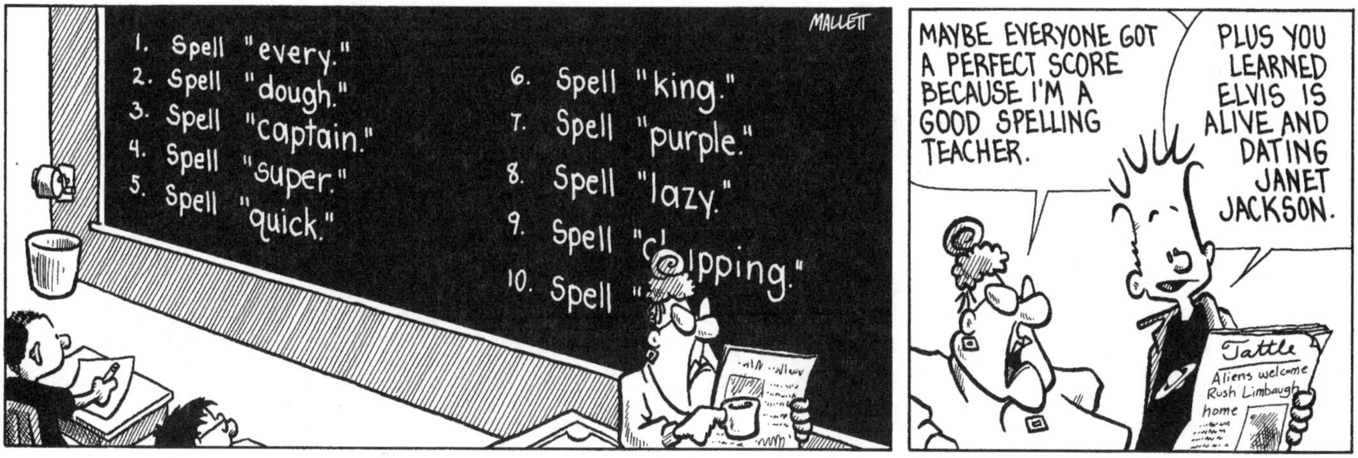
MALLETT
1. Spell "every."
2. Spell "dough."
3. Spell "captain."
4. Spell "super."
5. Spell "quick."
6. Spell "king."
7. Spell "purple."
8. Spell "lazy."
9. Spell
10. Spell
MAYBE EVERYONE GOT A PERFECT SCORE BECAUSE I'M A GOOD SPELLING TEACHER.
PLUS YOU LEARNED ELVIS IS ALIVE AND DATING JANET JACKSON.
Tattle
Aliens welcome Rush Limbaugh home

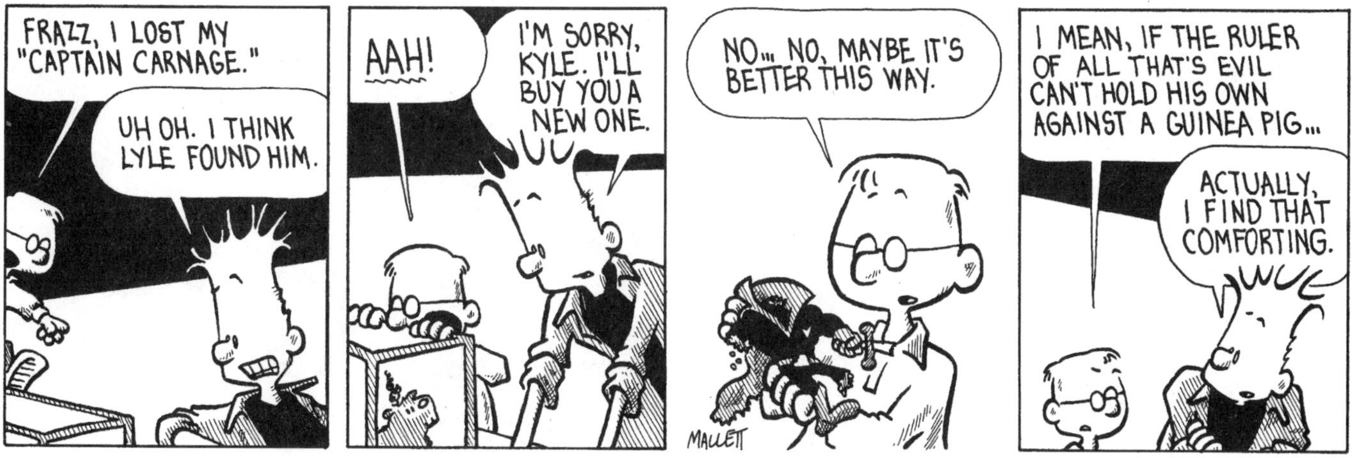
FRAZZ, I LOST MY "CAPTAIN CARNAGE."
UH OH. I THINK LYLE FOUND HIM.
AAH!
I'M SORRY, KYLE. I'LL BUY YOU A NEW ONE.
NO... NO, MAYBE IT'S BETTER THIS WAY.
MALLETT
I MEAN, IF THE RULER OF ALL THAT'S EVIL CAN'T HOLD HIS OWN AGAINST A GUINEA PIG...
ACTUALLY, I FIND THAT COMFORTING.

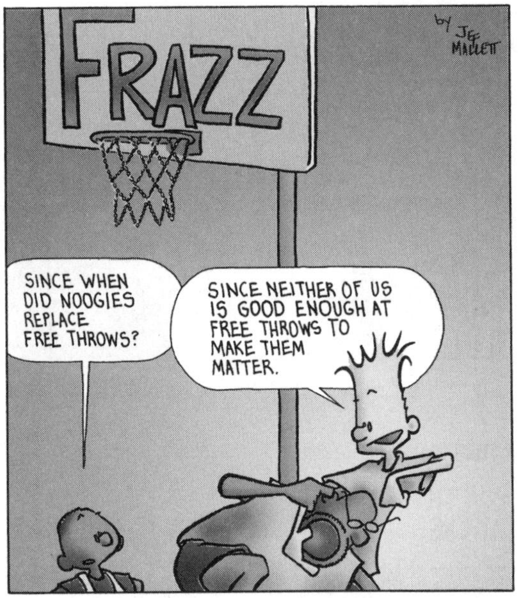
FRAZZ
by JEF MALLETT
SINCE WHEN DID NOOGIES REPLACE FREE THROWS?
SINCE NEITHER OF US IS GOOD ENOUGH AT FREE THROWS TO MAKE THEM MATTER.

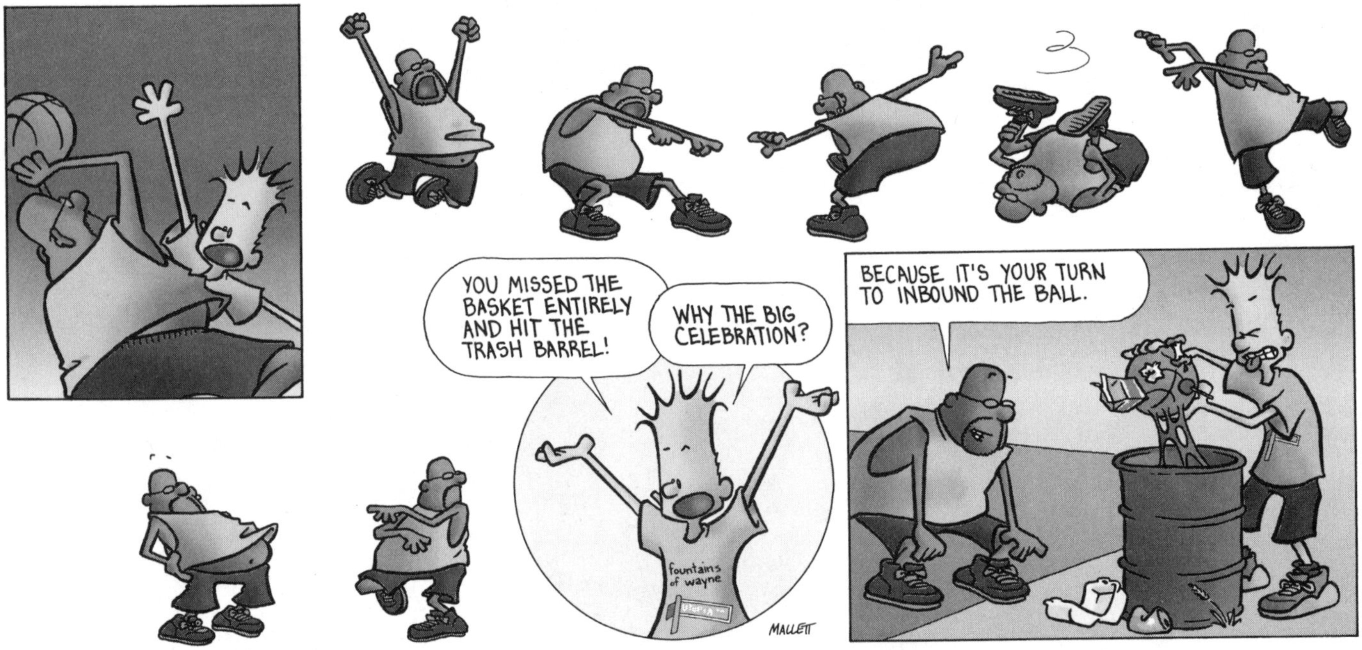
YOU MISSED THE BASKET ENTIRELY AND HIT THE TRASH BARREL!
WHY THE BIG CELEBRATION?
fountains of wayne
MALLETT
BECAUSE IT'S YOUR TURN TO INBOUND THE BALL.

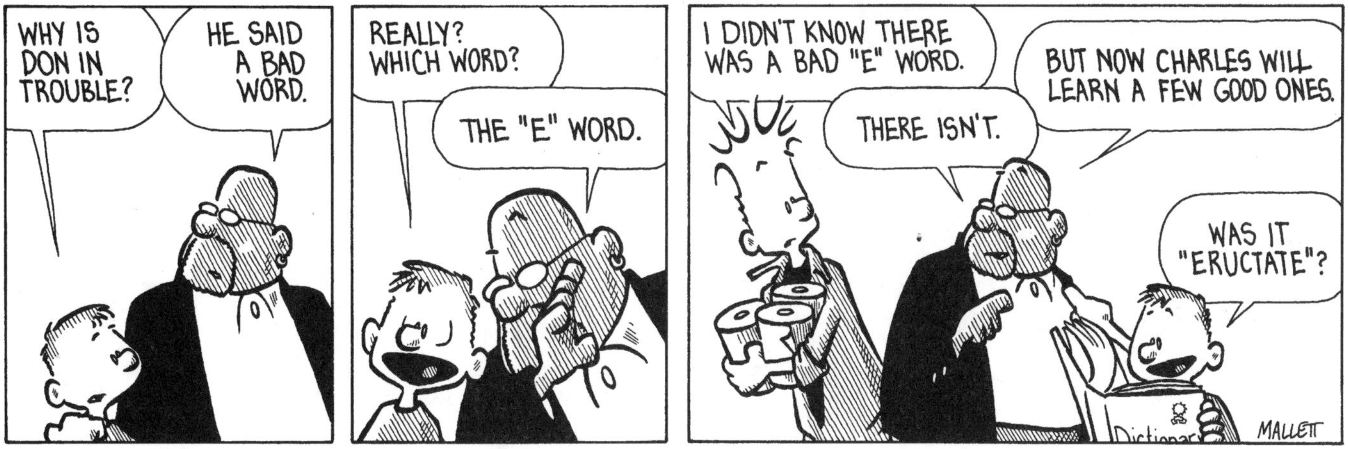
WHY IS DON IN TROUBLE?
HE SAID A BAD WORD.
REALLY? WHICH WORD?
THE "E" WORD.
I DIDN'T KNOW THERE WAS A BAD "E" WORD.
THERE ISN'T.
BUT NOW CHARLES WILL LEARN A FEW GOOD ONES.
WAS IT "ERUCTATE"?
Dictionary
MALLETT

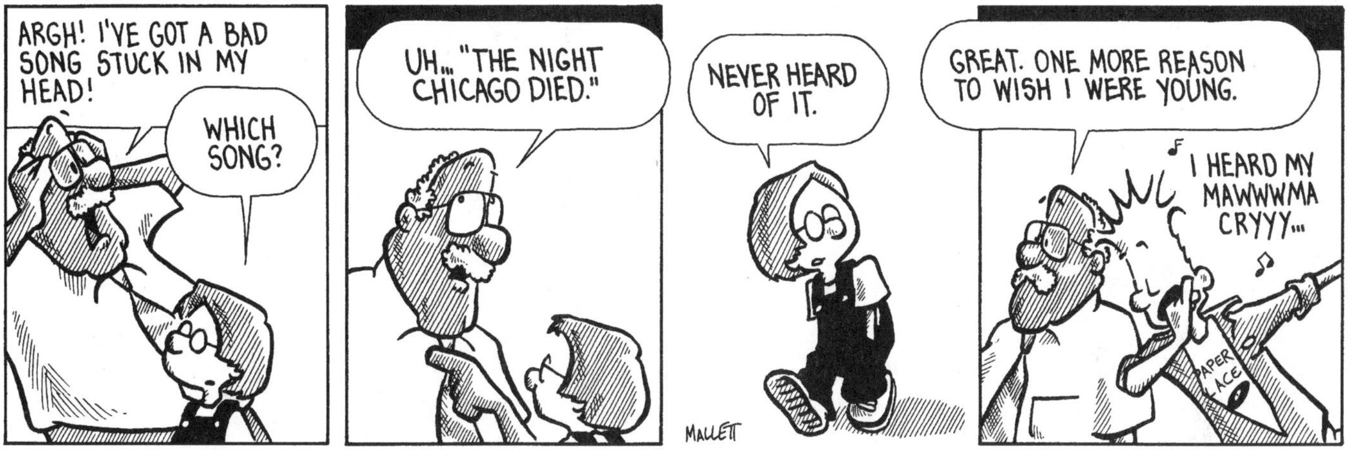
ARGH! I'VE GOT A BAD SONG STUCK IN MY HEAD!
WHICH SONG?
UH... "THE NIGHT CHICAGO DIED."
NEVER HEARD OF IT.
MALLETT
GREAT. ONE MORE REASON TO WISH I WERE YOUNG.
I HEARD MY MAWWWMA CRYYY...
PAPER LACE

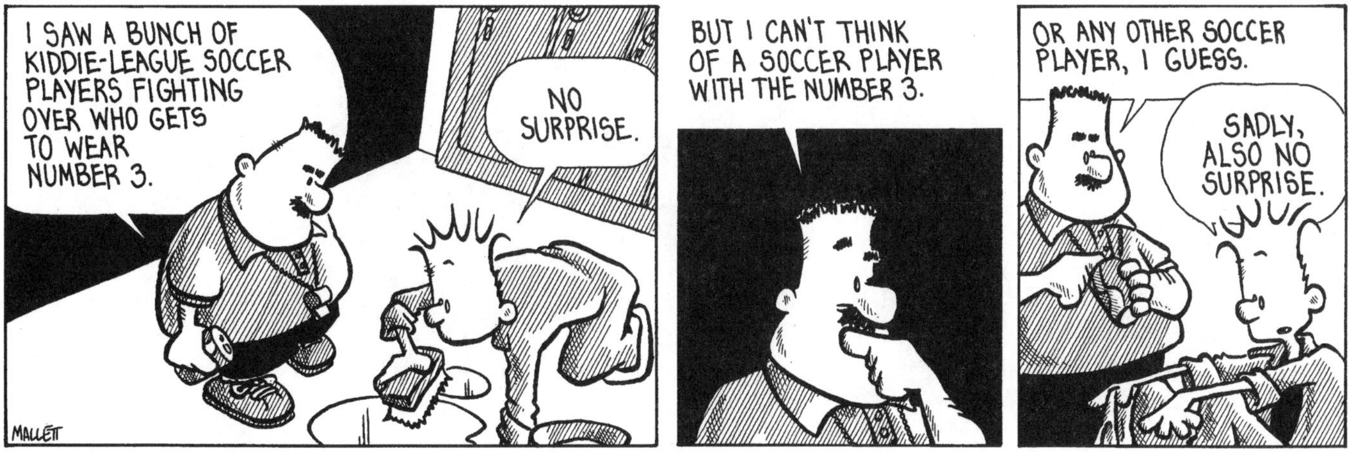
I SAW A BUNCH OF KIDDIE-LEAGUE SOCCER PLAYERS FIGHTING OVER WHO GETS TO WEAR NUMBER 3.
NO SURPRISE.
MALLETT
BUT I CAN'T THINK OF A SOCCER PLAYER WITH THE NUMBER 3.
OR ANY OTHER SOCCER PLAYER, I GUESS.
SADLY, ALSO NO SURPRISE.

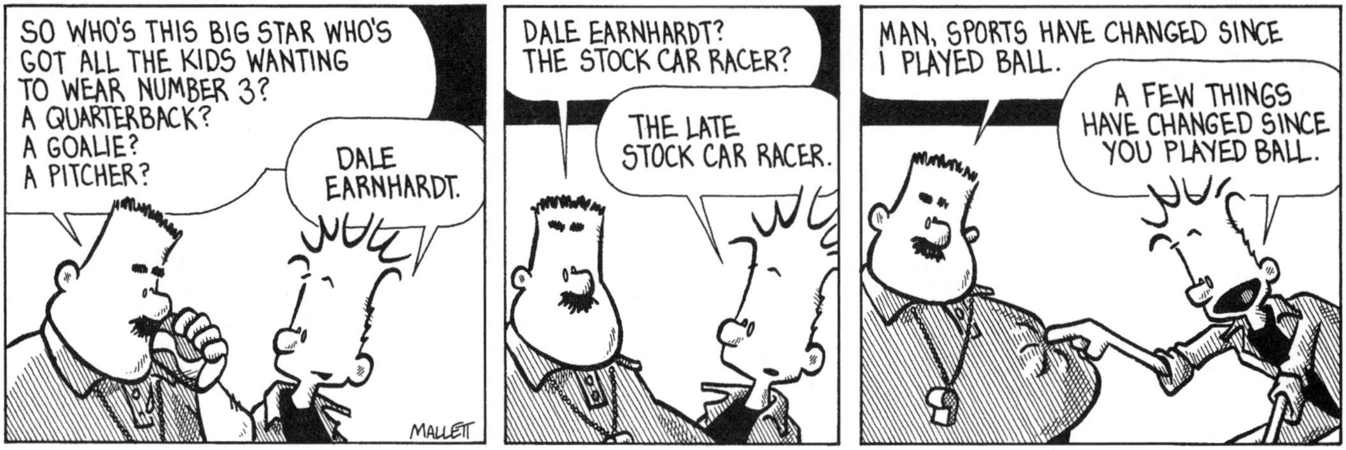
SO WHO'S THIS BIG STAR WHO'S GOT ALL THE KIDS WANTING TO WEAR NUMBER 3? A QUARTERBACK? A GOALIE? A PITCHER?
DALE EARNHARDT.
MALLETT
DALE EARNHARDT? THE STOCK CAR RACER?
THE LATE STOCK CAR RACER.
MAN, SPORTS HAVE CHANGED SINCE I PLAYED BALL.
A FEW THINGS HAVE CHANGED SINCE YOU PLAYED BALL.

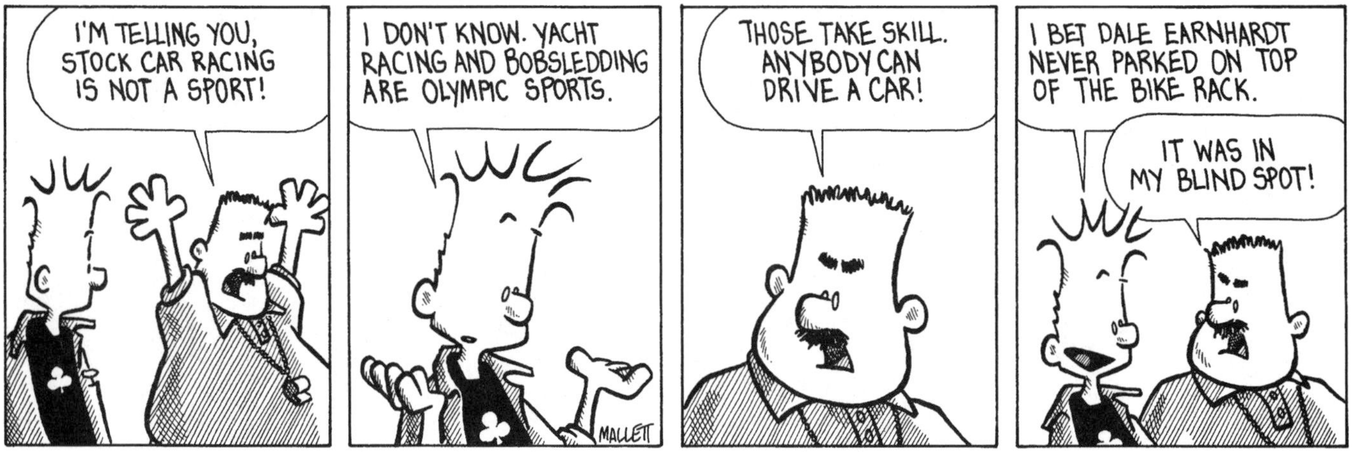
I'M TELLING YOU, STOCK CAR RACING IS NOT A SPORT!
I DON'T KNOW. YACHT RACING AND BOBSLEDDING ARE OLYMPIC SPORTS.
MALLETT
THOSE TAKE SKILL. ANYBODY CAN DRIVE A CAR!
I BET DALE EARNHARDT NEVER PARKED ON TOP OF THE BIKE RACK.
IT WAS IN MY BLIND SPOT!

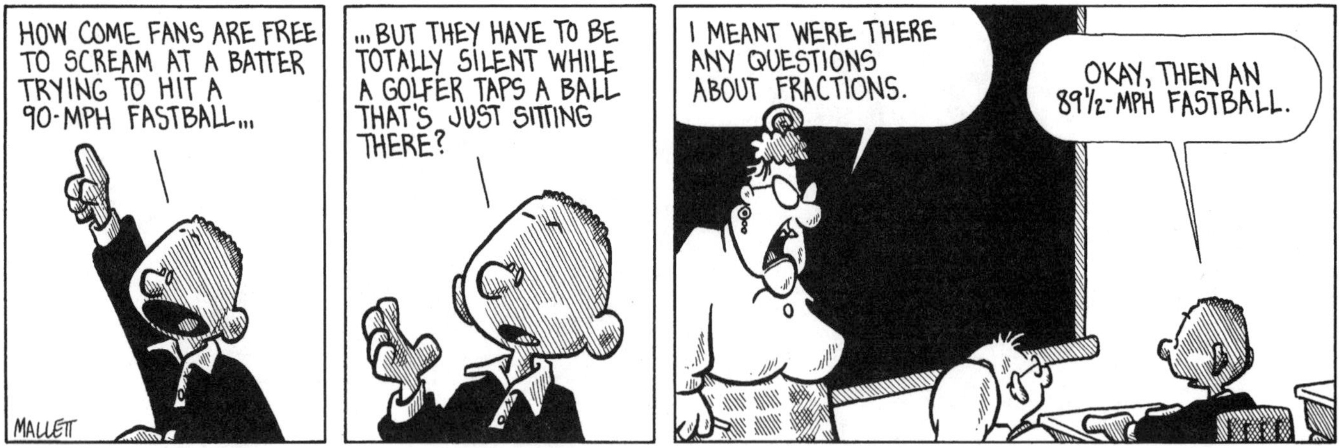
HOW COME FANS ARE FREE TO SCREAM AT A BATTER TRYING TO HIT A 90-MPH FASTBALL...
MALLETT
...BUT THEY HAVE TO BE TOTALLY SILENT WHILE A GOLFER TAPS A BALL THAT'S JUST SITTING THERE?
I MEANT WERE THERE ANY QUESTIONS ABOUT FRACTIONS.
OKAY, THEN AN 89½-MPH FASTBALL.

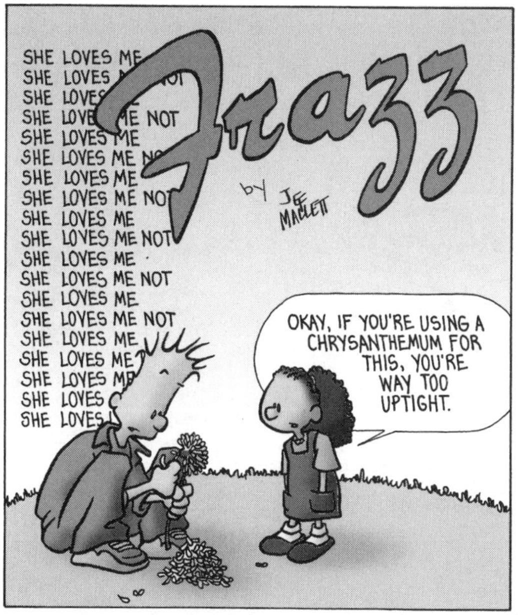
SHE LOVES ME
SHE LOVES ME NOT
SHE LOVES ME
SHE LOVES ME NOT
SHE LOVES ME
SHE LOVES ME NOT
SHE LOVES ME
SHE LOVES ME NOT
SHE LOVES ME
SHE LOVES ME NOT
SHE LOVES ME
SHE LOVES ME NOT
SHE LOVES ME
SHE LOVES ME NOT
SHE LOVES ME
SHE LOVES ME
SHE LOVES
SHE LOVES
SHE LOVES
Frazz
by JEF MALLETT
OKAY, IF YOU'RE USING A CHRYSANTHEMUM FOR THIS, YOU'RE WAY TOO UPTIGHT.

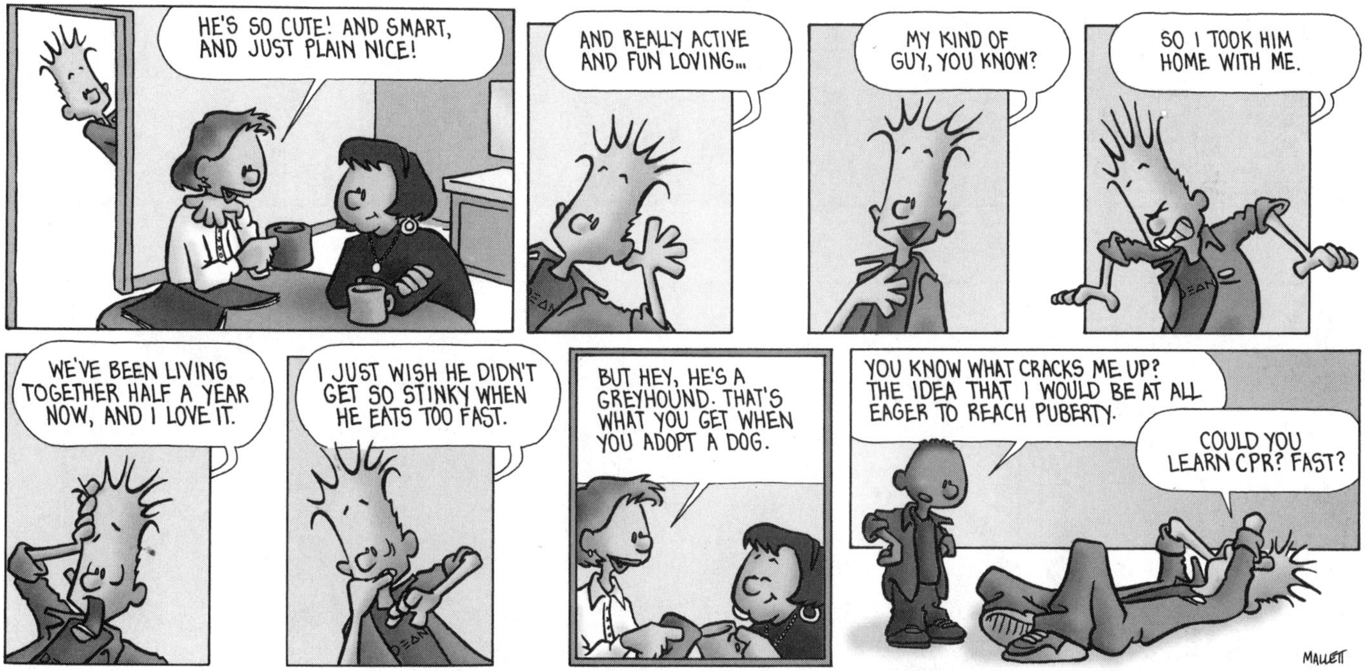
HE'S SO CUTE! AND SMART, AND JUST PLAIN NICE!
AND REALLY ACTIVE AND FUN LOVING...
MY KIND OF GUY, YOU KNOW?
SO I TOOK HIM HOME WITH ME.
WE'VE BEEN LIVING TOGETHER HALF A YEAR NOW, AND I LOVE IT.
I JUST WISH HE DIDN'T GET SO STINKY WHEN HE EATS TOO FAST.
BUT HEY, HE'S A GREYHOUND. THAT'S WHAT YOU GET WHEN YOU ADOPT A DOG.
YOU KNOW WHAT CRACKS ME UP? THE IDEA THAT I WOULD BE AT ALL EAGER TO REACH PUBERTY.
COULD YOU LEARN CPR? FAST?
MALLETT

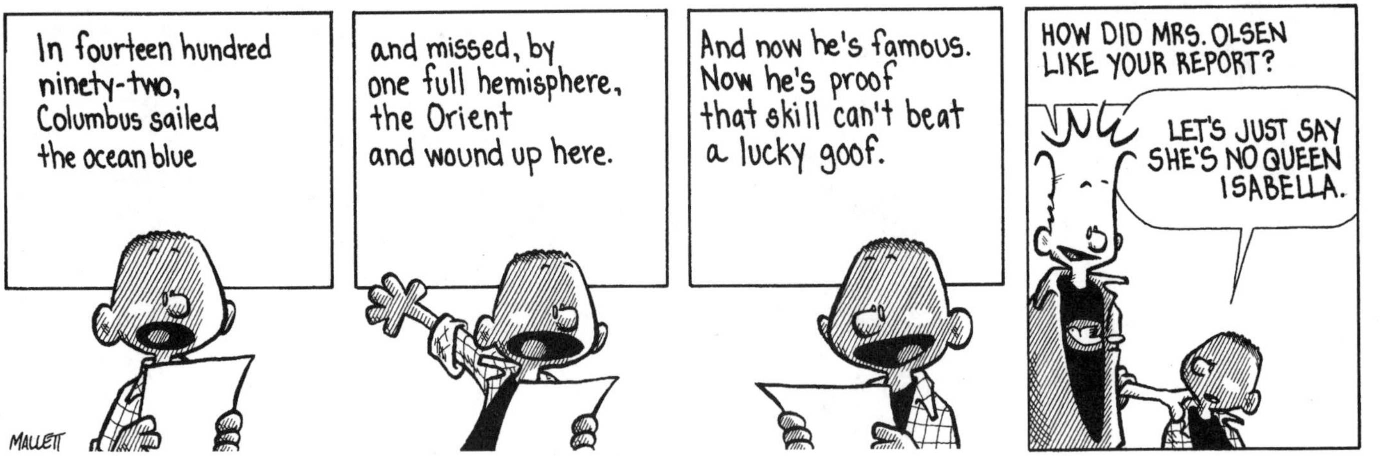
In fourteen hundred ninety-two, Columbus sailed the ocean blue
MALLETT
and missed, by one full hemisphere, the Orient and wound up here.
And now he's famous. Now he's proof that skill can't beat a lucky goof.
HOW DID MRS. OLSEN LIKE YOUR REPORT?
LET'S JUST SAY SHE'S NO QUEEN ISABELLA.

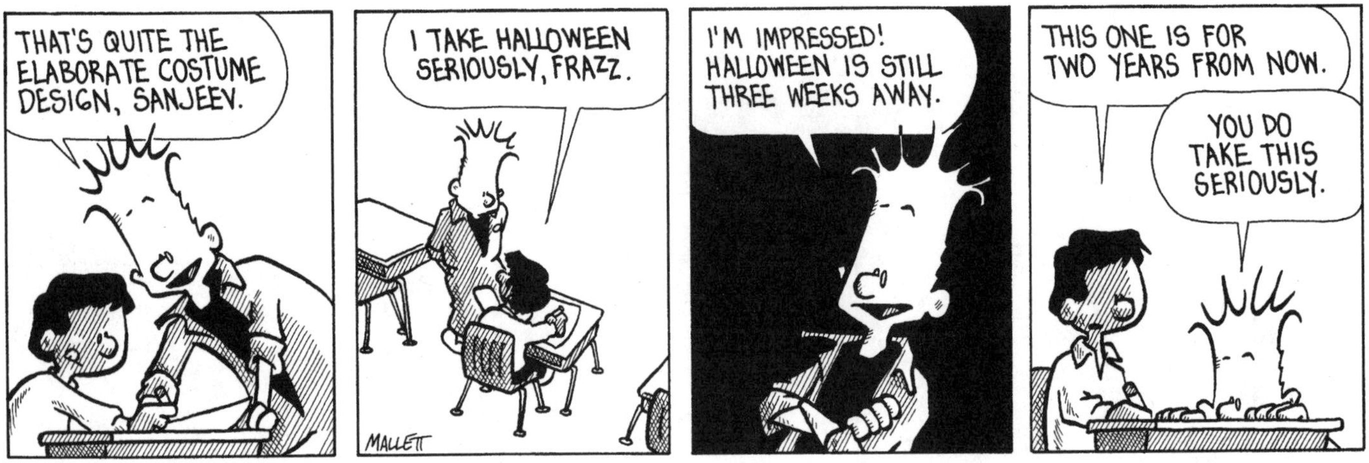
THAT'S QUITE THE ELABORATE COSTUME DESIGN, SANJEEV.
I TAKE HALLOWEEN SERIOUSLY, FRAZZ.
MALLETT
I'M IMPRESSED! HALLOWEEN IS STILL THREE WEEKS AWAY.
THIS ONE IS FOR TWO YEARS FROM NOW.
YOU DO TAKE THIS SERIOUSLY.

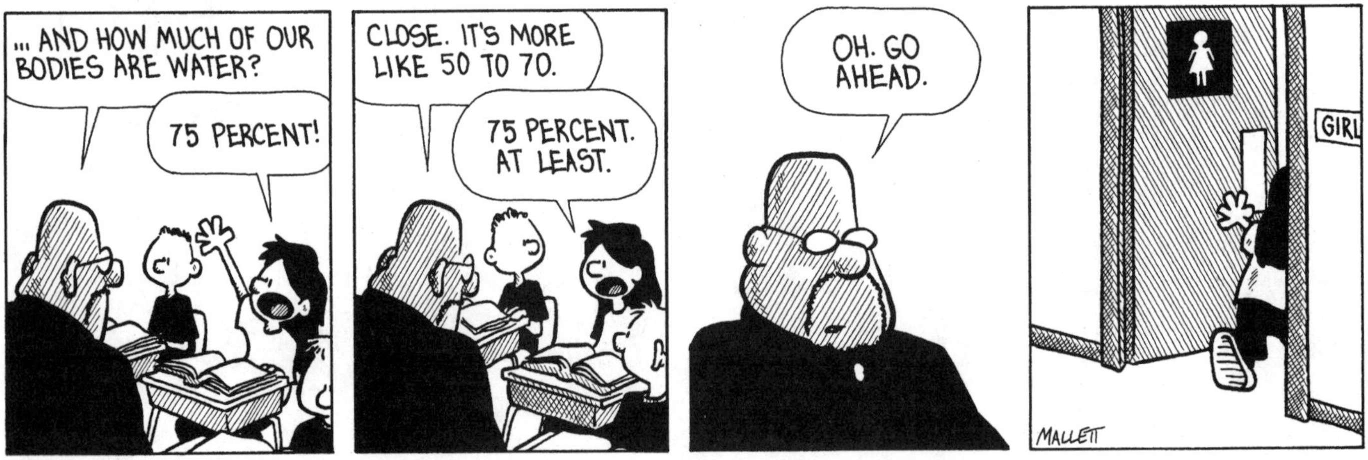
... AND HOW MUCH OF OUR BODIES ARE WATER?
75 PERCENT!
CLOSE. IT'S MORE LIKE 50 TO 70.
75 PERCENT. AT LEAST.
OH. GO AHEAD.
GIRL
MALLETT

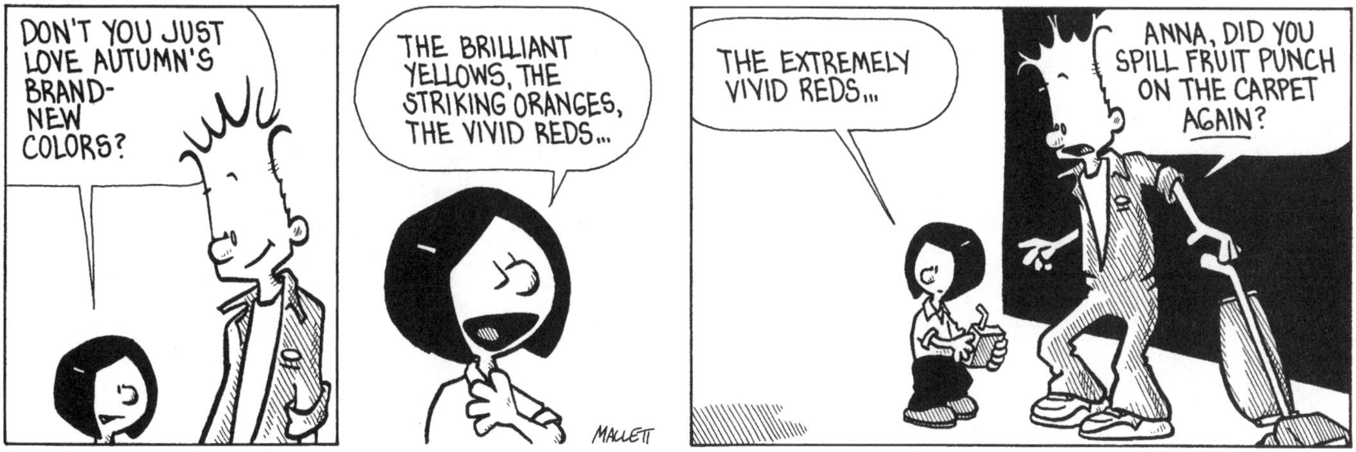
DON'T YOU JUST LOVE AUTUMN'S BRAND-NEW COLORS?
THE BRILLIANT YELLOWS, THE STRIKING ORANGES, THE VIVID REDS...
MALLETT
THE EXTREMELY VIVID REDS...
ANNA, DID YOU SPILL FRUIT PUNCH ON THE CARPET AGAIN?

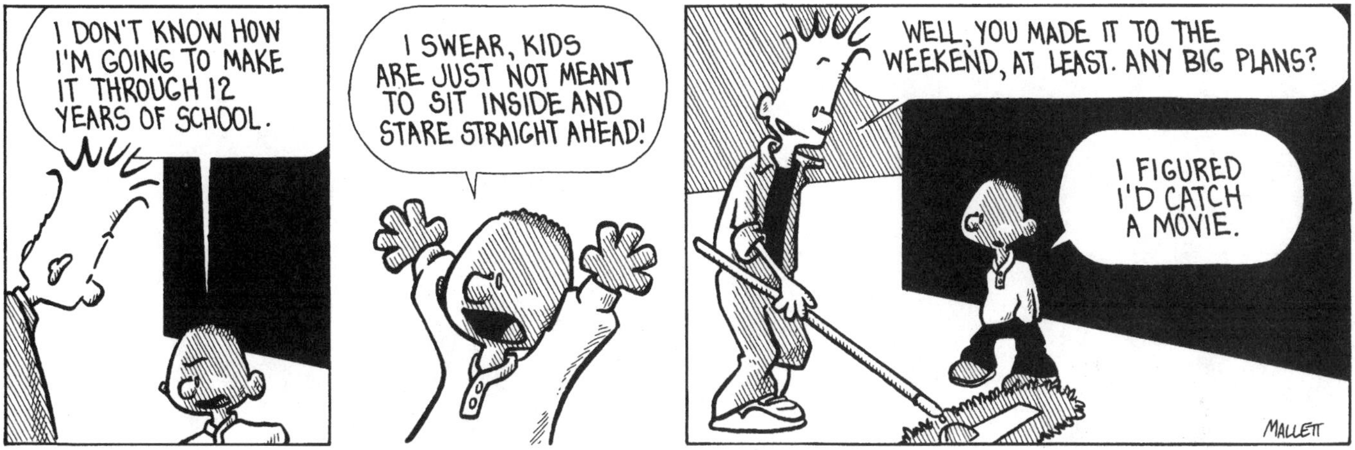
I DON'T KNOW HOW I'M GOING TO MAKE IT THROUGH 12 YEARS OF SCHOOL.
I SWEAR, KIDS ARE JUST NOT MEANT TO SIT INSIDE AND STARE STRAIGHT AHEAD!
WELL, YOU MADE IT TO THE WEEKEND, AT LEAST. ANY BIG PLANS?
I FIGURED I'D CATCH A MOVIE.
MALLETT

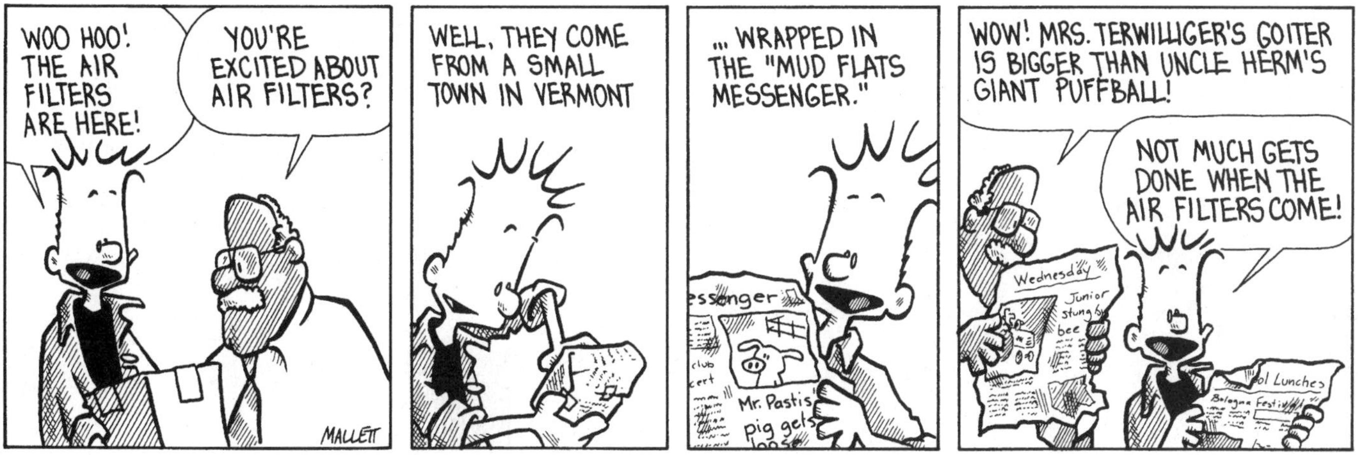
WOO HOO! THE AIR FILTERS ARE HERE!
YOU'RE EXCITED ABOUT AIR FILTERS?
MALLETT
WELL, THEY COME FROM A SMALL TOWN IN VERMONT
... WRAPPED IN THE "MUD FLATS MESSENGER."
Mr. Pastis'
WOW! MRS. TERWILLIGER'S GOITER IS BIGGER THAN UNCLE HERM'S GIANT PUFFBALL!
NOT MUCH GETS DONE WHEN THE AIR FILTERS COME!
Wednesday
Junior stung by bee

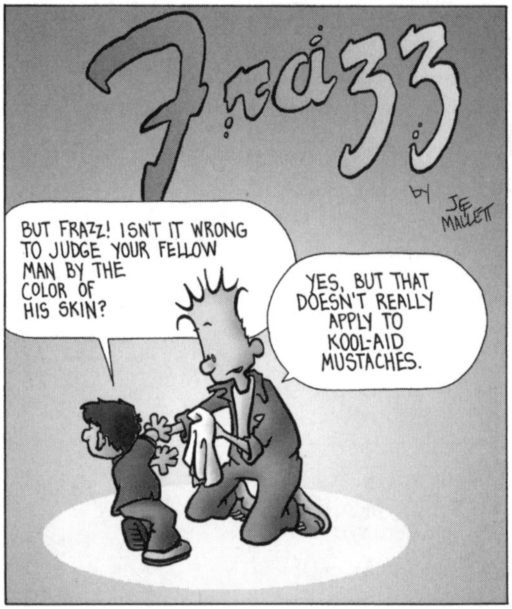
Frazz
by JEF MALLETT
BUT FRAZZ! ISN'T IT WRONG TO JUDGE YOUR FELLOW MAN BY THE COLOR OF HIS SKIN?
YES, BUT THAT DOESN'T REALLY APPLY TO KOOL-AID MUSTACHES.

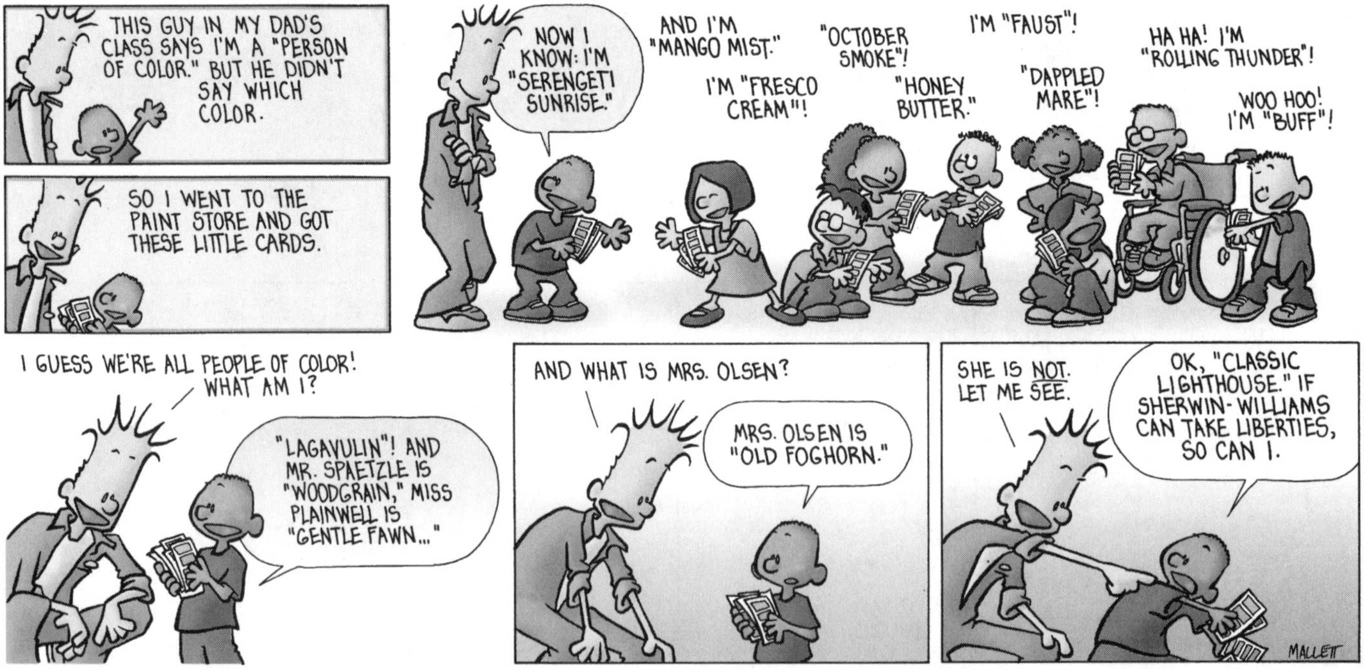
THIS GUY IN MY DAD'S CLASS SAYS I'M A "PERSON OF COLOR." BUT HE DIDN'T SAY WHICH COLOR.
SO I WENT TO THE PAINT STORE AND GOT THESE LITTLE CARDS.
NOW I KNOW: I'M "SERENGETI SUNRISE."
AND I'M "MANGO MIST."
I'M "FRESCO CREAM"!
"OCTOBER SMOKE"!
"HONEY BUTTER."
I'M "FAUST"!
"DAPPLED MARE"!
HA HA! I'M "ROLLING THUNDER"!
WOO HOO! I'M "BUFF"!
I GUESS WE'RE ALL PEOPLE OF COLOR! WHAT AM I?
"LAGAVULIN"! AND MR. SPAETZLE IS "WOODGRAIN," MISS PLAINWELL IS "GENTLE FAWN..."
AND WHAT IS MRS. OLSEN?
MRS. OLSEN IS "OLD FOGHORN."
SHE IS NOT. LET ME SEE.
OK, "CLASSIC LIGHTHOUSE." IF SHERWIN-WILLIAMS CAN TAKE LIBERTIES, SO CAN I.
MALLETT

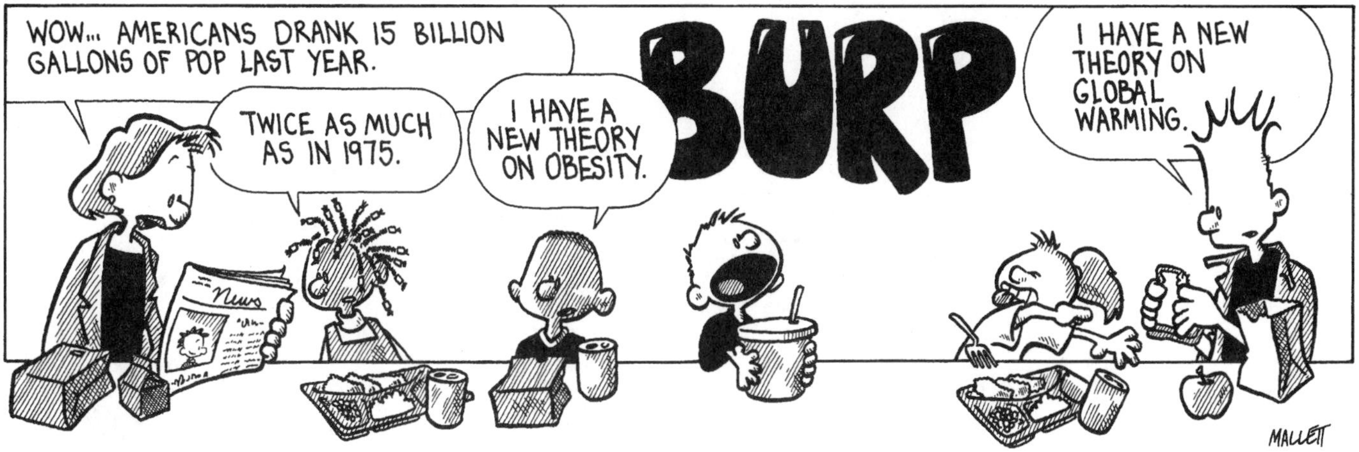
WOW... AMERICANS DRANK 15 BILLION GALLONS OF POP LAST YEAR.
TWICE AS MUCH AS IN 1975.
I HAVE A NEW THEORY ON OBESITY.
BURP
I HAVE A NEW THEORY ON GLOBAL WARMING.
MALLETT

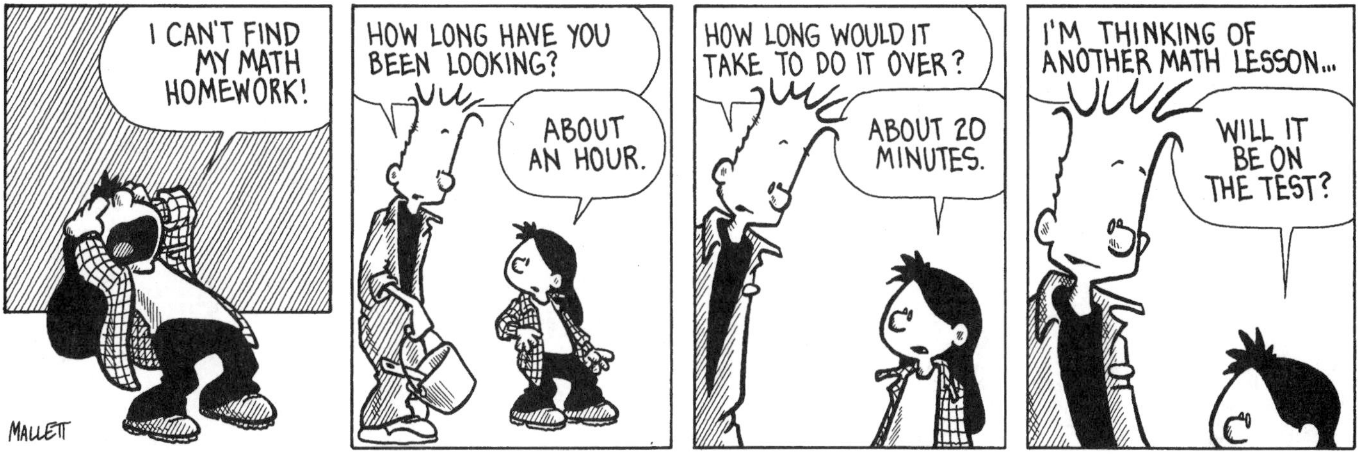
I CAN'T FIND MY MATH HOMEWORK!
MALLETT
HOW LONG HAVE YOU BEEN LOOKING?
ABOUT AN HOUR.
HOW LONG WOULD IT TAKE TO DO IT OVER?
ABOUT 20 MINUTES.
I'M THINKING OF ANOTHER MATH LESSON...
WILL IT BE ON THE TEST?

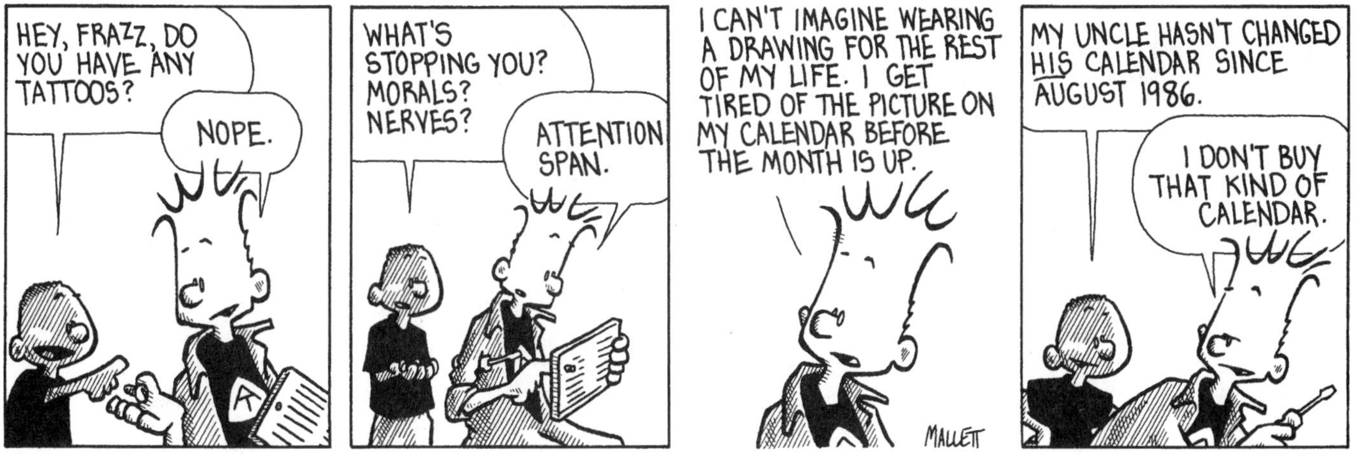
HEY, FRAZZ, DO YOU HAVE ANY TATTOOS?
NOPE.
WHAT'S STOPPING YOU? MORALS? NERVES?
ATTENTION SPAN.
I CAN'T IMAGINE WEARING A DRAWING FOR THE REST OF MY LIFE. I GET TIRED OF THE PICTURE ON MY CALENDAR BEFORE THE MONTH IS UP.
MALLETT
MY UNCLE HASN'T CHANGED HIS CALENDAR SINCE AUGUST 1986.
I DON'T BUY THAT KIND OF CALENDAR.

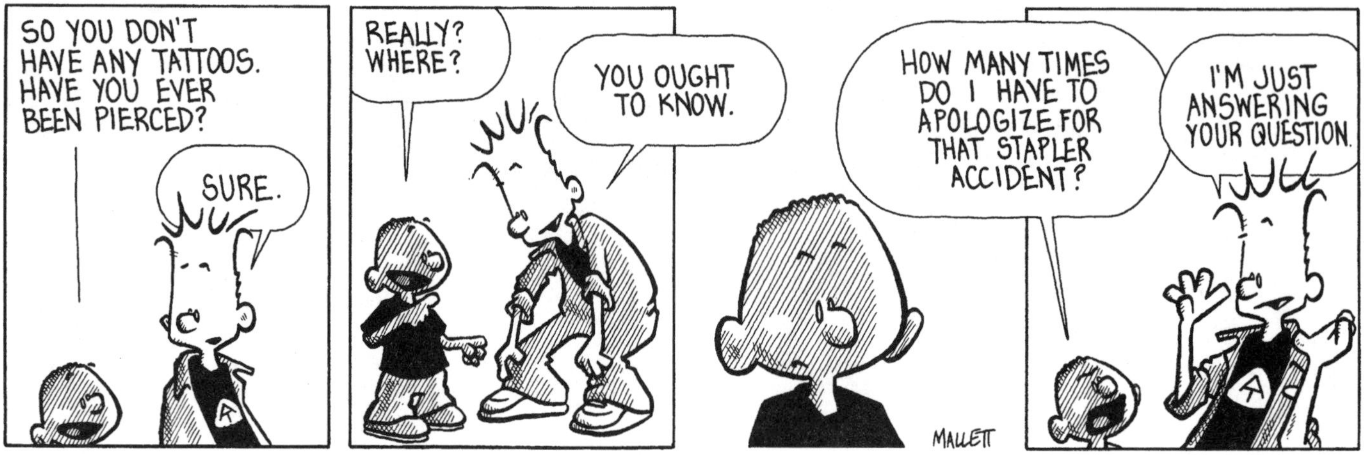
SO YOU DON'T HAVE ANY TATTOOS. HAVE YOU EVER BEEN PIERCED?
SURE.
REALLY? WHERE?
YOU OUGHT TO KNOW.
HOW MANY TIMES DO I HAVE TO APOLOGIZE FOR THAT STAPLER ACCIDENT?
I'M JUST ANSWERING YOUR QUESTION.
MALLETT

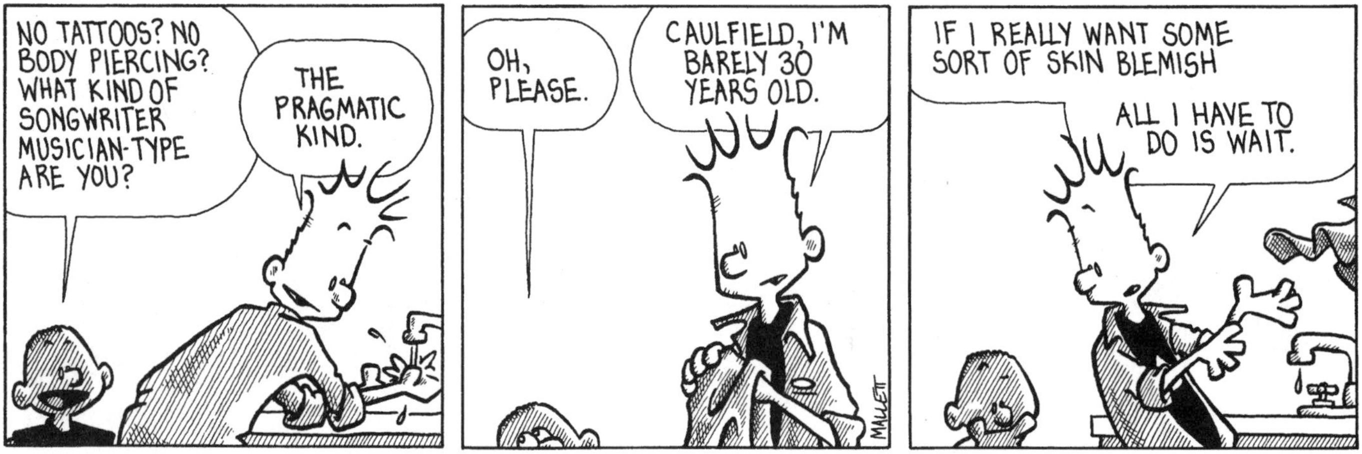
NO TATTOOS? NO BODY PIERCING? WHAT KIND OF SONGWRITER MUSICIAN-TYPE ARE YOU?
THE PRAGMATIC KIND.
OH, PLEASE.
CAULFIELD, I'M BARELY 30 YEARS OLD.
MALLETT
IF I REALLY WANT SOME SORT OF SKIN BLEMISH
ALL I HAVE TO DO IS WAIT.

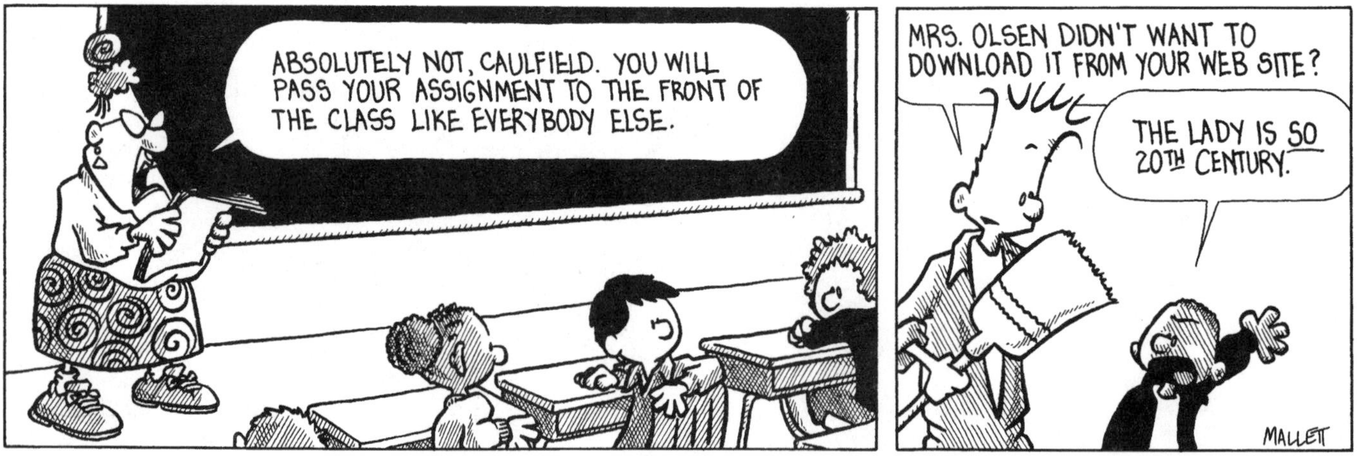
ABSOLUTELY NOT, CAULFIELD. YOU WILL PASS YOUR ASSIGNMENT TO THE FRONT OF THE CLASS LIKE EVERYBODY ELSE.
MRS. OLSEN DIDN'T WANT TO DOWNLOAD IT FROM YOUR WEB SITE?
THE LADY IS SO 20TH CENTURY.
MALLETT

Frazz — Jef Mallett

I THINK I'D LIKE SHAKESPEARE MORE IF HE DIDN'T USE SUCH WEIRD WORDS.

TRUE DAT, DAWG!

A ROSE BY ANY OTHER NAME WOULD SURELY SMELL AS SWEET.

YET FRAZZ'S HIGH-TECH MICROFIBER SOCKS STILL SMELL LIKE FEET.

WELL, NEXT TO CAULFIELD'S UNDERSHIRT THEY SMELL LIKE POTPOURRI.

AS IF! I SHOWER OFT TO URGE...

THE B.O. NOT TO BE.

MALLETT

SEE, SHAKESPEARE'S GENIUS ISN'T IN WHAT HE WROTE—IT'S IN WHAT HE INSPIRES US TO WRITE.

95

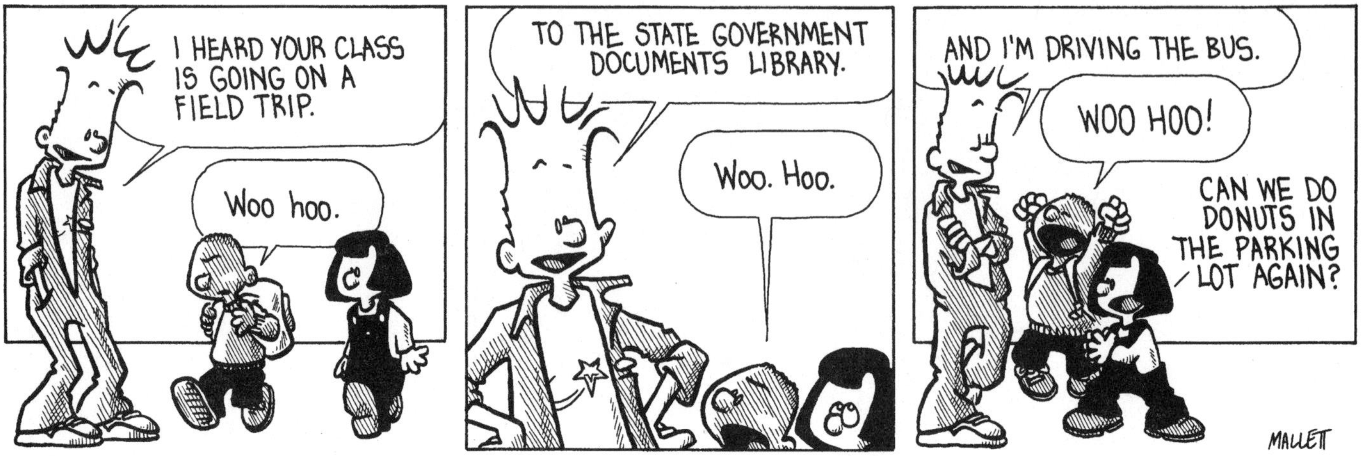
I HEARD YOUR CLASS IS GOING ON A FIELD TRIP.
Woo hoo.
TO THE STATE GOVERNMENT DOCUMENTS LIBRARY.
Woo. Hoo.
AND I'M DRIVING THE BUS.
WOO HOO!
CAN WE DO DONUTS IN THE PARKING LOT AGAIN?
MALLETT

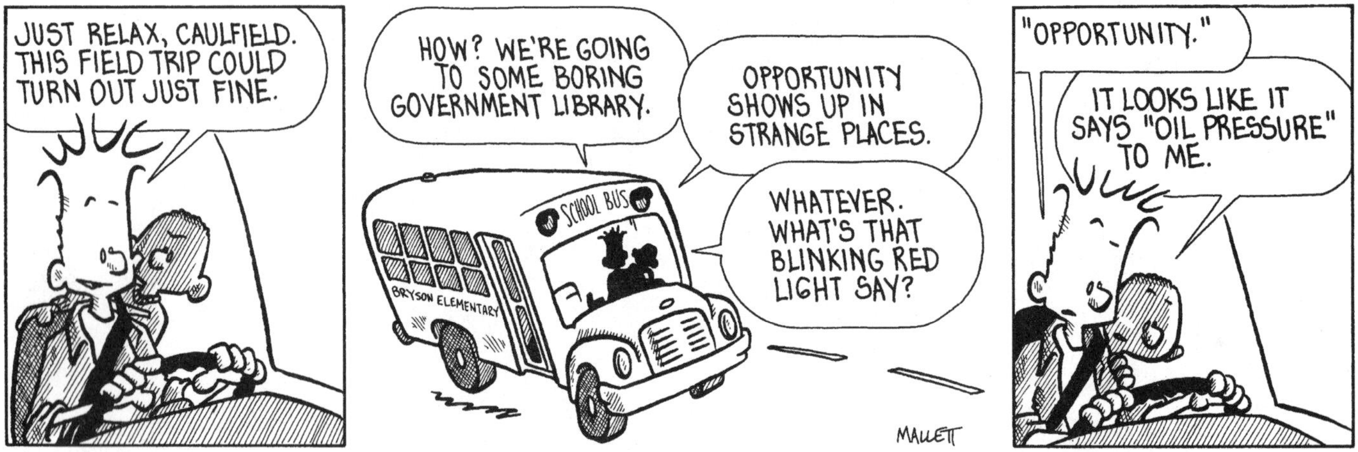
JUST RELAX, CAULFIELD. THIS FIELD TRIP COULD TURN OUT JUST FINE.
HOW? WE'RE GOING TO SOME BORING GOVERNMENT LIBRARY.
OPPORTUNITY SHOWS UP IN STRANGE PLACES.
SCHOOL BUS
BRYSON ELEMENTARY
WHATEVER. WHAT'S THAT BLINKING RED LIGHT SAY?
MALLETT
"OPPORTUNITY."
IT LOOKS LIKE IT SAYS "OIL PRESSURE" TO ME.

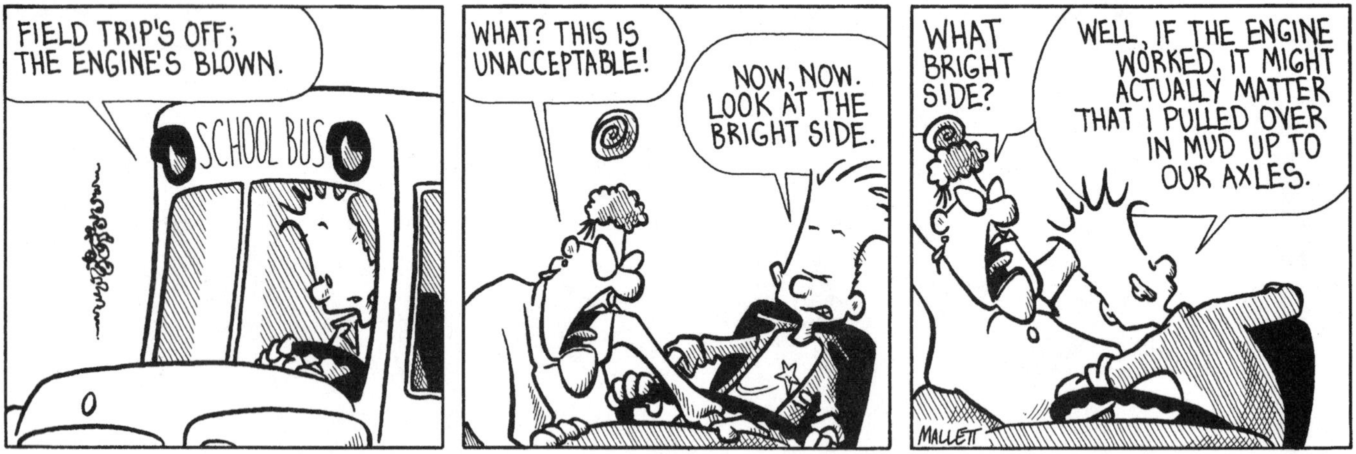
FIELD TRIP'S OFF; THE ENGINE'S BLOWN.
SCHOOL BUS
WHAT? THIS IS UNACCEPTABLE!
NOW, NOW. LOOK AT THE BRIGHT SIDE.
WHAT BRIGHT SIDE?
WELL, IF THE ENGINE WORKED, IT MIGHT ACTUALLY MATTER THAT I PULLED OVER IN MUD UP TO OUR AXLES.
MALLETT

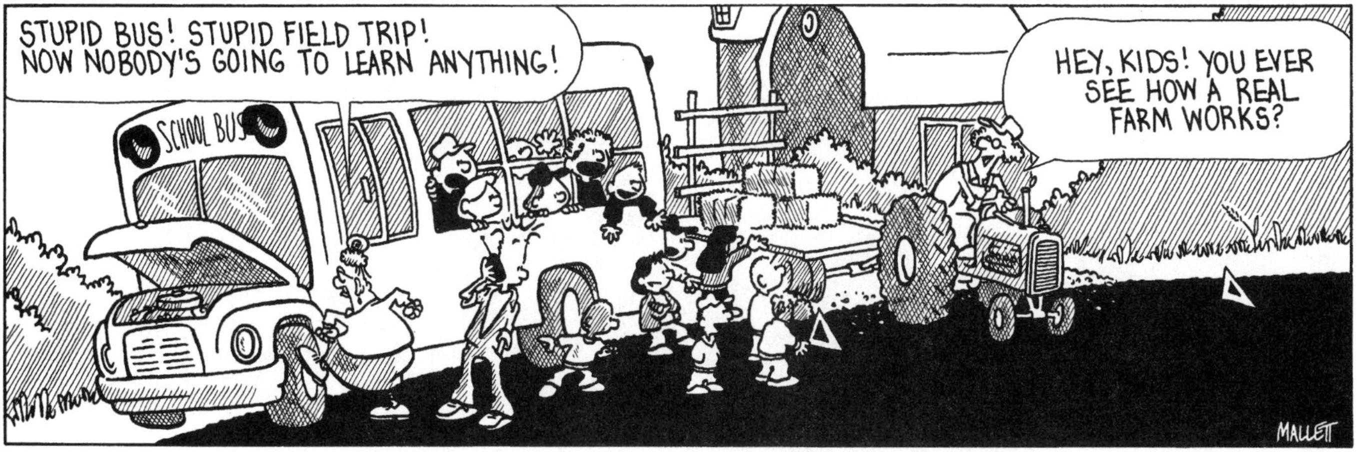
STUPID BUS! STUPID FIELD TRIP! NOW NOBODY'S GOING TO LEARN ANYTHING!
SCHOOL BUS
HEY, KIDS! YOU EVER SEE HOW A REAL FARM WORKS?
MALLETT

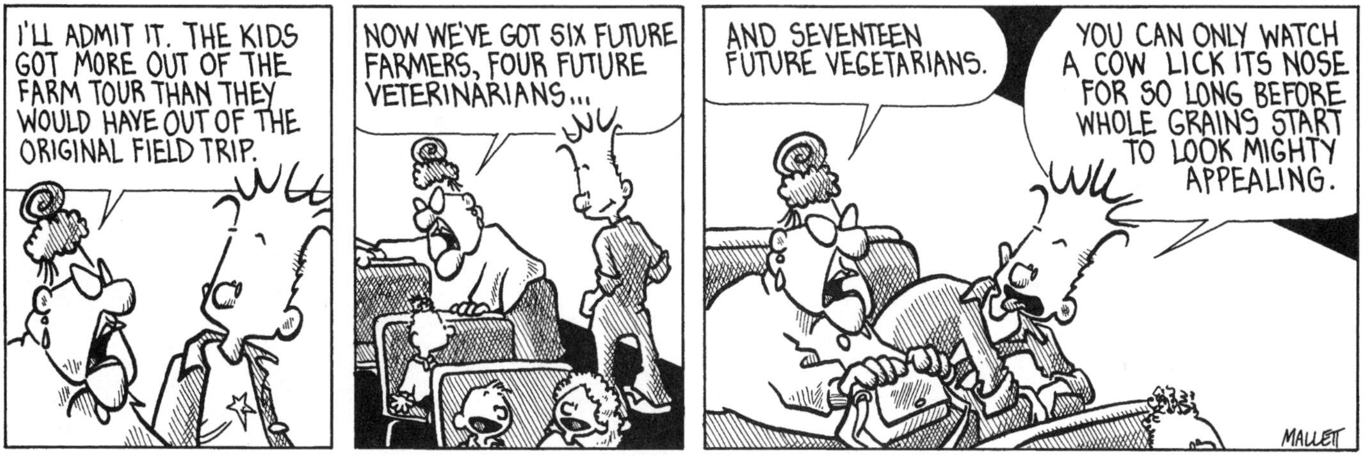
I'LL ADMIT IT. THE KIDS GOT MORE OUT OF THE FARM TOUR THAN THEY WOULD HAVE OUT OF THE ORIGINAL FIELD TRIP.
NOW WE'VE GOT SIX FUTURE FARMERS, FOUR FUTURE VETERINARIANS...
AND SEVENTEEN FUTURE VEGETARIANS.
YOU CAN ONLY WATCH A COW LICK ITS NOSE FOR SO LONG BEFORE WHOLE GRAINS START TO LOOK MIGHTY APPEALING.
MALLETT

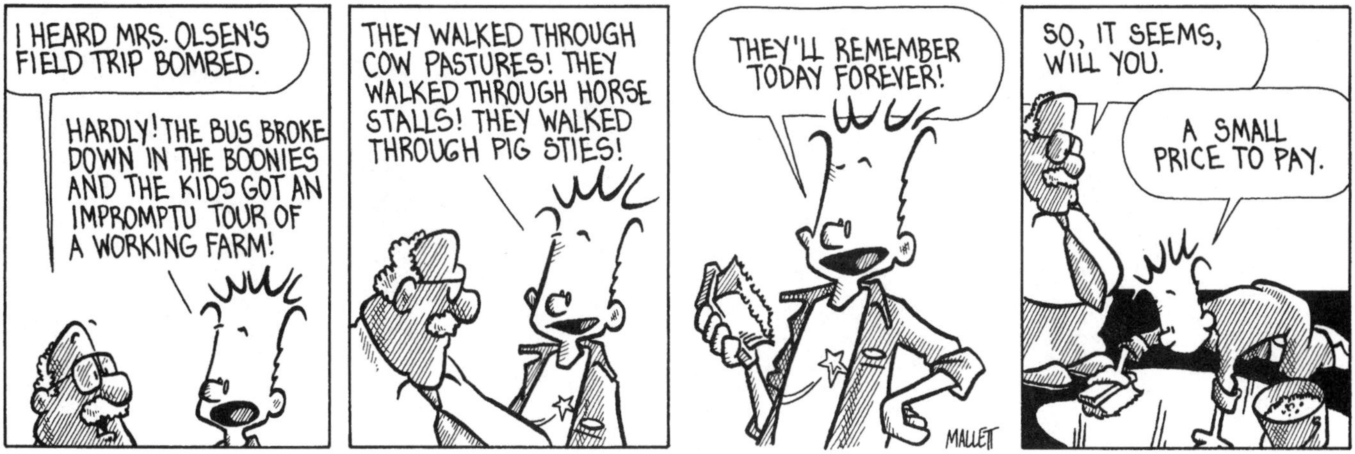
I HEARD MRS. OLSEN'S FIELD TRIP BOMBED.
HARDLY! THE BUS BROKE DOWN IN THE BOONIES AND THE KIDS GOT AN IMPROMPTU TOUR OF A WORKING FARM!
THEY WALKED THROUGH COW PASTURES! THEY WALKED THROUGH HORSE STALLS! THEY WALKED THROUGH PIG STIES!
THEY'LL REMEMBER TODAY FOREVER!
MALLETT
SO, IT SEEMS, WILL YOU.
A SMALL PRICE TO PAY.

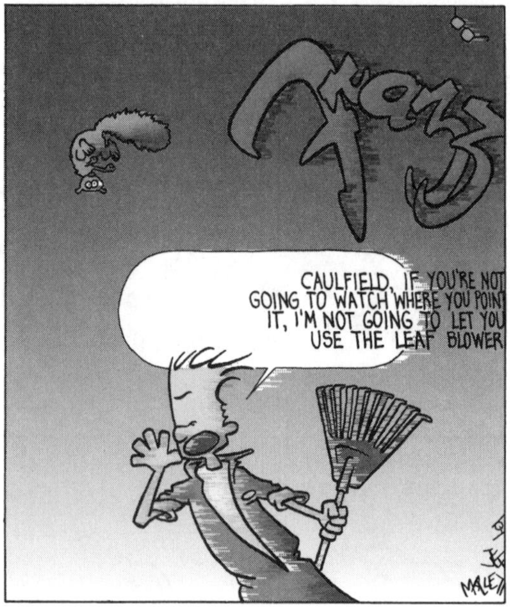
Frazz
CAULFIELD, IF YOU'RE NOT GOING TO WATCH WHERE YOU POINT IT, I'M NOT GOING TO LET YOU USE THE LEAF BLOWER.
MALLETT

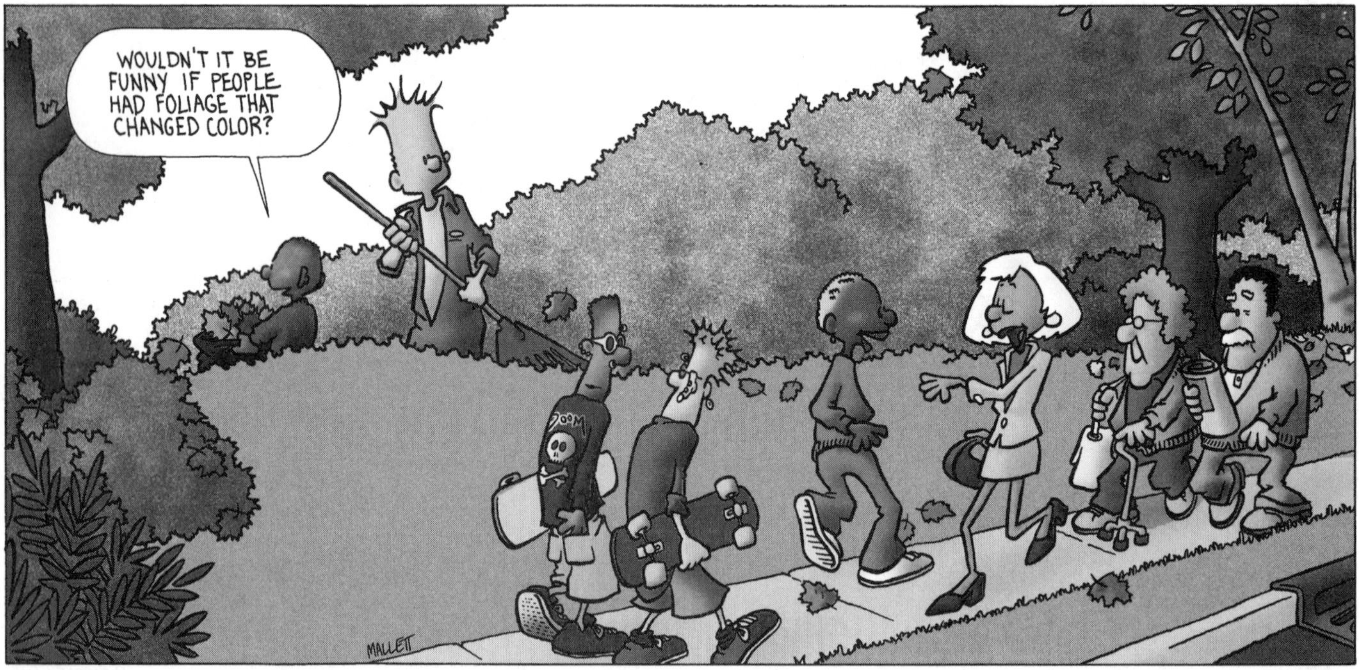
WOULDN'T IT BE FUNNY IF PEOPLE HAD FOLIAGE THAT CHANGED COLOR?
DOOM
MALLETT

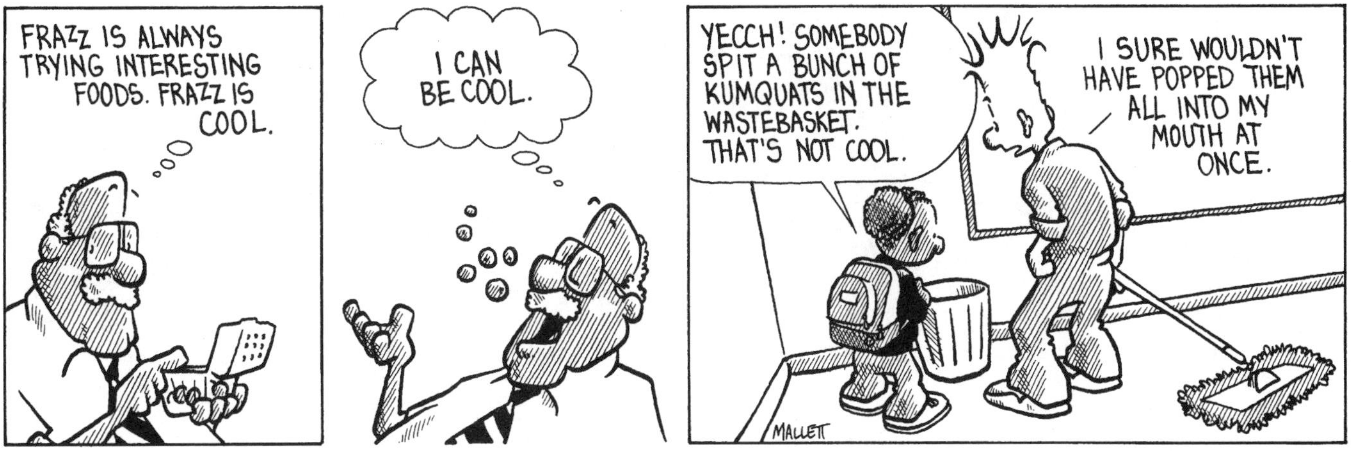
FRAZZ IS ALWAYS TRYING INTERESTING FOODS. FRAZZ IS COOL.
I CAN BE COOL.
YECCH! SOMEBODY SPIT A BUNCH OF KUMQUATS IN THE WASTEBASKET. THAT'S NOT COOL.
I SURE WOULDN'T HAVE POPPED THEM ALL INTO MY MOUTH AT ONCE.
MALLETT

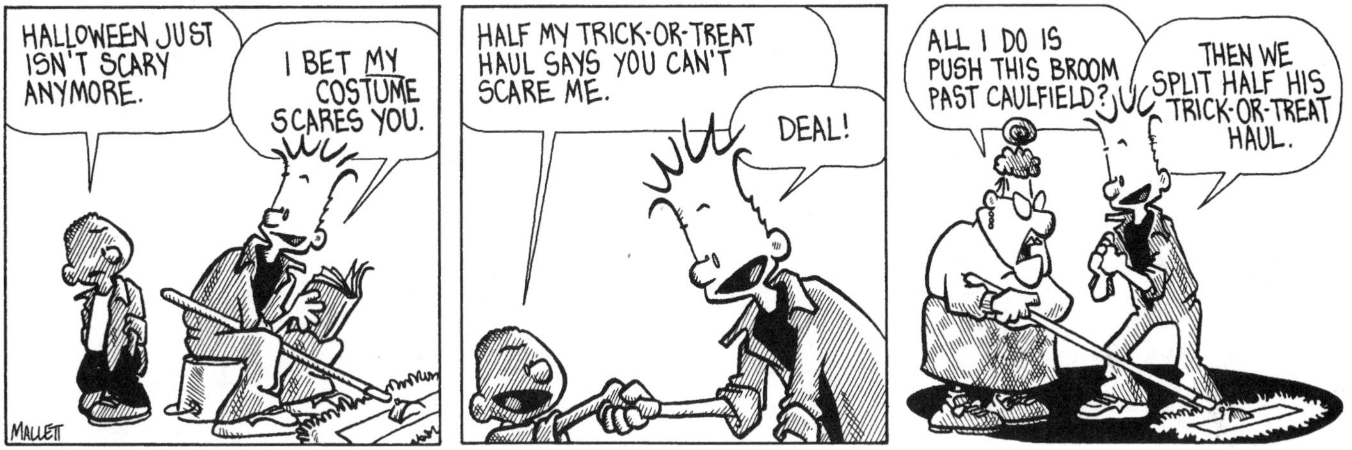
HALLOWEEN JUST ISN'T SCARY ANYMORE.
I BET MY COSTUME SCARES YOU.
HALF MY TRICK-OR-TREAT HAUL SAYS YOU CAN'T SCARE ME.
DEAL!
ALL I DO IS PUSH THIS BROOM PAST CAULFIELD?
THEN WE SPLIT HALF HIS TRICK-OR-TREAT HAUL.
MALLETT

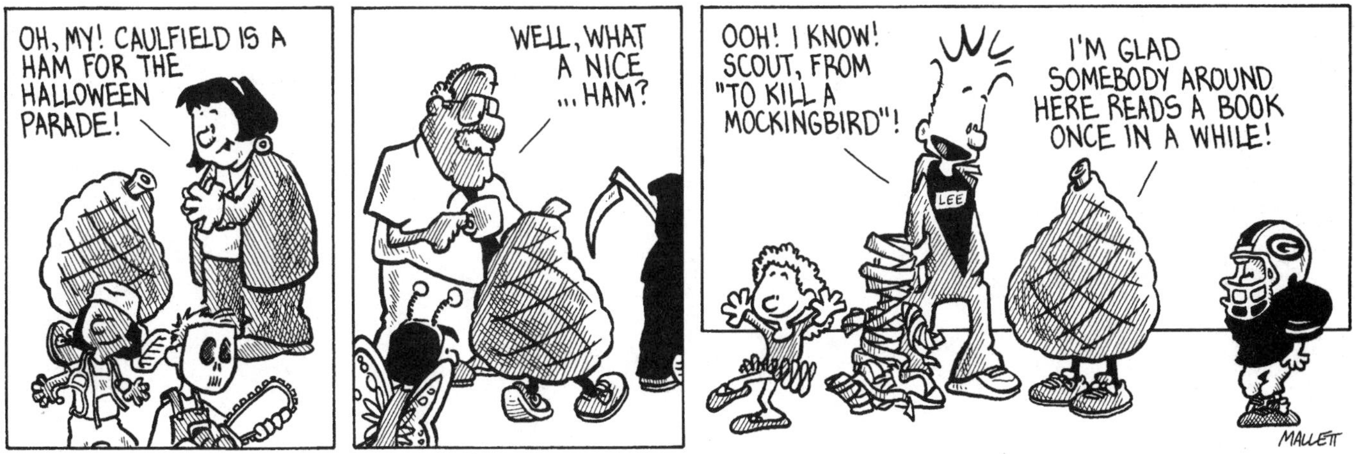
OH, MY! CAULFIELD IS A HAM FOR THE HALLOWEEN PARADE!
WELL, WHAT A NICE ...HAM?
OOH! I KNOW! SCOUT, FROM "TO KILL A MOCKINGBIRD"!
I'M GLAD SOMEBODY AROUND HERE READS A BOOK ONCE IN A WHILE!
LEE
MALLETT

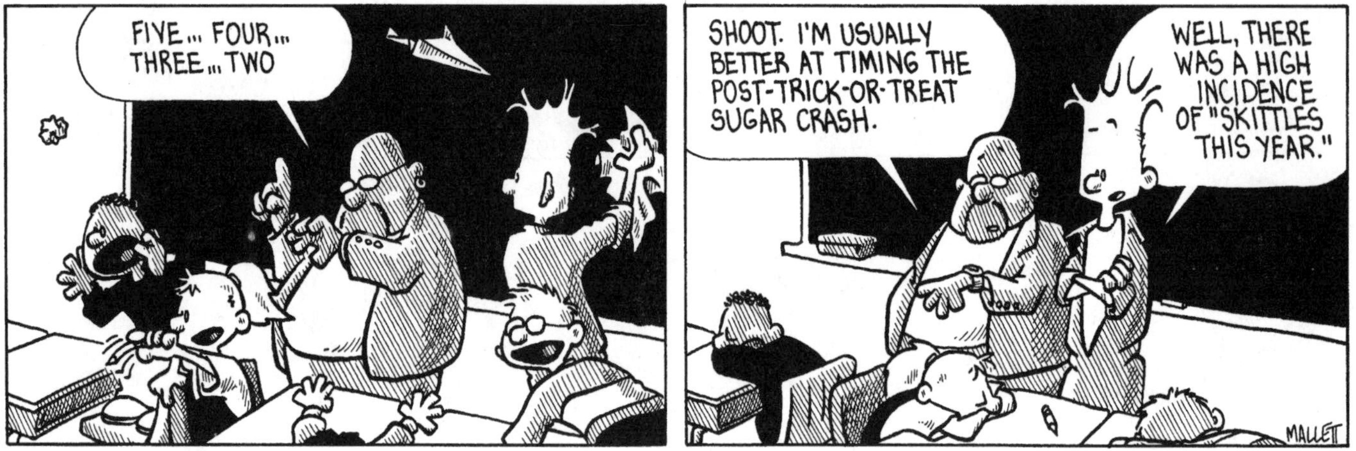
FIVE... FOUR... THREE... TWO
SHOOT. I'M USUALLY BETTER AT TIMING THE POST-TRICK-OR-TREAT SUGAR CRASH.
WELL, THERE WAS A HIGH INCIDENCE OF "SKITTLES THIS YEAR."
MALLETT

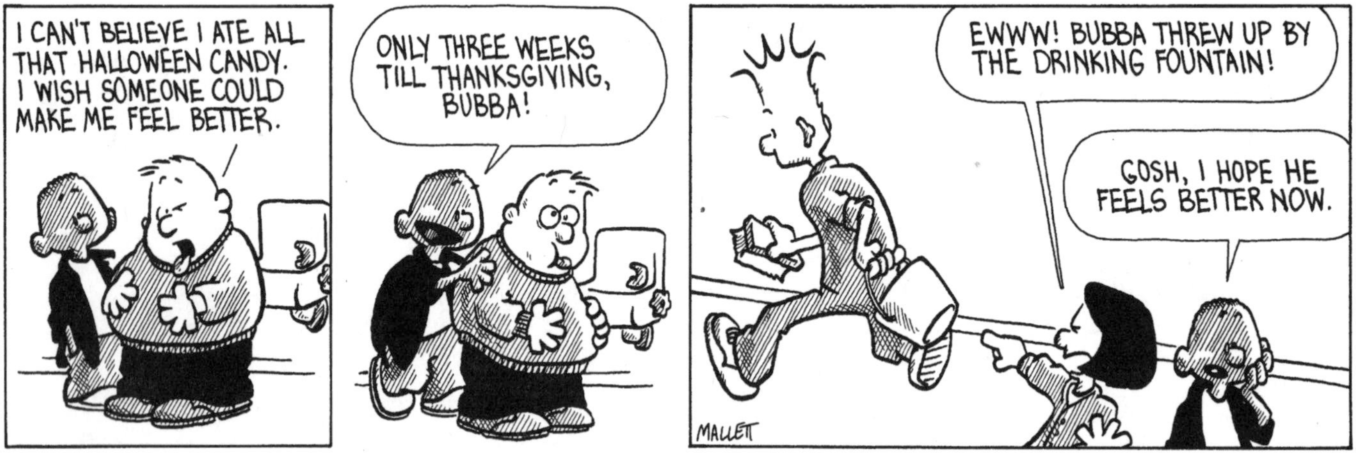
I CAN'T BELIEVE I ATE ALL THAT HALLOWEEN CANDY. I WISH SOMEONE COULD MAKE ME FEEL BETTER.
ONLY THREE WEEKS TILL THANKSGIVING, BUBBA!
EWWW! BUBBA THREW UP BY THE DRINKING FOUNTAIN!
GOSH, I HOPE HE FEELS BETTER NOW.
MALLETT

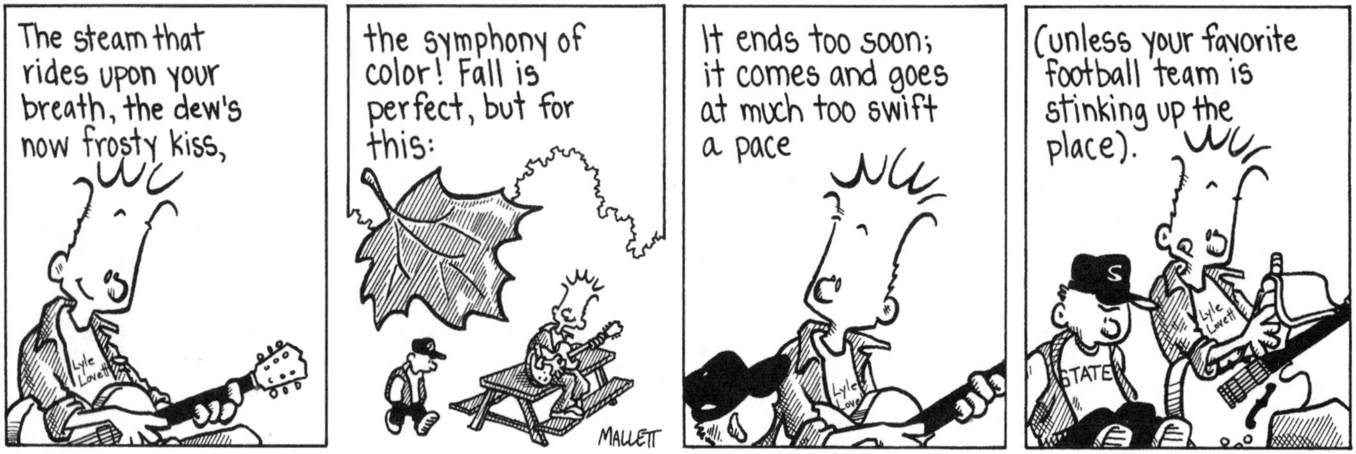
The steam that rides upon your breath, the dew's now frosty kiss,
Lyle Lovett
the symphony of color! Fall is perfect, but for this:
MALLETT
It ends too soon; it comes and goes at much too swift a pace
(unless your favorite football team is stinking up the place).
S
STATE
Lyle Lovett

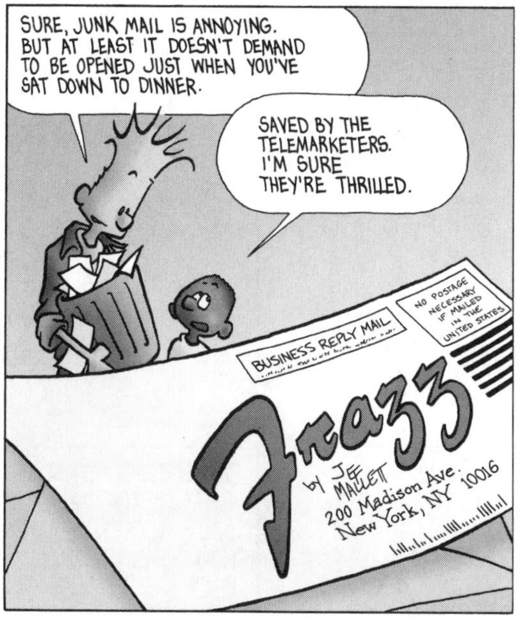
SURE, JUNK MAIL IS ANNOYING. BUT AT LEAST IT DOESN'T DEMAND TO BE OPENED JUST WHEN YOU'VE SAT DOWN TO DINNER.
SAVED BY THE TELEMARKETERS. I'M SURE THEY'RE THRILLED.
BUSINESS REPLY MAIL
NO POSTAGE NECESSARY IF MAILED IN THE UNITED STATES
Frazz
by JEF MALLETT
200 Madison Ave.
New York, NY 10016

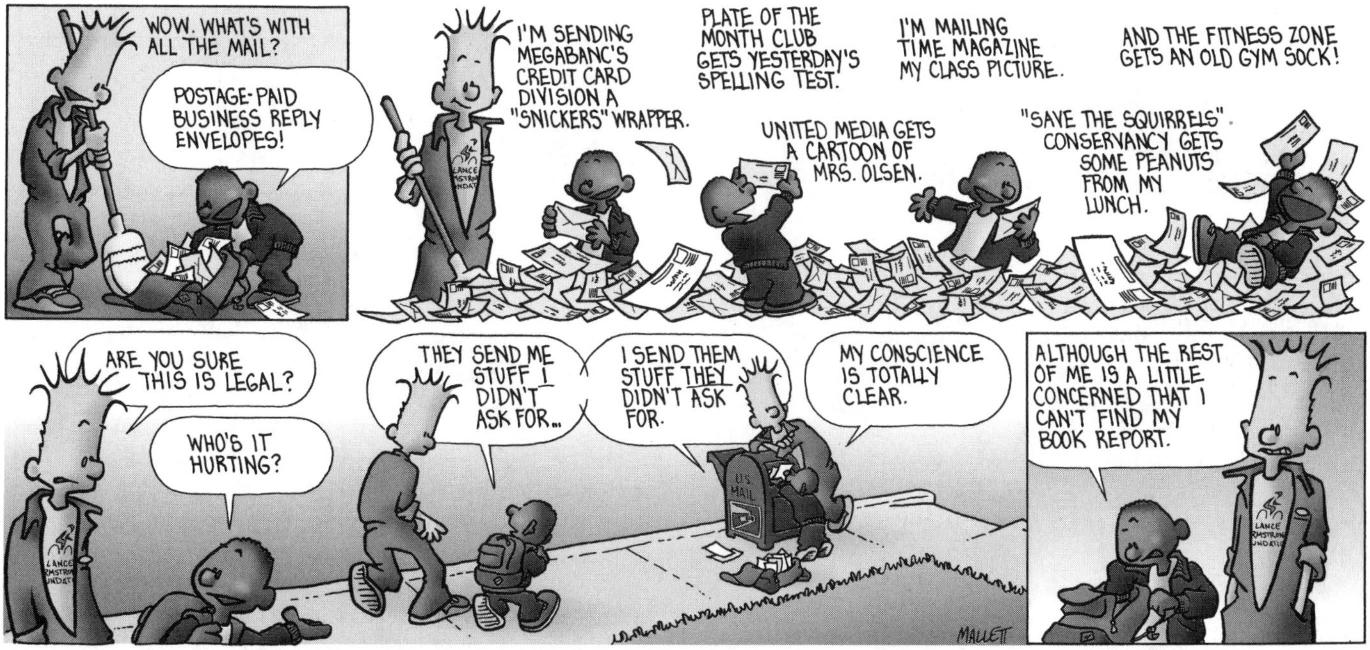
WOW. WHAT'S WITH ALL THE MAIL?
POSTAGE-PAID BUSINESS REPLY ENVELOPES!
I'M SENDING MEGABANC'S CREDIT CARD DIVISION A "SNICKERS" WRAPPER.
PLATE OF THE MONTH CLUB GETS YESTERDAY'S SPELLING TEST.
UNITED MEDIA GETS A CARTOON OF MRS. OLSEN.
I'M MAILING TIME MAGAZINE MY CLASS PICTURE.
"SAVE THE SQUIRRELS" CONSERVANCY GETS SOME PEANUTS FROM MY LUNCH.
AND THE FITNESS ZONE GETS AN OLD GYM SOCK!
ARE YOU SURE THIS IS LEGAL?
WHO'S IT HURTING?
THEY SEND ME STUFF I DIDN'T ASK FOR...
I SEND THEM STUFF THEY DIDN'T ASK FOR.
MY CONSCIENCE IS TOTALLY CLEAR.
ALTHOUGH THE REST OF ME IS A LITTLE CONCERNED THAT I CAN'T FIND MY BOOK REPORT.
U.S. MAIL
MALLETT

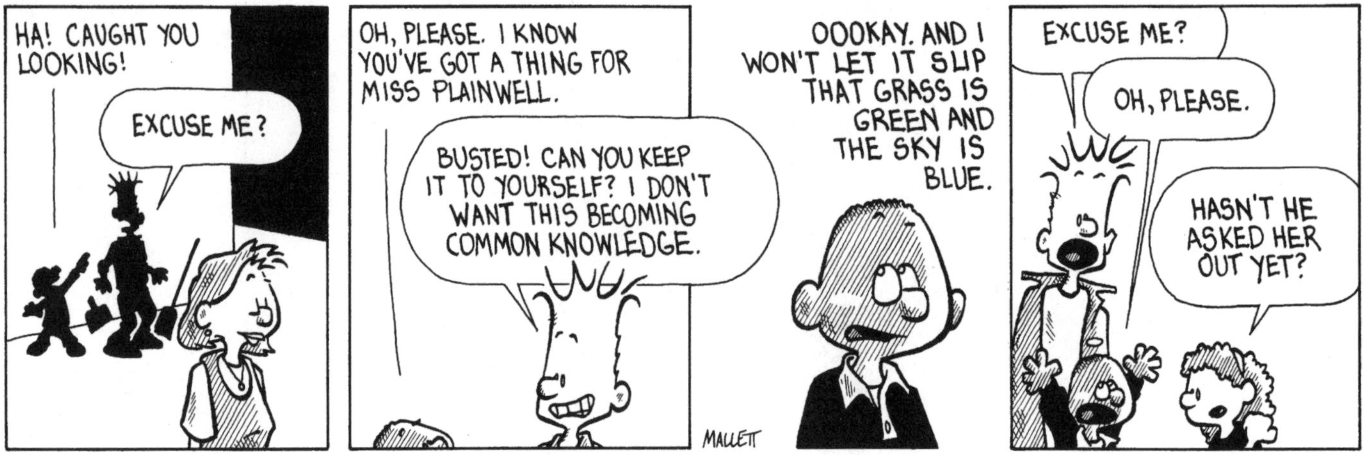
HA! CAUGHT YOU LOOKING!
EXCUSE ME?
OH, PLEASE. I KNOW YOU'VE GOT A THING FOR MISS PLAINWELL.
BUSTED! CAN YOU KEEP IT TO YOURSELF? I DON'T WANT THIS BECOMING COMMON KNOWLEDGE.
OOOKAY. AND I WON'T LET IT SLIP THAT GRASS IS GREEN AND THE SKY IS BLUE.
MALLETT
EXCUSE ME?
OH, PLEASE.
HASN'T HE ASKED HER OUT YET?

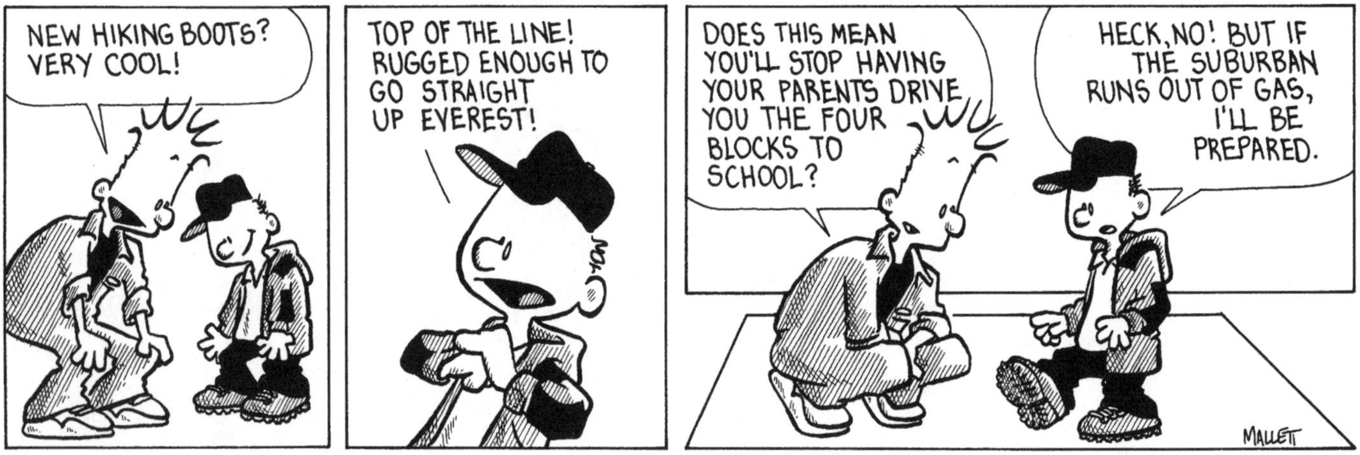
NEW HIKING BOOTS? VERY COOL!
TOP OF THE LINE! RUGGED ENOUGH TO GO STRAIGHT UP EVEREST!
DOES THIS MEAN YOU'LL STOP HAVING YOUR PARENTS DRIVE YOU THE FOUR BLOCKS TO SCHOOL?
HECK, NO! BUT IF THE SUBURBAN RUNS OUT OF GAS, I'LL BE PREPARED.
MALLETT

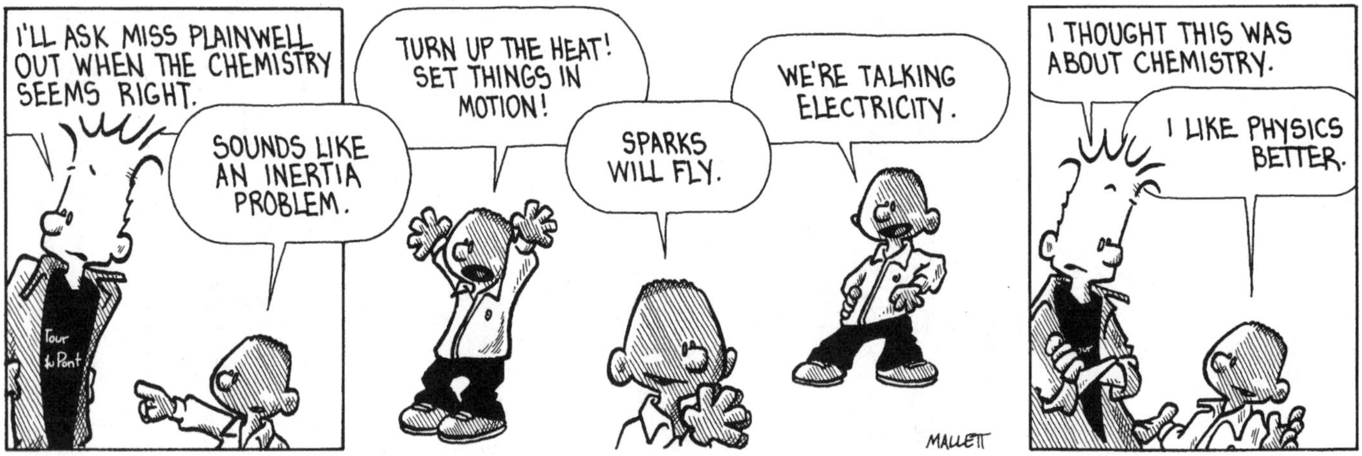
I'LL ASK MISS PLAINWELL OUT WHEN THE CHEMISTRY SEEMS RIGHT.
SOUNDS LIKE AN INERTIA PROBLEM.
TURN UP THE HEAT! SET THINGS IN MOTION!
SPARKS WILL FLY.
WE'RE TALKING ELECTRICITY.
MALLETT
I THOUGHT THIS WAS ABOUT CHEMISTRY.
I LIKE PHYSICS BETTER.

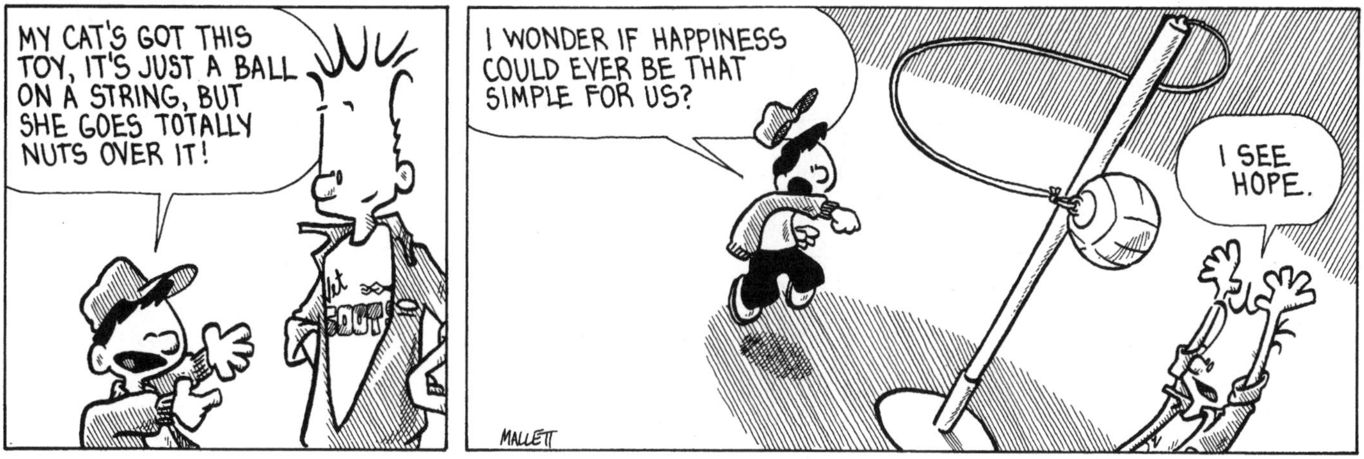
MY CAT'S GOT THIS TOY, IT'S JUST A BALL ON A STRING, BUT SHE GOES TOTALLY NUTS OVER IT!
I WONDER IF HAPPINESS COULD EVER BE THAT SIMPLE FOR US?
I SEE HOPE.
MALLETT

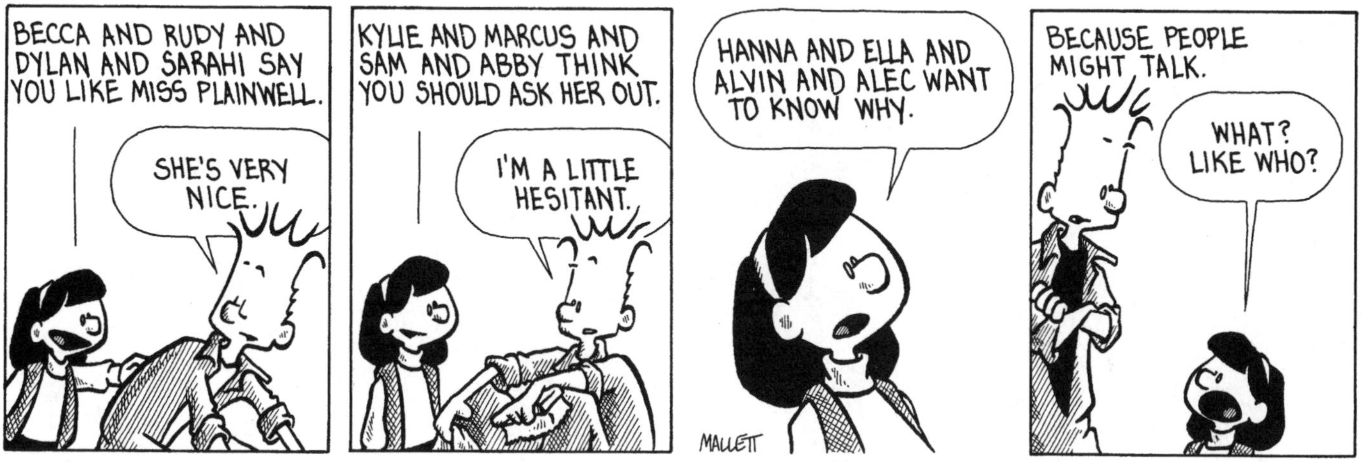
BECCA AND RUDY AND DYLAN AND SARAHI SAY YOU LIKE MISS PLAINWELL.
SHE'S VERY NICE.
KYLIE AND MARCUS AND SAM AND ABBY THINK YOU SHOULD ASK HER OUT.
I'M A LITTLE HESITANT.
HANNA AND ELLA AND ALVIN AND ALEC WANT TO KNOW WHY.
MALLETT
BECAUSE PEOPLE MIGHT TALK.
WHAT? LIKE WHO?

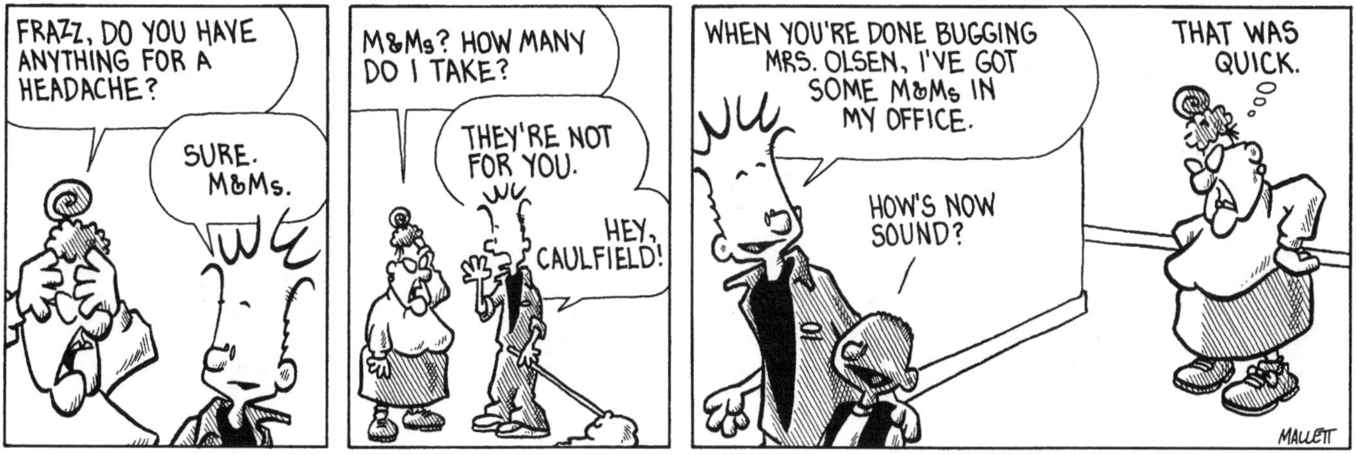
FRAZZ, DO YOU HAVE ANYTHING FOR A HEADACHE?
SURE. M&Ms.
M&Ms? HOW MANY DO I TAKE?
THEY'RE NOT FOR YOU.
HEY, CAULFIELD!
WHEN YOU'RE DONE BUGGING MRS. OLSEN, I'VE GOT SOME M&Ms IN MY OFFICE.
HOW'S NOW SOUND?
THAT WAS QUICK.
MALLETT

FRAZZ
by JEF MALLETT
IF WE'RE SERIOUS ABOUT VETERANS DAY, WHY DON'T WE GIVE VETERANS THE DAY OFF?
MAYBE WE'LL LEARN STUFF LIKE THAT IN SECOND GRADE.

HEY, FRAZZ! I WANT YOU TO MEET MY UNCLE LAZLO!
UNCLE LAZLO WAS AN INFANTRY SERGEANT IN VIETNAM!
REALLY? WOW. I CAN'T EVEN BEGIN TO IMAGINE WHAT YOU WENT THROUGH ON MY BEHALF!
I'M HUMBLED.
I'M GRATEFUL.
AND I'M VERY PROUD TO MEET Y...
OH, GEEZ.
I'M SORRY. DOES THAT HAPPEN A LOT?
NOT NEARLY ENOUGH, MY FRIEND. NOT NEARLY ENOUGH.
MALLETT

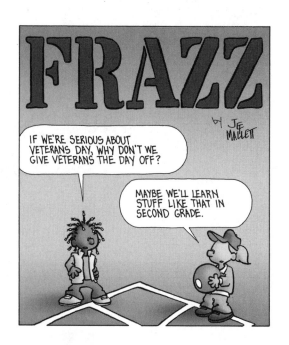

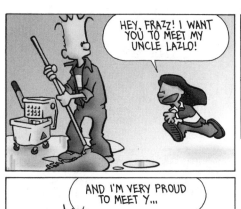

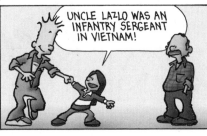

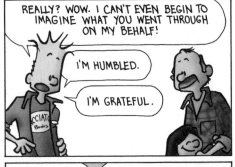

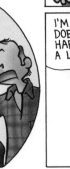

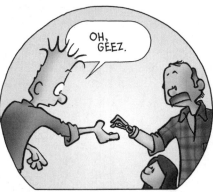

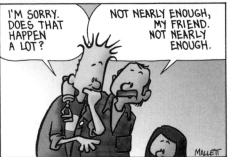

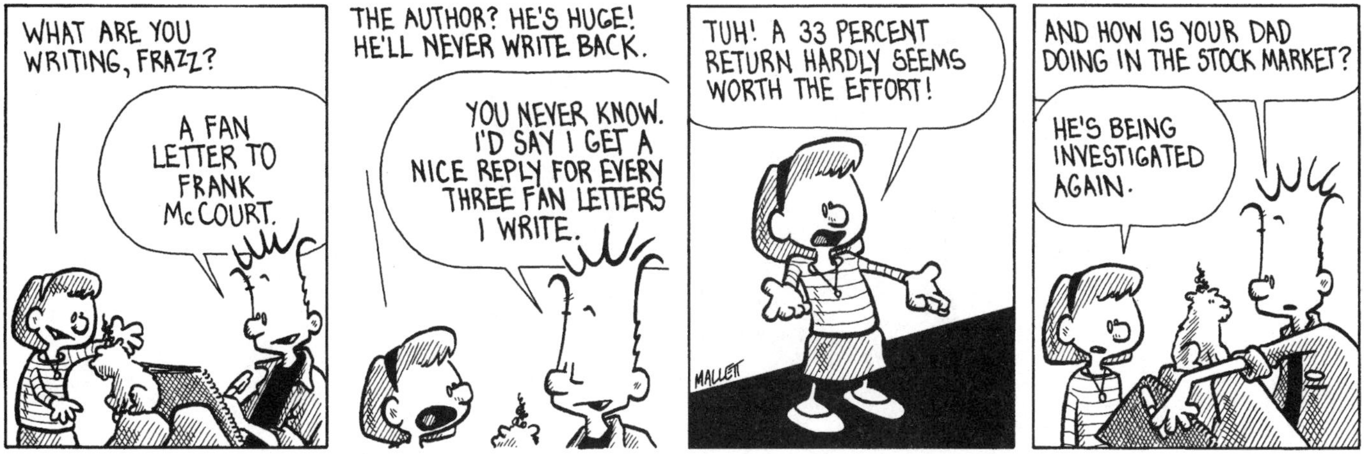
WHAT ARE YOU WRITING, FRAZZ?
A FAN LETTER TO FRANK McCOURT.
THE AUTHOR? HE'S HUGE! HE'LL NEVER WRITE BACK.
YOU NEVER KNOW. I'D SAY I GET A NICE REPLY FOR EVERY THREE FAN LETTERS I WRITE.
TUH! A 33 PERCENT RETURN HARDLY SEEMS WORTH THE EFFORT!
MALLETT
AND HOW IS YOUR DAD DOING IN THE STOCK MARKET?
HE'S BEING INVESTIGATED AGAIN.

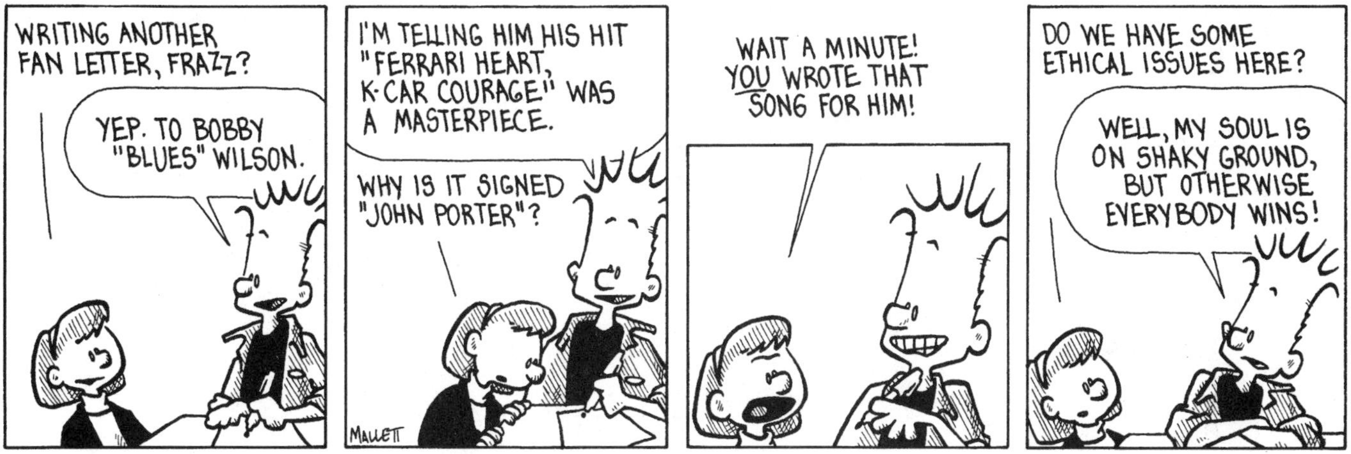
WRITING ANOTHER FAN LETTER, FRAZZ?
YEP. TO BOBBY "BLUES" WILSON.
I'M TELLING HIM HIS HIT "FERRARI HEART, K-CAR COURAGE" WAS A MASTERPIECE.
WHY IS IT SIGNED "JOHN PORTER"?
MALLETT
WAIT A MINUTE! YOU WROTE THAT SONG FOR HIM!
DO WE HAVE SOME ETHICAL ISSUES HERE?
WELL, MY SOUL IS ON SHAKY GROUND, BUT OTHERWISE EVERYBODY WINS!

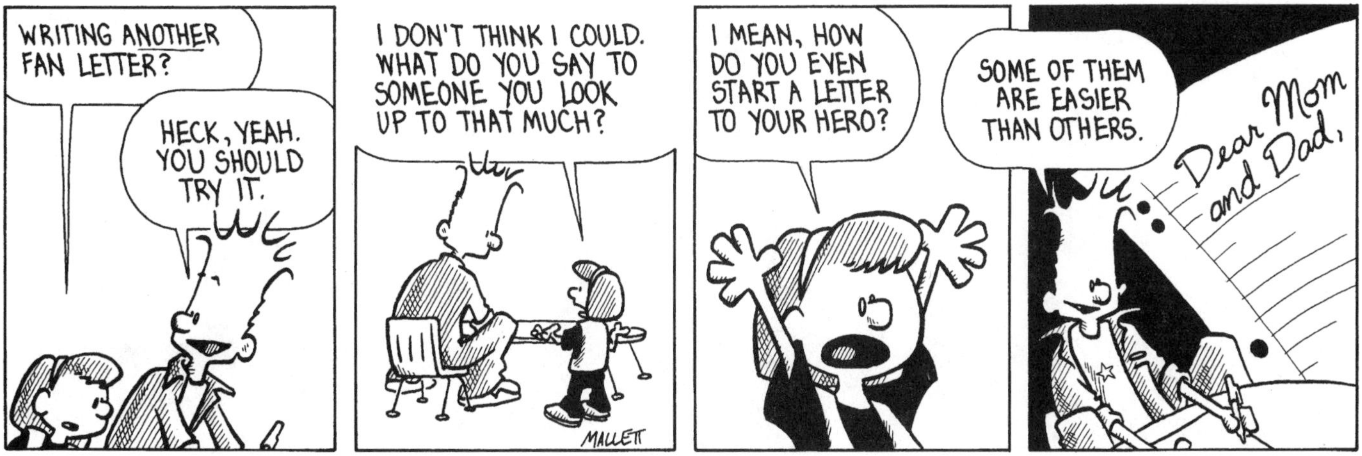
WRITING ANOTHER FAN LETTER?
HECK, YEAH. YOU SHOULD TRY IT.
I DON'T THINK I COULD. WHAT DO YOU SAY TO SOMEONE YOU LOOK UP TO THAT MUCH?
MALLETT
I MEAN, HOW DO YOU EVEN START A LETTER TO YOUR HERO?
SOME OF THEM ARE EASIER THAN OTHERS.
Dear Mom and Dad,

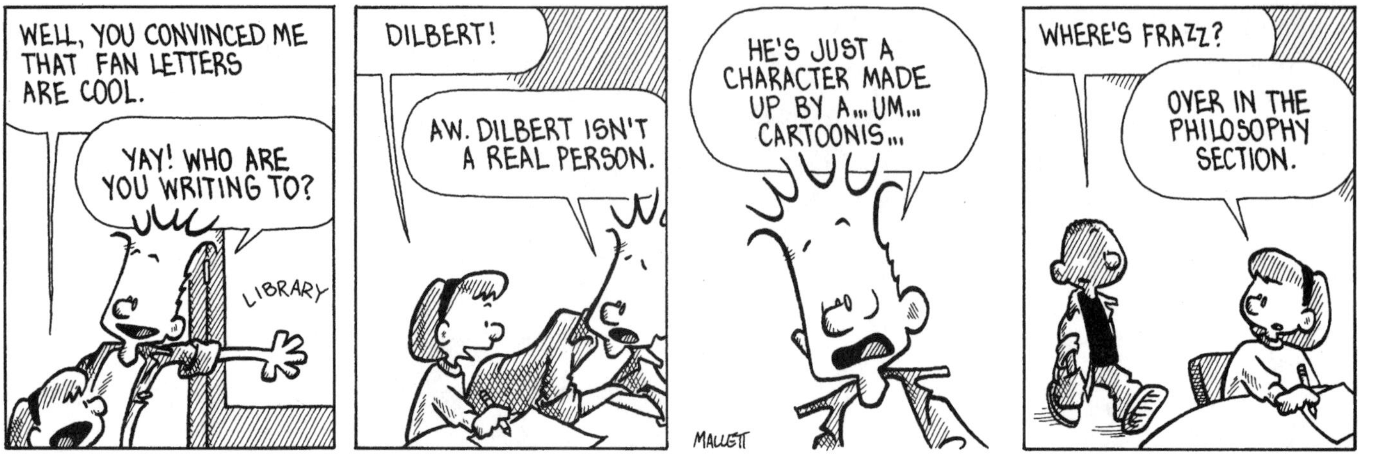
WELL, YOU CONVINCED ME THAT FAN LETTERS ARE COOL.
YAY! WHO ARE YOU WRITING TO?
LIBRARY
DILBERT!
AW. DILBERT ISN'T A REAL PERSON.
HE'S JUST A CHARACTER MADE UP BY A... UM... CARTOONIS...
MALLETT
WHERE'S FRAZZ?
OVER IN THE PHILOSOPHY SECTION.

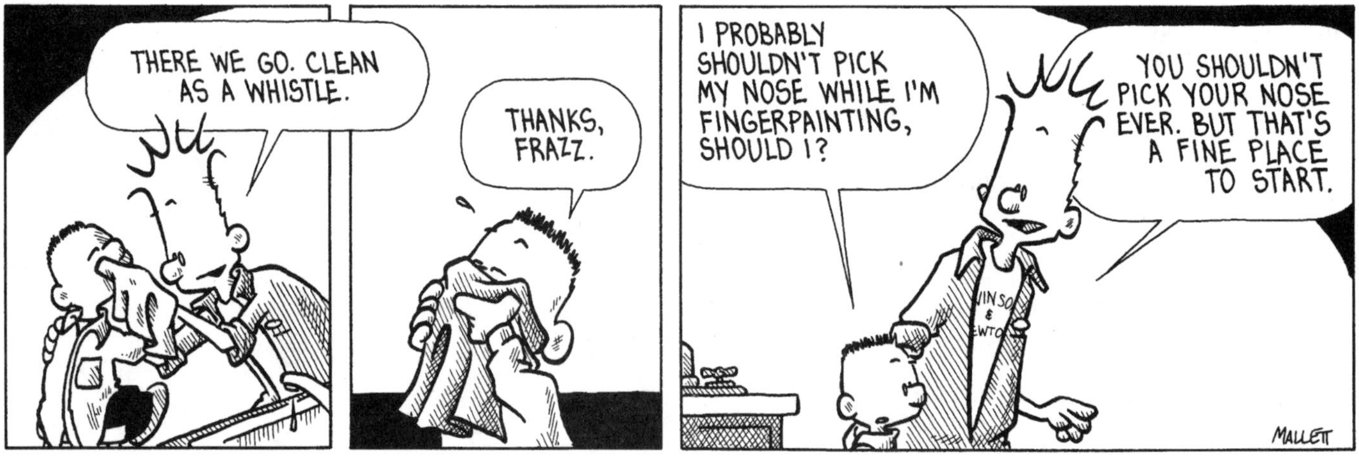
THERE WE GO. CLEAN AS A WHISTLE.
THANKS, FRAZZ.
I PROBABLY SHOULDN'T PICK MY NOSE WHILE I'M FINGERPAINTING, SHOULD I?
YOU SHOULDN'T PICK YOUR NOSE EVER. BUT THAT'S A FINE PLACE TO START.
MALLETT

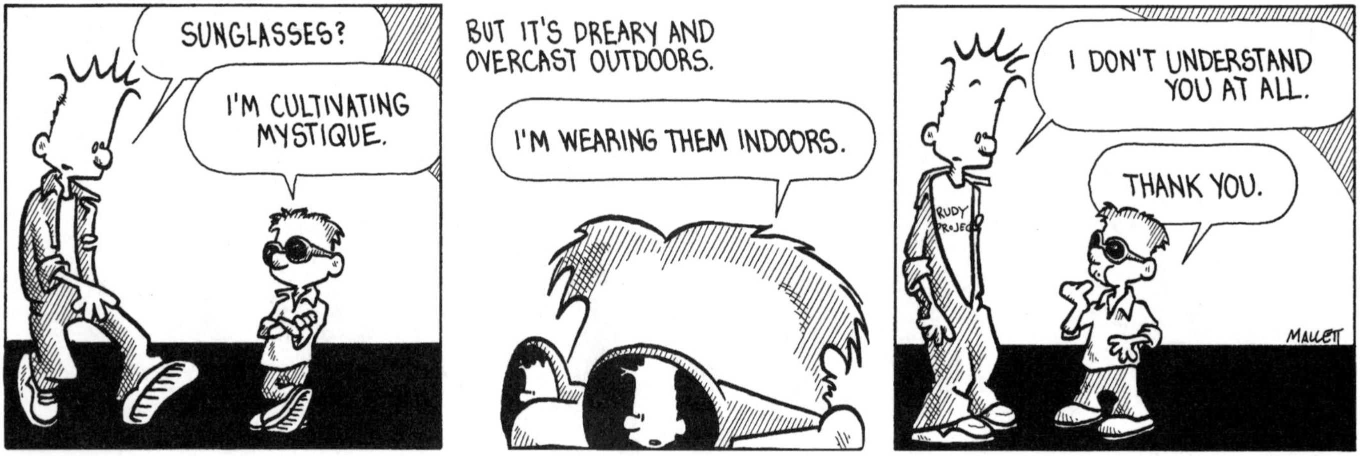
SUNGLASSES?
I'M CULTIVATING MYSTIQUE.
BUT IT'S DREARY AND OVERCAST OUTDOORS.
I'M WEARING THEM INDOORS.
I DON'T UNDERSTAND YOU AT ALL.
THANK YOU.
MALLETT

JEF MALLETT
z
zz
azz
razz
raz

©2001 Jef Mallett/Distributed by United Feature Syndicate, Inc.
SO IN THE SPRING, HOW DO SQUIRRELS FIND THE NUTS THEY BURIED IN THE FALL?
THEY DON'T.
WHAT? NO WAY!
WAY.
THEIR INSTINCT IS TO BURY IN THE FALL AND DIG IN THE SPRING, AND WITH ENOUGH SQUIRRELS INVOLVED, IT ALL WORKS OUT. BUT IF THEY FIND THEIR OWN STASH, IT'S PURELY BY ACCIDENT.
I'M NOT CONVINCED AN ANIMAL THAT DISORGANIZED COULD SURVIVE.
IT'S IN A BOOK IN MY OFFICE. COME ON.
MALLETT
OR MAYBE IT'S AT HOME.
DON'T WORRY. I'M CONVINCED.

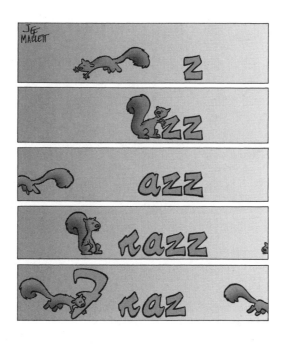

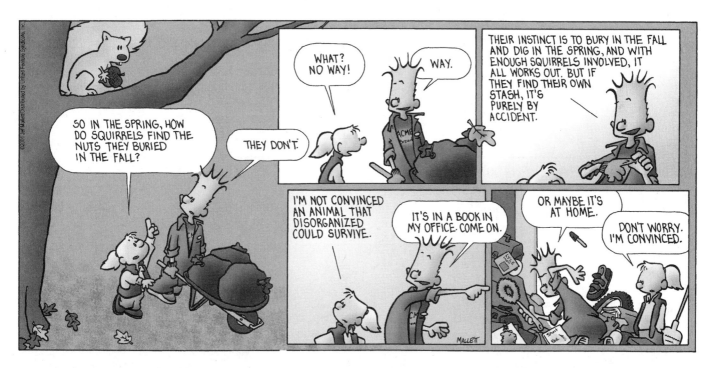

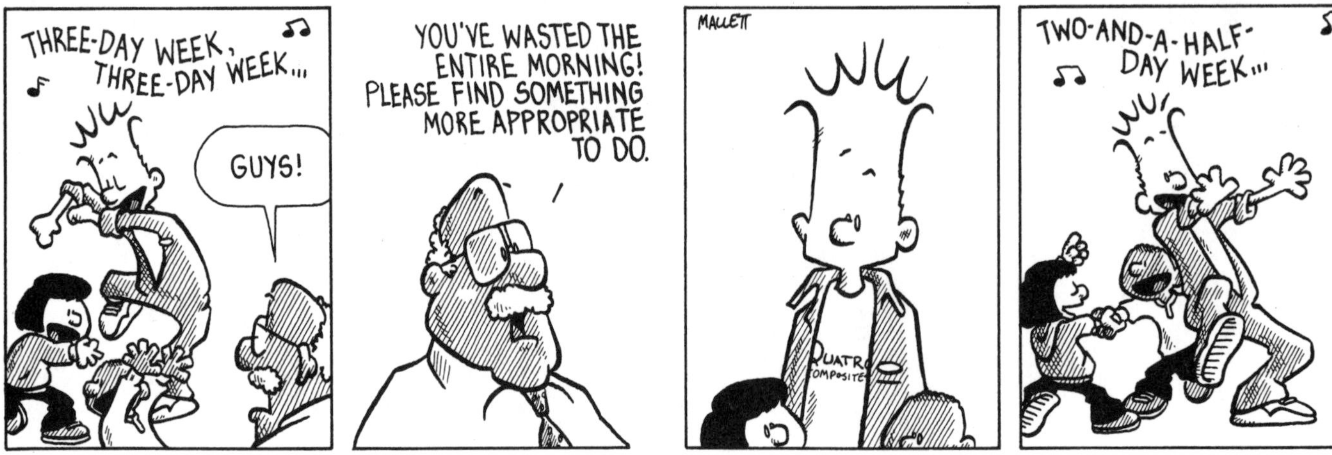
THREE-DAY WEEK, THREE-DAY WEEK...
GUYS!
YOU'VE WASTED THE ENTIRE MORNING! PLEASE FIND SOMETHING MORE APPROPRIATE TO DO.
MALLETT
TWO-AND-A-HALF-DAY WEEK...

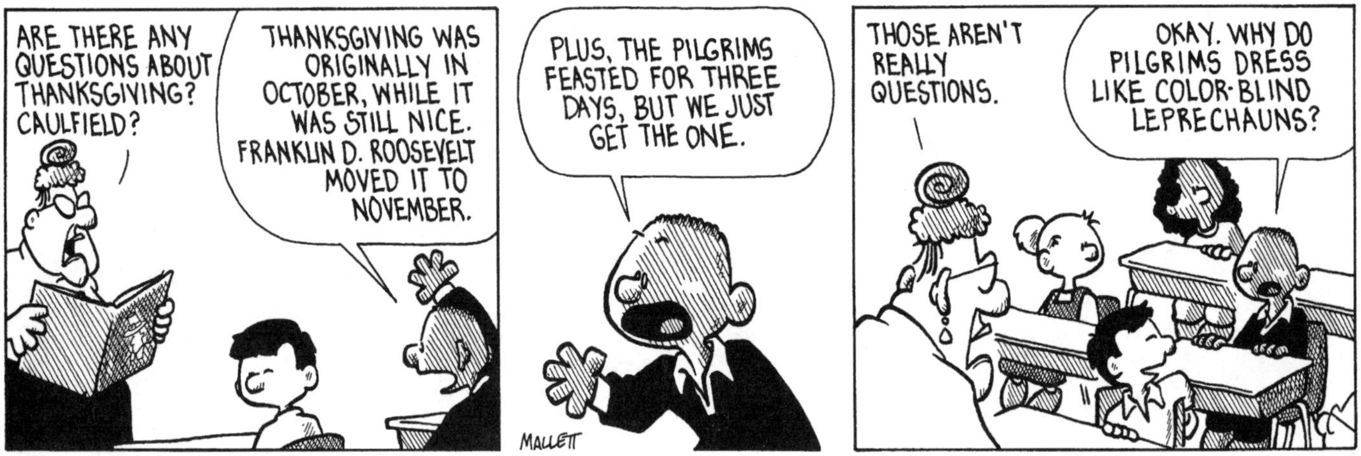
ARE THERE ANY QUESTIONS ABOUT THANKSGIVING? CAULFIELD?
THANKSGIVING WAS ORIGINALLY IN OCTOBER, WHILE IT WAS STILL NICE. FRANKLIN D. ROOSEVELT MOVED IT TO NOVEMBER.
PLUS, THE PILGRIMS FEASTED FOR THREE DAYS, BUT WE JUST GET THE ONE.
MALLETT
THOSE AREN'T REALLY QUESTIONS.
OKAY. WHY DO PILGRIMS DRESS LIKE COLOR-BLIND LEPRECHAUNS?

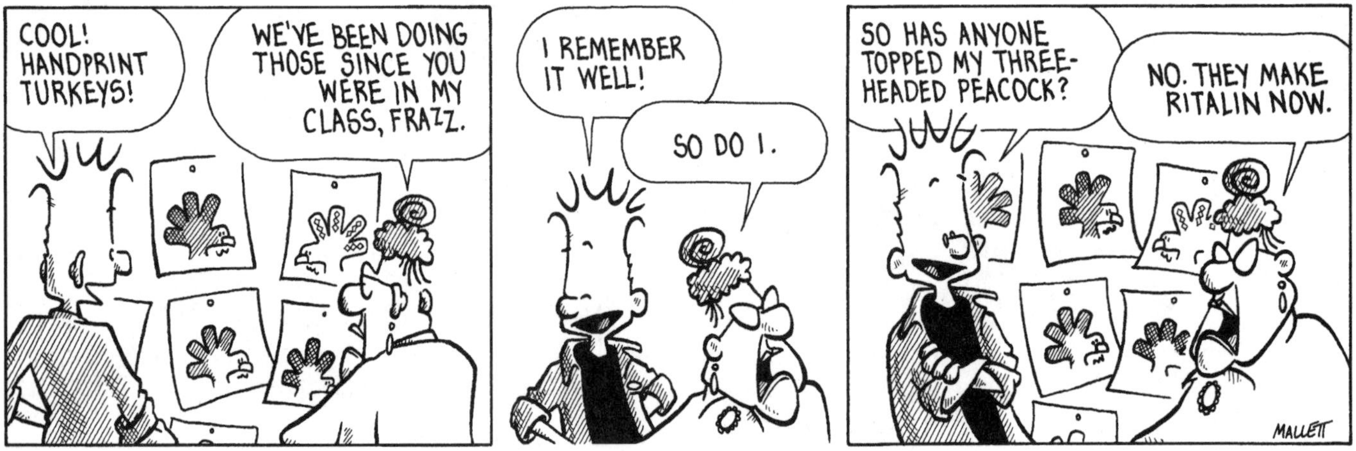
COOL! HANDPRINT TURKEYS!
WE'VE BEEN DOING THOSE SINCE YOU WERE IN MY CLASS, FRAZZ.
I REMEMBER IT WELL!
SO DO I.
SO HAS ANYONE TOPPED MY THREE-HEADED PEACOCK?
NO. THEY MAKE RITALIN NOW.
MALLETT

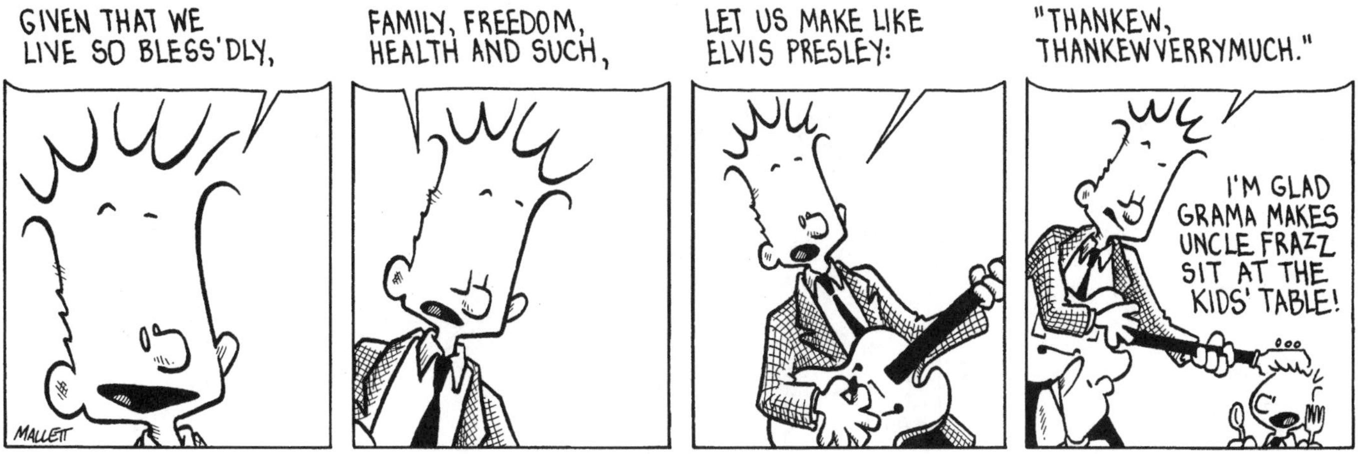
GIVEN THAT WE LIVE SO BLESS'DLY,
FAMILY, FREEDOM, HEALTH AND SUCH,
LET US MAKE LIKE ELVIS PRESLEY:
"THANKEW, THANKEWVERRYMUCH."
I'M GLAD GRAMA MAKES UNCLE FRAZZ SIT AT THE KIDS' TABLE!
MALLETT

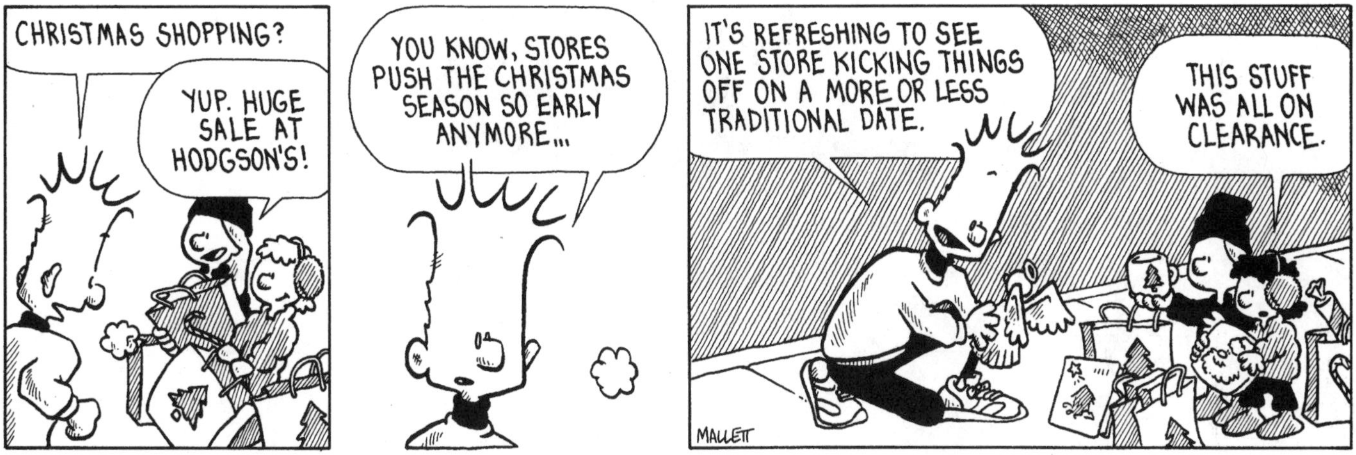
CHRISTMAS SHOPPING?
YUP. HUGE SALE AT HODGSON'S!
YOU KNOW, STORES PUSH THE CHRISTMAS SEASON SO EARLY ANYMORE...
IT'S REFRESHING TO SEE ONE STORE KICKING THINGS OFF ON A MORE OR LESS TRADITIONAL DATE.
THIS STUFF WAS ALL ON CLEARANCE.
MALLETT

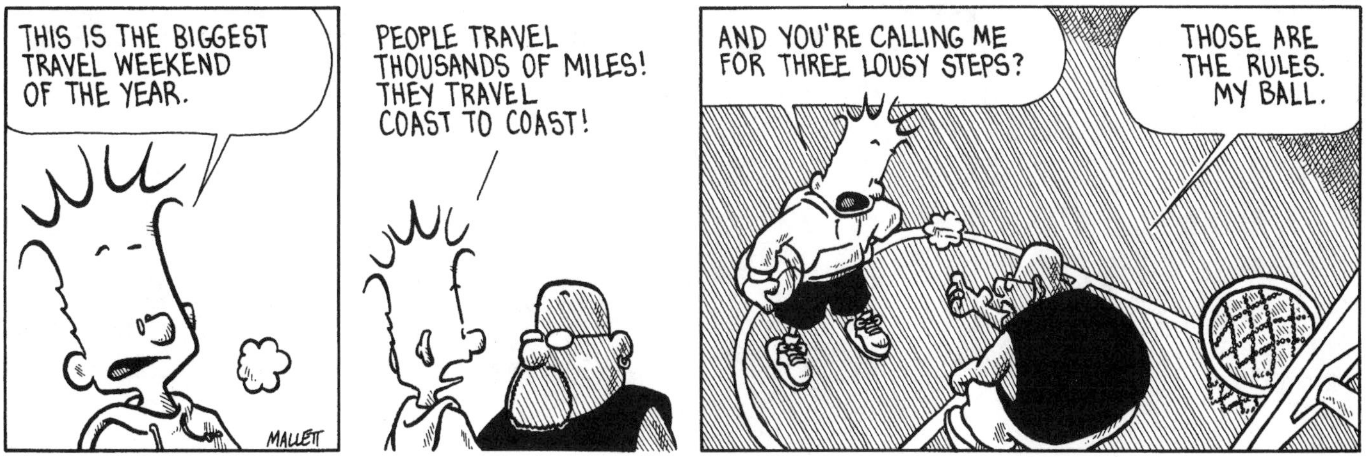
THIS IS THE BIGGEST TRAVEL WEEKEND OF THE YEAR.
MALLETT
PEOPLE TRAVEL THOUSANDS OF MILES! THEY TRAVEL COAST TO COAST!
AND YOU'RE CALLING ME FOR THREE LOUSY STEPS?
THOSE ARE THE RULES. MY BALL.

Frazz
JEF MALLETT
WHY DO YOU RIDE YOUR BIKE TO WORK, FRAZZ?
WHY, FOR THE FRESH AIR AND SOLITUDE.
IF YOU FIND ANY, LET ME KNOW.

FRAZZ, WHEN YOU RIDE TO WORK, DO YOU EVER WORRY ABOUT GETTING... YOU KNOW...
STINKY?
RHETA!
FAIR QUESTION! FIRST, IT'S ONLY A 5-MILE TRIP. AND I TAKE IT EASY ON MY WAY IN.
PLUS I SHOWER BEFORE I START OUT. SO ANY SWEAT I DO WORK UP CAN'T MINGLE WITH ANY OLD, RIPE STUFF.
SAME WITH MY CLOTHES. I'M NOT ABOUT TO LET 'EM FERMENT OVERNIGHT.
SO NO WORRIES, RHETA. I SHOW UP FRESH AS A DAISY!
'KAY.
MALLETT

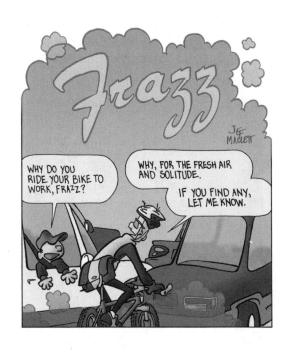

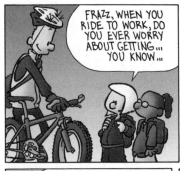

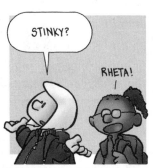

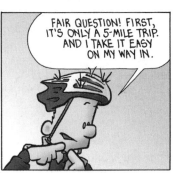

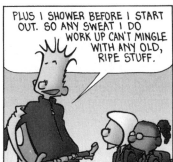

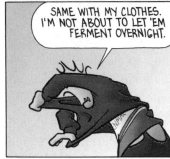

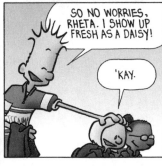

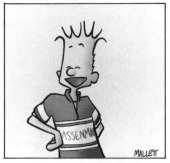

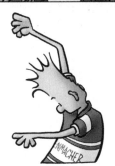

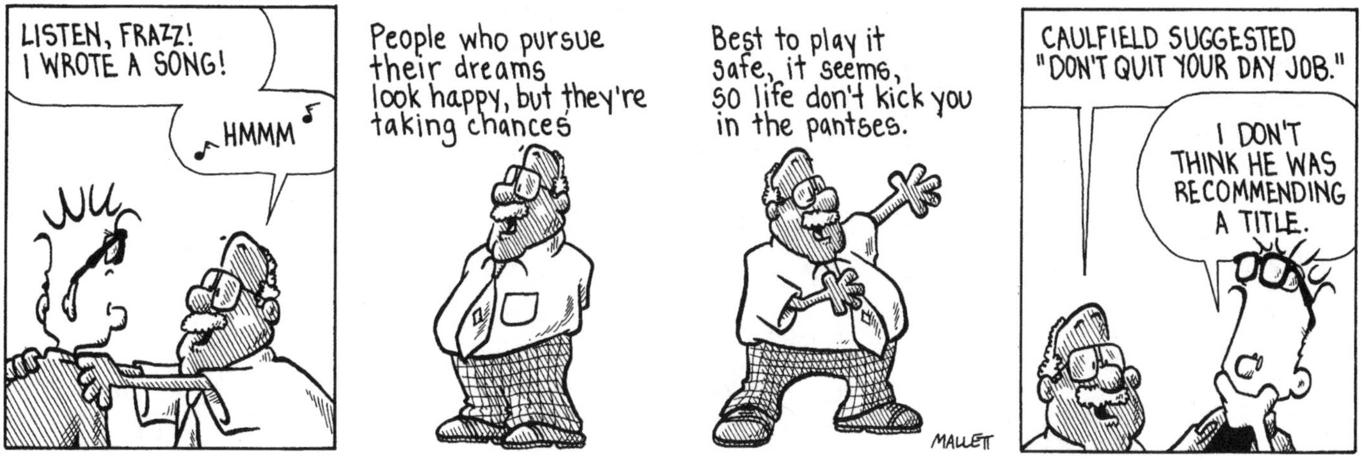
LISTEN, FRAZZ! I WROTE A SONG!
HMMM
People who pursue their dreams look happy, but they're taking chances
Best to play it safe, it seems, so life don't kick you in the pantses.
MALLETT
CAULFIELD SUGGESTED "DON'T QUIT YOUR DAY JOB."
I DON'T THINK HE WAS RECOMMENDING A TITLE.

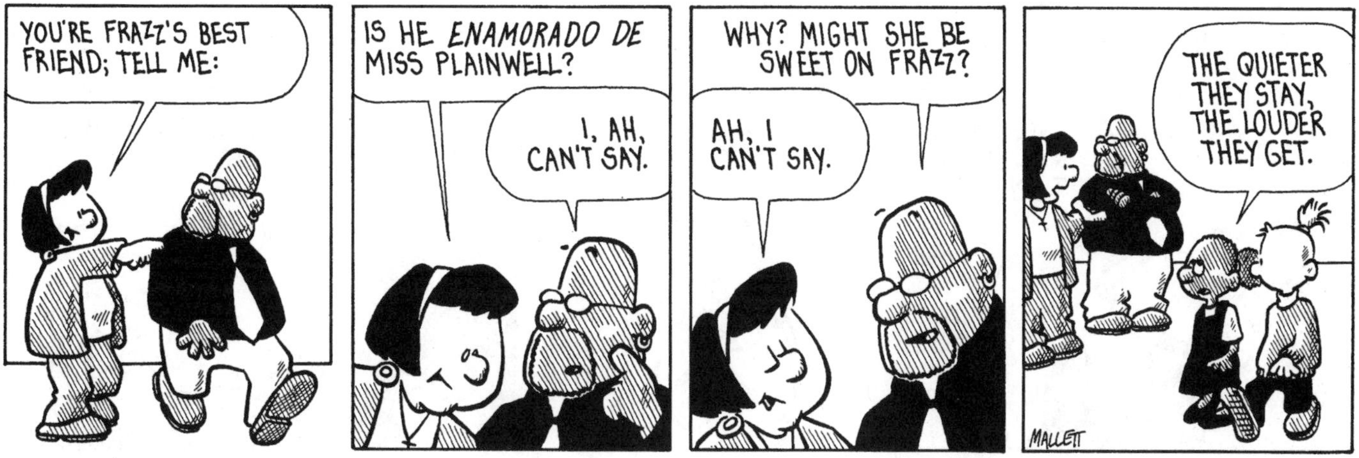
YOU'RE FRAZZ'S BEST FRIEND; TELL ME:
IS HE *ENAMORADO DE* MISS PLAINWELL?
I, AH, CAN'T SAY.
WHY? MIGHT SHE BE SWEET ON FRAZZ?
AH, I CAN'T SAY.
THE QUIETER THEY STAY, THE LOUDER THEY GET.
MALLETT

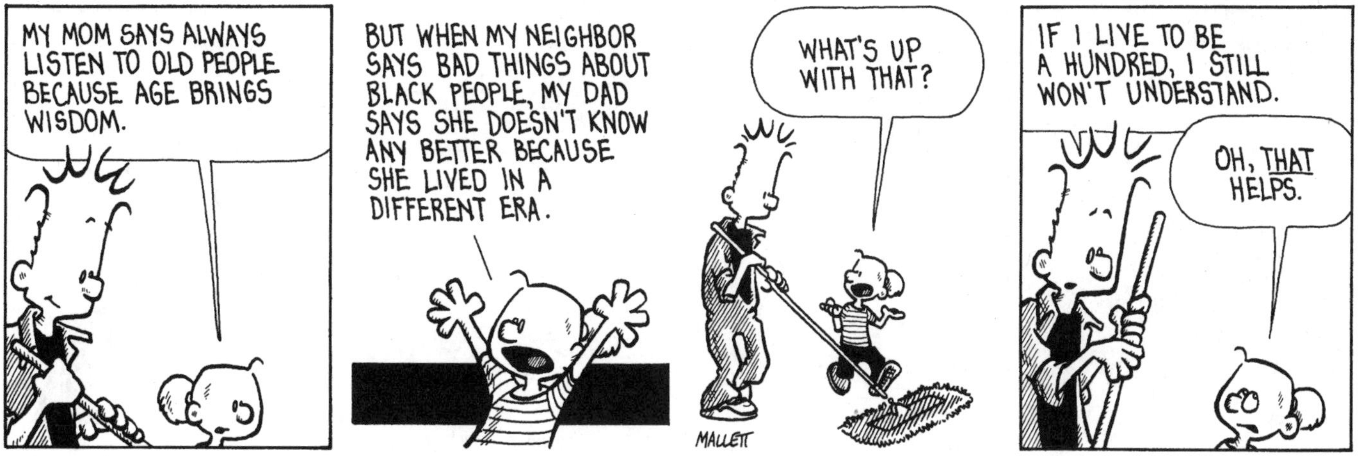
MY MOM SAYS ALWAYS LISTEN TO OLD PEOPLE BECAUSE AGE BRINGS WISDOM.
BUT WHEN MY NEIGHBOR SAYS BAD THINGS ABOUT BLACK PEOPLE, MY DAD SAYS SHE DOESN'T KNOW ANY BETTER BECAUSE SHE LIVED IN A DIFFERENT ERA.
WHAT'S UP WITH THAT?
MALLETT
IF I LIVE TO BE A HUNDRED, I STILL WON'T UNDERSTAND.
OH, THAT HELPS.

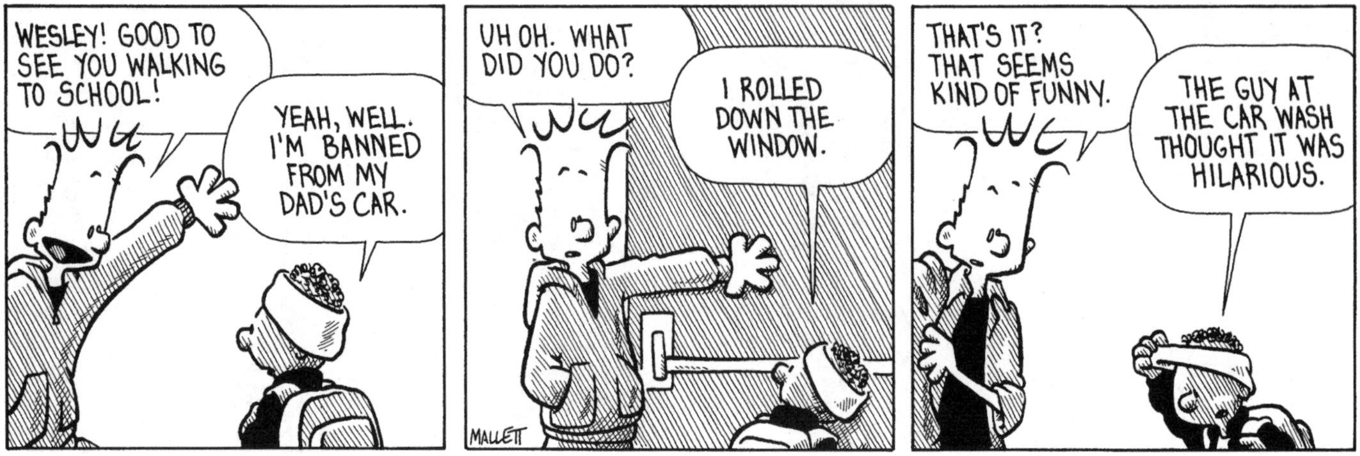
WESLEY! GOOD TO SEE YOU WALKING TO SCHOOL!
YEAH, WELL. I'M BANNED FROM MY DAD'S CAR.
UH OH. WHAT DID YOU DO?
I ROLLED DOWN THE WINDOW.
MALLETT
THAT'S IT? THAT SEEMS KIND OF FUNNY.
THE GUY AT THE CAR WASH THOUGHT IT WAS HILARIOUS.

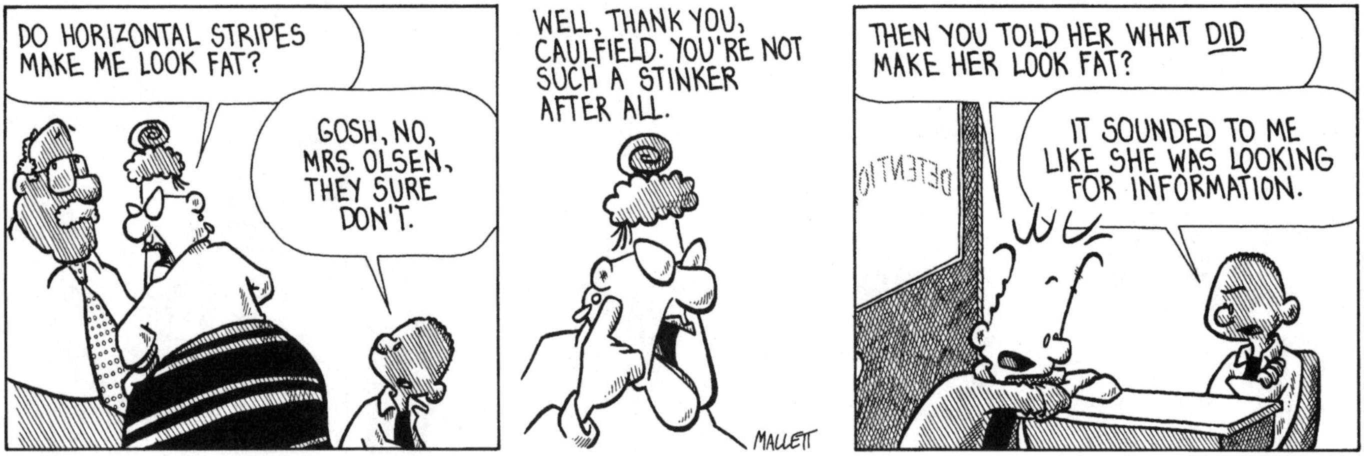
DO HORIZONTAL STRIPES MAKE ME LOOK FAT?
GOSH, NO, MRS. OLSEN, THEY SURE DON'T.
WELL, THANK YOU, CAULFIELD. YOU'RE NOT SUCH A STINKER AFTER ALL.
MALLETT
THEN YOU TOLD HER WHAT DID MAKE HER LOOK FAT?
IT SOUNDED TO ME LIKE SHE WAS LOOKING FOR INFORMATION.

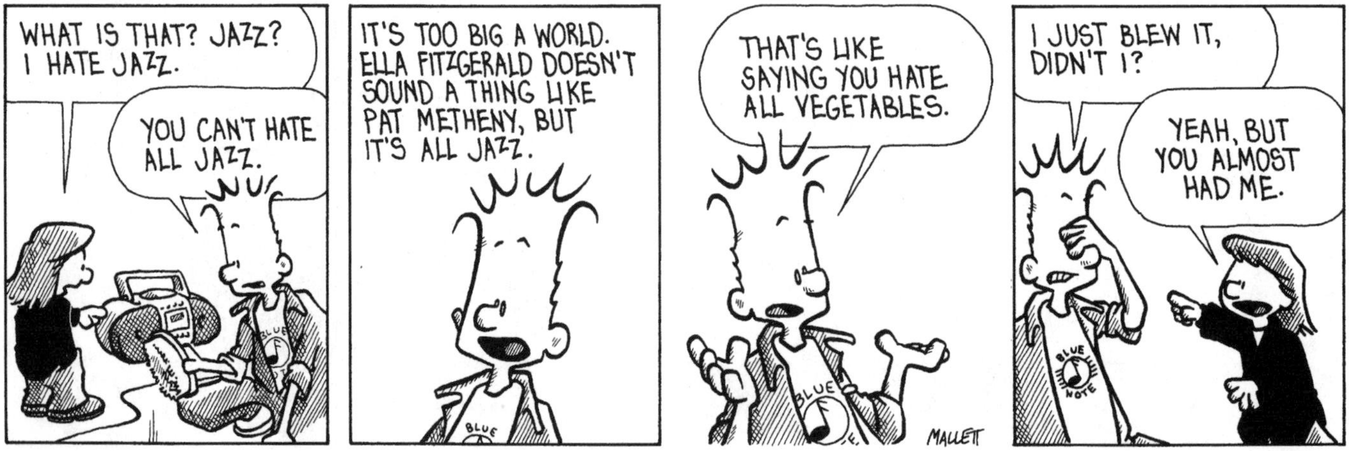
WHAT IS THAT? JAZZ? I HATE JAZZ.
YOU CAN'T HATE ALL JAZZ.
IT'S TOO BIG A WORLD. ELLA FITZGERALD DOESN'T SOUND A THING LIKE PAT METHENY, BUT IT'S ALL JAZZ.
THAT'S LIKE SAYING YOU HATE ALL VEGETABLES.
MALLETT
I JUST BLEW IT, DIDN'T I?
YEAH, BUT YOU ALMOST HAD ME.

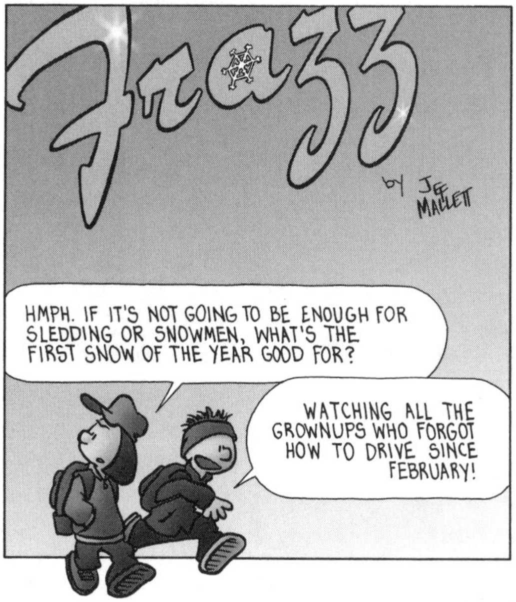
Frazz
by Jef Mallett
HMPH. IF IT'S NOT GOING TO BE ENOUGH FOR SLEDDING OR SNOWMEN, WHAT'S THE FIRST SNOW OF THE YEAR GOOD FOR?
WATCHING ALL THE GROWNUPS WHO FORGOT HOW TO DRIVE SINCE FEBRUARY!

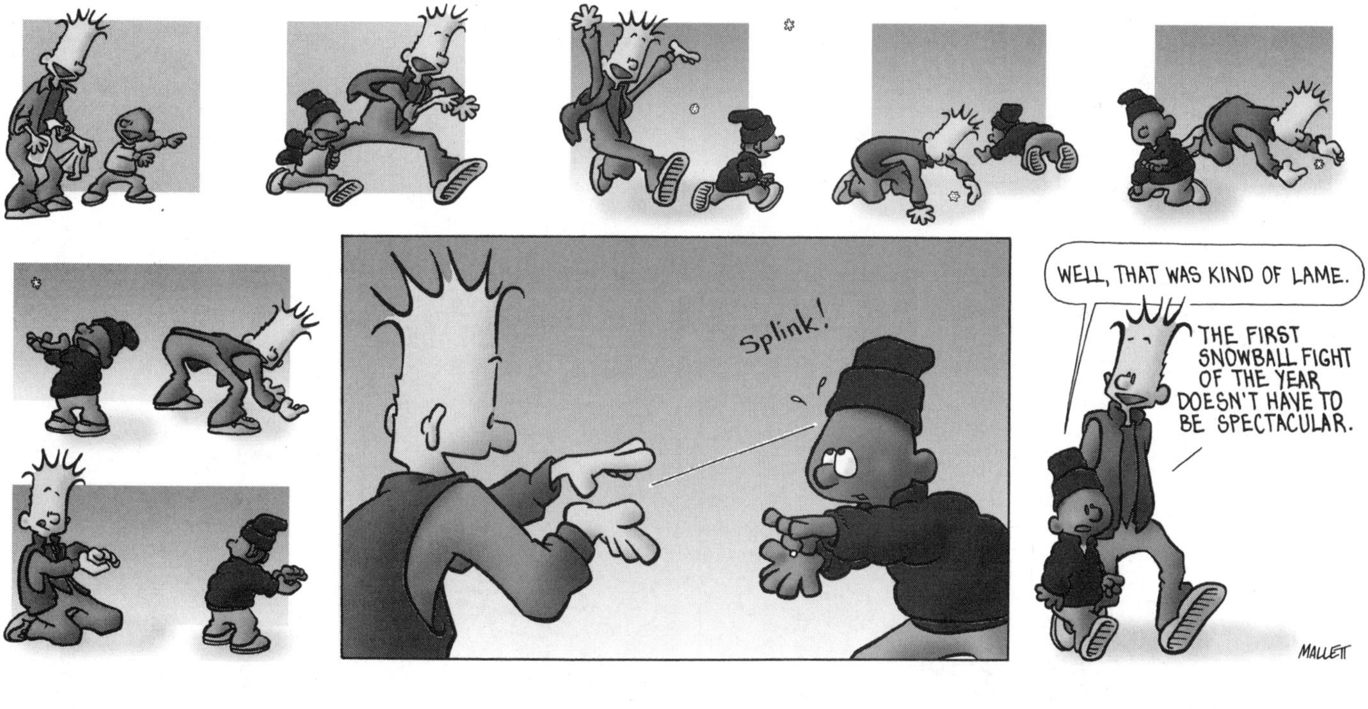
Splink!
WELL, THAT WAS KIND OF LAME.
THE FIRST SNOWBALL FIGHT OF THE YEAR DOESN'T HAVE TO BE SPECTACULAR.
MALLETT

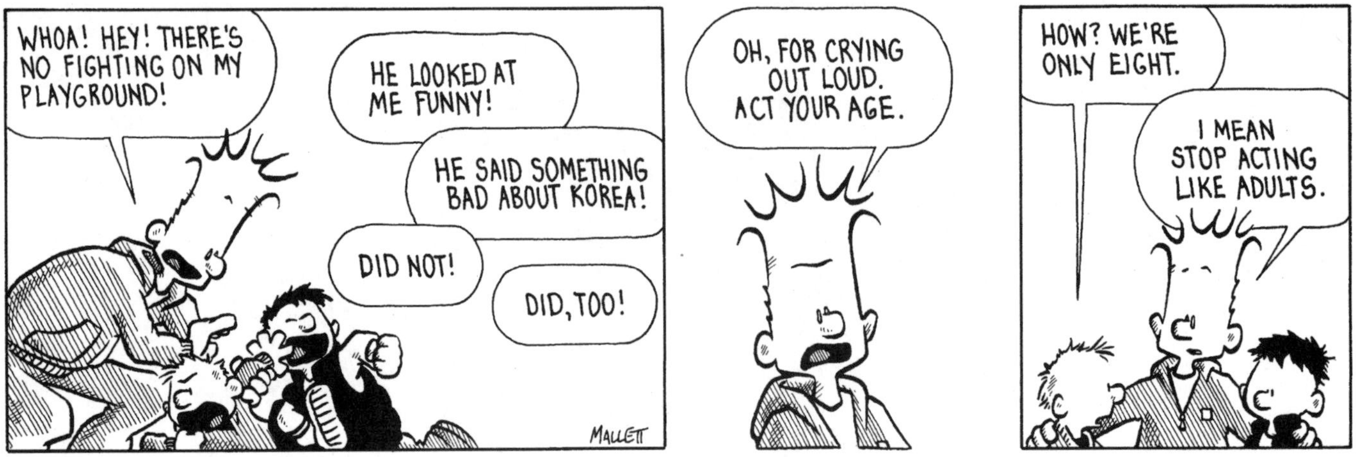
WHOA! HEY! THERE'S NO FIGHTING ON MY PLAYGROUND!
HE LOOKED AT ME FUNNY!
HE SAID SOMETHING BAD ABOUT KOREA!
DID NOT!
DID, TOO!
MALLETT
OH, FOR CRYING OUT LOUD. ACT YOUR AGE.
HOW? WE'RE ONLY EIGHT.
I MEAN STOP ACTING LIKE ADULTS.

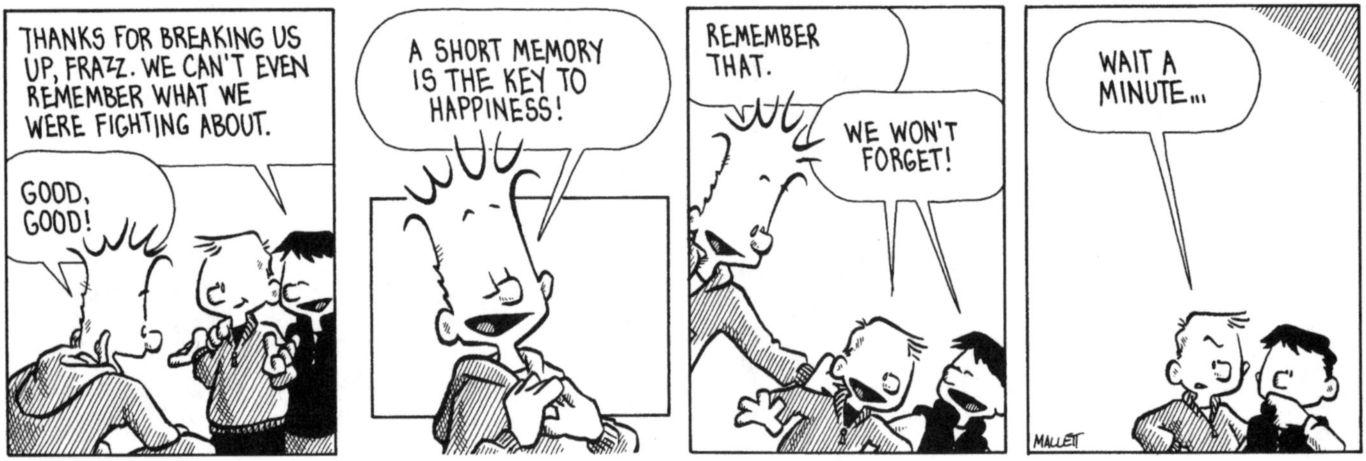
THANKS FOR BREAKING US UP, FRAZZ. WE CAN'T EVEN REMEMBER WHAT WE WERE FIGHTING ABOUT.
GOOD, GOOD!
A SHORT MEMORY IS THE KEY TO HAPPINESS!
REMEMBER THAT.
WE WON'T FORGET!
WAIT A MINUTE...
MALLETT

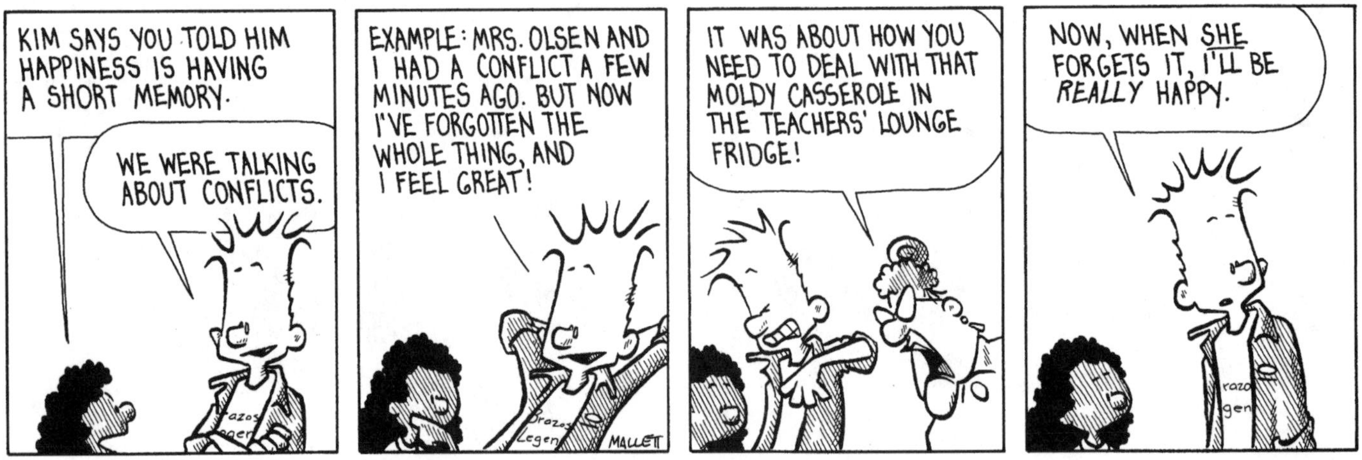
KIM SAYS YOU TOLD HIM HAPPINESS IS HAVING A SHORT MEMORY.
WE WERE TALKING ABOUT CONFLICTS.
EXAMPLE: MRS. OLSEN AND I HAD A CONFLICT A FEW MINUTES AGO. BUT NOW I'VE FORGOTTEN THE WHOLE THING, AND I FEEL GREAT!
MALLETT
IT WAS ABOUT HOW YOU NEED TO DEAL WITH THAT MOLDY CASSEROLE IN THE TEACHERS' LOUNGE FRIDGE!
NOW, WHEN SHE FORGETS IT, I'LL BE REALLY HAPPY.

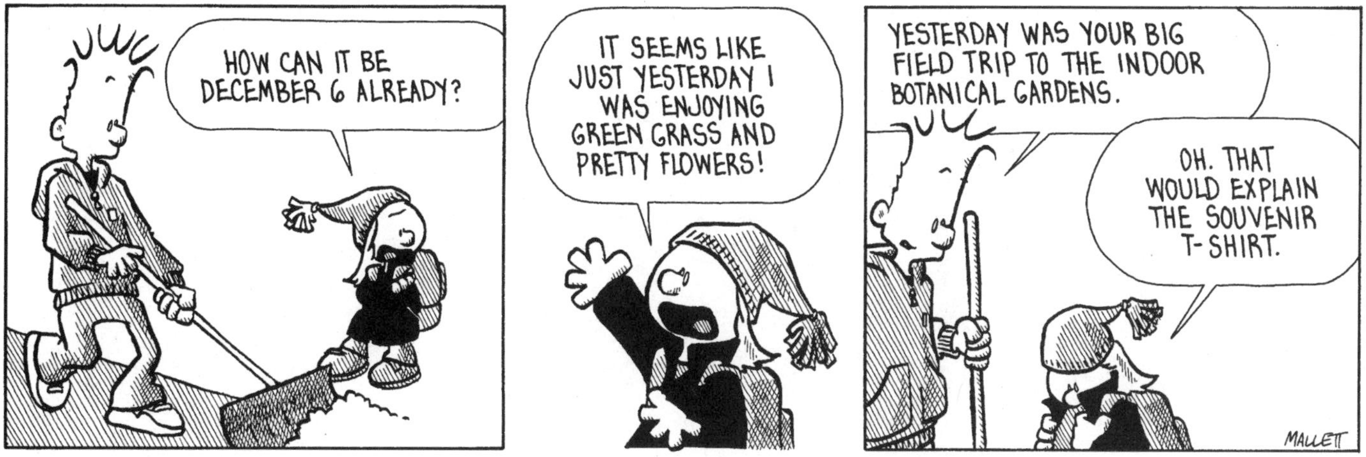
HOW CAN IT BE DECEMBER 6 ALREADY?
IT SEEMS LIKE JUST YESTERDAY I WAS ENJOYING GREEN GRASS AND PRETTY FLOWERS!
YESTERDAY WAS YOUR BIG FIELD TRIP TO THE INDOOR BOTANICAL GARDENS.
OH. THAT WOULD EXPLAIN THE SOUVENIR T-SHIRT.
MALLETT

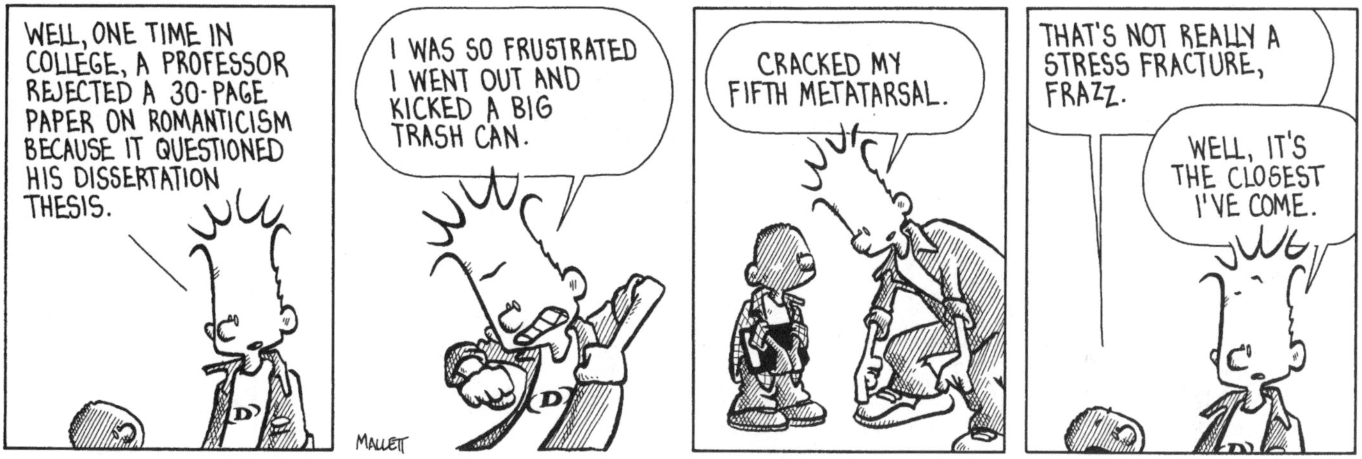
WELL, ONE TIME IN COLLEGE, A PROFESSOR REJECTED A 30-PAGE PAPER ON ROMANTICISM BECAUSE IT QUESTIONED HIS DISSERTATION THESIS.
I WAS SO FRUSTRATED I WENT OUT AND KICKED A BIG TRASH CAN.
CRACKED MY FIFTH METATARSAL.
THAT'S NOT REALLY A STRESS FRACTURE, FRAZZ.
WELL, IT'S THE CLOSEST I'VE COME.
MALLETT

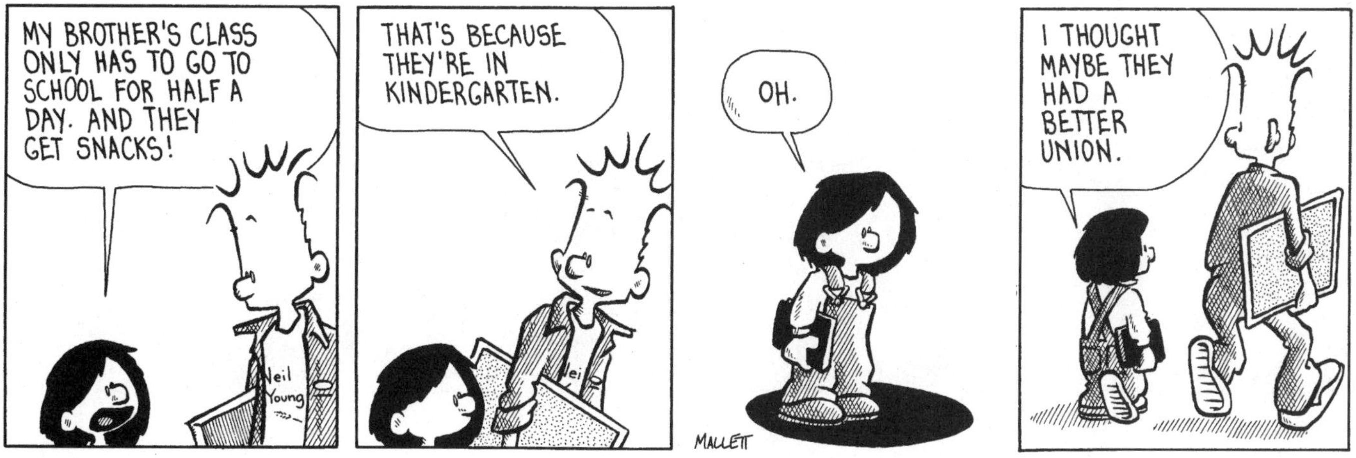
MY BROTHER'S CLASS ONLY HAS TO GO TO SCHOOL FOR HALF A DAY. AND THEY GET SNACKS!
Neil Young
THAT'S BECAUSE THEY'RE IN KINDERGARTEN.
OH.
I THOUGHT MAYBE THEY HAD A BETTER UNION.
MALLETT

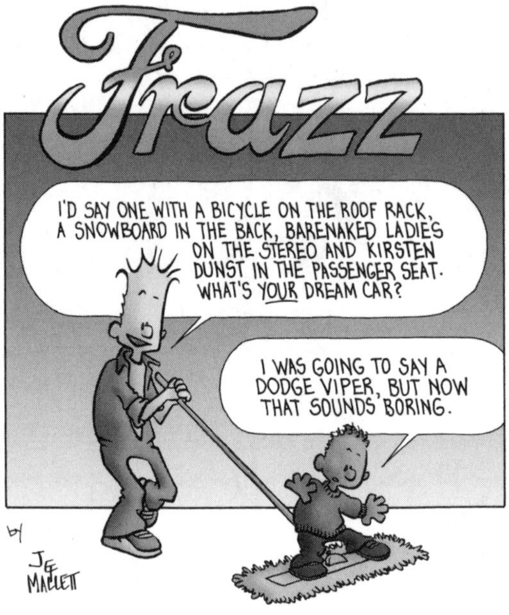
Frazz
I'D SAY ONE WITH A BICYCLE ON THE ROOF RACK, A SNOWBOARD IN THE BACK, BARENAKED LADIES ON THE STEREO AND KIRSTEN DUNST IN THE PASSENGER SEAT. WHAT'S YOUR DREAM CAR?
I WAS GOING TO SAY A DODGE VIPER, BUT NOW THAT SOUNDS BORING.
by JEF MALLETT

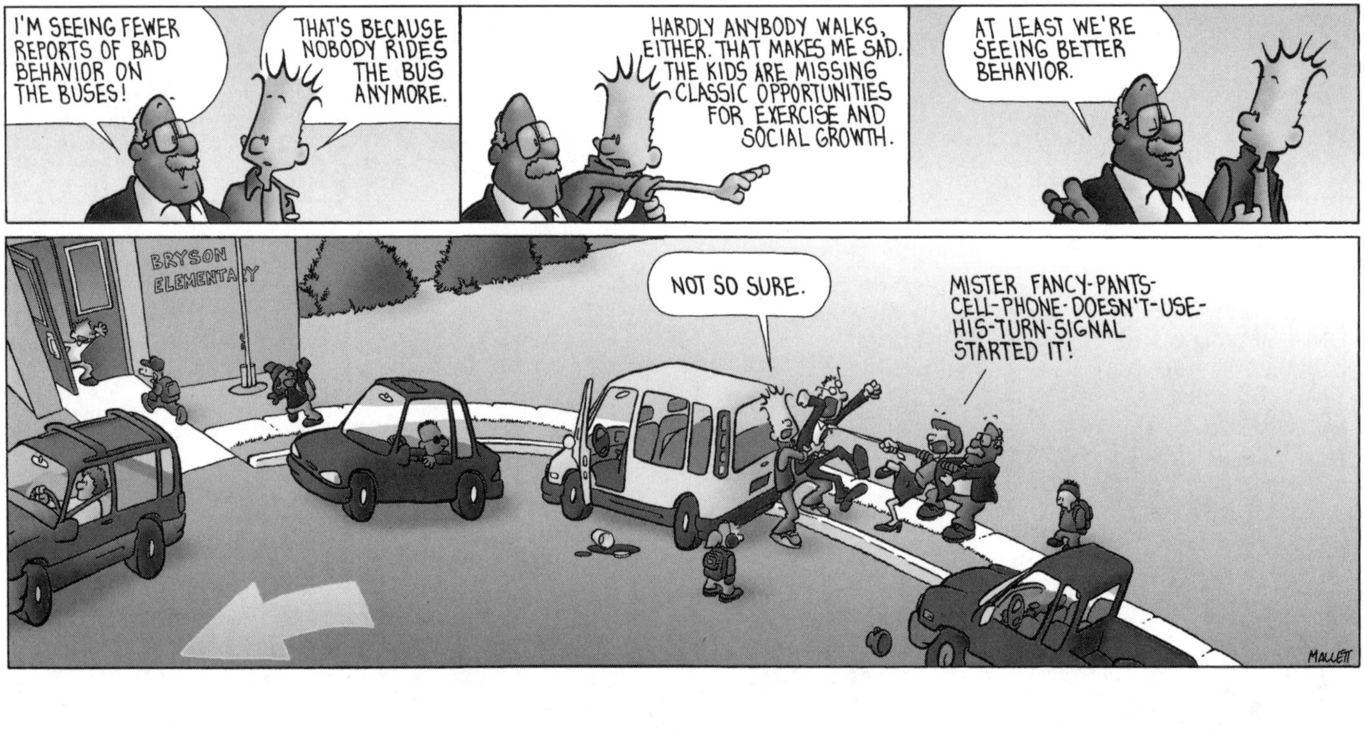
I'M SEEING FEWER REPORTS OF BAD BEHAVIOR ON THE BUSES!
THAT'S BECAUSE NOBODY RIDES THE BUS ANYMORE.
HARDLY ANYBODY WALKS, EITHER. THAT MAKES ME SAD. THE KIDS ARE MISSING CLASSIC OPPORTUNITIES FOR EXERCISE AND SOCIAL GROWTH.
AT LEAST WE'RE SEEING BETTER BEHAVIOR.
BRYSON ELEMENTARY
NOT SO SURE.
MISTER FANCY-PANTS-CELL-PHONE-DOESN'T-USE-HIS-TURN-SIGNAL STARTED IT!
MALLETT

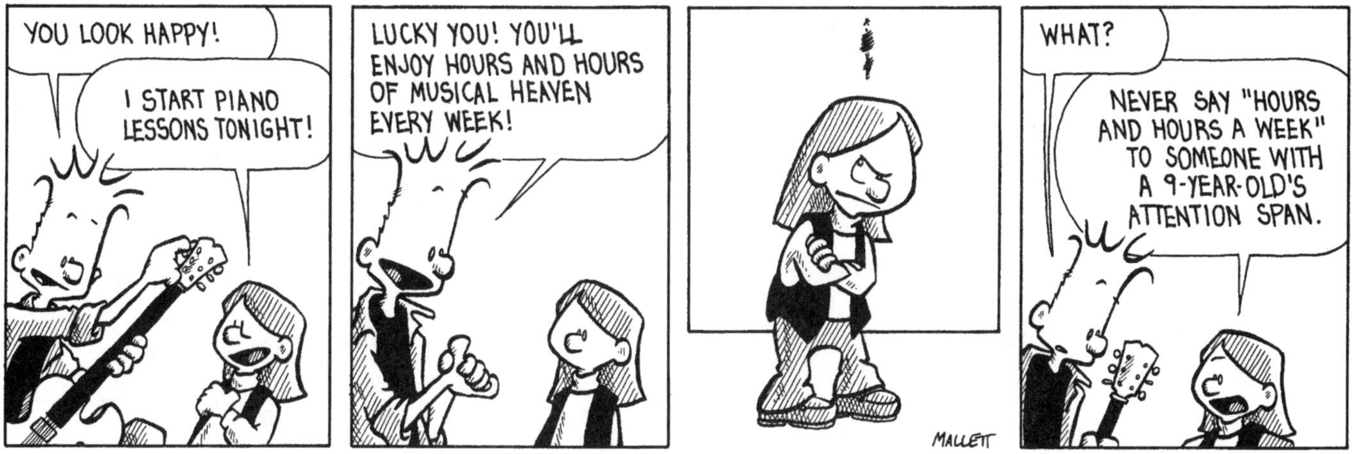
YOU LOOK HAPPY!
I START PIANO LESSONS TONIGHT!
LUCKY YOU! YOU'LL ENJOY HOURS AND HOURS OF MUSICAL HEAVEN EVERY WEEK!
WHAT?
NEVER SAY "HOURS AND HOURS A WEEK" TO SOMEONE WITH A 9-YEAR-OLD'S ATTENTION SPAN.
MALLETT

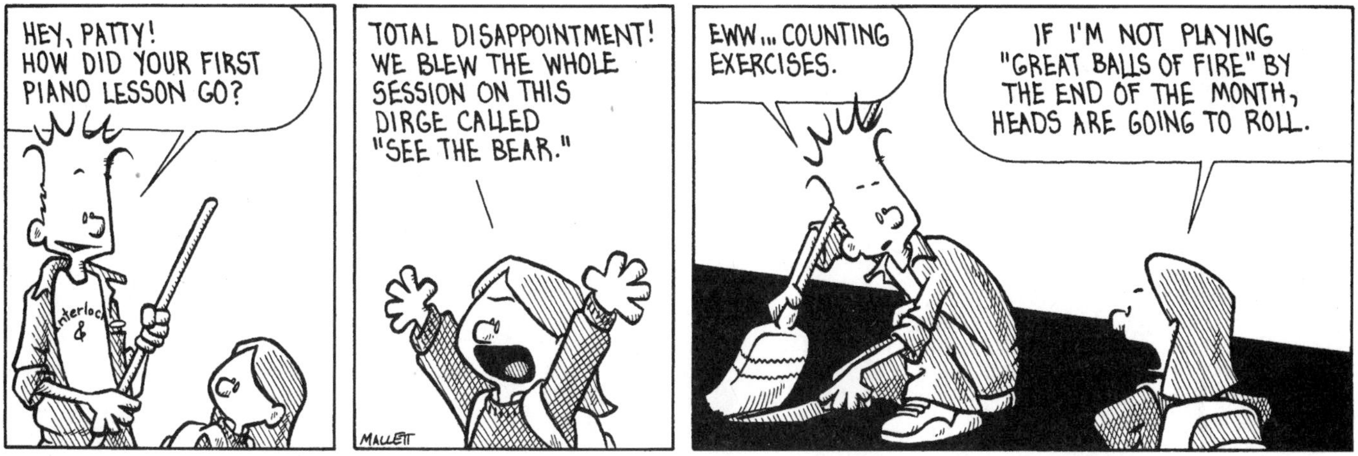
HEY, PATTY! HOW DID YOUR FIRST PIANO LESSON GO?
TOTAL DISAPPOINTMENT! WE BLEW THE WHOLE SESSION ON THIS DIRGE CALLED "SEE THE BEAR."
MALLETT
EWW... COUNTING EXERCISES.
IF I'M NOT PLAYING "GREAT BALLS OF FIRE" BY THE END OF THE MONTH, HEADS ARE GOING TO ROLL.

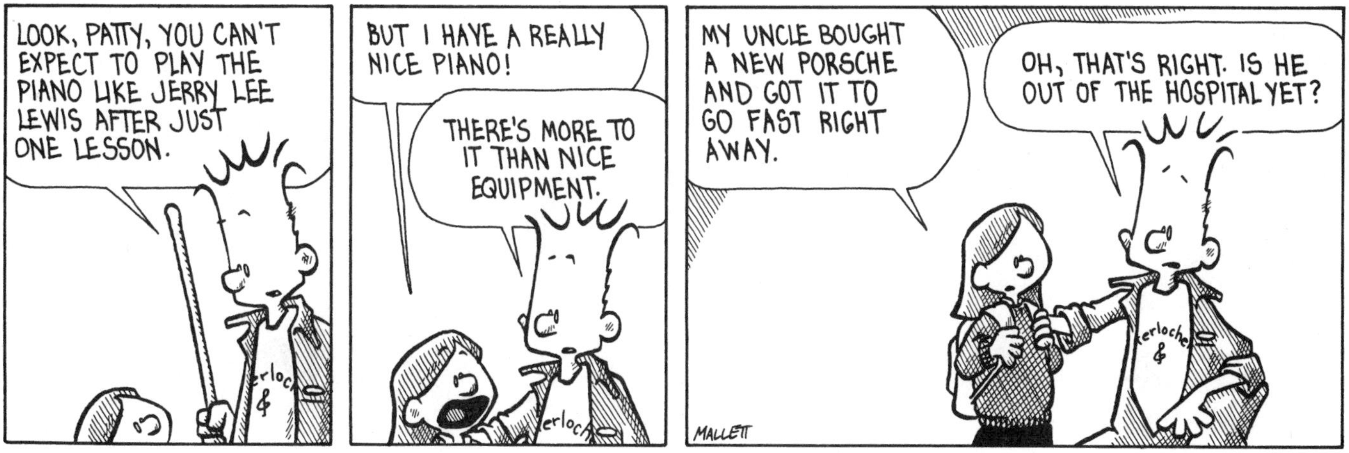
LOOK, PATTY, YOU CAN'T EXPECT TO PLAY THE PIANO LIKE JERRY LEE LEWIS AFTER JUST ONE LESSON.
BUT I HAVE A REALLY NICE PIANO!
THERE'S MORE TO IT THAN NICE EQUIPMENT.
MY UNCLE BOUGHT A NEW PORSCHE AND GOT IT TO GO FAST RIGHT AWAY.
OH, THAT'S RIGHT. IS HE OUT OF THE HOSPITAL YET?
MALLETT

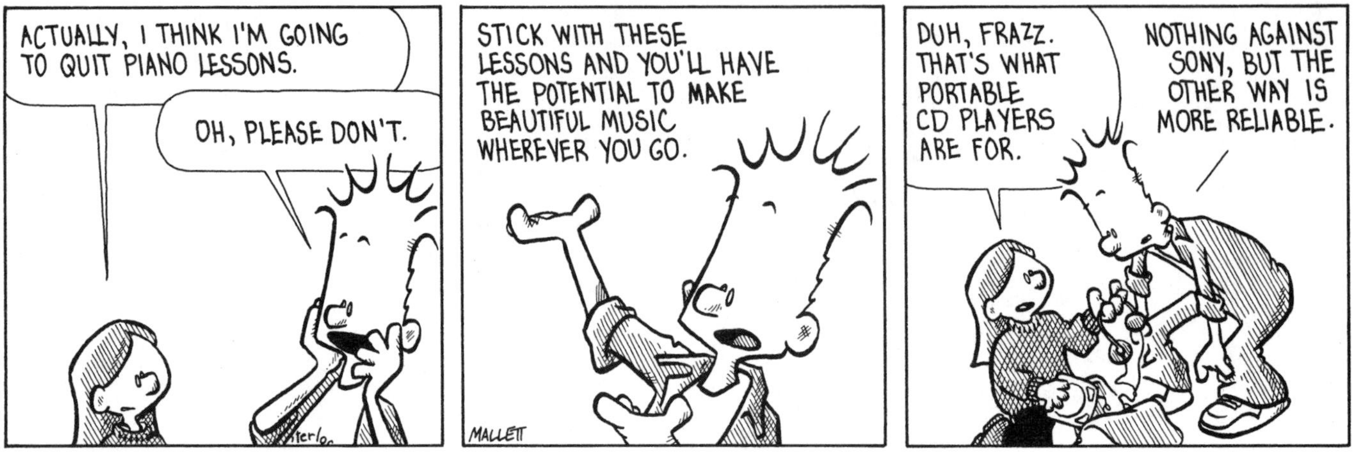
ACTUALLY, I THINK I'M GOING TO QUIT PIANO LESSONS.
OH, PLEASE DON'T.
STICK WITH THESE LESSONS AND YOU'LL HAVE THE POTENTIAL TO MAKE BEAUTIFUL MUSIC WHEREVER YOU GO.
MALLETT
DUH, FRAZZ. THAT'S WHAT PORTABLE CD PLAYERS ARE FOR.
NOTHING AGAINST SONY, BUT THE OTHER WAY IS MORE RELIABLE.

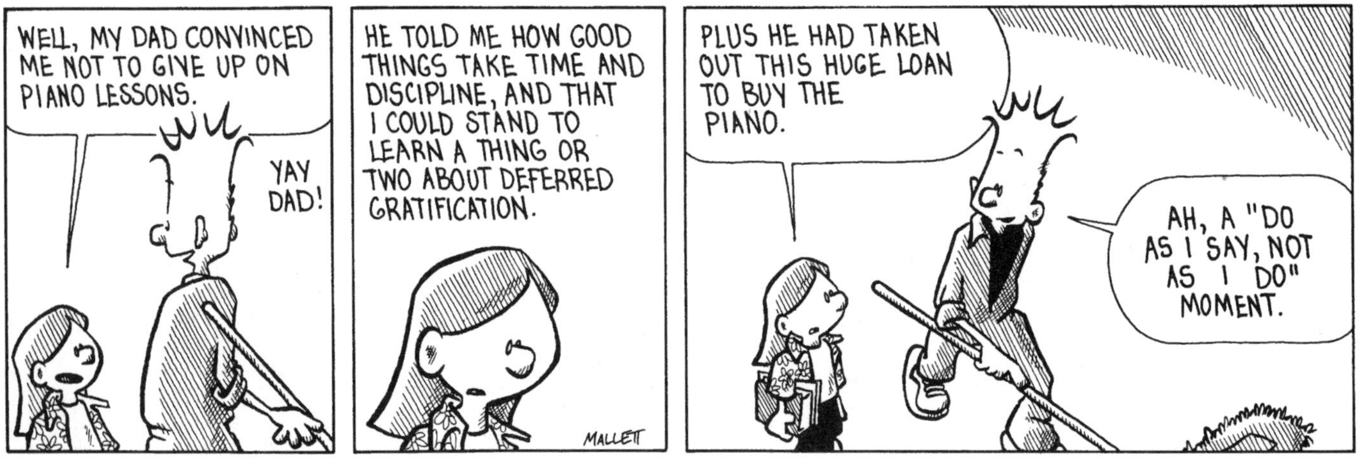
WELL, MY DAD CONVINCED ME NOT TO GIVE UP ON PIANO LESSONS.
YAY DAD!
HE TOLD ME HOW GOOD THINGS TAKE TIME AND DISCIPLINE, AND THAT I COULD STAND TO LEARN A THING OR TWO ABOUT DEFERRED GRATIFICATION.
MALLETT
PLUS HE HAD TAKEN OUT THIS HUGE LOAN TO BUY THE PIANO.
AH, A "DO AS I SAY, NOT AS I DO" MOMENT.

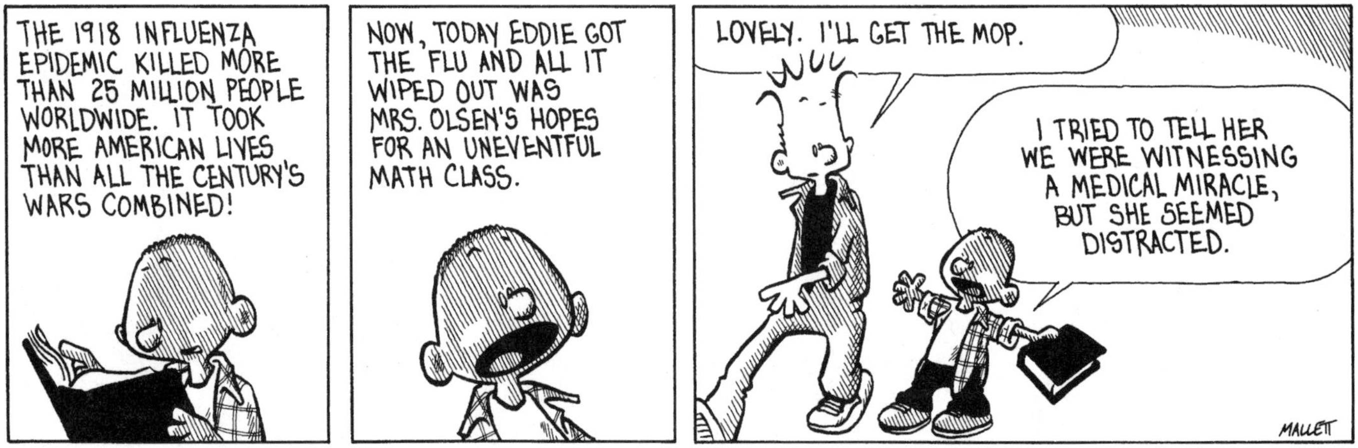
THE 1918 INFLUENZA EPIDEMIC KILLED MORE THAN 25 MILLION PEOPLE WORLDWIDE. IT TOOK MORE AMERICAN LIVES THAN ALL THE CENTURY'S WARS COMBINED!
NOW, TODAY EDDIE GOT THE FLU AND ALL IT WIPED OUT WAS MRS. OLSEN'S HOPES FOR AN UNEVENTFUL MATH CLASS.
LOVELY. I'LL GET THE MOP.
I TRIED TO TELL HER WE WERE WITNESSING A MEDICAL MIRACLE, BUT SHE SEEMED DISTRACTED.
MALLETT

Frazz by Jef Mallett

CHECK IT OUT, MR. HACKER! FRAZZ FOUND US SOME OF THAT COOL GREEN KETCHUP!

BIG DEAL. I JUST FOUND GREEN MAYONNAISE IN MY REFRIGERATOR.

GIVE YOU A TWIX BAR TO TRADE SEATS.

AS IF.

I HEARD YOU ATE PIG GUTS ONCE, FRAZZ.

WAS IT A DARE?

THEY'RE CALLED CHITLINS, AND NO.

I ATE THEM WHEN I WAS VISITING MY OLD ROOMMATE'S FAMILY IN THE DEEP SOUTH.

SEE, THE BEST WAY TO GET TO KNOW A CULTURE IS TO TRY THE FOOD.

SO WHEN I TRAVEL, I EAT ADVENTUROUSLY.

I LEARNED A LOT ABOUT MALAYSIA OVER A DURIAN.

I SURVIVED VEGEMITE IN AUSTRALIA.

IF I EVER GET TO SCOTLAND, YOU BETTER BELIEVE I'LL TRY HAGGIS.

WHY THIS NEW INTEREST IN MY DIET?

BECAUSE MRS. OLSEN BROUGHT IN A FRUITCAKE, AND MEG AND I HAVE A BET.

OKAY, THE TEACHERS' LOUNGE KITCHENETTE IS NOT "TRAVEL."

MALLETT

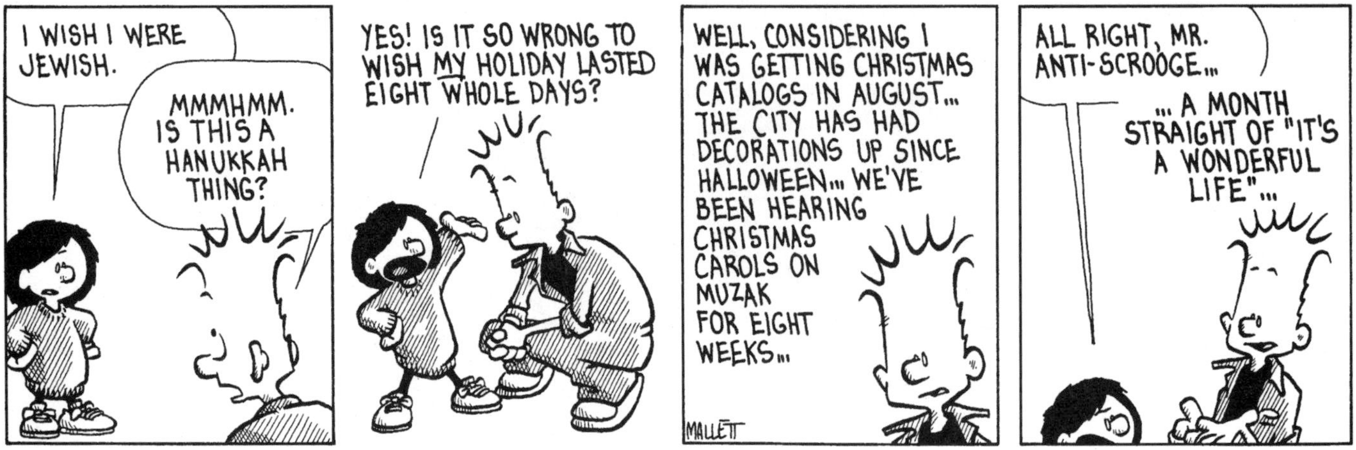
I WISH I WERE JEWISH.
MMMHMM. IS THIS A HANUKKAH THING?
YES! IS IT SO WRONG TO WISH MY HOLIDAY LASTED EIGHT WHOLE DAYS?
WELL, CONSIDERING I WAS GETTING CHRISTMAS CATALOGS IN AUGUST... THE CITY HAS HAD DECORATIONS UP SINCE HALLOWEEN... WE'VE BEEN HEARING CHRISTMAS CAROLS ON MUZAK FOR EIGHT WEEKS...
MALLETT
ALL RIGHT, MR. ANTI-SCROOGE...
... A MONTH STRAIGHT OF "IT'S A WONDERFUL LIFE"...

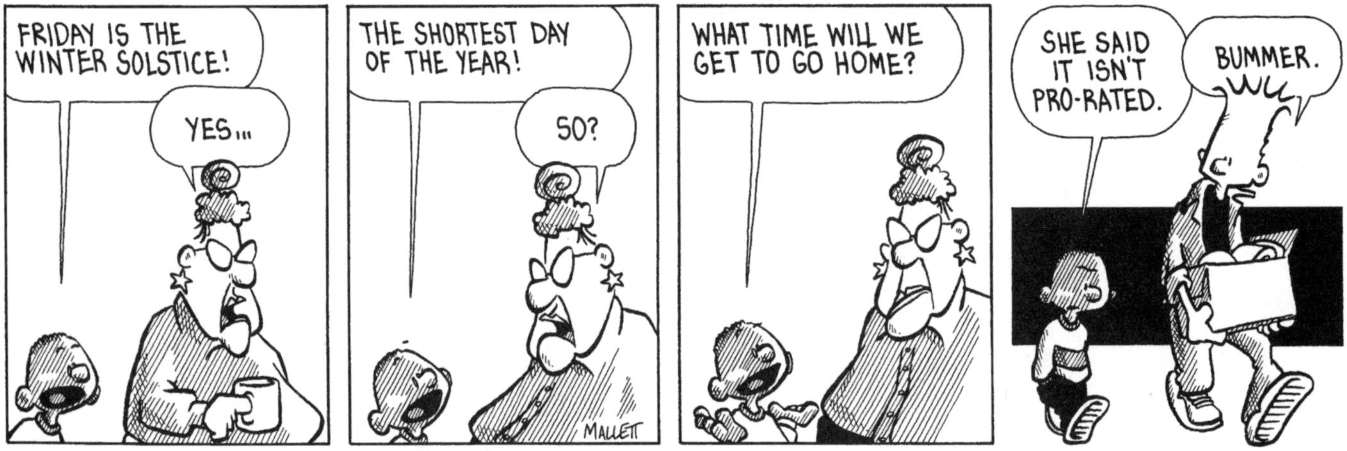
FRIDAY IS THE WINTER SOLSTICE!
YES...
THE SHORTEST DAY OF THE YEAR!
SO?
MALLETT
WHAT TIME WILL WE GET TO GO HOME?
SHE SAID IT ISN'T PRO-RATED.
BUMMER.

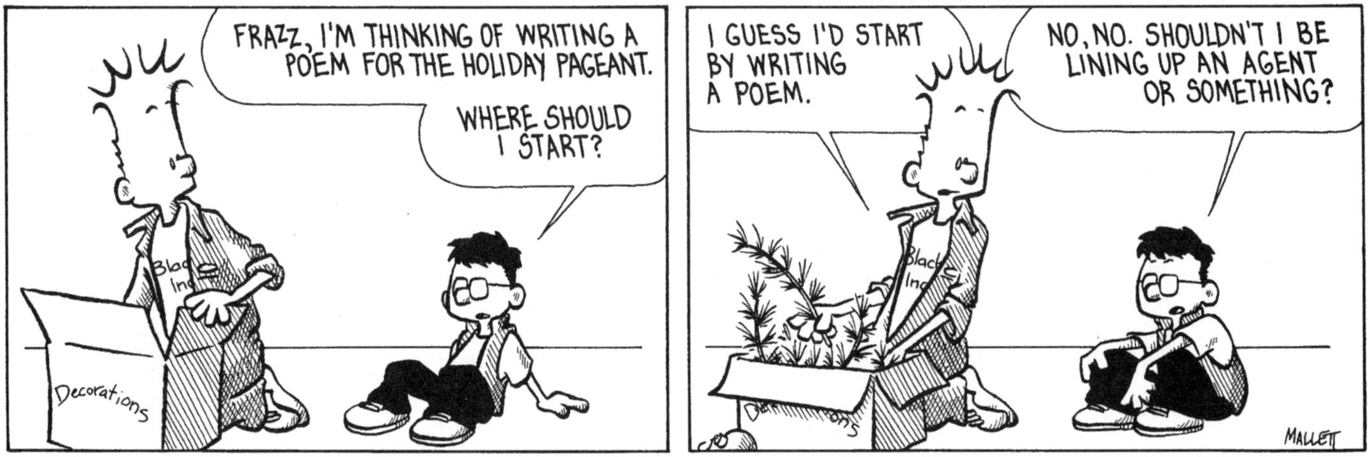
FRAZZ, I'M THINKING OF WRITING A POEM FOR THE HOLIDAY PAGEANT.
WHERE SHOULD I START?
Decorations
I GUESS I'D START BY WRITING A POEM.
NO, NO. SHOULDN'T I BE LINING UP AN AGENT OR SOMETHING?
MALLETT

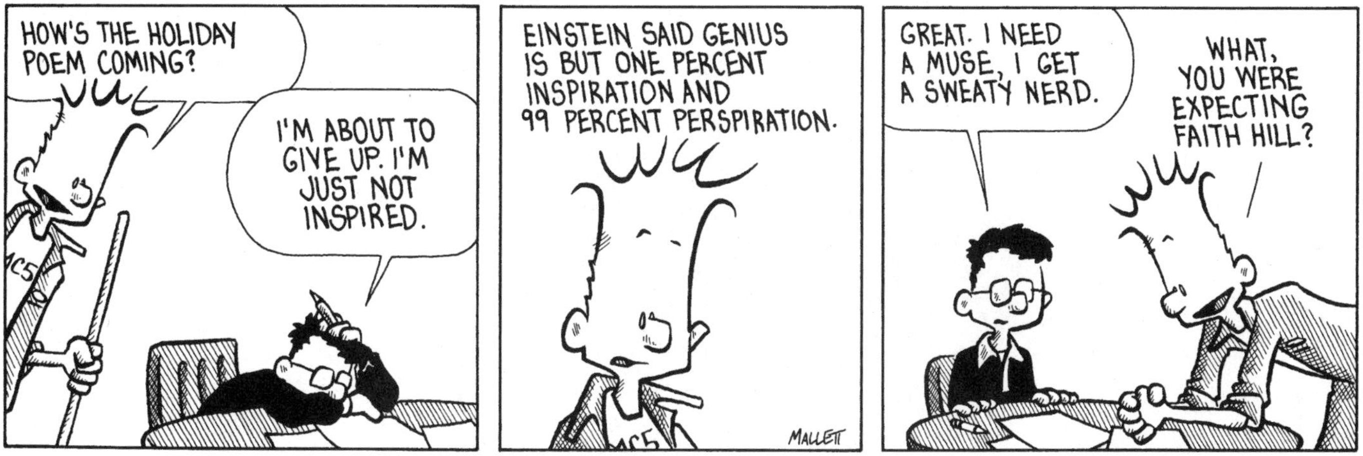
HOW'S THE HOLIDAY POEM COMING?
I'M ABOUT TO GIVE UP. I'M JUST NOT INSPIRED.
EINSTEIN SAID GENIUS IS BUT ONE PERCENT INSPIRATION AND 99 PERCENT PERSPIRATION.
MALLETT
GREAT. I NEED A MUSE, I GET A SWEATY NERD.
WHAT, YOU WERE EXPECTING FAITH HILL?

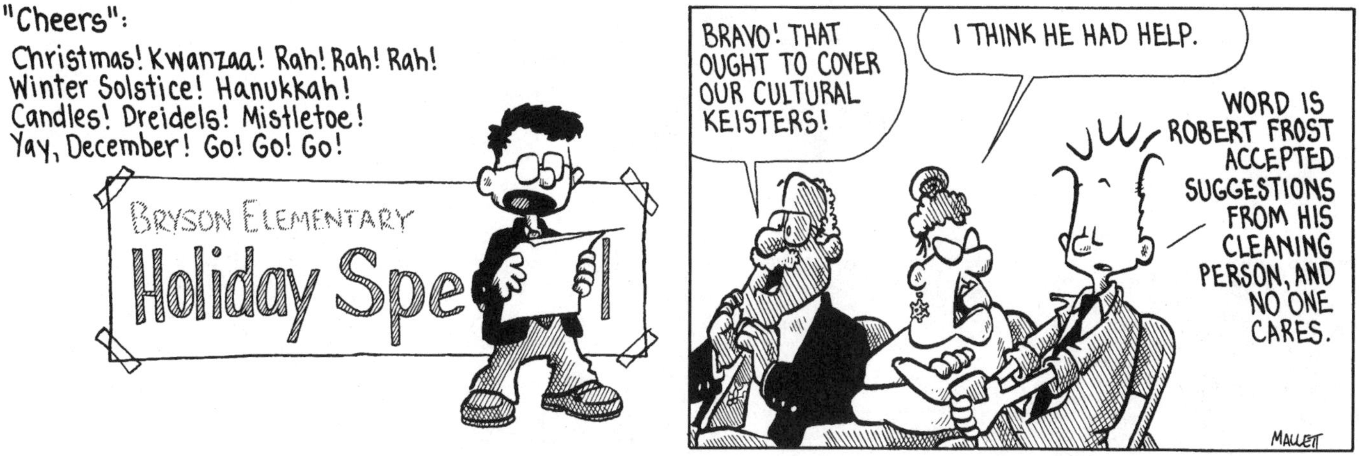
"Cheers":
Christmas! Kwanzaa! Rah! Rah! Rah!
Winter Solstice! Hanukkah!
Candles! Dreidels! Mistletoe!
Yay, December! Go! Go! Go!
BRYSON ELEMENTARY
Holiday Spe l
BRAVO! THAT OUGHT TO COVER OUR CULTURAL KEISTERS!
I THINK HE HAD HELP.
WORD IS ROBERT FROST ACCEPTED SUGGESTIONS FROM HIS CLEANING PERSON, AND NO ONE CARES.
MALLETT

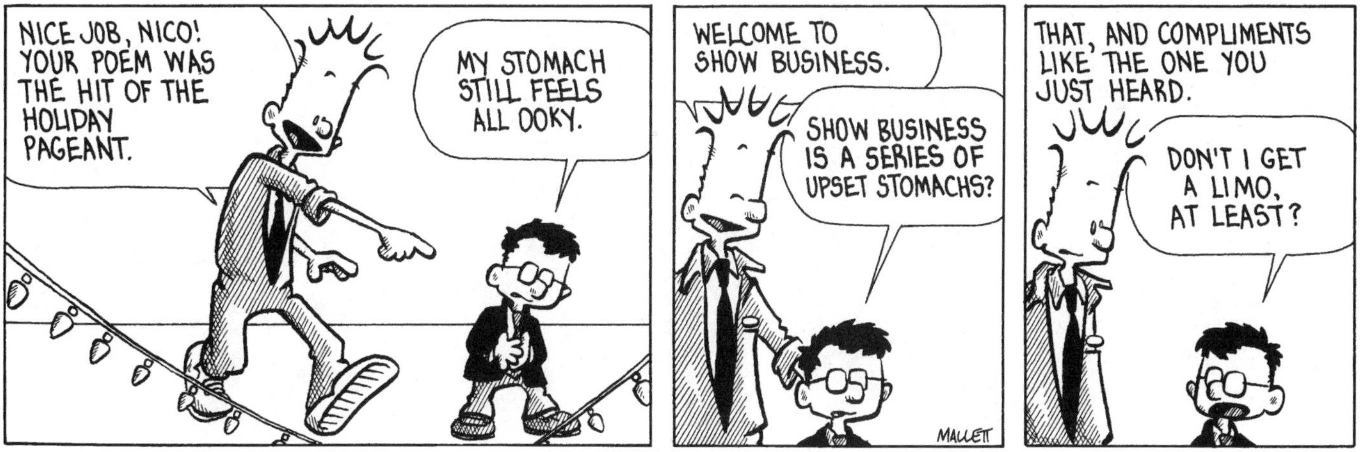
NICE JOB, NICO! YOUR POEM WAS THE HIT OF THE HOLIDAY PAGEANT.
MY STOMACH STILL FEELS ALL OOKY.
WELCOME TO SHOW BUSINESS.
SHOW BUSINESS IS A SERIES OF UPSET STOMACHS?
MALLETT
THAT, AND COMPLIMENTS LIKE THE ONE YOU JUST HEARD.
DON'T I GET A LIMO, AT LEAST?

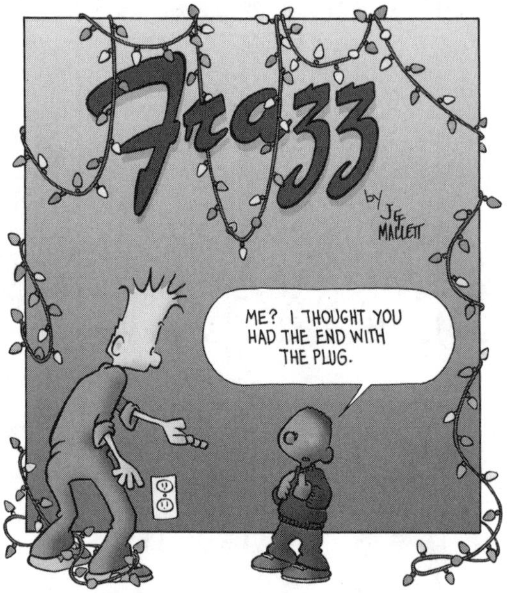
Frazz
by Jef Mallett
ME? I THOUGHT YOU HAD THE END WITH THE PLUG.

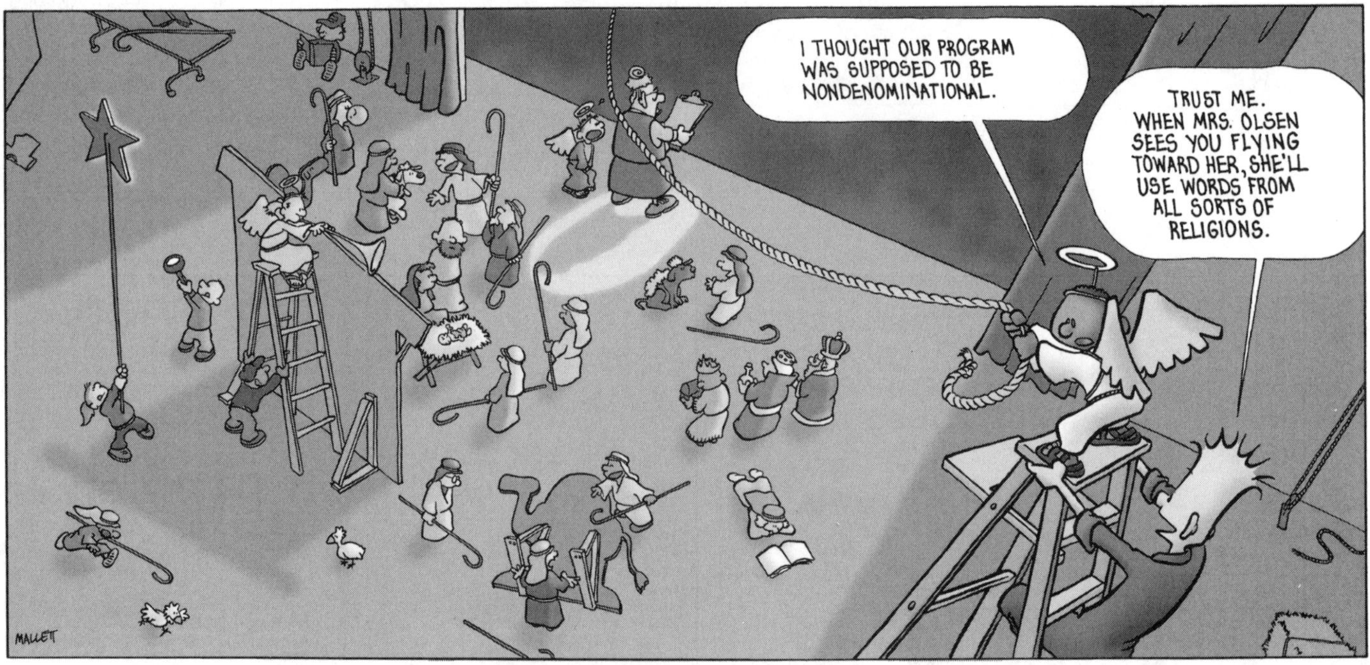
I THOUGHT OUR PROGRAM WAS SUPPOSED TO BE NONDENOMINATIONAL.
TRUST ME. WHEN MRS. OLSEN SEES YOU FLYING TOWARD HER, SHE'LL USE WORDS FROM ALL SORTS OF RELIGIONS.
MALLETT

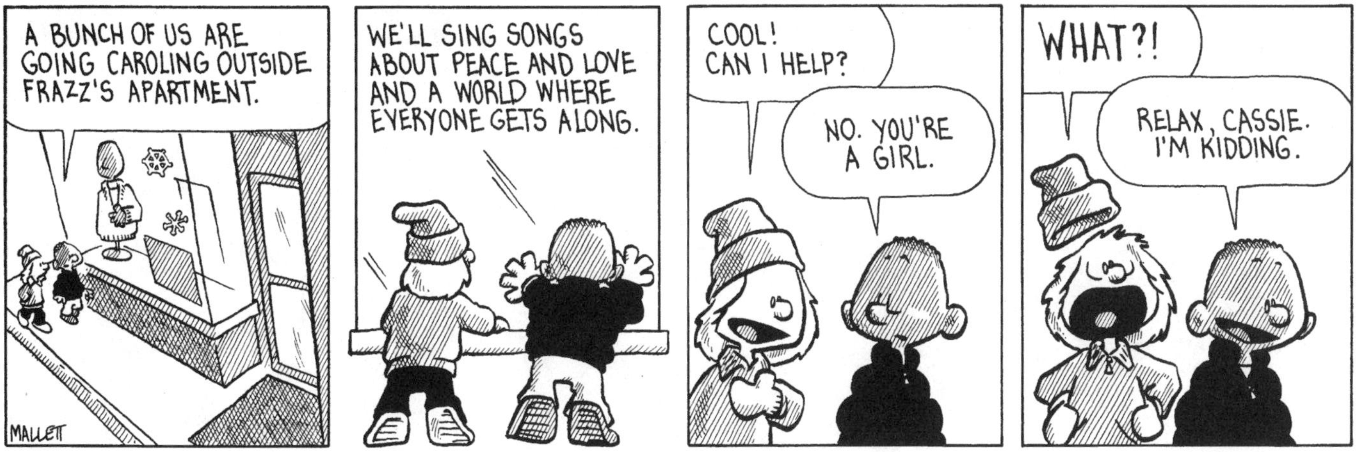
A BUNCH OF US ARE GOING CAROLING OUTSIDE FRAZZ'S APARTMENT.
MALLETT
WE'LL SING SONGS ABOUT PEACE AND LOVE AND A WORLD WHERE EVERYONE GETS ALONG.
COOL! CAN I HELP?
NO. YOU'RE A GIRL.
WHAT?!
RELAX, CASSIE. I'M KIDDING.

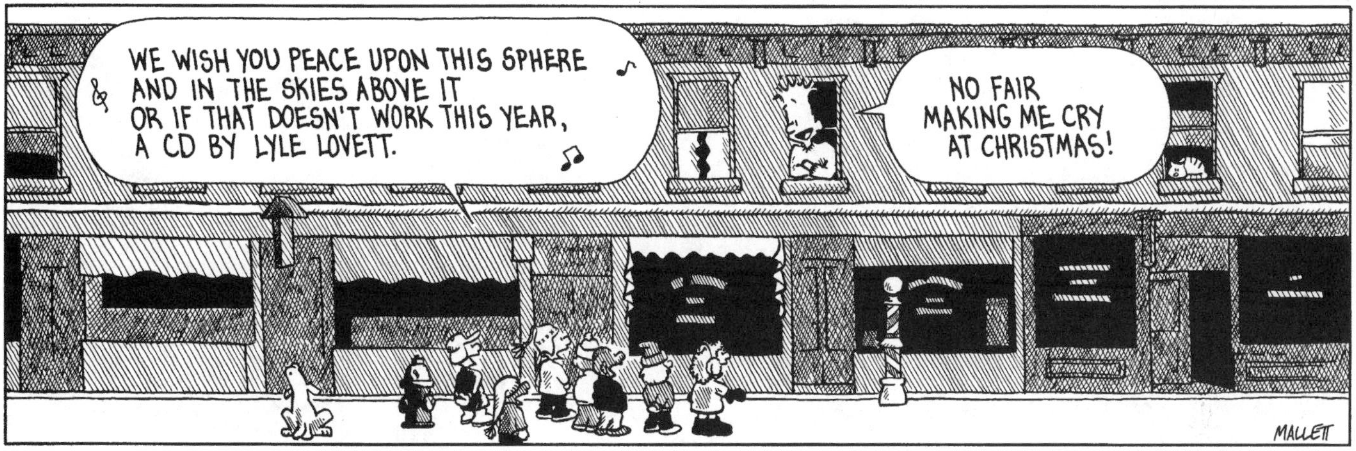
WE WISH YOU PEACE UPON THIS SPHERE AND IN THE SKIES ABOVE IT OR IF THAT DOESN'T WORK THIS YEAR, A CD BY LYLE LOVETT.
NO FAIR MAKING ME CRY AT CHRISTMAS!
MALLETT

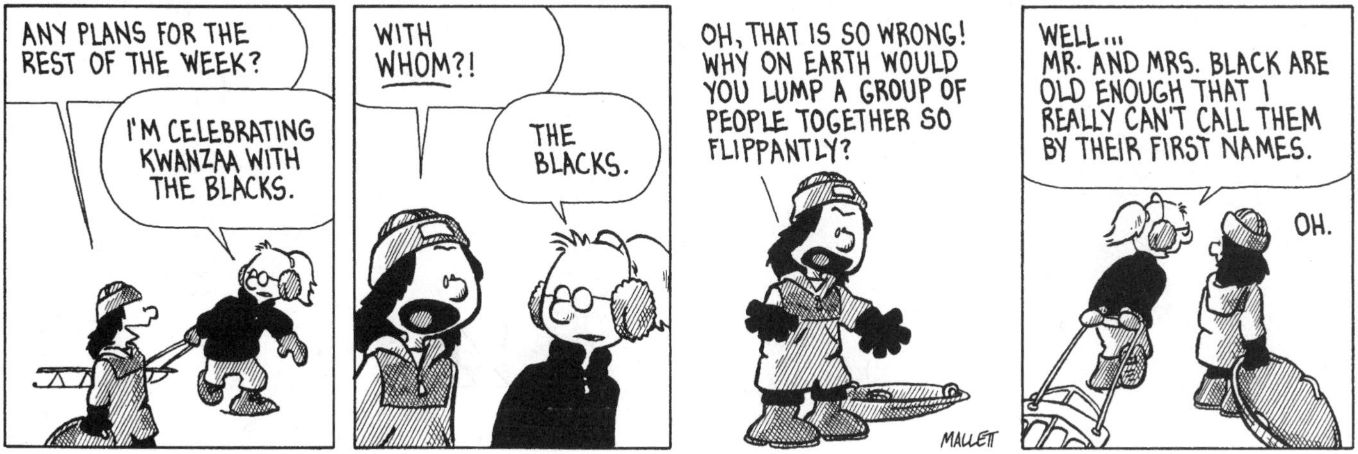
ANY PLANS FOR THE REST OF THE WEEK?
I'M CELEBRATING KWANZAA WITH THE BLACKS.
WITH WHOM?!
THE BLACKS.
OH, THAT IS SO WRONG! WHY ON EARTH WOULD YOU LUMP A GROUP OF PEOPLE TOGETHER SO FLIPPANTLY?
MALLETT
WELL... MR. AND MRS. BLACK ARE OLD ENOUGH THAT I REALLY CAN'T CALL THEM BY THEIR FIRST NAMES.
OH.

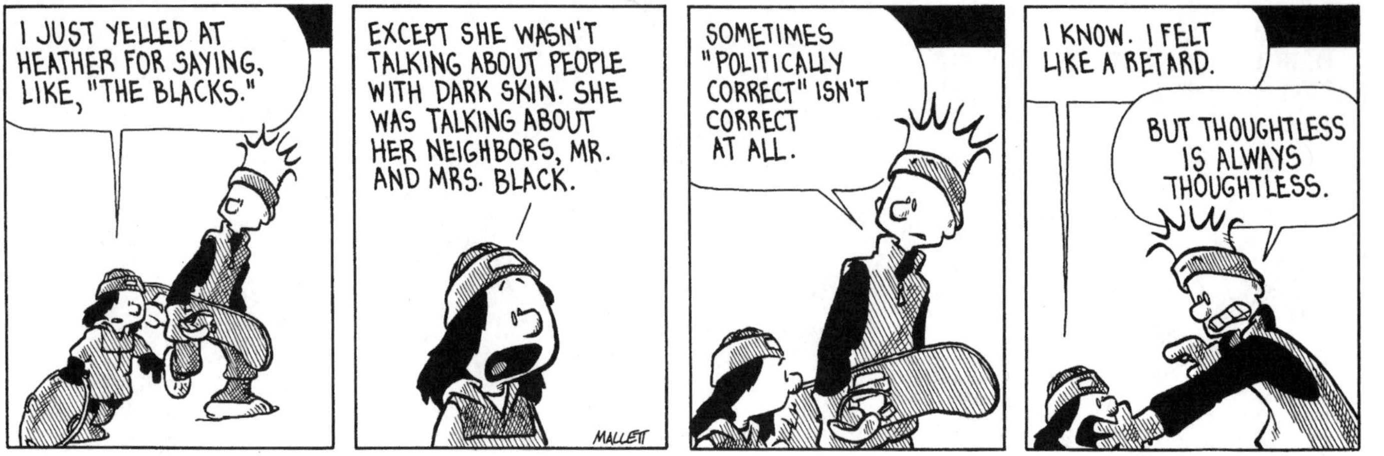
I JUST YELLED AT HEATHER FOR SAYING, LIKE, "THE BLACKS."
EXCEPT SHE WASN'T TALKING ABOUT PEOPLE WITH DARK SKIN. SHE WAS TALKING ABOUT HER NEIGHBORS, MR. AND MRS. BLACK.
MALLETT
SOMETIMES "POLITICALLY CORRECT" ISN'T CORRECT AT ALL.
I KNOW. I FELT LIKE A RETARD.
BUT THOUGHTLESS IS ALWAYS THOUGHTLESS.

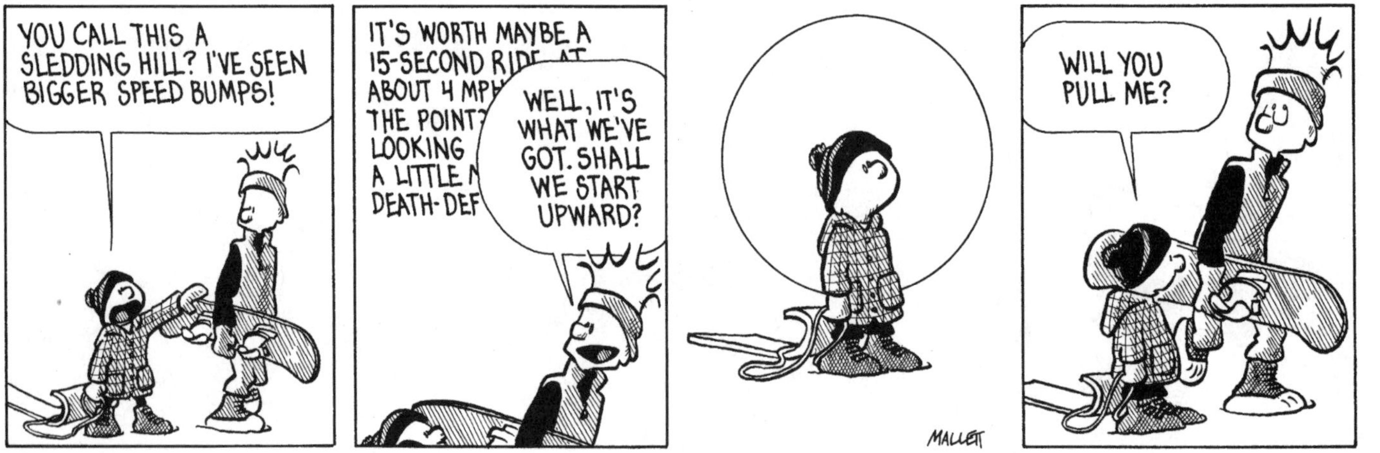
YOU CALL THIS A SLEDDING HILL? I'VE SEEN BIGGER SPEED BUMPS!
IT'S WORTH MAYBE A 15-SECOND RID AT ABOUT 4 MPH THE POINT? LOOKING A LITTLE DEATH-DEF
WELL, IT'S WHAT WE'VE GOT. SHALL WE START UPWARD?
WILL YOU PULL ME?
MALLETT

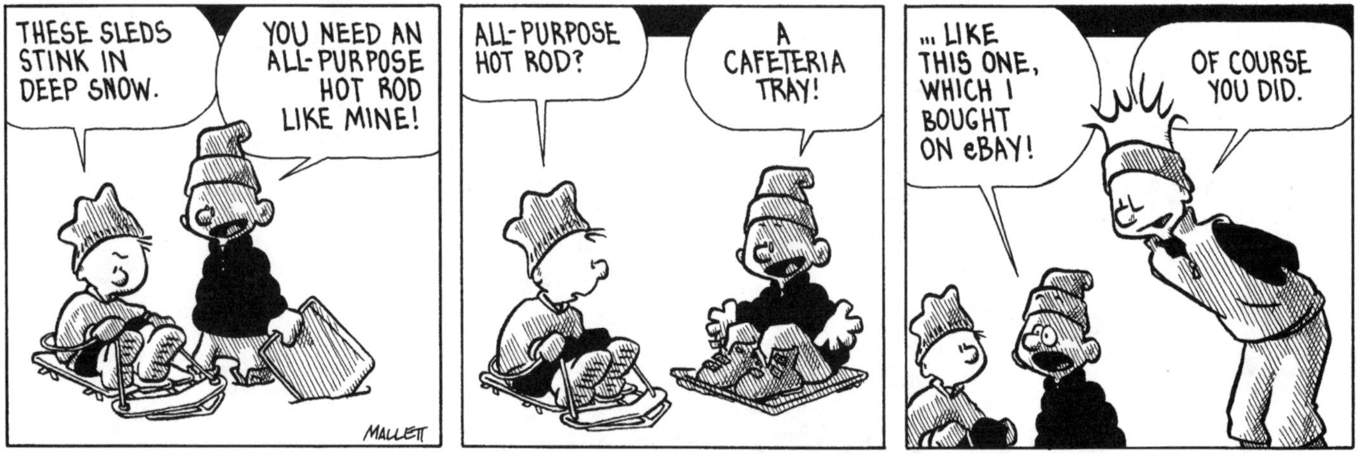
THESE SLEDS STINK IN DEEP SNOW.
YOU NEED AN ALL-PURPOSE HOT ROD LIKE MINE!
MALLETT
ALL-PURPOSE HOT ROD?
A CAFETERIA TRAY!
... LIKE THIS ONE, WHICH I BOUGHT ON eBAY!
OF COURSE YOU DID.

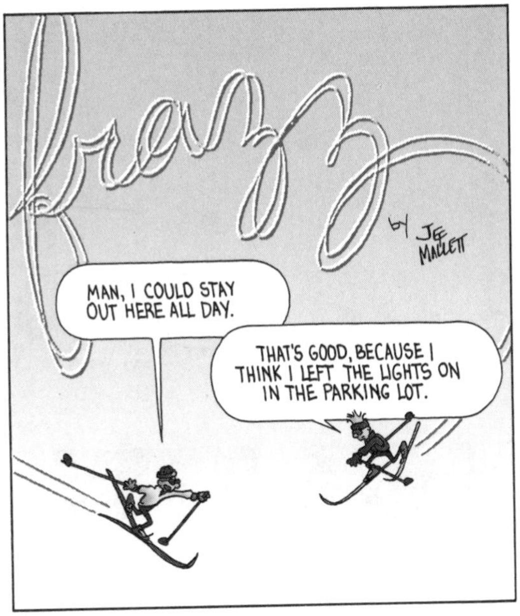
frazz
by JEF MALLETT
MAN, I COULD STAY OUT HERE ALL DAY.
THAT'S GOOD, BECAUSE I THINK I LEFT THE LIGHTS ON IN THE PARKING LOT.

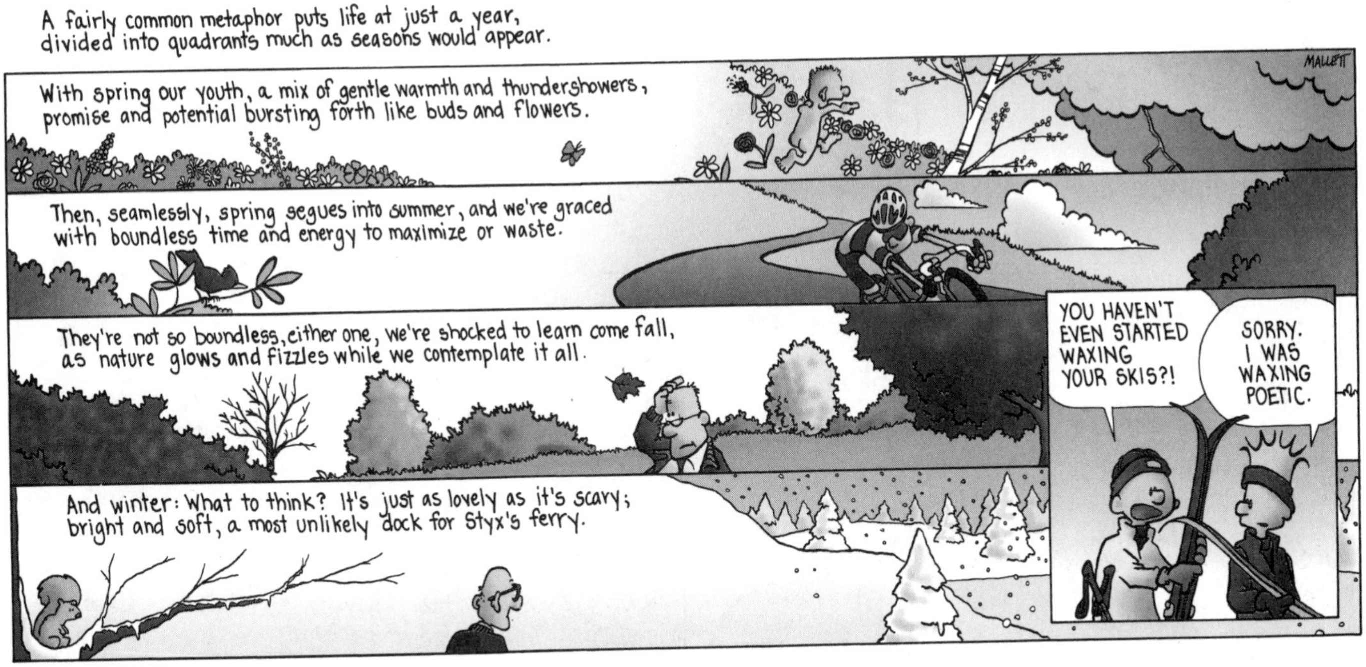
A fairly common metaphor puts life at just a year,
divided into quadrants much as seasons would appear.
MALLETT
With spring our youth, a mix of gentle warmth and thundershowers,
promise and potential bursting forth like buds and flowers.
Then, seamlessly, spring segues into summer, and we're graced
with boundless time and energy to maximize or waste.
They're not so boundless, either one, we're shocked to learn come fall,
as nature glows and fizzles while we contemplate it all.
And winter: What to think? It's just as lovely as it's scary;
bright and soft, a most unlikely dock for Styx's ferry.
YOU HAVEN'T EVEN STARTED WAXING YOUR SKIS?!
SORRY. I WAS WAXING POETIC.

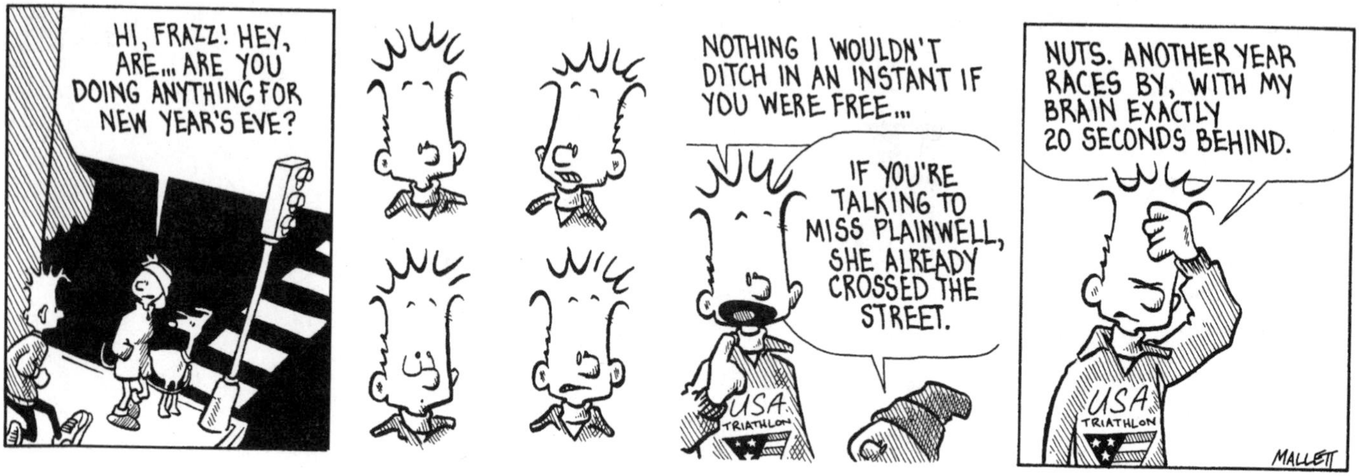
HI, FRAZZ! HEY, ARE... ARE YOU DOING ANYTHING FOR NEW YEAR'S EVE?
NOTHING I WOULDN'T DITCH IN AN INSTANT IF YOU WERE FREE...
IF YOU'RE TALKING TO MISS PLAINWELL, SHE ALREADY CROSSED THE STREET.
NUTS. ANOTHER YEAR RACES BY, WITH MY BRAIN EXACTLY 20 SECONDS BEHIND.
USA TRIATHLON
MALLETT

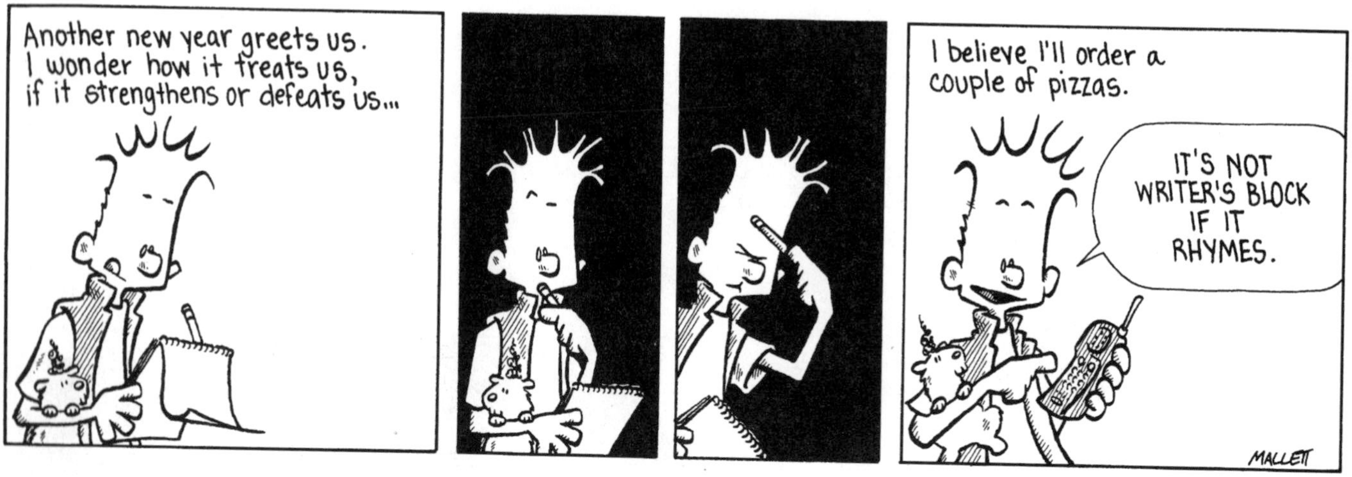
Another new year greets us. I wonder how it treats us, if it strengthens or defeats us...
I believe I'll order a couple of pizzas.
IT'S NOT WRITER'S BLOCK IF IT RHYMES.
MALLETT

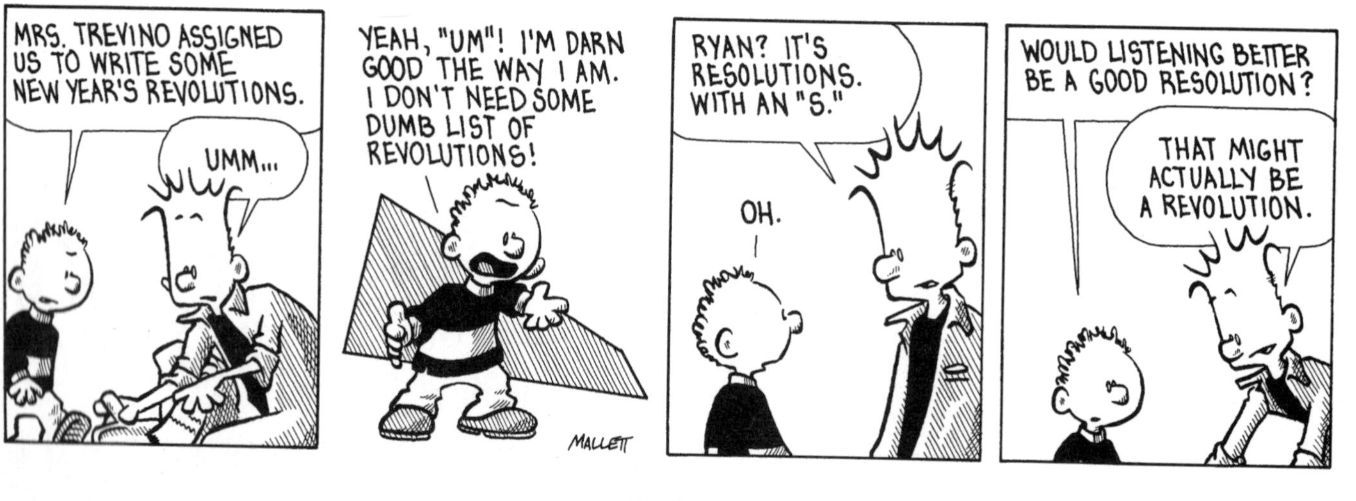
MRS. TREVINO ASSIGNED US TO WRITE SOME NEW YEAR'S REVOLUTIONS.
UMM...
YEAH, "UM"! I'M DARN GOOD THE WAY I AM. I DON'T NEED SOME DUMB LIST OF REVOLUTIONS!
MALLETT
RYAN? IT'S RESOLUTIONS. WITH AN "S."
OH.
WOULD LISTENING BETTER BE A GOOD RESOLUTION?
THAT MIGHT ACTUALLY BE A REVOLUTION.

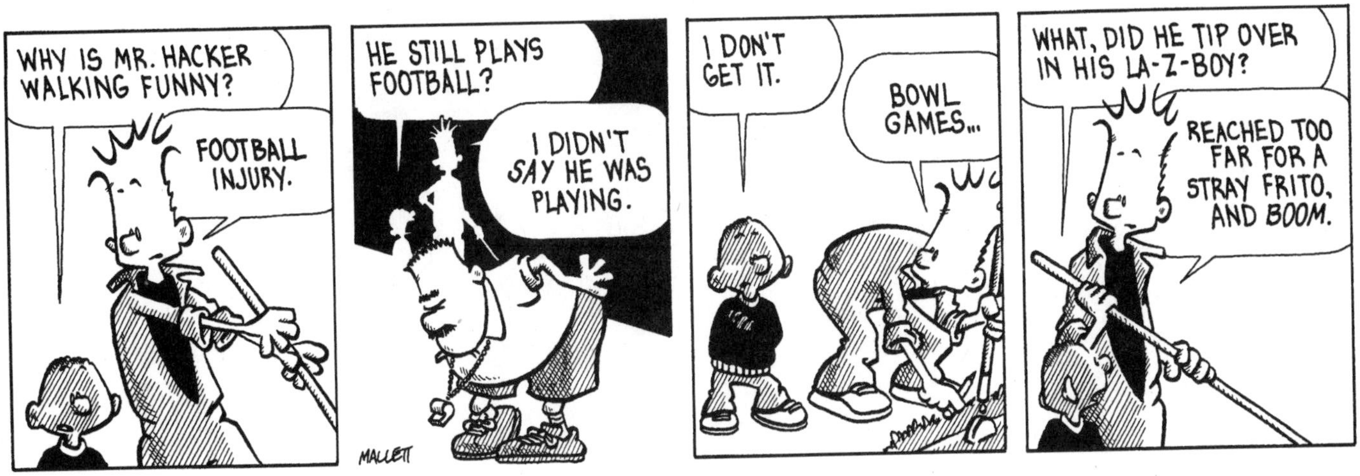
WHY IS MR. HACKER WALKING FUNNY?
FOOTBALL INJURY.
HE STILL PLAYS FOOTBALL?
I DIDN'T *SAY* HE WAS PLAYING.
I DON'T GET IT.
BOWL GAMES...
WHAT, DID HE TIP OVER IN HIS LA-Z-BOY?
REACHED TOO FAR FOR A STRAY FRITO, AND *BOOM*.
MALLETT

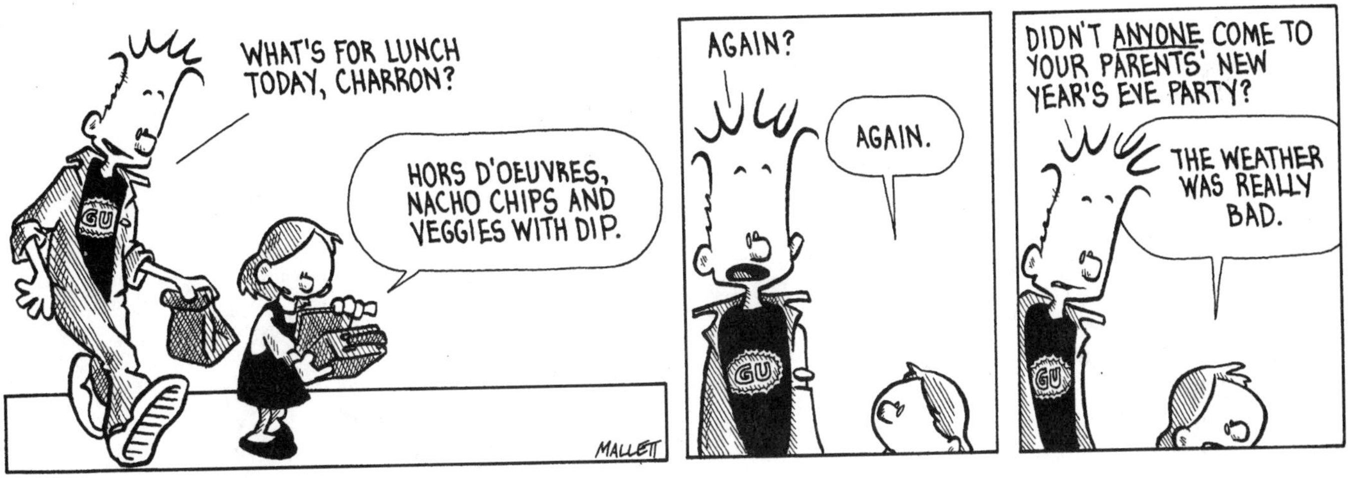
WHAT'S FOR LUNCH TODAY, CHARRON?
HORS D'OEUVRES, NACHO CHIPS AND VEGGIES WITH DIP.
MALLETT
AGAIN?
AGAIN.
DIDN'T ANYONE COME TO YOUR PARENTS' NEW YEAR'S EVE PARTY?
THE WEATHER WAS REALLY BAD.

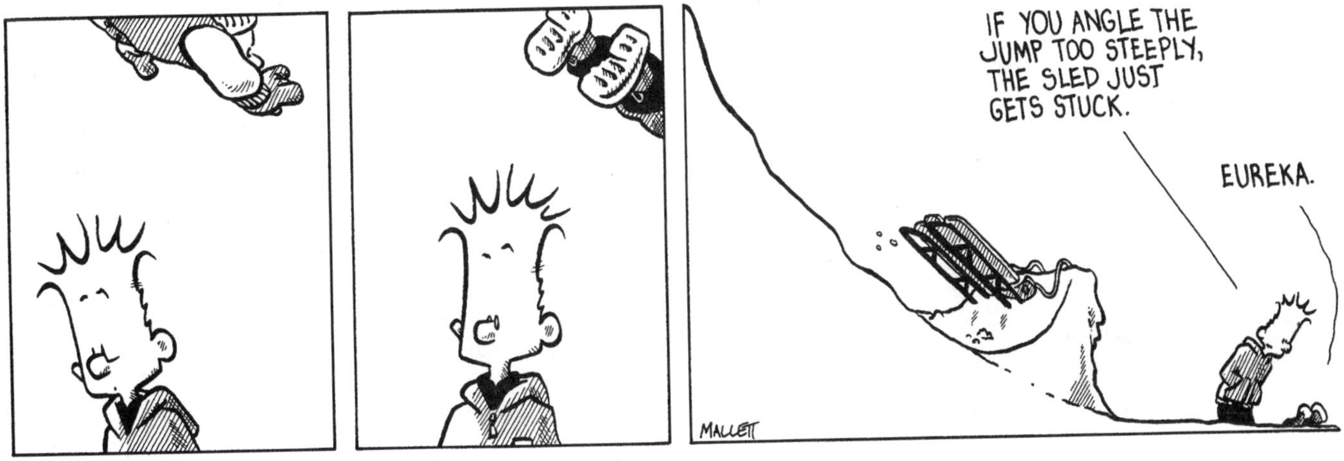
IF YOU ANGLE THE JUMP TOO STEEPLY, THE SLED JUST GETS STUCK.
EUREKA.
MALLETT

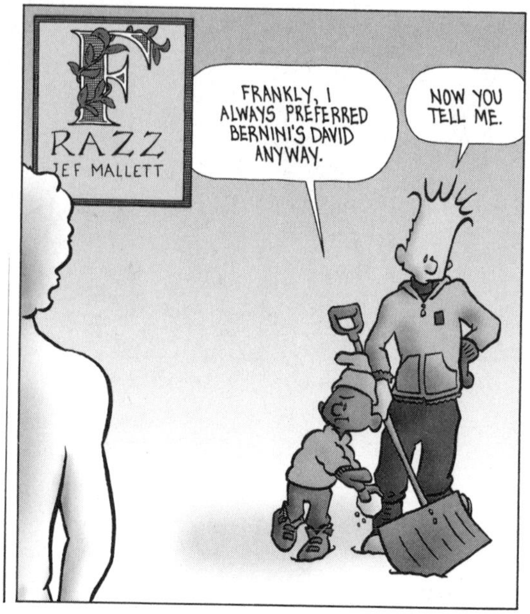
FRAZZ
JEF MALLETT
FRANKLY, I ALWAYS PREFERRED BERNINI'S DAVID ANYWAY.
NOW YOU TELL ME.

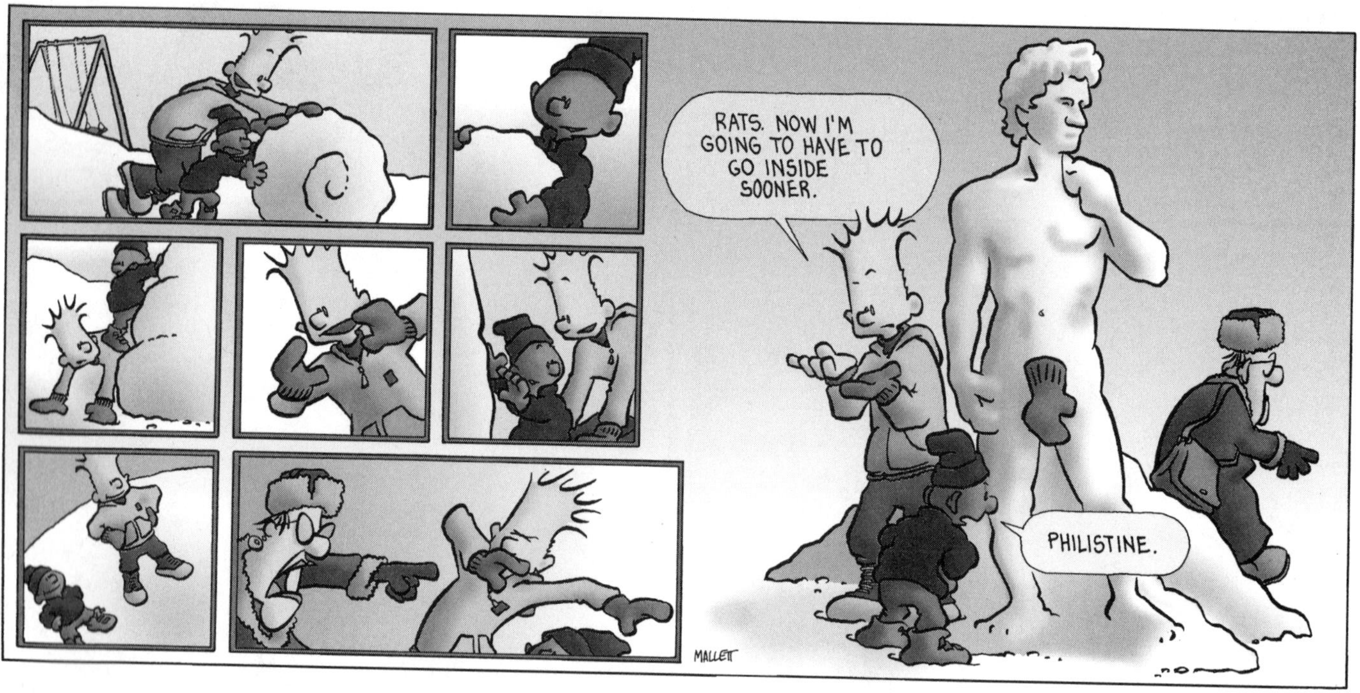
RATS. NOW I'M GOING TO HAVE TO GO INSIDE SOONER.
PHILISTINE.
MALLETT